THE URBAN CONDITION

People and Policy in the Metropolis

Edited by LEONARD J. DUHL, M.D.

with the assistance of JOHN POWELL

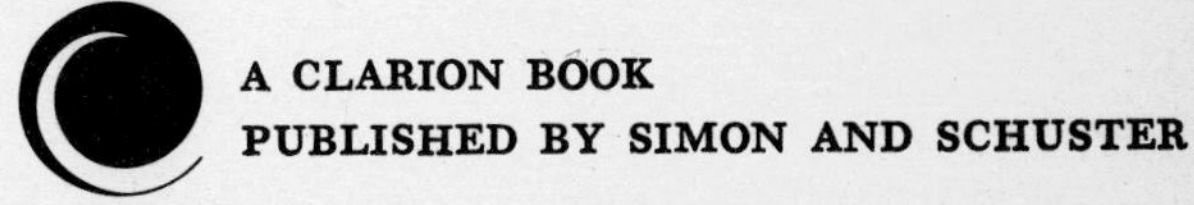

A CLARION BOOK
PUBLISHED BY SIMON AND SCHUSTER

A Clarion Book
Published by Simon and Schuster
Rockefeller Center, 630 Fifth Avenue
New York, New York 10020

Reprinted by arrangement with Basic Books, Inc., Publishers

THIRD PAPERBACK PRINTING

SBN 671-20243-X
Manufactured in the United States of America
Printed by The Murray Printing Co., Forge Village, Mass.
Bound by Electronic Perfect Binders, Inc., Brooklyn, N.Y.

TO MY FATHER, Louis Duhl,
who first made me aware of
the issues discussed in this book.

Introduction

LEONARD J. DUHL, M.D.

In this book we are concerned with one of the central problems which faces the world today: urbanization in an industrial society. While other issues, notably problems of international affairs and survival in the atomic age, are more immediate, more basic, and more critical, these are great problems which are likely to require renewed solutions and continuing vigilance with each generation. But the solutions we *now* achieve or fail to achieve regarding the urban environment are likely to have major consequences for a long future, less evident than life and death but of enormous significance for human welfare. Our immediate concern is with the problem-producing environment in which increasingly large numbers of human beings reside. And we address ourselves to some of the sources of problems in these urban environments and to some of the potential solutions of these problems.

The problems of the urban environment cannot wholly be separated from a host of other critical issues of human welfare such as education, health, and personal security. This book treats these concerns as part of the larger problem of the expanding metropolis and of the development of an urban America. All too often, a variety of problems associated with urban society are regarded as crises or critical needs in specific and limited areas of social life. For example, the importance of education in our society has lately led to many re-evaluations of our educational endeavors. Similarly, the expanding health and welfare programs have been viewed as a response both to overt and to covert inequities arising from the gap between widespread expectations and desires, and resources which are truly available to our population. Or, again, in the planning of our expanding cities, the mad urban sprawl, which leads to confusion in transportation, business activity, and taxation, has received some of the attention it so critically requires. But, for all of their special foci and their specific components, these issues have a great many common features and represent parts of a larger problem which can be conceived in terms of the development of the vast urban complexes with which we have only recently become familiar.

It is one thesis of this book that the crisis of urbanization of America is the crisis of size, of complexity, and of the large and varied administrative structures that are around us. As such, one cannot deal with it in parts. Many have bitterly attacked size and ask for a return to more rural patterns, or patterns that are more sensibly comprehended. Much as this return appeals to our sensibilities and to some of our values, it is impossible to turn the clock back or to stop the process which has resulted in this mass of organized complexity. What is now needed is a new way of viewing complexity, of viewing bigness and unravelling confusion.

Another theme is the attempt to separate and then to re-combine the rational and the irrational that is "man." On the one hand there is a widespread view that if man could be neatly compartmentalized and structured, and his society with it, man's own rationality could bring him out of the confusion and complexity. It is in response to this desire that the great organized technical machinery is developing. The giant computer, the new mechanism developed by the Department of Defense for metering their programs and coordinating their activities, is just the beginning of the massive use of our technological tools to bring some order out of chaos. On the other hand, as has been so beautifully demonstrated by the flight of Colonel Glenn, all the technical machinery in the world cannot replace the human being and his ability to make judgments. Despite and, in part, because of the high development of technology, there is a tremendous need for a new understanding of the needs of men, of the rational and irrational in human behavior, and of the ways in which human judgment is determined by a host of internal and external forces.

We are asking, therefore, in this book, for a reconciliation between the "social-irrational" man and his instincts, who was first deeply explored by Freud, and the "economic" or "rational" man, the man who uses the strength of his ego to control the environment, whom we may call the man of Adam Smith or of Karl Marx. But, strangely, one cannot do without either part; the rational and irrational must combine in a new pattern, which some have called "the administrative man."

This book is an attempt to deal with selected features of these very large and complex problems. In part, we are concerned with defining the *dimensions* of the problem, with looking at the parameters and at the possible ways of comprehending the fantastic interrelationships of all these phenomena. The book is certainly not alone in this endeavor. Others have examined the complex interplay of forces in industrial operations, military organization, schools and colleges, and other areas, in an attempt to unravel the interrelationships between social structure, culture, economic needs, physical planning, engineering, and the specific needs that make men human. Our own studies and discussions look for ways of comprehending this complexity, so that we can more clearly understand the ways in which judgments in one area affect all the others.

The "models" employed in this book are several. The one that seems to predominate is that which biologists call "ecology." The human environment of the metropolis is also ecological, in the sense that it is an open system, always in flux, never returning to the point from which it starts; and the broader ebb and flow in the process is more important than any specific cause and effect relationship. Thus it seemed advantageous to adopt the biologists' ecological model, rather than the more rigid linear cause-and-effect model of the "hard" sciences, such as physics. Admittedly, we are nowhere near full comprehension, but we have attempted to put together some of the ways in which we perceive these interrelationships.

To understand the totality, one has to look at the parts. But in looking at the parts, we recognize that they cannot be simply added together and the totality reconstructed from these parts. At best we can hope for partial insights into the complexity from a careful examination of its components. But it is only through concentrated attention to these details and special topics that we can hope to achieve that overview which can make a new and more global sense of phenomenal diversity and complexity. In these papers, we look at many segments of the major problem, but not at all. We have not looked at the work of the poet nor the business man. We have stayed away from the architect and the transportation expert. We have not considered specific problems of economics. We have chosen parts that seemed to us, in our various disciplines, to have the most relevance to understanding, and perhaps resolving, the problems nearest us.

We have looked at middle-class America, at the Negro, at new suburban communities, and at slums; and we have asked some questions. We have tried to show that some smaller projects can be prototypes for the study of much larger areas. We have even turned away from the city, at one point, to look at the college as a community; because here we can see the interrelationship between the irrational needs of man and the rational structures of the curriculum and the administrative process.

Since the context out of which the papers arose is that of mental health, we should explain its relevance to problems of the total urban environment. The traditional approach to the problem of mental illness is in terms of the individual patient, his family, and the institutions required to treat, care for, and cure him. The larger way to view the problem is in terms of the population from which the mentally ill come; the slum community, the poverty-stricken, the suburbs, industry, college, and so forth. Every problem has its own "community of solution." It is not always the community of the ill. When it is, we study and are concerned with the hospital, as a *total* institution. Now it seems that we must look further: at the total community, which is at risk of becoming ill, in order to determine all the factors, individual, social, administrative, and economic, that play a role. The discussion of poverty in this book is one such attempt; other papers reveal other facets of this approach. It is my strong feeling that for the mental patient, the significant community is not that of the mentally ill, but rather his primary community of identity, whether geographic area or functional group. And what holds true for the choice of "community of solution" for the non-hospitalized mentally ill is also true as we look at questions of delinquency, urban renewal, etc.

Having pointed to the complexity and to its parts, we then find that we must direct our attention to a long-neglected question: *How does one take what is known and turn this into social policy and social action?* The translation of research into social action is obviously one of the goals of people concerned with the behavioral and social sciences. The very process of planning, of pulling together known information, of evaluating the programs that exist, of searching for the gaps and unmet needs, of assessing the gains and losses of alternative solutions, of involving the relevant people in the planning process—all this is an important and vital part of the answer to that question.

It is our thesis that such planning must be done; we must learn which are the relevant factors that must be put into the judgmental system. We must try to learn how to reassess the hierarchy of values by which we make decisions. We must learn when the values that we associate with human well-being can and must be put above the values that we give to economic gain and physical development. It is only through this assessment that judgments can be made wisely.

Similarly, a democratic society cannot plan without involving people in the very process of planning. Admittedly, we wish to make use of expertise; but in an open society, where secrecy is at a minimum and communication at a maximum, people do and should become involved in decision-making, whether through community action, the courts, or the legislative process. It therefore behooves us to find ways of improving communication among people involved in the development of their own society, as well as to improve the process of community decision-making.

A further dilemma is how to strengthen our planning, and still at the same time optimize the freedom of individuals, groups, and cultures. We believe that the only way out of this complexity is organized rational planning in which governmental and quasi-governmental bodies, including business and labor, play important roles. Yet to some, equating planning with democracy seems paradoxical, since they claim that planning subjugates and makes people dependent. Planning in a *closed* society does have this effect. Planning in an *open* society can only facilitate democracy by reducing the inequities, maximizing the range of choice, educating people to use the choices they make, and making these choices more widely available.

These, then, are the concerns of this book. We have talked about our ecological view of complexity. Such a vantage point also represents a plea that we do not turn our backs on complexity in order to return to the more simple models, but rather that we *face* the complexity in all of its dimensions. We have at least the ability to begin to conceptualize the problem, to begin to investigate its parts, and to turn this information into social policy and action. I say we have this ability; but *the decision to do so* must ultimately be a political one.

Ultimately it is our political democratic structure that must make the decisions that will allow for the unravelling of the complexity of urban America. It is for this reason that we cannot divorce the concerns of mental health, delinquency, or even mental retardation from the broader questions of poverty, economics, city planning, transportation, or education. It is for this reason that this book, sponsored under mental health auspices, deals with mental health in so indirect a fashion. It is currently the fashion to be concerned with mental health as a total community phenomenon. This means a concern with involving the community in the prevention, care, and treatment of mental illness. However, the world of mental health is not unlike the world of city planning, economics, transportation, and the like, in its inability to see how its very solution is completely dependent upon solutions in spheres entirely foreign to its own. Ultimately, each solution must be sought within its relevant community *and also* as a part within an organized whole. It must be done with freedom and openness, through the same processes that have allowed America to cope with crisis after crisis throughout its history.

As each crisis occurs, whether for a society or an individual, men seek to cope with it by utilizing the skills and knowledge of the past. These skills and this knowledge may prove inadequate for coping with new problems and new crises, but we also have the opportunity to find new patterns of behavior and growth. Justice Douglas recently pointed out that in Chinese there are two characters used to write the one word, "crisis." One is for "danger" and the other for "opportunity." The crisis of urban America can force us to fall back on all the old inadequate concepts and methods of dealing with problems; or it can offer us the opportunity to find entirely new patterns compatible with our democratic structure, in the hope of organizing the mad complexity that seems to be around us. We have to face the fact that perfect solutions or cures are not to be found. What we have to accept is a continuing process of trying to cope, of a constant effort to adapt and readapt to the complexities and ambiguities as they ebb and flow in the urban scene.

Most of the papers in this book were originally presented at the Thirty-Ninth Annual Meeting of the American Orthopsychiatric Association in Los Angeles in March 1962. The opportunity to use this forum was especially welcome, because the Association itself has been increasingly concerned with the social context of its practice, and because we ourselves needed this stimulus to formulate ideas that we wanted to share with all persons concerned with the welfare of the metropolis and its people.

Primarily, however, the appearance of these papers is one culmination of the long-range program development concerns of the National Institute of Mental Health. Eight years ago, my own interest in the relationship of these many disciplines to mental health, along with John Calhoun's concern with the impact of the physical environment on behavior, led to the creation of this group. The participants are drawn from almost as many fields as they are individuals. They are psychoanalysts, public health physicians, psychologists, animal ecologists, sociologists, biologists, city planners, journalists, humanists, scientists. With all of these, however, this collection of papers still leaves out of account many people concerned with urban life—the architect, the poet, the minister, the businessman, for examples.

The group has become a community of scholars discussing mental health in relation to their own occupations and preoccupations; we are all concerned with different aspects of the same problem. Yet we cannot divorce our concerns with mental health from the general objectives of our society, such as justice, education, and the general welfare.

Though each of the articles stands in its own right, it is our deep hope that they will also be seen as a whole—precisely as they have tried to see the American Metropolis.

LEONARD J. DUHL, M.D.
Professional Services Branch
National Institute of Mental Health
Bethesda, Maryland

Acknowledgments

Besides the continuing long-range help and support of the National Institute of Mental Health, I want to acknowledge here my indebtedness to Edward Greenwood, the psychiatrist who started me on the path of being concerned with broader issues than the individual patient; C. J. Van Slyke, Associate Director of the National Institutes of Health, now retired, who taught me the ways of large-scale program development, by both teaching and example; and Joseph Bobbitt, National Institute of Mental Health, without whose insights, leadership, and support none of this work could have been done.

I want to thank also the many members of the group who participated through the years but who are not represented in this volume. These include Miss Catherine Bauer, Berkeley, California; Dr. Henrik Blum, Contra Costa County Health Department, Martinez, California; Judge David L. Bazelon, United States Court of Appeals, Washington; Dr. Herbert Birch, Albert Einstein College of Medicine, New York City; Dr. Scott Buchanan, Santa Barbara, California; Dr. Ernest W. Casperi, University of Rochester, New York; Mr. Albert Deutsch (deceased); Dr. Austin Henschel, Quartermaster Research and Development Center, Natick, Massachusetts; Mr. Robert Goe, Los Angeles; Mr. John B. Jackson, Sante Fe, New Mexico; Dr. Alexander Meikeljohn, Berkeley, California; Mr. Louis Miniclier, Washington; Dr. Theodore Schneirla, New York City; Dr. Nicholas Rashevsky, Chicago; and Dr. John Q. Stewart, Princeton University.

I am also indebted to Dr. Judd Marmor of Los Angeles, who chaired one of the meetings there.

Without the excellent editorial assistance of John Powell of the University of Miami, this book would not be.

Isadora Moore and Jean Koch, secretaries during the time this book was in process, were of inestimable help in preparing the manuscript.

Finally, I would like to thank my wife, who was a real part of the group and who has helped to nurture me and the group in our endeavors.

L. J. D.

Contributors

JOHN B. CALHOUN, PH.D., Laboratory of Psychology, National Institute of Mental Health

ROBERT H. CONNERY, PH.D., Department of Political Science, Duke University

DONALD A. COOK, PH.D., Director of Research, Basic Systems, Inc.

EDWARD S. DEEVEY, JR., PH.D., Department of Biology, Yale University

BRUCE P. DOHRENWEND, PH.D., Department of Psychiatry, College of Physicians and Surgeons, Columbia University

LEONARD J. DUHL, M.D., Professional Services Branch, National Institute of Mental Health

MARC FRIED, PH.D., Research Director, Center for Community Studies, Massachusetts General Hospital

HERBERT J. GANS, PH.D., Institute for Urban Studies, University of Pennsylvania

THOMAS GLADWIN, PH.D., Research Utilization Branch, National Institute of Mental Health

ROBERT GUTMAN, PH.D., Institute of Urban Studies, Rutgers University

A. B. HOLLINGSHEAD, PH.D., Chairman, Department of Sociology, Yale University

HENRY E. HOLMQUIST, M.A., Office of Program Policy, United States Housing and Home Finance Agency

HAROLD R. ISAACS, Center for International Studies, Massachusetts Institute of Technology

ERICH LINDEMANN, M.D., PH.D., Professor of Psychiatry, Harvard University School of Medicine

ELLEN LURIE, Community Relations Consultant, New York City

IAN L. MC HARG, Chairman, Department of Landscape Architecture, University of Pennsylvania

PETER MARRIS, Institute of Community Studies, London

RICHARD L. MEIER, PH.D., Mental Health Research Institute, University of Michigan

HARVEY S. PERLOFF, PH.D., Resources for the Future, Inc.

RICHARD W. POSTON, Research Professor, Cooperative Community Research, Southern Illinois University

LLOYD H. ROGLER, PH.D., Department of Sociology, Yale University

EDNA G. ROSTOW, Consultant in Psychiatry, Division of Student Mental Hygiene, Yale University Department of University Health

EUGENE V. ROSTOW, LL.D., Dean, School of Law, Yale University

EDWARD J. RYAN, PH.D., Center for Community Studies, Massachusetts General Hospital

JOHN R. SEELEY, Chairman, Department of Sociology, York University, Toronto

BENSON R. SNYDER, M.D., Psychiatrist-in-Chief, Medical Department, Massachusetts Institute of Technology

HERBERT E. STRINER, PH.D., Director of Program Development, The W. E. Upjohn Institute for Employment Research, Washington

SIR GEOFFREY VICKERS, V.C., Chairman, Research Committee, Mental Health Research Fund, Goring-on-Thames, England

ROSABELLE PRICE WALKLEY, PH.D., School of Public Health. University of California, Los Angeles

ROBERT C. WEAVER, PH.D., Administrator, United States Housing and Home Finance Agency

MELVIN M. WEBBER, Department of City and Regional Planning, University of California, Berkeley

DANIEL M. WILNER, PH.D., School of Public Health, University of California, Los Angeles

Contents

PART ONE

Man and His Environment

This is a book about the mental health of our urban society; not about the treatment of mental illness, but about new insights into the kind of planning needed for the "metroplex" as a whole and for the health of its social relationships and processes. The new orientation proposed by these writers is that of ecology, the concept developed by the physical and life sciences to deal with the complex and self-limiting interplay of physical or biological forces within a balanced environment. The writers have recognized that man's environment is *out* of balance. Many of his problems seem almost to have passed the point of no return. The failure of the nineteenth-century theory of irreversible "progress" has made it clear that our old methods of seeking solutions were inadequate and have to be replaced by far more complex and sophisticated perceptions of the interplay between man and his environment. Each paper by itself provides but a small beginning toward the needed understanding. As a collection of papers interrelating with each other, in which themes tend to recur and be examined from a variety of points of view, they may clarify the complexity of some of the central issues of the problem.

The first group of papers deals with the broad challenge to new ways of thinking about urban problems. Erich Lindemann treats the evolution of therapy, from the treatment of specific mental diseases to the search for the factors in family, institution, or community that may either alienate or sustain the individual in his attempts to adapt to stress. In its broadening of the field to include many non-medical disciplines and influences, the paper is also, in effect, a history of the interdisciplinary colloquies among the group that produced these papers.

John Seeley challenges the notion of an "objective" social science in his account of the interplay between the "outer" world and the inner milieu from which decision arises. A later paper by Benson Snyder illustrates this interplay in the context of college life, in terms of the strategy of psychiatric intervention called for with disturbed college freshmen, whose perception of the outer environment is often dictated by the inner one.

An account of the ecological approach is given by Edward Deevey, with analogies and illustrations. It is followed by John Calhoun's illustrative account of mice, not men; mice, unlike men, do not change their behavior because they are being observed; but even so the approach here suggests a methodology that might be adapted for human observation.

Ian McHarg, as a landscape architect, brings a challenge to the homocentric philosophy that has led to—or supported—man's unnatural behavior toward Nature, to say nothing of his inhumanity to man. Leonard Duhl's paper challenges conventional notions about disease, its nature, its role, its sources and treatment, and its significance in a total view of the society in which it occurs.

Finally, a student of cities, Donald Cook, offers another challenge: a reminder that the city's "problems" are also its opportunities for viable "mutations" in ways of adapting to the stress of change.

Many of the themes that are woven through these papers will recur in the more specific papers to follow: the meaning and role of therapy; the problem of where urban or social planning should draw the line between "inner" and "outer" experience, or between the subjective and the objective values of the environment; the variety and complexity of personal and environmental stress, which may under differing circumstances lead to either illness or opportunity. Underlying the book is the determination to find the points of *strategic intervention*, to the end of bringing about what therapists call "favorable change" in man's ability to interact freely and purposively with his environments: human, natural, and physical.

Mental Health and the Environment

ERICH LINDEMANN

This book grew out of a series of meetings held in Washington over a period of several years. The purpose of these meetings is more simply stated than achieved: to marshal the resources of human ecology, biophysics, the therapeutic sciences, and various of the social sciences, in order to understand—for the purpose ultimately of controlling—the chaotic and perplexing interplay of the environmental forces which affect individual well-being. These may, in many ways, be responsible for the loss or the lack of mental health. The group that attended these semi-annual discussions was quite comprehensive in its make-up; it included psychiatrists, psychologists, biologists, sociologists, economists, lawyers, and men and women from the fields of education, social action, social planning, architecture, and city planning.

Because ours is now largely an urban culture, and because most Americans live within a metropolitan environment, this was the context the group undertook to explore in a search for new insights, perceptions of relationship, and avenues of access and intervention. My own approach was initially that of my profession, one that focuses upon the emotionally disturbed individual. As a psychiatrist, I am accustomed to speculate on the background of a given state of unhappiness or mental disorder and try to sort a great variety of causes of social and personal processes into convenient diagnostic groupings that will offer therapeutic and prognostic guidelines. But the psychiatrist who begins to explore the broad question of the role of the total environment in the control of mental illness finds that he has opened his windows on vistas he might never have thought of as relevant to his own profession. Exactly the same kind of discovery, of course, awaits the architect who gets drawn into this wider search. It was this mutual unfolding of new perceptions that was the occupation of our group; and in this paper I want to trace some of what were, to me at least, major themes that emerged as the group progressed.

When the psychiatrist looks for population-wide measures to control mental disorders, he discovers a range of studies in epidemiology and in the geographical and social distribution of illnesses: studies that locate within the city certain areas typified by high frequency of disease, studies that compare stationary and migrant sections of the population, and studies that try to locate areas of illness within the social structure—particularly the class structure. The social scientists who have pursued such studies thus become the psychiatrist's colleagues in the wider search.

Next, he becomes aware of the debatability of diagnoses, the uncertainty of the criteria for mild and severe conditions. He begins to wonder how often a given psychiatric diagnosis is actually a social judgment reflecting the values and concepts of the diagnostician. Whether he considers a patient a good case to study or a good case to treat, an illness a "good" illness or an uninteresting condition, depends upon the skill the psychiatrist brings to his practice, his likes and dislikes, his style of communication, and all the unwitting determinants of attitude and goal that derive from his own cultural and class background.

Having accepted this as true for established diseases, he turns next to an even more perplexing effort to look at "mental health" as a *positive continuum,* extending from freedom from recognized illness to increasing degrees of well-being, productivity, creativity, and satisfaction. For no matter how uncertain our diagnoses may be, we do believe that conditions leading to impaired well-being also lay the groundwork for deterioration of emotional health.

The beginnings of this kind of thinking can be traced from Hughlings Jackson, who distinguished "positive" symptoms from "negative" ones, through the notion of "mal-adaptive reaction patterns" put forth by Meyer and Freud, to the notion of "homeostasis" anticipated by Claude Bernard and formulated by Walter Cannon. The concepts of traumatic experience, and of safety margins of the physiological and psychological systems of the organism, indicate that disease may be formulated as the result of disequilibrium, and disorganization related to a number of time-variables and configurational patterns in a field of energy exchange. The development of General Systems Theory, much enriched by Information Theory, had made it possible to relate as open systems individual organisms and social organizations. All strive for survival and internal cohesion, for the maintenance of inner order; all are involved in exchange within certain limits across their boundaries.

Many investigators have found it convenient to assume the existence of basic drives that might be specified, and to assume further that the satisfaction or disappointment of these drives could be related to the achievement and maintenance of an essential physical condition. Leighton has enumerated striving sentiments concerned with physical security, with sexual satisfaction, with belonging to a human group and a moral order, and having a defined location in a society affording opportunities for recognized achievement, for winning and giving love, and for suitable expression of hostility. These form a recent framework for community-wide studies relating to an essentially stationary condition. This kind of framework assumes that a society or community which provides a steady flow of opportunities for such satisfactions, compatible with the dominant strivings of its members, should be mentally healthy.

It is obvious, however, that this relatively steady state of opportunities for satisfaction and reward is rarely given in reality. There are marked fluctuations in interaction, in communication, in the ordering of mutually relevant human clusters. There are also precipitous changes due to such unpredictable causes as disasters, bereavement, sickness, change of employment, and indeed the problems encountered in the ordinary advance from way-station to way-station in the normal course of growth and development. Erikson's concept of "identity crisis" and Lindemann and Caplan's theory of "situational crisis" both deal with challenges presented to individuals by precipitous changes within the organism itself or within the individual's emotionally relevant network of relationships.

It will readily be seen that these new levels of insight were pushing our group to steadily deeper and more complex perceptions of the problem. We were, clearly, concerned with a psychogenic potential in the human and physical environment. Studies of mourning and grief in response to disaster revealed how people adapted to changes in role and in rate of interaction. They also illuminated the enormous variety of individual and societal factors that may turn an adaptive response into a maladaptive response, or illness. The notion of crisis as the state of a number of persons within a population exposed to the hazard of precipitous change in social context became an important source of insight. This notion formed a basis for organizing psychiatric observations relating to widely differing events within a community, ranging from a premature birth within a family to the forced relocation of a population from one habitat to another. Such problems could be studied in terms of drift theory and upward mobility of individuals, to account for the high incidence of pathology in some urban regions, or in terms of the interaction between housing arrangements and opportunities for communication and recreation, these being viewed as safeguards against ill health.

A dramatic shift in the dimension of inquiry arose from the question, what would our own group consider to be mental health for itself and its members? What would be the best realization of our potential, the greatest opportunity for happiness and achievement and making life worth while? The inquiry here turned on the difference between freeing people *from* something and being free *for* something, as Alexander Meiklejohn puts it. In the matter of choices, it soon becomes apparent that many choices have little relevance to well-being, and that many alternatives are foisted upon us by a prosperity-oriented society through advertising and the persuasive voices of the mass media. What is needed is the opportunity for *strategic* choice and for the freedom that permits the consideration of alternatives before one commits onself. Choice must precede commitment; and mental health appears to demand free commitment to an endeavor in terms of objectives shared within a reference group.

The capacity to make such choices is not inborn; and opportunity without capacity will produce stress rather than satisfaction. It is less important, then, that the environment match the needs of the individual than that individuals be prepared to meet the challenge of the environment. Mental health, in short, is seen to require education for liberty, not in the sense of license and unbridled competition, but in the sense of preparation for free and responsible participation in striving for shared goals. In this light, the environment emerges as an organization of human beings banded together by these goals and complementary purposes, providing a network of roles and statuses and appropriate divisions of labor. The uppermost concerns would then become the nature of freedom, the relationship of planning to free action, the role of law in providing freedom rather than merely imposing constraint, and, finally, the extent of tolerance within varying cultures for forms of deviance other than "sickness."

In considering the general phenomena of delinquency and crime, for instance, particularly within illegal organizations of considerable size, one comes upon the notion—disturbing as it may seem—that when these social deviations arise out of circumstances in which there is no opportunity for wider forms of responsibility, they may themselves constitute mental health: that is, they may provide responsible participation in small, highly-structured reference groups with their own codes of conduct, their own goals, their own high level of mutual obligation.

The reality of the human ecology is thus seen as a network of overlapping communities, with compatible or clashing goals, in several of which one individual may be a responsible participant—under compatible or clashing codes of conduct. The compatible or conflicting opportunities for participation in so many communities presents an order of complexity in which criteria of "mental health" could be applied equally to the individual actors and to the social systems of which they are at once the authors and the victims.

But this brings us back to the issue of education and the choice between alternative possible mental health orientations. Are we to be oriented toward a survival-of-the-fittest elite, or toward providing the maximum feasible potential of mental health values for the many? Should education focus on future social and intellectual leaders, or on maximizing the adaptive potential of the whole body of students? It is obvious that these questions permit no easy "yes" or "no," but involve us in choices between different kinds of "good," in each case at the expense of some persons or groups.

What emerged from these considerations was the perception that the mental health of the individual and its concomitants in the environment cannot be separated—despite current usage, which restricts the term *health* to persons and uses terms like disorganization or disintegration when it is the community or social structure that is under study. This became even clearer when the group turned to the needs and customs of peoples in other cultures; it tried to use the tools of anthropology to distinguish the basic value-orientations of different cultures and ethnic groups, in order to understand more clearly the nature of mental health planning in our own society. Particularly relevant differences were noted, for example, in India, where the methods of the medical schools evidenced profound differences in attitude toward the evaluation of mental health and the medical care of the mentally ill. Their attitudes grow out of equally profound differences in values; these are taken for granted, as ours are, and become apparent only when the two cultures confront each other in operation. This is very clear with respect to time-orientation: the East values tradition and the past, the West strives after the future. It shows clearly again in attitudes toward the productive role of the individual: in the East, large segments of the population are not expected to be productive, and prolonged preoccupation with subjective experience is highly valued. The Indian mind lacks the optimism about the conquest of nature so familiar to us. Finally, while the integration of the individual into the joint family as a tight seniority-oriented social unit seems natural in India, productive membership in a task-oriented team has to be learned with much effort. The social ills and emotional health hazards of industrialization are greatly feared there, and the West is pitied for the deplorable level of its mental health.

Yet note was taken, too, of the resistances to change within our own culture, whether it be against water fluoridation in New England, against the redistricting of states to give urban areas a fairer proportion of political power, against the abandoning of obsolete local jurisdictions in favor of regionalization, or whatever it may be. Studies of relocated populations within American cities show further striking differences of response among ethnic groups.

What was most significant, at least for the psychiatrists within this richly interdisciplinary group, was the growth of awareness that within communities and other social structures, the determinants of priorities for planning and action are as unconscious, as powerful, as complex, and as difficult to reach as are the unconscious forces in the individual psychic apparatus. The identification and description of these forces has only just begun; but it is indispensable for the programming of mental health services. Their clarification depends upon the joint efforts of psychiatrists and social scientists acting in close collaboration. As in psychotherapy, the task of intervening in social forces is a matter of dealing with resistances; an existing balance may be upset, and the "therapists" may have to cope with the vexing problem of deciding when information is useful and when it is destructive, as well as what information is relevant. There is research suggesting that the untimely use of information can result in hostility, destructive responses, and retardation of progress.

This newly raised problem of the relation of information to decision-making, thus becomes the central theme for a new phase of these studies, in which planners, public officials, and experts in the law are drawn in to use the thinking of the social scientists and the psychodynamic experts. It is obvious that much research is needed to buttress social planning; but the new information has to be used with due regard to the existing power structure and to the tolerance for disturbance of the equilibrium of ongoing social processes. We must not be surprised that social science investigation is often taken as spying, that persons in power will label certain data as classified, or that persons being questioned are reluctant to divulge more or less private information for fear it might be used against them. The vaunted claim of scientific endeavor to be objective and free from value-bias is seriously endangered whenever social information goes beyond the clarification of principles for general policy and becomes involved with individual social problems. The social scientist—and even more, the psychiatrist—who becomes a consultant to leaders of political or social action can easily be tempted to succumb to twin dangers: the preferential use of information, and the disregard of other data to suit the value priorities of the ruling groups.

The considerations I have outlined were, then, some of the central themes of the long series of discussions from which the present book has emerged. Theoretical formulations were usually buttressed by accounts of concrete research in progress on a wide variety of matters. A few of these were basic ecological factors in individual and group survival, epidemiological studies of actual mental illness, individual and social ills such as alcoholism, the operation of law concerning the borderline between illness and culpability, and the study of popuations in voluntary migration or enforced relocation.

We were faced throughout with a growing awareness of unforeseen complexities, but at the same time we experienced a growing sense of mutually-derived competence in coming to grips with the problems of planning suitable environments with due consideration for mental health and social values. Of particular help was the felt presence and eager participation of a man who never attended a single meeting, but who took part through correspondence and occasional visits with individual members. This was Sir Geoffrey Vickers, whose integrative insight into both historical and economic forces in industrial society kept the group reminded of the ways in which the values of profit in industry and of power in politics influence social choices of priority in measures adopted for the well-being of society. He encouraged us also to find a positive approach to planning which, amid the confusion of interests, would preserve the balance between planned control and individual initiative.

To return to my own role in this enterprise, I have come to understand with much more clarity how the mental health worker, be he psychiatrist, psychologist, or social worker, becomes in this pattern of common endeavor an understanding and accepted co-worker in programming. In anticipating hazards to mental health in proposed physical and social arrangements for specific groups of citizens, he can remain a true agent of preventive medicine even while his consultative efforts appear mainly in the fields of welfare and education. And beyond this, he may be able, in some measure, to enhance the opportunities for emotional well-being and positive mental health of the many communities with which he is concerned.

Bibliography

Birnbach, M., *Neo-Freudian Social Philosophy,* Stanford, Calif.: Stanford Univ. Press, 1961.

Cohen, E., ed., *Mental Health Teaching in Schools of Public Health,* New York: Columbia Univ. Press, 1961.

———, "Epidemiological and Statistical Information," *WHO Chronicle,* *16*:15-18, 1962.

Leighton, A., *My Name is Legion,* New York: Basic Books, 1959.

Miller, G., *et al., Plans and the Structure of Behavior,* New York: Holt, 1960.

Parsons, T., *et al., Theories of Society,* New York: The Free Press of Glencoe, 1961.

Thornton, E., ed., *Planning and Action for Mental Health,* London: World Federation of Mental Health, 1961.

Vickers, G., *The Undirected Society,* Toronto: Univ. of Toronto Press, 1959.

Weinberg, A., *Migration and Belonging,* The Hague: Martinus Nijhoff, 1961.

Personal Science 2

JOHN R. SEELEY

I hope I do not exaggerate when I argue that these papers represent, broadly, a meeting between those whose business it is to set the soul right that the world may be right, and those whose preoccupation has been to set the world well that the soul may be sound: a sort of meeting between the orthogenic school and the orthophenic school. It is not so much a case of the lion and the lamb lying down together as of their seeking to form a committee on a common strategy: my limited zoological training brings the figure to a halt.

Perhaps we are at the dawn or pre-dawn of a new synthesis, but even if so—or perhaps particularly if so—we had best cast a lingering, and I hope clarifying, backward glance at the thesis and antithesis that are to be so conjoined and transformed. It is not only the new society, to use a Marxian phrase, whose shape may be discerned in the womb of the old: it is as well, or more particularly, the new ideology, the gospel, the emergent doctrine. Let me draw fine, therefore—but not too fine—the counterposed contentions, the preferential preoccupations, that are in some sense represented here.

I hope my psychiatric friends will not take it ill if, as a first approximation, I represent them not as persons but as role-players in a division of labor—as occupying a curious, anomalous, interesting, and effective position: a strategic stand. Looking backward, they represent the virtual impotence of the psyche; looking forward, its virtual omnipotence. In the early stages of therapy, the psychotherapist as a sort of attorney for the prisoner, his patient, brings to the patient a vivid realization of his own inevitability as product of a conjuncture of forces he had no power sensibly to affect. The relief from (irrational) guilt, the capacity to perceive the self as it is (or at least in some reasonable relation to reality) depends upon a lively perception of self as *product*, a substantive shifting of blame onto, at every point, "the environment," as over against the ego. The culmination of this procedure would be attested by the return of a soul-deep "yes" to the question: "Canst thou say in thine heart thou hast seen with thine eyes, with what manner of art, thou wast shaped in what wise . . . ?"

In a second stage—now with society rather than the patient as the client for whom the psychotherapist is attorney—the "participation" of the patient in the process that is simultaneously his achievement and his fate is brought into focus. That psyche which was most emphatically product is now seen partly as producer, calling out (in virtue of what it had been made to be, but, nonetheless, therefore was) the *shaping* responses that would make it further what it would be. The psyche is no longer seen altogether passively as ". . . fashioned in love on my bosom and shown on my breast to the skies," but as author and authored, maker and made—"I, the plough and the furrow, the plough-cloven clod and the plough-share drawn thorough; the germ and the sod. . . ."

Lastly, no matter what may be *said,* the virtual omnipotence of the psyche is asserted. One is where one is, one does what one does, one's experience is such as it is, because most generally this is what one wants. Not that the therapist denies "reality" or permits his patient to do so, but that he now represents a special aspect of reality, its virtually infinite capacity for transformation in experience as a function of the manner of its apprehension. It is not precisely a directive to count "the world" well lost for the sake of that inner world which is the ultimate only home; but it *is* clearly enough a directive to remold the world in perception as an indispensable prelude to doing anything worth doing about it. The attitude is a secular analogue of "Seek ye first the Kingdom of God and His righteousness and all these things shall be added unto you": it *is* an enjoinder to seek an inner order as a precondition for effect upon the world. At the very least, there is a selective focus upon the fact—a fact *constituted* by faith in it—of *agency:* upon those aspects of experience that are brought into being, that are given their existence, by human endowment.

The test of the success of such a procedure is the relative diminution in importance of what might be entitled the brute world, *as such.* When a friend of mine contended that his test for therapeutic success was increased vulnerability in his patients, he meant that he counted upon an increased *willingness* to be wounded (for the sake of other goods), which is only another name for increased invulnerability, in the sense of relative indifference to and diminished importance for psychic pain.

The generalized upshot of the whole procedure is a double reduction in the significance of the external world: its *importance* is reduced in that the agent's paramount role in defining and regulating its impact is given due place; and its *significance* is reduced in that the caring eye is focused (not altogether, but primarily) on the inner experience, which is a transmutation rather than a reflection of the outer.

Paradoxically, it is thus, and perhaps only thus, that the world, the world that matters, can be made over, reconstituted, transformed, and re-formed. It is first diminished, abandoned, left, until following a transformation that is in but not of that world, it can be returned to, re-engaged, re-wed, and finally, transfigured.

I must now turn with equal devotion and with equal risk of offense to my friends among the planners.

They begin at a different point, move by a different procedure, and come, I think, to a different conclusion.

If the psychiatrist's first object of attention is the incredible internal chaos created in the individual psyche by the efforts of the well-intentioned people who have deliberately directed their attention upon it, the planner's first arresting object is the equally incredible external chaos men create for each other in the pursuit of lives and careers that may well make sense for each of them severally. It is this luxuriating foliage of success and achievement, the other-choking consequences of individual potency and production, the jungle of embodied goods and assets, that confronts him at the outset.

In a sense, then, he comes first upon man the producer—rather than man the produced—but man as the producer of the ills from which he suffers: the congestion, the disorder, the all-pervading nexus of unintended and unwanted consequence; and hence, ultimately, upon man the victim, the helpless and hapless product of his own production. The problems that arise for him are primarily problems of public acts rather than private feelings, problems that *do* have their roots in the world of brute fact, and their solution, if any, there also. The planner comes thus in the second instance to the position that the psychotherapist came to in the first: to man as the captive, the product, of forces or situations that not only transcend but, in their immensity, dwarf the resistive resources of the individual. Indeed, on this view, it is "the environment" that endows man with *its* characteristics, and in effect brings any individual into being, maintains and alters him. If anything is to be in any large sense better for anyone, the improvement must proceed from (and ultimately be reflected in) the reorganization of that external environment, in ways that will conduce to the internal satisfactions that it is idle or self-defeating to seek directly. Not only is no large-scale individual regeneration necessary as a prelude, but it is, *ex hypothesi,* impossible. Such personal regeneration as is necessary will flow from the rearrangement of objective circumstance, and that rearrangement does not necessitate any radical increase in individual rationality. What it does require is a social division of labor in which the burden of rationality is—in a rational recognition of one's own permanent irrationality—externalized, thrust upon a body of professionals, and hence set beyond one's own capacity to mismanage. In effect one is to become rational, not by some internal and personal struggle, but by setting in motion a public process that, once started, one cannot arrest—a process in which one selects an elite to procure for oneself and others that environment that is most conducive to rational behavior.

Whether or not it is thought that I have exaggerated, it is impossible not to distinguish two dominant themes—two themes that have played in and out of Western history, as they have played in and out in the lives of all of us. One theme virtually asserts that "if each before his own door sweeps, the village will be clean"; the other, that if the village institutes a proper sanitation service, each one will be clean—at least as far as his dooryard, and probably beyond. In dogmatic form these views are asserted not simply in terms of "if," but in terms of "if and only if"—i.e., a way becomes The Way. One formula runs roughly: good persons (or "mature" or "productive" or whatever new word for "good" you want) make a good society, which inevitably makes a good physical ordering—or, if not, it does not matter since virtue is its own sufficient reward. The other, obviously: a good physical ordering leads toward a good society, which produces (or educes) good persons—or, if not, it does not matter since a good external order is a, perhaps sufficient, good in itself.

By and large, we dignify theories of the first kind, if they are well developed, by calling them religions; and we denigrate theories of the second sort by calling them ideologies. We are, of course, in origin and dominant outlook (or certainly for polemical purposes) a religious society. An ideological society (e.g., the Soviet Union) would view the matter otherwise—again for polemical purposes. I have to enter the stricture because closer examination reveals what may be called a counter-theme to each: in the West, where people are supposed to account for circumstances, a great deal of weight is allowed in the adjudication of guilt or innocence to the theorem that circumstances account for people; in Soviet (and Chinese) trials, *per contra,* where circumstances are held to account for people, problems of personal guilt seem to be of focal if not exclusive interest.

In any case, we find ourselves in some uneasy relation to the two types of theory, or clusters of theories, and to the practices based upon them. One manifestation of the unease is the phenomenon I have just pointed to: the holding to one theory while behaving in terms of the unacknowledged other. Another is a sort of migration or wandering back and forth between the two, in the lives of persons, and in the history of society.

I am not quite right, I believe, in the equal emphasis I allowed to rest on both words when I spoke of "a wandering *back* and *forth.*" The two-way wandering occurs, but there is or seems to be a net migration toward the planner-ideological end of the spectrum and away from the psychologist-religious end. There seems to be a greater appeal, for those at or near the religio-psychological pole, in the goings-on near the other pole. Indeed, there is some reason to think that this is the direction in which entropy lies—although it is always possible to interpret the data otherwise. One might view Western history as a succession of runnings-down toward the external-naturalistic ideology, interspersed with a series of windings-up by great religious or secular-religious figures (I would count Freud and his immediate though not post-mediate followers among them) returning the society to a more charged, a less natural, a more improbable state or position.

If what I say is true, in whole or in large part, it would be interesting to speculate as to the reason or reasons for the greater attraction in one direction. The *fact* of the attraction may be taken, of course, either as a *prima facie* warrant of desirability or as a ground for caution, if not suspicion. Examination of the nature of the attraction may illuminate even when it cannot settle the issue. Let us take a brief look.

It is not too difficult to begin a listing of the evident virtues of the institutional position.

The immediate relief from a burden of guilt and responsibility is very like that of the first stage of psychotherapy, but enduring or permanent. It *is* so much easier to institute and institutionalize outside controls than inside ones, that once the idea has occurred to one, one is left wondering at one's prior folly. It *is* so much easier to love men in general and at a distance than to love anyone in particular and near at hand that, if both are equally effective, it is the better part of the most elementary wisdom to choose the former. There is of course not only psychological but material economy: it is in every sense cheaper to institute a process for the millions than to make a similar number of parallel individual efforts. These virtues are, however, but pale gleams beside the central shining star of attraction, the *virtu virtutis*, that sheds its light directly over only one pole: the star of "science," with all that the term popularly connotes.

There is a sense, a proper sense, I think, in which one may say that the matters of scientific discourse—indeed the scientific discourse itself—are out in the plain light of day, instead of somewhere in the stilled gloom of the non-scientific crypt. The references are to things seen, rather than to shades sensed. The world of science is the world of common consent (even if common sense must by training be rarefied to ensure it), and the reassurance in it is a communal reassurance which is perhaps harder to doubt than a self-reassurance. It is a world of reliabilities. It is a world of certainty, even when the certain extends only over a probability table, or a set of probabilities of probabilities. It is essentially a democratic, non-élitist world, where the passport of average intelligence renders every man approximately equal in his potentiality of compassing what is known. It is a world where very ordinary virtues pay, higher virtues are hardly required, and ordinary vices are handily insured against by being robbed of their normal payoffs. It is a world where the views reached seem independent of the self, hence not the responsibility of the self, hence not to be held at personal peril. It is, largely, a certified world.

I do not deny that such a world exists—*in reference to physics*. I do not deny that, insofar as it exists, we should be drawn to it. I do say (to those who might be otherwise drawn from vital enterprises) that *in reference to the affairs of men*, with regard to the social sciences, and such planning and managing procedures as are founded on them, the picture is far different. Not in any important point of comparison is there any resemblance between the natural and the social sciences. I can but summarize briefly.

As crucial a formulation as any in the social sciences is W. I. Thomas' recognition that social action depends on what he calls "the definition of the situation." If I extend my hand toward you, and you define such a movement as the beginning of a friendly approach, the probability of one chain of actions over another is quite different from what it would be if the extended hand is held to prefigure—and *therefore* probably does prefigure—an attack. Nothing *objective* in the situation affects the outcome. If I hug a teenager it may be most proper if I am defined as her father, but so improper as to lead toward jail if I am defined otherwise, and the difference is held to be critical. Such definitions are, of course, social definitions rather than idiosyncratic ones, definitions held in consensus.

It would be entirely wrong to think of a society as an "aggregate of persons," though I know such a view is common. The society *is*—it extends as far as, it lives and moves and has its being in—*the shared definitions of situations*. At the center of that network is, as for the person, its *self*-definition. Now, whatever else the social scientist does, he *redefines* and thereby, and to this extent, *alters* the society. Indeed, insofar as he functions as a social scientist, he does nothing else: even when he seems to function otherwise, when he "merely" records the going definitions of his society, he has altered the general level of self-consciousness in reference to the definition, he has brought it into or, to the threshold of, critical awareness, and thereby altered it functionally about as radically as it can be altered. So the social scientist is, willy-nilly, in the business of altering society. We can repeat Boyle's law indefinitely without changing the molecular dance; we cannot describe the activity of status-seeking without changing the system and its "laws." So, in the very performance of his scientific role, the social scientist is a social actor, a crucial actor, a mover and shaker, parallel in function to any formally designated politician, and probably eventually more powerful. Who was it said, "Let me write the songs of a nation. . . ." ? Better, in our day, he should have said: "Let me write its definitions . . . ," for the right to define is the right to make and unmake, create or destroy.

Even when this inescapable entanglement in action is recognized, a second effort is made to save some special, extraordinary, and in some sense superior status or standpoint for the social scientist. It is held, briefly, that he is under the discipline of his data (and his method), and that these drive him to a position very little dependent on his personal predilections and preferences. It is usually allowed that "interest" may well direct enquiry up to the point where an object of attention is selected, but that beyond that point the scientific process somehow takes over and controls outcome.

Even if the claim were conceded, it would be almost infinitely damaging to the asserted role of the social scientist; for the right to attend to this and not that *is* the right to direct attention hither and not thither, i.e., to adjudicate on the basis of personal sensibilities and preferences. Suppose a judge declared a free power to direct attention to whatever in the evidence interested him; it would be nearly equivalent to a proclamation that he will decide the outcome in terms of his private program.

But the claim cannot be allowed; the scientific process does *not* somehow take over once the object is focused under the eyepiece. For there is still the selection of the light in which the object is to be viewed, the context in which it is to be seen (actually *put*), and the setting of canons for discrimination between true and false, or more and less plausible propositions. I am not saying that "reality" constrains the social scientist in no way at all; but I am saying that the constraint is not much, if at all, tighter than the corresponding reality lays upon the artist, say a portraitist or painter. There is in each case a literal infinity of non-false representations that can be made; and *which* will be made in actuality is as much poetic in motive and political in effect as any other essentially expressive action. For that is what social science is: a ritualized acting out of an internal choice or necessity, in which the ritual in some sense orders and hence renders comprehensible, while in another sense it frees and hence allows the largest latitude for the personal. I shall not document these statements here, but it should be obvious that one may, for instance, "account for" delinquency, say, in countless ways: as an expression of the delinquent's wish or character or need; as a consequence of his parents' acts or unconscious motivations, or those of *their* parents; as a result of differential association or communication; as a function of the slum, the economic system, advertising, the police system, the rating and dating scheme; as a result of want of care in the folks stolen from or beat up —the victim makes the crime!—or the presence of alleys or want of light at the site; as an artifact of unreasonable laws. And so, literally, *ad infinitum*. The putting of all these true propositions together in one book, as in most texts on the subject, does not alter the status of the whole over that of the parts, for the ratio of one to infinity is the same as the ratio of ten to infinity. It should be obvious, too, that what is selected for exposition out of this interminable tangle is not free of either personal motive or political consequence: indeed, it arises almost altogether out of the first and eventuates almost altogether in the second. (The word "almost" is meant to bar patently false propositions, the exclusion of these being indeed one of the virtues of social science over less scrupulous propaganda.)

I have not presumed explicitly to adjudicate between the two competing emphases in the generalized melioristic enterprise that we all share. We are all, I am sure, would-be orthogenists—most so, those who would deny it. The poles represent selective concentration upon the *system of the person* as the unit and an *art* of improvement upon it, at one end, and selective concentration upon a *transpersonal system*—the social or political or economic or cultural order—and a *science* about it and how it can be engineered at the other. I have not adjudicated—though clearly I have tried to affect an outcome—for all the usual reasons: personal, political, and, ultimately, poetic. I *have* tried to make clear that no one should too readily transfer his residence from one to the other pole in the belief that things are far different and far better at the place where one is not. It is not so. All the agonies that attend any art anywhere, all the necessities and all the constraints that what one *is* lays upon what one *does,* all the dubieties of what one senses over the certainties of what one sees, all the hazards of commitment and the helplessness of fate, all these and more attend no less those who would deal by reason with the many at one time, than those who would deal by intuition with individuals at many times. However we propose to enhance goods or mitigate ills, let us at least not continue in the illusion that there is some position from which, some method whereby, or some system wherein the costs upon us personally may be reduced and some cut-rate victory had. That it might be so is an enduring hope, but since nothing in history or prospect warrants it, it is a will-o'-the-wisp whose pursuit it were better to abandon.

General and Urban Ecology

3

EDWARD S. DEEVEY, JR.

The systems we are concerned with in this group of papers—mind, personality, the city, society—have at least one thing in common: they are all Latin nouns of the third declension, and the Romans thought of them all as feminine. The grammatical point is not as completely irrelevant as it seems, for the way these nouns were inflected two thousand years ago has a bearing on the way we think about them today. *Civitas,* city, is third declension because it is an abstraction, like *societas,* and it is worth noticing that the world itself connotes, not the physical city, for that is *urbs,* but the complex set of relationships that this symposium is about.

The city, in its sense of *civitas,* conceals some excessively abstract notions under its urbane facade, and this is my excuse for sketching some models that are pretty fancy themselves, being in fact models designed to show how to make models. It is comforting to remember that Los Angeles, the scene of this symposium, is a city that likes fancy models, mostly of feminine gender, and one in which no one insists that a model have any definable resemblance to reality.

The kind of model that I propose is appropriate for the outer environs of Hollywood, for I believe I first saw its simplest form in a vintage *Mickey House,* or probably even earlier, in one or all of those *Aesop's Fables* that used to enliven Saturday afternoons in my boyhood. It is the standard sequence of the bulging house, not simply bulging but rapidly swelling and shrinking as the combat rages furiously inside. Now, *ecology* is derived from *oikos;* it is "the study of houses." But it is interested only in inhabited houses, house and inhabitants being regarded, abstractly of course, as a set of interactions. And here is a house whose inhabitants are interacting, with each other and with the walls, so that the walls wobble. I'll get my imagery out of the kindergarten presently, but I want to suggest that some wobble is found in all really interesting houses, whether we can see it easily or need a cartoonist to emphasize it for us. Wobble is intrinsic because it is an unavoidable consequence of the way complex systems maintain themselves as systems. What I am suggesting about the city, and the only license an ecologist has to contribute to a symposium on the city, is that the city is a *system*—another abstract feminine noun—and that the long historical view that ecology provides, if made sufficiently abstract but adequately illustrated by models, may give students of urban systems ways of thinking about them that will make this matter of wobble less agonizing.

Man is a visualizing animal, and likes his models visible. The wobbling walls are visible but somewhat unrealistic. A better place to start would be with the *temperature* of a house. Perhaps I should first explain, parenthetically, that where I live it is customary to heat houses, and the conventional device is an automatic oil furnace regulated by a gadget on the wall called a *thermostat*, an electric relay that turns the furnace on and off when the temperature falls below or rises above a pre-set level. The temperature is not visible, but the thermostat is, and if we distrust our skin as an instrument of sensation, we can read a thermometer at intervals and draw a graph, thus making a visual model that embodies quite a few debatable concepts, including the divisibility of time and its progression from left to right. Sidestepping any debate on the handedness of time, I hurry on to point to the thermostat as a model with most of the features I need. Because, of course, the temperature is not constant, but oscillates, and it oscillates more in the remote recesses of the house than it does in the living room where the thermostat is. This is because the air in the house is not circulated rapidly and completely, but only with some delays. So if an underheated bedroom needs heat, it takes some time for it to communicate this, by slow mixing, to the air in the living room, which responds by getting cooler, eventually notifying the thermostat that it is time to turn on the furnace. Meanwhile the underheated room continues its downward wobble, and is bound to get cooler before it gets warmer.

The language in which I describe this everyday experience is full of abstract notions of which the models are words; unintentionally, I use the metaphors of information theory when I speak of needs and responses and of air communicating, just as the engineer does when he says the thermostat is calling for heat. But this is just noted in passing; for now I am concerned to emphasize the time-delay in response and the wobble that results.

From the point of view of the bedroom, the living room is a poor place for a thermostat, because it is insulated from the place where the real decisions should be made, and the flow of air takes too much time. Suppose we build an asbestos box around the thermostat. Now the time-delay in transmitting warm or cold air from the house to the thermostat is unreasonably long, and the temperature in the living room oscillates too, while the little man inside the box, being perfectly comfortable himself, wonders what all the fuss is about outside. As we play with this model in imagination, we begin to hear mutters about the remoteness of the seat of authority, breaking down the barriers to allow flow of information, and so on. But if it were desirable, from the standpoint of improving the whole system, to *increase* the wobble—in order to detect it at all, for instance; or to design a device to protect the nursery from excessive wobble while the grown-ups enjoy a fire in the living room fireplace—the fact of interest is that insulating the thermostat *lengthens* the time-delay in the system but *shortens* the time the engineer needs to find out the answers.

I promised to get my imagery out of the kindergarten, and here we are still in the nursery. I confess that I had not realized before how literally ecology is the study of houses. Very soon I shall have to come to grips with the real problems, as social scientists see them; by now most readers will have got well ahead of me, and rejected all my implied analogies with social systems, not as false, maybe, but as unhelpful. Society, the city, and the personality are systems, granted; but they are far more complex than the elastic house or the insulated thermostat. And social science can have no engineering until it has some science; social scientists cannot know in advance how their systems work, since they weren't allowed to design them, and they certainly do not know where the thermostats are, what they regulate, or what their time-delays are. I do not pretend to have the answers to those questions; but I maintain that they cannot be answered by the human mind without the aid of models. I also suspect that social science is better than some social scientists realize. Anyway, the thermostat has *most* of the features I need, though not all of them.

Now I want to look briefly at population biology, which belongs to an older tradition of ecology and yet has always been a social science, otherwise named demography.

The great achievement of nineteenth-century demography was Verhulst's perception that populations grow by a self-limiting process. Malthus, in the eighteenth century, merely wished he could be sure of that, and Pearl, in the early twentieth century, contributed some illustrations of Verhulst's abstruse statement, which he had rediscovered for himself after some engaging studies of fruit-flies in milk bottles and of hens in a henhouse. Since Pearl's death in 1940, some animal ecologists have been doing interesting things: they have found Verhulst's model not wrong, but inadequate, and inadequate in some instructive ways. As always, application of the model to a variety of animals has proved informative, and it seems that while it serves very well for ideally simple animals, such as one-celled protozoans, the farther up the scale one goes the more serious are the inadequacies.

A close look at Verhulst's model shows at once some things that are not quite right. It says simply that growth results from successive doublings of mass or numbers, 1, 2, 4, 8, and so on, but that the closer the approach to some limiting value, in a finite environment, the more the doubling rate is depressed, so that in equal intervals of time the numbers are more like 1, 1.9, 3.5, 6.5, and so on. That is what is meant by self-limitation—the population limits its own rate of increase. And Paramecium in a drop of pond water, with food kept constant, does seem to obey this kind of law. But Paramecium is a semi-imaginary animal that seems to have been invented to fit the model. When one individual divides, death and reproduction occur in the same instant. So the animal defines population increase, with mathematical elegance, as "birth = death." If death and reproduction are separated in time, or befall different individuals at any moment, as they ordinarily do, one may anticipate trouble with the model's definition of increase. And even with Paramecium that matter of the upper limit conceals a paradox: at maximum or equilibrium population, when we say that the carrying capacity of the water drop has been reached, births must exactly equal deaths, so any individual that dies makes room for one new one; but if there is no room for a new Paramecium, none can be born, but neither can any old one die. What fun Aristophanes would have had with a model that predicts Tithonus' fate to be universal! *The Grasshoppers,* he might have called the play, and Athens would have laughed for weeks.

For a population coasting along at equilibrium, then, births in a sense regulate deaths and deaths regulate births, the thermostats are interlocked, or coupled, and yet some small degree of wobble is intrinsic. One feels intuitively that the more widely births and deaths are separated in space or time, or the more different the other devices that regulate births and deaths, the greater the wobble, since increasing the time-delay in regulation amounts to insulating a thermostat. Daphnia, the water flea, is an animal designed by nature to prove this point; it sounds partly imaginary, too, being parthenogenetic, but of course all good abstractions are of feminine gender. What happens, roughly, is this: a well-fed female Daphnia can drop a clutch of fifty young, and do so every couple of days throughout a life of a month or so; but with food supply constant, the oftener she and her daughters try *that* trick, the less likely any are to be well fed. Verhulst's limitation is obeyed, but not very scrupulously, and a few mistimed clutches can make some wide misses that need to be corrected. Conversely, on the downward swing that ensues, a starved Daphnia stops reproducing and eventually dies, but the death of one adult female encourages the more rapid growth, and quicker reproduction, of several smaller and less voracious young, provided of course there are any young around to respond. Everything that happens is both a cause and a consequence of some particular relation of numbers, sizes, and ages to food supply; but, whether an individual Daphnia responds to a change in food supply by altering her rate of growth or reproduction, or by dying, depends not only on what the change is, but on her age, size, and previous history of growth and reproduction. Result: some pretty spectacular wobbles, not necessarily regular, but approximately predictable if we know the age and size of the members and the time it takes for a given set of conditions to exert their effects. As these times are all different, and differ for every age and size, the system is full of coupled regulators. Any one regulator takes a little time, and guarantees a certain amount of wobble in whatever it is that it regulates; but any given wobble is a message that triggers some other regulator to correct, or over-correct, the wobble.

Having hinted again, by the word *message,* that wobble is information, propagated through a system with some time lag, or friction, I refrain again from enlarging on the point, and use it only to emphasize that vertebrate populations contain more kinds of information than Daphnia is likely to find meaningful, and hence more kinds of friction. Daphnia populations, anyway the ones that L. B. Slobodkin[1] deals with, can be handled by a model that includes only a few kinds of sticky regulators; just as all Paramecia look alike to a mathematician, all Daphnia of a particular age or size can be treated as equivalent. Vertebrates, though, have individualities, and, knowing each other personally, are capable of responding to each other's individualities. In an elementary demonstration of this proposition, Marjorie Douglis[2] showed, a few years ago, that hens can be made to take up part-time residence in several different flocks, meeting like bridge clubs for an hour or so each week, and can learn to occupy a different place in the peck-order of each. Once personality, even if categorized as social role, is admitted to the list of properties that regulate behavior, or are regulated by it, the potential array of slow messages increases astronomically—presumably as something to the power of n to the mth power, where n is the number of kinds of messages and m is the number of personalities, or roles.

Evidently we shall be a long time in understanding this kind of language; but part of its vocabulary has been identified in a general way, and may be called *social stress*. Just as a dog's snarl is unambiguous, whether the dog is a French poodle or a Russian wolfhound, the import of stress can be freely translated without knowing what all the words mean. And what it seems to imply, for vertebrates, is a coupling of endocrine responses within the body to messages from outside, so that an array of social messages transforms the personality and in turn is transformed, or regulated, by the personality. This would mean, among other things, that overcrowding in a population of mammals contains the power to regulate itself; as social stress pushes some individuals beyond their personal limit of endurance, their reproductive success declines—male sterility, abortion, and infanticide by exposure and by cannibalism are all verified in populations of badly overcrowded mice. And even if the death rate remains unchanged, the overcrowding is not likely to last indefinitely. Beyond that, there is a terrifying new possibility, supported by several recent studies with mice, that social stress is perceived, or at any rate responded to, by individuals still unborn; my former student, Kim Keeley,[3] has shown that the stress of crowding is transmitted from crowded mother to fetus across the placenta, not through the milk.

The behavior of the young mice in these experiments is modified throughout their own lives. I'm happy to be able to say that so far the modifications are trivial—possibly, since the offspring of crowded mice leave fewer droppings, according to one test, we may call the modification beneficial—but *any* prenatal influence on behavior opens vistas, and an audience of psychiatrists needs no help from me in bringing those vistas into focus.

It should be noted that I have not said that social forces are the only kind of stress, or that all oscillation of numbers of mammals is induced by stress. I mention this in deference to some of my zoological colleagues. Field zoologists, especially those who study the fluctuating populations of Arctic mammals, have been slow to accept social behavior as the source of the wobble they see, and this caution is proper. Although migrating lemmings are undeniably sick animals, the situation may be the one so familiar to psychiatrists, namely, that we see only the psychotics who present themselves for treatment. The suggestion I made[4] a couple of years ago, that lemmings migrate and snowshoe hares oscillate in numbers because they are socially stressed at home, was the kind of journalistic suggestion that is easier to make than to investigate. In the laboratory, though, what happens to crowded mice and rats is unmistakable, and the notion of social stress does not stand or fall by what happens in wild nature. Neither does the fact that most people of my acquaintance are well adjusted alter the problem of public mental health. In fact, not having known any lemmings personally, I am prepared to believe their home life idyllic, except for the weasels and jaegers; I would rather expect most vertebrate populations to wobble less than Daphnia does, simply because they have more ways of correcting wobble. But under unusual circumstances, such as captivity, some of these regulators are disconnected, just as one might unhook one thermostat and insulate another to increase the wobble and pinpoint its source. Intensifying social stress in the laboratory is an engineers' trick—a comparatively safe, comfortable, and useful trick—for tinkering with the machinery of a complex system.

One may or may not agree that my model of vertebrate populations is coming to grips with social systems; but at least my imagery has finally got out of the kindergarten. Infanticide by cannibalism has an ugly sound, even to those who specialize in disturbed personalities. I said I hoped to be helpful, though, and a murine version of Swift's *Modest Proposal* for meeting the population problem is not what I have in mind. If I'm right in thinking that sociologically trained readers are still ahead of my argument, their next objection is well taken: population biology is complex enough to be interesting, no doubt, but it is an experimental science, which social science is not. Engineers' tricks for testing for sticky regulators are simply not available. What do ecologists do when confronted by systems that are both complex and unmanageable, like female intuition or the city of Los Angeles?

The answer, briefly, is that they do just what social scientists do—substitute inference from history for experimental control. If that is too general a way of putting it, let me say that ecologists look for wobble, and use it wherever they find it. That is why I want students of cities to take their intellectual models from ecology, instead of from physics and chemistry. For classical physics, at any rate, wobble is just a symptom of faulty experimental design, whereas for us who cannot experiment, it is the golden key. Perhaps I can make the point clearer by turning to a system that is even more complex than society.

The biosphere may sound like the abstraction to end all abstractions, but some of it is perfectly visible, all men are part of it, and it is approachable at many points. Suppose we start at what may seem an unlikely place, the climate of the last century, which is known to have been getting warmer. The trend is hard to detect in middle latitudes, but very obvious in the Arctic; evidently there is a sticky thermostat in our living room, and Greenland is an underheated bedroom, temporarily being overheated. The thermostat is partly made of salt water, which holds more heat than air, and there is more water, containing far more heat, in middle latitudes than in the Arctic. As we take account of ocean currents, wind forces and directions, distribution of land and sea, and a few dozen other measurable variables, we can account for the zonation of climates, the difference between maritime and continental regimes, and so on, and we can even explain that *if* there is a perturbation in the system, Greenland ought to see it as more violent than California does. But the elegant equilibrium theories that physics provides for each variable in the system predict equilibrium for the lot, if the time is long enough, and we know that the climate has not varied much in the ten thousand years since the ice sheets vacated the United States and western Europe. Ten thousand years should be ample time for equilibrium; why, then, does the climate wobble at all?

The pure physics of the situation contains one obvious source of wobble, the annual variations in the relation of earth and sun. But nothing is more predictable than the march of the seasons, and celestial mechanics provides no clue to a net change of climate over a series of years. A minor component of the system that might be critical, though, is the carbon dioxide content of the air. Like glass in a greenhouse, carbon dioxide traps long-wave radiation that otherwise might go back to space. And carbon dioxide is a fuel that builds vegetation—a messy substance that meteorologists would prefer to ignore, because if life is interlocked with the physical system, its physics is no longer pure. Moreover, carbon dioxide has been poured into the atmosphere at an alarming rate, since the Industrial Revolution, the quantity now present having increased about 10 per cent in a hundred years. It has been calculated that if the amount in the air should double, the climate would warm up enough to melt the world's glaciers, sea level would rise by about a hundred meters, and Los Angeles would be one of many Cities in the Sea, to be explored by bewildered skin divers. Could the 10 per cent increase of carbon dioxide be the perturbation that has warmed the climate during the same century?

Yes, it could, but I doubt that it is. For one thing, this recent wobble of climate looks like any of a dozen others that took place in the last few thousand years, before the combustion of coal and petroleum began on any such scale.[5] And the fossil fuels have produced labeled carbon, carbon that is millions of years old and has lost all its radioactive carbon-14 long ago. Taking advantage of this label, we know that only about 2 per cent of the air's carbon dioxide is from this source, whereas enough carbon has been burned to account for all the 10 per cent increase. So the rest of the added fossil carbon must be in the sea and in vegetation. The carbon dioxide in air exchanges rapidly, within a few years, with the much bigger supply in the ocean, and if there is more in the air than there used to be, there may be less in the sea, or in plants. Perhaps, then, the change of climate came first, and has by now boiled off more carbon dioxide from a slightly warmer ocean, or has oxidized a little more peat or humus; or again, perhaps the climatic change is secondary, and the clearing of land for agriculture has oxidized more humus, or slowed up the fixation of carbon by plants, so that more stays behind in the air.

If I were to build a model of this system,[6] I should have to start with a long list of sticky regulators, including the sluggish circulation of the deep ocean, the production and decay of humus, the whole photosynthetic machinery, and the making of reefs of carbonate rock by corals. In addition, I should have to look closely at any process that changes the acidity of sea water, such as the pollution of the atmosphere with sulfur dioxide from coal and petroleum. Two things have been learned in the last few years that put sulfur in the big picture: that human activities account for about a quarter of all the sulfur that enters the ocean, and that sulfur bacteria annually metabolize a major fraction of the sulfur in the air, just as green plants metabolize the carbon. I won't build this model formally, though, for it would wheeze and cough like a Model-T Ford, and end in a crashing anticlimax; without enough of the right numbers the model still will not tell us why the climate wobbles, or whether the extra industrial carbon dioxide is an irrelevancy.

What I can do, without actually making the model of the biosphere, is to mention a couple of engineers' tricks that amount to tinkering with its history. That may sound like the neatest trick of the ages, but I mean it metaphorically; it is something that social science, especially comparative anthropology, does all the time. For instance, some of the climatic wobble is preserved in the peat of bogs, not only as interbedded pollen grains, which give the history of the vegetation, but as layers of fossil carbohydrate, the peat itself, formed under alternating wet and drier climates. The water that supplied these bogs all came from the sky, and sulfur was one of the airborne chemicals that came along with it. If the sulfur sticks to the peat, the same isotopic labels that prove the oceanic sulfur in the air to be partly bacterial may tell us how much of the air was maritime when each layer of peat was formed.

The same kind of trick, applied to the carbon in the peat, might tell us at once what that extra 10 per cent of carbon dioxide is doing in our twentieth-century atmosphere. The idea would be to measure the carbon dioxide of the air through several oscillations of climate. Unfortunately that carbon is needed first to date the peat, and can't give the atmospheric carbon content at the same time. But tree rings are made of carbon that is already dated, and if we look at the isotopic labels in this carbon, over the last few centuries, we see some fascinating wobble. It may be just what is needed to explain the climate, and then it may not; it is carbon-14 that varies, and we may only be seeing fluctuations in the strength of the cosmic rays that make this isotope. Not that *that* wouldn't be interesting; but there comes a point when even an ecologist begins to wonder which is queerer—the house or its inhabitants.

I thought social scientists might find it refreshing to see that the so-called hard sciences can be as difficult as their own, and for the same reason—that *life is interlocked with physical systems.* Physics and chemistry are not hard-difficult as well as hard-rigorous; as compared with the ecological and behavioral sciences, they have gained rigor by avoiding the complexity that would make them difficult. Once the complexity is admitted, as I have tried to show, rigor in isolating cause and effect is necessary but insufficient. One needs a more imaginative model than a Bunsen burner under a beaker of water. My recipe, then, is to look for coupled regulators, and capitalize on wobble as the clue to the way they work.

I hope I am not expected to be much more specific than this. I have suggested that the model of the biosphere is faulty because it lacks numbers, and I know that numbers are harder to come by in social science than they are in ecology. But numbers are abstractions too, often useful but sometimes misleading, and in social science the things that wobble and are regulated are not necessarily understood by counting something. A couple of crude examples must suffice, for I have already got beyond my depth.

The political situation in Africa contains some fairly distressing wobble. At first sight this is surprising; for, as ethnologists know, the native tribesmen are brilliant political strategists in tribal contexts, and the practical theorists who worked out their kinship and kingship systems made their European contemporaries look like naive schoolboys. And then one remembers the long economic history that Africa has been forced to bypass. It looks as though economic development, including feudalism as a stage, is a sticky regulator, and colonialism is the insulator that intensifies political oscillation. This gross oversimplification is loaded with debatable abstractions, of course, and is not even new, but in its very language the model suggests ways of tinkering with history to see what less obvious regulators may turn up.

Consider, finally, that gorgeous array of jittery regulators that make a city so entertaining. To take an example more or less at random, the concepts of the city as *urbs* and as *civitas*, though they are abstractions as cloudy as any invented by the human mind, can act on each other physically as coupled regulators. I mean that *urbs* is structure and *civitas* is function, and the realization of some function—any function—as structure precludes some other function, which immediately wants to tear down the structure and build a new one. If it succeeds, envy and economics will make the victory a fleeting one. Hence the wavering between hard concrete and fluid personalities, between crossroads and massive communication centers, that we see especially in the central city.

Different cities have bargained differently with history, so that what wobbles in one may seem to be smoothly regulated in another. As long as some social force is smoothly regulated, with little time-delay, we are likely to overlook it entirely, and so the cities where it wobbles more are instructive, in the same way that Daphnia populations and Greenland's climate are instructive. When I urge social scientists to allow themselves to be instructed by wobble, I do not mean that they must sit like bird watchers, expecting that if wobble is watched for long enough it will go away. In that long historical view I spoke of, it probably will; but some time before that, or even before Los Angeles is drowned by a hundred meters of salt water, I think there are some genuine engineers' tricks to be tried. Any engineer who tries to smooth perturbations out of existence, though, is working on a dangerously naive model, for if there were no perturbations there would be nothing left to be regulated.

References

1. Slobodkin, L. B., *Growth and Regulation of Animal Populations*, New York: Holt, 1961.
2. Douglis, M. B., "Social Factors Influencing the Hierarchies of the Domestic Hen: the Interaction Between Resident and Part-time Members of Organized Flocks," *Physiological Zoology*, 21:147-182, 1948.
3. Keeley, K., "Prenatal Influence on Behavior of Offspring of Crowded Mice," *Science*, 135:44-45, 1962.

4. Deevey, E. S., "The Hare and the Haruspex," *Yale Review,* 59:161-179, 1960.
5. ———, "Bogs," *Scientific American,* 199:114-122, 1958.
6. De Vries, H., "Measurement and Use of Natural Radiocarbon," in *Researches in Geochemistry,* P. H. Abelson, ed., New York: Wiley, 1959.

Population Density and Social Pathology

4

JOHN B. CALHOUN

In the celebrated thesis of Thomas Malthus, vice and misery impose the ultimate natural limit on the growth of populations. Students of the subject have given most of their attention to misery, that is, to predation, disease, and food supply as forces that operate to adjust the size of a population to its environment. But what of vice? Setting aside the moral burden of this word, what are the effects of the social behavior of a species on population growth—and of population density on social behavior?

Some years ago I attempted to submit this question to experimental inquiry. I confined a population of wild Norway rats in a quarter-acre enclosure. With an abundance of food and places to live and with predation and disease eliminated or minimized, only the animals' behavior with respect to one another remained as a factor that might affect the increase in their number. There could be no escape from the behavioral consequences of rising population density. By the end of 27 months the population had become stabilized at 150 adults. Yet adult mortality was so low that 5,000 adults might have been expected from the observed reproductive rate. The reason this larger population did not materialize was that infant mortality was extremely high. Even with only 150 adults in the enclosure, stress from social interaction led to such disruption of maternal behavior that few young survived.

With this background in mind I turned to observation of a domesticated albino strain of the Norway rat under more controlled circumstances indoors. The data for the present discussion come from the histories of six different populations. Each was permitted to increase to approximately twice the number that my experience had indicated could occupy the available space with only moderate stress from social interaction. In each case my associates and I maintained close surveillance of the colonies for 16 months in order to obtain detailed records of the modifications of behavior induced by population density.

The consequences of the behavioral pathology we observed were most apparent among the females. Many were unable to carry pregnancy to full term or to survive delivery of their litters if they did. An even greater number, after successfully giving birth, fell short in their maternal functions. Among the males the behavior disturbances ranged from sexual deviation to cannibalism and from frenetic overactivity to a pathological withdrawal from which individuals would emerge to eat, drink and move about only when other members of the community were asleep. The social organization of the animals showed equal disruption. Each of the experimental populations divided itself into several groups, in each of which the sex ratios were drastically modified. One group might consist of 6 or 7 females and 1 male, whereas another would have 20 males and only 10 females.

The common source of these disturbances became most dramatically apparent in the populations of our first series of three experiments, in which we observed the development of what we called a behavioral sink. The animals would crowd together in greatest number in one of the 4 interconnecting pens in which the colony was maintained. As many as 60 of the 80 rats in each experimental population would assemble in one pen during periods of feeding. Individual rats would rarely eat except in the company of other rats. As a result extreme population densities developed in the pen adopted for eating, leaving the others with sparse populations.

Eating and other biological activities were thereby transformed into social activities in which the principal satisfaction was interaction with other rats. In the case of eating, this transformation of behavior did not keep the animals from securing adequate nutrition. But the same pathological "togetherness" tended to disrupt the ordered sequences of activity involved in other vital modes of behavior such as the courting of sex partners, the building of nests and the nursing and care of the young. In the experiments in which the behavioral sink developed, infant mortality ran as high as 96 per cent among the most disoriented groups in the population. Even in the absence of the behavioral sink, in the second series of three experiments, infant mortality reached 80 per cent among the corresponding members of the experimental populations.

The design of the experiments was relatively simple. The three populations of the first series each began with 32 rats; each population of the second series began with 56 rats. In all cases the animals were just past weaning and were evenly divided between males and females. By the twelfth month all the populations had multiplied and each comprised 80 adults. Thereafter removal of the infants that survived birth and weaning held the populations steady. Although the destructive effects of population density increased during the course of the experiments, and the mortality rate among the females and among the young was much higher in the sixteenth month than it was earlier, the number of young that survived to weaning was always large enough to offset the effects of adult mortality and actually to increase the population. The evidence indicates, however, that in time failures of reproductive function would have caused the colonies to die out. At the end of the first series of experiments eight rats—the four healthiest males and the four healthiest females in each of two populations—were permitted to survive. These animals were 6 months old at the time, in the prime of life. Yet, in spite of the fact that they no longer lived in overpopulated environments, they produced fewer litters in the next 6 months than would normally have been expected. Nor did any of the offspring that were born survive to maturity.

The males and females that initiated each experiment were placed, in groups of the same size and sex composition, in each of the 4 pens that partitioned a 10-by-14-foot observation room. The pens were complete dwelling units; each contained a drinking fountain, a food hopper and an elevated artificial burrow, reached by a winding staircase and holding five nest boxes. A window in the ceiling of the room permitted observation, and there was a door in one wall. With space for a colony of 12 adults in each pen—the size of the groups in which rats are normally found—this setup should have been able to support 48 rats comfortably. At the stabilized number of 80, an equal distribution of the animals would have found 20 adult rats in each pen. But the animals did not dispose themselves in this way.

Biasing factors were introduced in the physical design of the environment to encourage differential use of the 4 pens. The partitions separating the pens were electrified so that the rats could not climb them. Ramps across three of the partitions enabled the animals to get from one pen to another and so traverse the entire room. With no ramps to permit crossing of the fourth partition, however, the pens on each side of it became the end pens of what was topologically a row of 4. The rats had to make a complete circuit of the room to go from the pen we designated 1 to the pen designated 4 on the other side of the partition separating the two. This arrangement of ramps immediately skewed the mathematical probabilities in favor of a higher population density in pens 2 and 3 than in pens 1 and 4. Pens 2 and 3 could be reached by two ramps, whereas pens 1 and 4 had only one each.

The use of pen 4 was further discouraged by the elevation of its burrow to a height greater than that of the burrow in the other end pen. The two middle pens were similarly distinguished from each other, the burrow in pen 3 being higher than that in pen 2. But here the differential appears to have played a smaller role, although pen 2 was used somewhat more often than pen 3.

With the distribution of the rats biased by these physical arrangements, the sizes of the groups in each pen could have been expected to range from as few as 13 to as many as 27. With the passage of time, however, changes in behavior tended to skew the distribution of the rats among the pens even more. Of the 100 distinct sleeping groups counted in the tenth to twelfth month of each experiment, only 37 fell within the expected size range. In 33 groups there were fewer than 13 rats, and in 30 groups the count exceeded 27. The sex ratio approximated equality only in those groups that fell within the expected size range. In the smaller groups, generally composed of 8 adults, there were seldom more than 2 males. In the larger groups, on the other hand, there were many more males than females. As might be expected, the smaller groups established themselves in the end pens, whereas the larger groups were usually observed to form in the middle pens. The female members of the population distributed themselves about equally in the 4 pens, but the male population was concentrated almost overwhelmingly in the middle pens.

One major factor in the creation of this state of affairs was the struggle for status that took place among the males. Shortly after male rats reach maturity, at about 6 months of age, they enter into a round robin of fights that eventually fixes their position in the social hierarchy. In our experiments such fights took place among the males in all the pens, both middle and end. In the end pens, however, it became possible for a single dominant male to take over the area as his territory. During the period when the social hierarchy was being established, the subordinate males in all pens adopted the habit of rising early. This enabled them to eat and drink in peace. Since rats generally eat in the course of their normal wanderings, the subordinate residents of the end pens were likely to feed in one of the middle pens. When, after feeding, they wanted to return to their original quarters, they would find it very difficult. By this time the most dominant male in the pen would probably have awakened, and he would engage the subordinates in fights as they tried to come down the one ramp to the pen. For a while the subordinate would continue its efforts to return to what had been its home pen, but after a succession of defeats it would become so conditioned that it would not even make the attempt. In essence, the dominant male established his territorial dominion and his control over a harem of females, not by driving the other males out, but by preventing their return.

Once a male had established his dominion over an end pen and the harem it contained, he was usually able to maintain it. Although he slept a good deal of the time, he made his sleeping quarters at the base of the ramp. He was, therefore, on perpetual guard. Awakening as soon as another male appeared at the head of the ramp, he had only to open his eyes for the invader to wheel around and return to the adjoining pen. On the other hand, he would sleep calmly through all the comings and goings of his harem; seemingly he did not even hear their clatterings up and down the wire ramp. His conduct during his waking hours reflected his dominant status. He would move about in a casual and deliberate fashion, occasionally inspecting the burrow and nests of his harem. But he would rarely enter a burrow, as some other males did, merely to ferret out the females.

A territorial male might tolerate other males in his domain provided they respected his status. Such subordinate males inhabited the end pens in several of the experiments. Phlegmatic animals, they spent most of their time hidden in the burrow with the adult females, and their excursions to the floor lasted only as long as it took them to obtain food and water. Although they never attempted to engage in sexual activity with any of the females, they were likely, on those rare occasions when they encountered the dominant male, to make repeated attempts to mount him. Generally the dominant male tolerated these advances.

In these end pens, where population density was lowest, the mortality rate among infants and females was also low. Of the various social environments that developed during the course of the experiments, the brood pens, as we called them, appeared to be the only healthy ones, at least in terms of the survival of the group. The harem females generally made good mothers. They nursed their young, built nests for them, and protected them from harm. If any situation arose that a mother considered a danger to her pups, she would pick the infants up one at a time and carry them in her mouth to a safer place. Nothing would distract her from this task until the entire litter had been moved. Half the infants born in the brood pens survived.

The pregnancy rates recorded among the females in the middle pens were no lower than those recorded in the end pens. But a smaller percentage of these pregnancies terminated in live births. In the second series of experiments 80 per cent of the infants born in the middle pens died before weaning. In the first series 96 per cent perished before this time. The males in the middle pens were no less affected than the females by the pressures of population density. In both series of experiments the social pathology among the males was high. In the first series, however, it was more aggravated than it was in the second.

This increase in disturbance among the middle-pen occupants of the first series of experiments was directly related to the development of the phenomenon of the behavioral sink—the outcome of any behavioral process that collects animals together in unusually great numbers. The unhealthy connotations of the term are not accidental: a behavioral sink does act to aggravate all forms of pathology that can be found within a group.

The emergence of a behavioral sink was fostered by the arrangements that were made for feeding the animals. In these experiments the food consisted of small, hard pellets that were kept in a circular hopper formed by wire mesh. In consequence, satisfaction of hunger required a continuous effort lasting several minutes. The chances therefore were good that while one rat was eating another would join it at the hopper. As was mentioned earlier, rats usually eat intermittently throughout their waking hours, whenever they are hungry and food is available. Since the arrangement of the ramps drew more rats into the middle pens than into the end ones, it was in these pens that individuals were most likely to find other individuals eating. As the population increased, the association of eating with the presence of other animals was further reinforced. Gradually the social aspect of the activity became determinant: the rats would rarely eat except at hoppers already in use by other animals.

At this point the process became a vicious circle. As more and more of the rats tended to collect at the hopper in one of the middle pens, the other hoppers became less desirable as eating places. The rats that were eating at these undesirable locations, finding themselves deserted by their group-mates, would transfer their feeding to the more crowded pen. By the time the three experiments in the first series drew to a close half or more of the populations were sleeping as well as eating in that pen. As a result there was a decided increase in the number of social adjustments each rat had to make every day. Regardless of which pen a rat slept in, it would go to one particular middle pen several times a day to eat. Therefore it was compelled daily to make some sort of adjustment to virtually every other rat in the experimental population.

No behavioral sinks developed in the second series of experiments, because we offered the rats their diet in a different way. A powdered food was set out in an open hopper. Since it took the animals only a little while to eat, the probability that two animals would be eating simultaneously was considerably reduced. In order to foster the emergence of a behavioral sink I supplied the pens with drinking fountains designed to prolong the drinking activity. The effect of this arrangement was unquestionably to make the animals social drinkers; they used the fountain mainly when other animals lined up at it. But the effect was also to discourage them from wandering and to prevent the development of a behavioral sink. Since rats generally drink immediately on arising, drinking and the social interaction it occasioned tended to keep them in the pens in which they slept. For this reason all social pathology in the second series of experiments, although severe, was less extreme than it was in the first series.

Females that lived in the densely populated middle pens became progressively less adept at building adequate nests and eventually stopped building nests at all. Normally rats of both sexes build nests, but females do so most vigorously around the time of parturition. It is an undertaking that involves repeated periods of sustained activity, searching out appropriate materials (in our experiments strips of paper supplied an abundance), transporting them bit by bit to the nest and there arranging them to form a cup-like depression, frequently sheltered by a hood. In a crowded middle pen, however, the ability of females to persist in this biologically essential activity became markedly impaired. The first sign of disruption was a failure to build the nest to normal specifications. These females simply piled the strips of paper in a heap, sometimes trampling them into a pad that showed little sign of cup formation. Later in the experiment they would bring fewer and fewer strips to the nesting site. In the midst of transporting a bit of material they would drop it to engage in some other activity occasioned by contact and interaction with other individuals met on the way. In the extreme disruption of their behavior during the later months of the population's history they would build no nests at all but would bear the litters on the sawdust in the burrow box.

The middle-pen females similarly lost the ability to transport their litters from one place to another. They would move only part of their litters, and would scatter them by depositing the infants in different places or by simply dropping them on the floor of the pen. The infants thus abandoned throughout the pen were seldom nursed. They would die where they were dropped, and were thereupon generally eaten by the adults.

The social stresses that brought about this disorganization in the behavior of the middle-pen females were imposed with special weight on them when they came into heat. An estrous female would be pursued relentlessly by a pack of males, unable to escape from their soon unwanted attentions. Even when she retired to a burrow, some males would follow her. Among these females there was a correspondingly high rate of mortality from disorders in pregnancy and parturition. Nearly half of the first- and second-generation females that lived in the behavioral-sink situation had died of these causes by the end of the sixteenth month. Even in the absence of the extreme stresses of the behavioral sink, 25 per cent of the females died. In contrast, only 15 per cent of the adult males in both series of experiments died.

A female that lived in a brood pen was sheltered from these stresses even though during her periods of estrus she would leave her pen to mate with males in the other pens of the room. Once she was satisfied, however, she could return to the brood pen. There she was protected from the excessive attention of other males by the territorial male.

For the effect of population density on the males there is no index as explicit and objective as the infant and maternal mortality rates. We have attempted a first approximation of such an index, however, by scoring the behavior of the males on two scales: that of dominance and that of physical activity. The first index proved particularly effective in the early period of the experiments, when the males were approaching adulthood and beginning the fights that eventually fixed their status in the social hierarchy. The more fights a male initiated and the more fights he won, the more likely he was to establish a position of dominance. More than half the animals in each experiment gave up the struggle for status after a while, but among those that persisted a clear-cut hierarchy developed.

In the crowded middle pens no one individual occupied the top position in this hierarchy permanently. In every group of 12 or more males one was the most aggressive and most often the victor in fights. Nevertheless, this rat was periodically ousted from his position. At regular intervals during the course of their waking hours the top-ranking males engaged in free-for-alls that culminated in the transfer of dominance from one male to another. In between these tumultuous changings of the guard relative calm prevailed.

The aggressive, dominant animals were the most normal males in our populations. They seldom bothered either the females or the juveniles. Yet even they exhibited occasional signs of pathology, going berserk, attacking females, juveniles and the less active males, and showing a particular predilection—which rats do not normally display—for biting other animals on the tail.

Below the dominant males both on the status scale and in their level of activity were the homosexuals—a group perhaps better described as pansexual. These animals apparently could not discriminate between appropriate and inappropriate sex partners. They made sexual advances to males, juveniles and females that were not in estrus. The males, including the dominants as well as the others of the pansexuals' own group, usually accepted their attentions. The general level of activity of these animals was only moderate. They were frequently attacked by their dominant associates, but they very rarely contended for status.

Two other types of male emerged, both of which had resigned entirely from the struggle for dominance. They were, however, at exactly opposite poles as far as their levels of activity were concerned. The first were completely passive and moved through the community like somnambulists. They ignored all the other rats of both sexes, and all the other rats ignored them. Even when the females were in estrus, these passive animals made no advances to them. And only very rarely did other males attack them or approach them for any kind of play. To the casual observer the passive animals would have appeared to be the healthiest and most attractive members of the community. They were fat and sleek, and their fur showed none of the breaks and bare spots left by the fighting in which males usually engage. But their social disorientation was nearly complete.

Perhaps the strangest of all the types that emerged among the males was the group I have called the probers. These animals, which always lived in the middle pens, took no part at all in the status struggle. Nevertheless, they were the most active of all the males in the experimental populations, and they persisted in their activity in spite of attacks by the dominant animals. In addition to being hyperactive, the probers were both hypersexual and homosexual, and in time many of them became cannibalistic. They were always on the alert for estrous females. If they were none in their own pens, they would lie in wait for long periods at the tops of the ramps that gave on the brood pens and peer down into them. They always turned and fled as soon as the territorial rat caught sight of them. But even if they did not manage to escape unhurt, they would soon return to their vantage point.

The probers conducted their pursuit of estrous females in an abnormal manner. Mating among rats usually involves a distinct courtship ritual. In the first phase of this ritual the male pursues the female. She thereupon retires for a while into the burrow, and the male lies quietly in wait outside, occasionally poking his head into the burrow for a moment but never entering it. (In the wild forms of the Norway rat this phase usually involves a courtship dance on the mound at the mouth of the burrow.) The female at last emerges from the burrow and accepts the male's advances. Even in the disordered community of the middle pens this pattern was observed by all the males who engaged in normal heterosexual behavior. But the probers would not tolerate even a short period of waiting at the burrows in the pens where accessible females lived. As soon as a female retired to a burrow, a prober would follow her inside. On these expeditions the probers often found dead young lying in the nests; as a result they tended to become cannibalistic in the later months of the population's history.

Although the behaviorial sink did not develop in the second series of experiments, the pathology exhibited by the populations in both sets of experiments, and in all pens, was severe. Even in the brood pens, females could raise only half their young to weaning. Nor does the difference in infant mortality between the middle pens of the first and second series—96 per cent in the first as opposed to 80 per cent in the second—represent a biologically significant improvement. It is obvious that the behavioral repertory with which the Norway rat has emerged from the trials of evolution and domestication must break down under the social pressures generated by population density. In time, refinement of experimental procedures and of the interpretation of these studies may advance our understanding to the point where they may contribute to the making of value judgments about analogous problems confronting the human species.

Man and Environment 5

IAN L. MCHARG

The nature and scale of this enquiry can be simply introduced through an image conceived by Loren Eiseley. Man, far out in space, looks back to the distant earth, a celestial orb, blue-green oceans, green of verdant land, a celestial fruit. Examination discloses blemishes on the fruit, dispersed circles from which extend dynamic tentacles. The man concludes that these cankers are the works of man and asks, "Is man but a planetary disease?"

There are at least two conceptions within this image. Perhaps the most important is the view of a unity of life covering the earth, land and oceans, interacting as a single superorganism, the biosphere. A direct analogy can be found in man, composed of billion upon billion of cells but all of these operating as a single organism. From this the full relevance of the second conception emerges, the possibility that man is but a dispersed disease in the world-life body.

The conception of all life interacting as a single superorganism is as novel as is the conception of man as a planetary disease. The suggestion of man the destroyer, or rather brain the destroyer, is salutary to society which has traditionally abstracted brain from body, man from nature, and vaunted the rational process. This, too, is a recent view. Yet the problems are only of yesterday. Pre-atomic man was an inconsequential geological, biological, and ecological force; his major power was the threat of power. Now, in an instant, post-atomic man is the agent of evolutionary regression, a species now empowered to destroy all life.

In the history of human development, man has long been puny in the face of overwhelmingly powerful nature. His religions, philosophies, ethics and acts have tended to reflect a slave mentality, alternately submissive or arrogant toward nature. Judaism, Christianity,

Humanism tend to assert outrageously the separateness and dominance of man over nature, while animism and nature worship tend to assert total submission to an arbitrary nature. These attitudes are not urgent when human societies lack the power to make any serious impact on environment. These same attitudes become of first importance when man holds the power to cause evolutionary regressions of unimaginable effect or even to destroy all life.

Modern man is confronted with the awful problem of comprehending the role of man in nature. He must immediately find a *modus vivendi,* he must seek beyond for his role in nature, a role of unlimited potential yet governed by laws which he shares with all physical and organic systems. The primacy of man today is more based upon his power to destroy than to create. He is like an aboriginal, confronted with the necessity of operating a vast and complex machine, whose only tool is a hammer. Can modern man aspire to the role of agent in creation, creative participant in a total, unitary, evolving environment? If the pre-atomic past is dominated by the refinement of concern for man's acts towards man, the inauguration of the atomic age increases the dimension of this ancient concern and now adds the new and urgent necessity of understanding and resolving the interdependence of man and nature.

While the atomic threat overwhelms all other considerations this is by no means the only specter. The population implosion may well be as cataclysmic as the nuclear explosion. Should both of these threats be averted there remain the lesser processes of destruction which have gathered momentum since the nineteenth century. In this period we have seen the despoilation of continental resources accumulated over aeons of geological time, primeval forests destroyed, ancient resources of soil mined and sped to the sea, marching deserts, great deposits of fossil fuel dissipated into the atmosphere. In the country, man has ravaged nature; in the city, nature has been erased and man assaults man with insalubrity, ugliness and disorder. In short man has evolved and proliferated by exploiting historic accumulations of inert and organic resources, historic climaxes of plants and animals. His products are reserved for himself, his mark on the environment is most often despoliation and wreckage.

The Duality of Man and Nature

Conceptions of man and nature range between two wide extremes. The first, central to the Western tradition, is man-oriented. The cosmos is but a pyramid erected to support man on its pinnacle, reality exists only because man can observe it, indeed God is made in the image of man. The opposing view, identified with the Orient, postulates a unitary and all-encompassing nature within which man exists, man in nature.

These opposing views are the central duality, man and nature, West and East, white and black, brains and testicles, Classicism and Romanticism, orthodoxy and transnaturalism in Judaism, St. Thomas and St. Francis, Calvin and Luther, anthropomorphism and naturalism. The Western tradition vaunts the individual and the man-brain, and denigrates nature, animal, non-brain. In the Orient nature is omnipotent, revered, and man is but an aspect of nature. It would be as unwise to deny the affirmative aspects of either view as to diminish their negative effects. Yet today this duality demands urgent attention. The adequacy of the Western view of man and nature deserves to be questioned. Further, one must ask if these two views are mutually exclusive.

The opposition of these attitudes is itself testimony to an underlying unity, the unity of opposites. Do our defining skin and nerve ends divide us from environment or unite us to it? Is the perfectibility of man self-realizable? Is the earth a storeroom awaiting plunder? Is the cosmos a pyramid erected to support man?

The inheritors of the Judaic-Christian-Humanist tradition have received their injunction from Genesis, a man-oriented universe, man exclusively made in the image of God, given dominion over all life and non-life, enjoined to subdue the earth. The naturalist tradition in the West has no comparable identifiable text. It may be described as holding that the cosmos is unitary, that all systems are subject to common physical laws yet having unlimited potential; that in this world man is simply an inhabitant, free to develop his own potential. This view questions anthropocentrism and anthropomorphism; it does not diminish either man's uniqueness or his potential, only his claims to primacy and exclusive divinity. This view assumes that the precursors of man, plant and animal, his co-tenant contemporaries, share a cosmic role and potential.

From its origin in Judaism, extension in Classicism, reinforcement in Christianity, inflation in the Renaissance and absorption into the nineteeth and twentieth centuries, the anthropomorphic-anthropocentric view has become the tacit view of man versus nature.

Evolution of Power

The primate precursors of man, like their contemporary descendants, support neither a notably constructive, nor a notably destructive role in their ecological community. The primates live within a complex community which has continued to exist; no deleterious changes can be attributed to the primate nor does his existence appear to be essential for the support of his niche and habitat. When the primates abandoned instinct for reason and man emerged, new patterns of behavior emerged and new techniques were developed. Man acquired powers which increased his negative and destructive effect upon environment, but which left unchanged the possibility of a creative role in the environment. Aboriginal peoples survive today: Australian aborigines, Dravidians and Birbory in India, South African Bushmen, Veda in Ceylon, Ainu in Japan, Indians of Tierra del Fuego; none of these play a significantly destructive role in the environment. Hunters, primitive farmers, fishermen—their ecological role has changed little from that of the primate. Yet from aboriginal people there developed several new techniques which gave man a significantly destructive role within his enviroment. The prime destructive human tool was fire. The consequences of fire, originated by man, upon the ecology of the world cannot be measured, but there is reason to believe that its significance was very great indeed.

Perhaps the next most important device was that of animal husbandry, the domestication of grazing animals. These, sheep, goats, and cattle, have been very significant agents historically in modifying the ecology in large areas of the world. This modification is uniformly deleterious to the original environment. Deforestation is perhaps the third human system which has made considerable impact upon the physical environment. Whether involuntary, that is, as an unconscious product of fire, or as a consequence of goat and sheep herding, or as an economic policy, this process of razing forests has wrought great changes upon climate and microclimate, flora and fauna. However, the regenerative powers of nature are great; and while fire, domestic animals, and deforestation have denuded great areas of world surface, this retrogression can often be minimized or reversed by the natural processes of regeneration. Perhaps the next consequential act of man in modifying the natural environment was large-scale agriculture. We know that in many areas of the world agriculture can be sustained for many centuries without depletion of the soil. Man can create a new ecology in which he is the prime agent, in which the original ecological community has been changed, but which is nevertheless self-perpetuating. This condition is the exception. More typically agriculture has been, and is today, an extractive process in which the soil is mined and left depleted. Many areas of the world, once productive, are no longer capable of producing crops. Extractive agriculture has been historically a retrogressive process sustained by man.

The next important agent for modifying the physical environment is the human settlement, hamlet, village, town, city. It is hard to believe that any of the pre-classical, medieval, renaissance, or even eighteenth-century cities were able to achieve a transformation of the physical environment comparable to the agents mentioned before—fire, animal husbandry, deforestation, or extensive agriculture. But with the emergence of the nineteenth-century industrial city, there arose an agent certainly of comparable consequence, perhaps even of greater consequence, even more destructive of the physical environment and the balances of ecological communities in which man exists, than any of the prior human processes.

The large modern metropolis may be thirty miles in diameter. Much, if not all, of the land which it covers is sterilized. The micro-organisms in the soil no longer exist; the original animal inhabitants have largely been banished. Only a few members of the plant kingdom represent the original members of the initial ecology. The rivers are foul; the atmosphere is polluted; the original configuration of the land is only rarely in evidence; climate and micro-climate have retrogressed so that the external microclimate is more violent than was the case before the establishment of the city. Atmospheric pollution may be so severe as to account for 4,000 deaths in a single week of intense "fog," as was the case in London. Floods alternate with drought. Hydrocarbons, lead, carcenogenic agents, carbon dioxide, carbon monoxide concentrations, deteriorating conditions of atmospheric electricity—all of these represent retrogressive processes introduced and supported by man. The epidemiologist speaks of neuroses, lung cancer, heart and renal disease, ulcers, the stress diseases, as the badges of urban conditions. There has also arisen the specter of the effects of density and social pressure upon the incidence of disease and upon reproduction. The modern city contains other life-inhibiting aspects whose effects are present but which are difficult to measure: disorder, squalor, ugliness, noise.

In its effect upon the atmosphere, soil as a living process, the water cycle, climate and micro-climate, the modern city represents a transformation of the original physical environment certainly greater over the area of the city than the changes achieved by earlier man through fire, animal husbandry, deforestation, and extensive agriculture.

Indeed, one can certainly say that the city is at least an ecological regression, although as a human institution it may represent a triumph. Whatever triumphs there are to be seen in the modern city as an institution, it is only with great difficulty that one can see any vestige of triumph in the modern city as a physical environment. One might ask of the modern city that it be humane; that is, capable of supporting human organisms. This might well be a minimum requirement. In order for this term to be fully appropriate—that is, that the city be compassionate and elevating—it should not only be able to support physiological man, but also should give meaning and expression to man as an individual and as a member of an urban society. I contend that far from meeting the full requirements of this criterion, the modern city inhibits life, that it inhibits man as an organism, man as a social being, man as a spiritual being, and that it does not even offer adequate minimum conditions for physiological man; that indeed the modern city offers the least humane physical environment known to history.

Assuredly, the last and most awful agent held by man to modify the physical environment is atomic power. Here we find post-atomic man able to cause evolutionary regressions of unimaginable effect and even able to destroy all life. In this, man holds the ultimate destructive weapon; with this, he can become the agent of destruction in ecological community, of all communities, of all life. For any ecological community to survive, no single member can support a destructive role. Man's role historically has been destructive; today or tomorrow it can be totally, and for all life existent, irrevocably destructive.

Now, wild nature, save a few exceptions, is not a satisfactory physical environment. Where primitive peoples exist in a wild nature little adapted by man, their susceptibility to disease, life expectancy, vulnerability to climatic vagaries, and to the phenomena of drought and starvation is hardly ideal. Yet the certainty that man must adapt nature and himself does not diminish his dependence upon natural, non-human processes. These two observations set limits upon conceptions of man and nature. Man must adapt both through biological and cultural innovation but these adaptations occur within a context of natural, non-human processes. It is not inevitable that adapting nature to support human congregations must of necessity diminish the quality of the physical environment.

Creation of a physical environment by organisms as individuals and as communities is not exclusively a human skill. The chambered nautilus, the beehive, and the coral formation are all efforts by organisms to take inert materials and dispose them to create a physical environment. In these examples the environments created are complimentary to the organisms. They are constructed with great economy of means; they are expressive; they have, in human eyes, great beauty, and they have survived periods of evolutionary time vastly longer than the human span. Can we hope that man will be able to change the physical environment to create a new ecology in which he is primary agent, but which will be a self-perpetuating and not a retrogressive process? We hope that man will be able at least to equal the chambered nautilus, the bee, and the coral—that he will be able to build a physical environment indispensable to life, constructed with economy of means, having lucid expression, and containing great beauty. When man learns this single lesson he will be enabled to create by natural process an environment appropriate for survival—the minimum requirement of a humane environment. When this view is believed, the artist will make it vivid and manifest. Medieval faith, interpreted by artists, made the Gothic cathedral ring with holiness. Here again we confront the paradox of man in nature and man transcendent. The vernacular architecture and urbanism of earlier societies and primitive cultures today, the Italian hill town, medieval village, the Dogon community, express the first view, a human correspondence to the nautilus, the bee and coral. Yet this excludes the Parthenon, Hagia Sofia, Beauvais, statements which speak of the uniqueness of man and his aspirations. Neither of these postures is complete, the vernacular speaks too little of the consciousness of man, yet the shrillness of transcendence asks for the muting of other, older voices.

Perhaps when the achievements of the past century are appraised, there will be advanced as the most impressive accomplishment of this period the great extension of social justice. The majority of the population of the Western world moved from an endemic condition of threatening starvation, near desperation, and serfdom, to relative abundance, security, and growing democratic freedoms. Human values utilized the benison of science, technology, and industry, to increase wealth absolutely and distribute it more equitably. In the process, responsibility and individual freedom increased, brute hunger, bare suppression, and uncontrolled disease were diminished. It is a paradox that in this period of vastly increased wealth, the quality of the physical environment has not only failed to improve commensurately, but has actually retrogressed. If this is true, and I believe that there is more than ample evidence to support this hypothesis, then it represents an extraordinary failure on the part of Western society. The failure is the more inexplicable as the product of a society distinguished by its concern for social justice; for surely the physical environment is an important component of wealth and social justice. The modern city wears the badges which distinguish it as a product of the nineteenth and twentieth centuries. Polluted rivers, polluted atmosphere, squalid industry, vulgarity of commerce, diners, hot dog stands, second-hand car lots, gas stations, sagging wire and billboards, the whole anarchy united by ugliness—at best neutral, at worst offensive and insalubrious. The product of a century's concern for social justice, a century with unequaled wealth and technology, is the least humane physical environment known to history. It is a problem of major importance to understand why the nineteenth and twentieth centuries have failed in the creation of a physical environment; why the physical environment has not been, and is not now, considered as a significant aspect of wealth and social justice.

Renaissance and Eighteenth Century

If we consider all the views in our Western heritage having an anti-environmental content, we find they represent a very impressive list. The first of these is the anthropomorphic view that man exclusively is made in the image of God (widely interpreted to mean that God is made in the image of man). The second assumption is that man has absolute dominion over all life and non-life. The third assumption is that man is licensed to subdue the earth. To this we add the medieval

Christian concept of other-worldliness, within which life on earth is only a probation for the life hereafter, so that only the acts of man to man are of consequence to his own soul. To this we add the view of the Reformation that beauty is a vanity; and the Celtic, and perhaps Calvinistic, view that the only beauty is natural beauty, that any intent to create beauty by man is an assumption of God's role, is a vanity, and is sacrilegious. The total of these views represents one which can only destroy and which cannot possibly create. The degree to which there has been retention of great natural beauty, creation of beauty and order, recognition of aspects of natural order, and particularly recognition of these aspects of order as a manifestation of God, would seem to exist independently of the Judaic-Christian view. They may be animist and animitist residues that have originated from many different sources; but it would appear, whether or not they are espoused by Christian and Jews, that they do not have their origins in Judaism or Christianity. It would also appear that they do not have their origins in classical or humanist thought, or even in eighteenth-century rationalist views.

These two opposed views of man's role in the natural world are reflected in two concepts of nature and the imposition of man's idea of order upon nature. The first of these is the Renaissance view most vividly manifest in the gardens of the French Renaissance and the projects of André Lenôtre for Louis XIV. The second is the eighteenth-century English picturesque tradition. The gardens of the Renaissance clearly show the imprint of humanist thought. A rigid symmetrical pattern is imposed relentlessly upon a reluctant landscape. If this pattern was, as is claimed, some image of a perfect paradisiac order, it was a human image which derived nothing from the manifest order and expression of wild nature. It was rather, I suggest, an image of flexed muscles, a cock's crow of power, and an arrogant presumption of human dominance over nature. Le Roi Soleil usurped none of the sun's power by so claiming. Art was perverted to express a superficial pattern while claiming this as an expression of a fundamental order.

If the Renaissance sought to imprint upon nature a human order, the eighteenth-century English tradition sought to idealize wild nature, in order to provide a sense of the sublime. The form of estates in the eighteenth century was of an idealized nature, replacing the symmetrical patterns of the Renaissance. The form of ideal nature had been garnered from the landscape painting of Poussin and Salvator Rosa;

developed through the senses of the poets and writers, such as Pope, Cowley, Thomson, Addison, Gray, Dyer, Stocker, Shaftesbury, and the Orientalist, Sir William Temple—a eulogy of the campagna from the painters; a eulogy of the natural countryside and its order from the writers; and from Temple, the occult balance discovered in the Orient. However, the essential distinction between the concept of the Renaissance, with its patterning of the landscape, and that of eighteenth-century England was the sense that the order of nature itself existed and represented a prime determinant, a prime discipline for man in his efforts to modify nature. The search in the eighteenth century was for creation of a natural environment which would evoke a sense of the sublime. The impulse of design in the Renaissance was to demonstrate man's power over nature; man's power to order nature; man's power to make nature in his human image. With so inadequate an understanding of the process of man relating to nature, his designs could not be self-perpetuating. Where the basis for design was only the creation of a superficial order, inevitably the consequence was decoration, decay, sterility, and demise. Within the concepts of eighteenth-century England, in contrast, the motivating idea was to idealize the laws of nature. The interdependence of micro-organisms—plants, insects and animals, the association of particular ecological groupings with particular areas and particular climates—this was the underlying discipline within which the aristocrat–landscape architect worked. The aim was to create an idealized nature which spoke to man of the tranquility, contemplation, and calm which nature brought, which spoke of nature as the arena of sublime and religious experience, essentially speaking to man of God. This represents, I believe, one of the most healthy manifestations of the Western attitude toward nature. To this eighteenth-century attitude one must add a succession of men who are aberrants in the Western tradition, but whose views represent an extension of the eighteenth-century view—among them, Wordsworth and Coleridge, Thoreau and Emerson, Jonathan Edwards, Jonathan Marsh, Gerald Manley Hopkins, and many more.

Natural Science and Naturalism

It might be productive to examine the natural scientist's view of the evolution of nature and certain aspects of this order. The astronomer gives us some idea of immensity of scale, a hundred billion galaxies receding from us at the speed of light. Of these hundred billion galaxies is one which is our own, the Milky Way. Eccentric within the immensity of the Milky Way, the inconspicuous solar system exists. Within the immensity of the solar system, revolves the minute planet, Earth. The astronomer and geologist together give us some sense of the process during which the whirling, burning gases increased in density, coalesced with cooling, condensed, gave off steam, and finally produced a glassy sphere, the Earth. This sphere with land and oceans had an atmosphere with abundant carbon dioxide, with abundant methane, and little or no free oxygen. A glassy sphere with great climatic ranges in temperature, diurnal and seasonal, comparable to an alternation between Arctic and Equatorial conditions. From the biologist we learn of the origins of life. The first great miracle of life was this plant-animal in the sea; the emergence of life on land, the succession of fungi, mosses, liverworts, ferns. The miracle beyond life is photosynthesis, the power by which plants, absorbing carbon dioxide, give out oxygen and use the sun's energy to transform light into substance. The substance becomes the source of food and fuel for all other forms of life. There seems to be good reason to believe that the Earth's atmosphere, with abundant oxygen, is a product of the great evolutionary succession of plants. On them we depend for all food and fossil fuels. From the botanist we learn of the slow colonization of the Earth's surface by plants, the degree to which the surface of the Earth was stabilized, and, even more significantly, how plants modified the climatic extremes to support the amphibian, reptilian, and subsequent mammalian evolutionary sequence.

The transcendental view of man's relation to nature implicit in Western philosophies is dependent upon the presumption that man does in fact exist outside of nature, that he is not dependent upon it. In contemporary urban society the sense of absolute dependence and interdependence is not apparent, and it is an extraordinary experience to see a reasonably intelligent man become aware of the fact that his survival is dependent upon natural processes, not the least of which are based upon the continued existence of plants. This relationship can be demonstrated by experiment with three major characters: light, man, and algae. The theater is a cylinder in which is a man, a certain quantity of algae, a given quantity of water, a given quantity of air, and a single input, a source of light corresponding to sunlight (in this case a fluorescent tube). The man breathes the air, utilizes the oxygen, and exhales carbon dioxide. The algae utilize the carbon dioxide and exhale oxygen. There is a closed cycle of carbon dioxide and oxygen. The man consumes water, passes the water, the algae consume the water, the water is transpired, collected, and the man consumes the water. There is a closed water cycle. The man eats the algae, the man passes excrement, the algae consume the excrement, the man consumes the algae. There is a closed cycle of food. The only input is light. In this particular experiment the algae is as dependent upon the man as the man is upon the algae. In nature this is obviously not true. For some two billion years nature did exist without man. There can, however, be absolutely no doubt about the indispensability of the algae or plant photosynthesis to the man. It is the single agent able to utilize radiant energy from the sun and make it available as products to support life. This experiment very clearly shows the absolute dependence of man on nature.

Man has claimed to be unique. Social anthropologists have supported this claim on the ground that he alone has the gift of communication, and again that he alone has values. It might be worthwhile considering this viewpoint. A very famous biologist, Dr. David Goddard, said that a single human sperm, weighing one billionth of a gram, contains more information coded into its microscopic size than all of the information contained in all of the libraries of all men in all time. This same statement can be made for the seed of other animals or plants. This is a system of communication which is not rational, but which is extraordinarily delicate, elegant, and powerful, and which is capable of transmitting unimaginable quantities of information in microscopic volume.

This system of communication has enabled all species to survive the evolutionary time span. All forms of extant life share this system of communication; man's participation in it is in no sense exceptional.

Man also claims a uniqueness for himself on the grounds that he alone, of all of the animals, has values from which cultural objectives are derived. It would appear that the same *genetic* system of communication also contains a *value system*. Were this not so, those systems of organic life which do persist today would not have persisted; the genetic information transmitted is the information essential for survival. That information insures the persistence of the organism within its own ecological community. The genetic value system also contains the essential mutation; that imperfection essential for evolution and survival. This system of communication is elegant, beautiful, and powerful, capable of sifting enormous numbers of conflicting choices. Man participates in and shares this system, but his participation is in no sense exceptional.

Yet another aspect of man's assumption that he is independent of natural processes is the anthropomorphic attitude which implies a finite man who is born, grows, and dies, but who during his life is made of the same unchanging stuff—himself. Not so. If we simply measure that which man ingests, uses, and rejects, we begin to doubt this premise. Hair, nails, skin, and chemical constituents are replaced regularly. He replaces several billion cells daily. The essential stuff of man is changed very regularly indeed. In a much more fundamental way, however, man is a creature of environment. We have learned that he is absolutely dependent upon stimuli—light, shadow, color, sound, texture, gravity; and upon his sense of smell, taste, touch, vision, and hearing. These constantly changing environmental conditions are his references. Without them there would be hallucination, hysteria, perhaps mental disintegration, certainly loss of reality.

The Ecological View

It remains for the biologist and ecologist to point out the interdependence which characterizes all relationships, organic and inorganic, in nature. It is the ecologist who points out that an ecological community is only able to survive as a result of interdependent activity between all of the species which constitute the community. To the basic environment (geology, climate), is added an extraordinary complexity of inert materials, their reactions, and the interaction of the organic members of the community with climate, inert materials, and other organisms. The characteristic of life is interdependence of all of the elements of the community upon each other. Each one of these is a source of stimulus; each performs work; each is part of a pattern, a system, a working cycle; each one is to some lesser or greater degree a participant and contributor in a thermodynamic system. This interdependence common to nature—common to all systems—is in my own view the final refutation of man's assumption of independence. It appears impossible to separate man from this system. It would appear that there is a system, the order of which we partly observe. Where we observe it, we see interdependence, not independence, as a key. This interdependence is in absolute opposition to Western man's presumption of transcendence, his presumption of independence, and, of course, his presumption of superiority, dominion, and license to subdue the earth.

A tirade on the theme of dependence is necessary only to a society which views man as independent. Truly there is in nature no independence. Energy is the basis for all life; further, no organism has, does, or will live without an environment. All systems are depletive. There can be no enduring system occupied by a single organism. The minimum, in a laboratory experiment, requires the presence of at least two complementary organisms. These conceptions of independence and anthropocentrism are baseless.

The view of organisms and environment widely held by natural scientists is that of interdependence—symbiosis. Dr. Paul Sears of Yale University has written:

> Any species survives by virtue of its niche, the opportunity afforded it by environment. But in occupying this niche, it also assumes a role in relation to its surroundings. For further survival it is necessary that its role at least be not a disruptive one. Thus, one generally finds in nature that each component of a highly organized community serves a constructive, or, at any rate, a stabilizing role. The habitat furnishes the niche, and if any species breaks up the habitat, the niche goes with it. . . . That is, to persist they [ecological communities] must be able to utilize radiant energy not merely to perform work, but to maintain the working system in reasonably good order. This requires the presence of organisms adjusted to the habitat and to each other, so organized as to make the fullest use of the influent radiation and to conserve for use and re-use the materials which the system requires. The degree to which a living community meets these conditions is therefore a test of its efficiency and stability.[1]

Man, too, must meet this test. Dr. Sears states:

> Man is clearly the beneficiary of a very special environment which has been a great while in the making. This environment is more than a mere inert stockroom. It is an active system, a pattern and a process as well. Its value can be threatened by disruption no less than by depletion.

The natural scientist states that no species can exist without an environment, no species can exist in an environment of its exclusive creation, no species can survive, save as a non-disruptive member of an ecological community. Every member must adjust to other members of the community and to the environment in order to survive. Man is not excluded from this test.

Man must learn this prime ecological lesson of interdependence. He must see himself linked as a living organism to all living and all preceding life. This sense may impel him to understand his interdependence with the micro-organisms of the soil, the diatoms in the sea, the whooping crane, the grizzly bear, sand, rocks, grass, trees, sun, rain, moon, and stars. When man learns this he will have learned that when he destroys he also destroys himself; that when he creates, he also adds to himself. When man learns the single lesson of interdependence he may be enabled to create by natural process an environment appropriate for survival. This is a fundamental precondition for the emergence of man's role as a constructive and creative agent in the evolutionary process. Yet this view of interdependence as a basis for survival, this view of man as a participant species in an ecological community and environment, is quite contrary to the Western view.

I have reminded the reader that the creation of a physical environment by organisms, as individuals and as communities, is not exclusively a human skill; it is shared with the bee, the coral, and the chambered nautilus, which take inert materials and dispose them to create a physical environment, complementary to—indeed, indispensable to—the organism.

When man abandoned instinct for rational thought, he abandoned the powers that permitted him to emulate such organisms; if rationality alone sufficed, man should at least be able to equal these humble organisms. But thereby hangs a parable:

> The nuclear cataclysm is over. The earth is covered with gray dust. In the vast silence no life exists, save for a little colony of algae hidden deep in a leaden cleft long innured to radiation. The algae perceive their isolation; they reflect upon the strivings of all life, so recently ended, and on the strenuous task of evolution to be begun anew. Out of their reflection could emerge a firm conclusion: "Next time, no brains."

Reference

1. Sears, Paul B., "The Process of Environmental Change by Man," in *Man's Role in Changing the Face of the Earth,* W. L. Thomas, Jr., ed., Chicago: Univ. of Chicago Press, 1956.

6 The Changing Face of Mental Health

LEONARD J. DUHL

We are at the beginning of a new era in mental health programming. Since World War II, there has been a steady increase in the acceptance of the need for mental health services, in financial support of research and training, and in the initiation of expanded roles for clinic, hospital, and community. This new era looks toward the development of what I would like to call an *ecological* view of mental health.

What we have traditionally called mental health programs are only part of the needed program. The true perspective would include *community* mental health. In developing this argument, I want to make five points:

1. Our heritage is both scientific and humanitarian. The latter refers to our broad societal concerns. The science of our field has only recently moved from the concept of *single causality* to a more comprehensive approach.

2. This more comprehensive perspective is called "ecology," the study of the multiple factors of environment, both internal and external, that affect the normal development and behavior of the individual and his society. "Mental health" thus becomes not the study of mental disease alone, but the study of man in society.

3. Disease is, in fact, a *socially defined* condition. Its definition varies with the tools of measurement of the individual's ability to cope with stresses; but also with the values of those whom society selects to define disease, and with society's own ability to accept deviation from the norm it considers "healthy."

4. Psychiatry has been moving toward a broader socio-biologic concern with human behavior. Among its newer orientations are the psy-

Presented at the Detroit Regional Meeting of the American Psychiatric Association, October 29–31, 1959.

choanalytic approach, the advent of new drugs and biophysical discoveries, the discovery that the hospital not only cures but also contributes to mental illness (what is called its "iatrogenic" factor, meaning that the therapeutic procedures may also exacerbate certain features of the disease), and the beginnings of a public health point of view toward both prevention and emergency service in regard to mental disease. We need now to include the consideration of the total community, its decision-making processes, and the ways in which it causes, affects, defines, and corrects the behavior of its members.

5. Prior research has been devoted to parts of the total problem of human behavior, assuming that adding them together would give a whole. The concept of ecology requires that we include many more variables, from the genetic and biological to the way in which man creates the very society that in turn shapes him. We need a new way of conceptualizing the *organized complexities* of life. As Warren Weaver has written,

> The problems . . . in the biological, medical, psychological, economic, and political sciences are just too complicated to yield to the old nineteenth-century techniques which were so dramatically successful on two, three, or four-variable problems of simplicity. These new problems, moreover, cannot be handled as problems of disorganized complexity. These new problems—and the future of the world depends on many of them—require science to make a third great advance, an advance that must be even greater than the nineteenth century conquest of problems of simplicity or the twentieth century victory over problems of disorganized complexity. Science must, over the next fifty years, learn to deal with problems of organized complexity.[1]

The changes we create must be understood in both their therapeutic effect and in their long-term implications.

In what follows, I have permitted myself the luxury of speculation on what may be the many-sided developments of mental health during the coming years, and the privilege of asking many more questions than I can answer. If it seems unduly visionary to leave the realm of psychiatry for those of public health, social science, and, in fact, science and life themselves, this is done as part of a plan. I want to tie together the concerns of the psychiatrist and psychoanalyst with those of biological and sociological concerns in public health.

The Historical Perspective

Medicine, in its long history from the time of Hippocrates in the fourth century B.C., was concerned with the interplay of man and his environment. Man's health depended on his living in harmony with his external environment. *Physis*, the Greek root of the word physician, means "nature." Hippocrates asked that every practitioner of medicine "be skilled in nature and must strive to know what man is in relation to food, drink, occupation, and which effect each of these has on the other." Though this history emphasizes the importance of the internal and external environment of man in understanding health and disease, the recent era in medicine forsook this heritage and became primarily concerned with finding a single cause for illness. The period of dominance of the germ theory, however, is gradually coming to an end. Increasingly, research in medicine and psychiatry is concerned with the whole man, psychologically, biologically, and socially. One may say we are entering an era of environmental health, a stage where psychiatric and humanitarian concerns merge into the developing perspective of an ecology of man.

Ecology

Research and observation have made it clear that man is the result of a continual process, both biological and psychological, of learning by adaptation. In this process, the basic constitution is modified by the external environment. But that environment itself is increasingly man's creation, and reacts upon him in turn to affect him in innumerable ways. Clearly, the etiology of disease can no longer be looked for in single factors, but rather in the permutations and combinations of multiple, interacting factors ranging from individual biological differences to environmental changes, and to the interactive relationships among individuals.

Novelists often see this more clearly than scientists. Tolstoy writes, in *War and Peace*,

> Since the real causes of phenomena are hidden beyond the reach of the human mind, historians can at most describe the behavior of individuals and certain limited relationships; but they must abandon the futile search for the specific causality of human events.

The scientific discipline of ecology, developed in the biological study of animal populations, serves as a model for understanding the complexities of the multi-factored relationships in the causality of human behavior. Since man is unique among the animals, he is not only part of an ecological network, but he modifies it, creates large parts of it, has giant technical tools to cope with it, and is in turn modified by it. Quite clearly, in the ecology of man, his fellow man, groups of men, the creations of man, even his by-products and his wastes, become tremendously important variables. Thus the changed patterns of cities, the armies, the satellites circling the globe, smog, insecticides, the automobile, cigarettes, and IBM machines are variables we cannot ignore. One major problem we face is how to predict which variables are important.

Park, Wirth, Shaw, Faris, Dunham, Hollingshead, and many others in sociology have utilized the basically biological concept of ecology in sociological studies of the community and its problems. This is a major accomplishment; but it is not yet enough. These accomplishments must be integrated with psychological insights, as is being increasingly done, and re-integrated with biological science, which at this time has a more sophisticated understanding of individual differences than it once did.

More than a proliferation of researches, ecology requires a new theoretical model of man. Lawrence Frank has written that any real advance in social order, as in culture, "occurs when members of the group accept a new or different model which they attempt to realize in daily living." Frank continues,

> The most valuable contribution . . . is to provide new models of social order which will guide the activities and expectations, not only of citizen members, but more especially of the administrators, policy makers, legislators, planners, technicians, and the various helping professions.[2]

The mental health field certainly needs such new theories for its future development.

A science of man, or a program concerned with man, cannot with any hope of success try to deal with all things at all times. We cannot always be generalists. We must be prepared to be specific in our orientation, and to deal, as need dictates, with single aspects of single problems. But if we can also see the problem as a whole, we may find the part that is most open to solution, which factor is the key holding back the others. Knowledge of the whole problem may permit us the choice of one or another specific point of intervention which, if attacked, may deal with the general phenomenon. However, the great wealth of materials available in the field of mental health allows for no truly comprehensive expertise. What is required in communication among the many related disciplines—along with clarity of thinking, and a common fund of definitions—is a dictionary that all can use. Training is needed for both generalists and specialists, with adequate emphasis on criticism. We need to clarify the progress from definition to design to a clear vision of goals and means.

Disease

For purposes of discussion, I offer here an operational definition of disease: Departure from the normal biological, psychological, or social means of coping with stresses of the internal and external environment are defined (by those to whom society has given authority) as disease only when the individual's or group's biological, psychological, or social survival is jeopardized, and/or when there occurs permanent or semi-permanent damage to the psychosocial or biological functions of man.

Let me illustrate. Bacteria, alcohol, or paranoid-like behavior, so long as they maintain peaceful coexistence (i.e., so long as relative homeostasis is maintained), do not result in disease. Infection with *C. diphtheriae* does not necessarily result in the disease, diphtheria. Alcohol usage does not become "alcoholism" unless jeopardy to biological or psychosocial survival occurs. Thus, when peaceful coexistence of bug and bug, or bug and human, or alcohol and human, breaks down under some form of stress, disease is said to occur. Often disease is a matter of definition alone: in Nazi Germany, nonconformity to the system was labeled disease, while what we called disease was the acceptance of the values of that state itself.

The idea that social deviance is disease, and not sin, has become increasingly prevalent; it has, in fact, enlarged the dimensions of what are called mental health problems. This is, in fact, one source of danger: the concept of normality has become the criterion of mental health. But since the middle class is most often the source of what is considered "normal," we are in peril of utilizing "mental health" to perpetuate middle-class values.

Stress may arise out of a total change of environment, or from a momentary crisis which threatens the survival of the organism. If the organism succeeds in coping with the threat without breakdown, disease is averted and perhaps a new and healthy mechanism of adaptation developed. If the threat is manageable only through biological or psychosocial mechanisms that themselves threaten survival, a disease is in the making. Or if the stress is unmanageable even by these means, again disease occurs.

When man's homeostatic balance "looks" for ways of adaptation or breakdown, it has only a limited number of courses of action it can take. Its prime resource is its basic genetic and biological structure, together with the psychological and social ways of coping which it has learned. The actions of other men around him, as part of his environmental resources, can help modify earlier learned responses. Given a little more time, and another reshuffling of factors, there can be yet another outcome. Disease may thus take many forms. It can indeed be defined as a group of symptoms allowed at the moment by the play of ecological forces. Dealing with a single symptom is like putting a finger in a hole in the dyke. The need is not to plug the hole—though one may have to in emergencies—but to deal with the pressures and to find ways in which they may be controlled or prevented. Multiple treatment, simultaneous or successive, may deal with the problem; but I certainly am not advocating "shot-gun" medicine.

Psychiatric illness has been subject to fads, as all diseases have. As infectious diseases come under control, cancer and heart disease gain prominence. As people live longer, and suffer other kinds of illness, they may reproduce and pass on propensities for disease. For these reasons, mental illness may soon show a relative increase; and there are other reasons too. Mental illness may be the only form of reaction open to otherwise "healthy" people; delinquency, or alcohol, may be the one freedom of action available to some. Some have said that in Denmark, where most prominent concerns are cared for, and have solutions; where everyone is educated, and few are left sick, alone, or underfed, damage to one's body through depression, alcoholism, or even suicide is the only remaining means of "self-expression." This is a very dangerous generalization; I mention it only to raise a further question, the speculative relation of societal change to an ecological understanding of man. How do climate and geography—both of which show correlations with changing patterns of disease—and economics, community planning, laws, education, government, business practices, crime, recreation, all fit into our programs of mental health? We certainly do not have the answers to these questions; but they point to a need.

Mental Health Programs and Practices

A review of our practices in this field, aimed at extending our concepts of mental health programming, cannot omit the changes in professional preparation and attitudes.

I would like, however, to mention the "mental health movement" briefly before returning to the changes in professional mental health practice. The movement, humanitarian and middle class in its values, has been primarily concerned with services for the mentally ill. However, through its fifty-year history, concern with housing, education, and societal values have come up again and again as a leitmotif, reminding us, if but quietly, that there is more to a mental health program than services to the ill.

The professional, the psychiatrist and his colleagues in the past twenty years, have shown a change in their interests. Prior to World War II, some psychiatrists had been community oriented, and mental health clinics were developed; but much of psychiatry was hospital oriented. After the war, psychiatrists became primarily patient-centered. Where on the one hand psychoanalytic theory opened up questions of multiple causation and was truly ecologically oriented, practice, on the other hand, became committed to office therapeutics with little recognition of the possibility of working with environmental factors.

In this last decade, as funds have become increasingly available for programs, research, and training, and public awareness has been on the upgrade, a major revolution has occurred. The era we are now completing has experienced a reawakening in two directions: increased interest in the biologic aspect of mental illness, and a sociopsychological concern with family, the hospital, and the broader community.

More personnel were trained; the psychiatrist went more and more into private practice, as well as working in clinics and some of the larger mental hospitals. Colleagues such as psychologists and social workers joined hands to make a joint operation more effective by pooling the effective skills of each. More psychiatric personnel, again aided by colleagues in a variety of disciplines, probed into biological areas that provided clues about individual difference, genetic transmission of traits, neurophysiological pathways, new drugs, etc. Psychosocially, the major changes in psychiatric services have been in developments in the mental hospital, in family therapy, and in the development of public health programs.

In the mental hospitals, awareness developed that the institutional structure itself has both curative and iatrogenic characteristics. The impact of administrative procedures, hospital design, and total staff-patient relationships on the progress of the hospitalized patient began to be recognized. The total staff, the milieu, and the role of the hospital were questioned and re-evaluated. The move to open doors wide, with doctors and patients passing in and out of the hospital to the community, was seen first in Europe and now, increasingly, in the United States. Hospitals can be seen as part of the larger community. Hospitals can be used not as final dumping grounds (and museums of pathology), but as places for the living, where hospitalization is considered a healthy move and where the patient may get refurbished to meet the outside world when he has been prepared to do so by a variety of mental health workers. As part of the total community, some hospitals see their function as being the major mental health resource for an area, rather than as a reservoir of its guilt. We see day hospitals, night hospitals, and new kinds of institutions, such as work camps and schools for the emotionally disturbed, on the drawing board.

Our hospitals are our most exciting places, for here social psychiatry has proven itself. It has shown that the institution cures, hinders, and develops pathologies of its own. It has aided us in looking toward other social institutions where people get helped. It has served as a model for studies of school and college where we are trying to understand the impact of the total institution, and its parts, on the students as they go through. In many social institutions, among them the schools and colleges, we learn inadequate patterns of coping, as well as good ones. It is here we lay down the patterns which, in addition to those developed in early family life, plague or aid people through a lifetime.

The second area of change can be termed family therapy. Work with families first developed in child guidance activities. However, therapy in the hospitals, with schizophrenics, and now more often in private practice, has shown that the difficulties of the patient reside in both the patient and the total family situation. Not only are families being studied and helped by teams of personnel, but, more frequently, families are being seen together in joint treatment with one therapist. Clinics recognizing the importance of total family configurations in both health and disease are more family-oriented in treatment, in record-keeping, and in research. We see isolated attempts to integrate family social services or recreational activities for individual and family with hospital and medical services. We even remember, and are learning to use, the lessons of the former Peckham Health Center in England in new programs where recreation, health, family services, and education are part of one total program.

In these two areas, and in the third that I am about to mention, there is increasing awareness that treatment is not an individual but a social problem.

The third area may be labeled public health. Early observable activities have been the development of psychiatric emergency services, the use of public health nurses in the community in various roles, including following up of hospital discharges, and the increasing concern of social workers, who were for a period primarily patient oriented, with the family environment and the society within which the patient got sick and to which he must return.

Public health programs have developed beyond these advances. They are geared to the prevention of illness in a total community. As I view it, there are six levels of preventive measures which can be taken.

1. The general promotion of mental health by increasing the strength and toleration to stress of individuals and communities in a non-specific manner. This goal can be accomplished in a variety of ways: through community organizations and improved and broadened educational programs, by the maintenance of a high level of community morale, through varied cultural and social programs run by people aware of the psychological and emotional needs of the community, and by the establishment of recreation and leisure-time activities for citizens of all ages. Community changes causing psycho-

logical disruption should always be made with an understanding of the ways in which changes in society affect the way people think and behave.

2. The elimination of deprivations. In many ways, the community can help restore and make up for the psychological and social deprivations suffered by its people. Both official agencies and the unofficial helpers are important in this work. Specific programs which might be instituted are: the provision of housekeepers for families in which the mother is ill, keeping families together in time of disaster rather than following the "women and children first" dictum, use of substitute mothers in children's wards in hospitals, pre- and post-delivery programs for pregnant women, and a variety of other ways of helping people to maintain emotional equilibrium in times of crisis.

3. The interruption of pathogenic trains of events by diminishing or eliminating stress which leads to disaster. A neighborhood in which rising tensions seem sure to precipitate violence would need this sort of program. Temporary relocation of agitating or sparking personalities in such a situation might very well interrupt the rising tide of emotion, and permit the neighborhood to restore some sort of emotional balance.

4. The prevention of major mental illness, delinquency, drug addiction, and so forth, by early detection and referral to available community resources. People with incipient mental illness or emotional disturbance can be detected by an interested community through the work of public health nurses, through welfare activities, by the minister, through schools, business, and industry. Some people so detected can be helped by minor treatments that get to them in time, and through the work of guidance and other personnel minimally trained in psychology or psychiatry. Others require more highly skilled help. For these people at home, at school, at work, or at play, a psychiatric emergency service, with skilled people available at a moment's notice, might be most helpful.

5. The arrest of illness by treatment, and the subsequent rehabilitation of the ill through coordinated activities of private practitioners, institutions, clinics, and the community.

6. The prevention of permanent disability by the treatment of psychological disturbance. This treatment would consist chiefly of recognition of full-blown illness and referral for treatment.

Working on these six levels, each community, depending upon its special needs and problems, can organize a series of over-all planning and preventive programs. From planning highways to organizing the schools, from establishing treatment and rehabilitation clinics to setting up industrial mental health programs, the whole range of a community's activities can be oriented in terms of the basic psychological and social needs of its population.

In preventive work there are a wide variety of activities that can help cope with the problems we face. In reviewing the specific tools we have to prevent categorical diseases, it is clear that at this time they are minimal. Syphilitic paresis, pellagra, psychosis, post-infectious encephalitis, and cephalic poisons are a few of the diseases for which we have found specific preventive methods. However, our actions in early diagnosis, treatment, and rehabilitation have also become more effective.

Action programs concerned with specific areas and executed without a comprehensive theoretical base may be wasteful and even misleading. All groups concerned with the well-being of man, who at the same time either consider themselves scientists or are responsible for the administration of a scientific program, should allocate energy and manpower to the development of such theories. Within such holistic ecological frameworks, theories of mental illness would be more productive.

If one returns to the ecological model of man I presented earlier, and becomes concerned with the developmental processes rather than disease, we have a different yet very important preventive mechanism. In this approach, we are concerned with the "learning process" and how it is modified by past experience and by the experience of the crisis itself. If we can help individuals in periods of crisis, perhaps new, more acceptable coping devices can be learned by the individual.

To organize such a program, geared to helping people learn through crisis, it becomes important to know something about where people turn for help.

Looking into the college, we find only a small percentage of the student body (perhaps 11 per cent) turning to the psychiatric services provided; others turn to the psychological services, the deans' offices, the religious counselors, and the heads of dormitories. The myriad of problems faced never get to the psychiatrists' doors unless, perhaps, when all other hope is lost. Clearly a large number of the population never gets to, nor should get to, a psychiatrist. One question is, who should be referred to a psychiatrist, and who can be aided elsewhere?

We find "caretakers" in all our communities and in our community institutions. Official or unofficial, these caretakers play a role in the continuous drama of problems, simple and severe, in which people turn to others for help. Psychiatrists more and more are playing a new role (for which they are often untrained) as consultants. Their role is "helping people to help others," and developing a network of resources that a community uses and can use when its members are under stress. We see evidence of greater understanding and appreciation of the role of the caretakers in our society. We are recognizing the value of consultation, and of skills we all possess. We see encouraging glimmerings that this process is not making junior psychiatrists out of this large group of caretakers, but rather individuals who use their own skills as these are strengthened by help we can give them. We foresee the development of new institutions run by such people, with minimal consultative help, giving real service and assistance in neglected areas.

In the Armed Forces there is a well organized program of frontline psychiatry. It was found that if consultation was available at the time of crisis, the individual was more easily returned to normal functioning than if the effects of the crisis were allowed to "fix" through hospitalization.

There are many key institutions and services in society that affect the way people learn how to cope with stress, and that can offer the possibility of learning new techniques of adaptation to crisis. Among them are the nursery school, public school, and college; marriage and premarital counselors; the obstetrician and pediatrician; work; recreation; the church. Many crises affect most segments of the population at one time or another, and are dealt with by a variety of institutions. Such crises are retirement, death of a close family member, the awakening of puberty with menstruation and sexual urges, new siblings, etc. Turning to either official or unofficial caretakers may provide new methods of coping with these problems and, in fact, prevent future difficulties.

There are, however, difficulties standing in the way of providing adequate services of this kind.

On its simplest level, the problem is manpower. We need numbers of trained people to provide the most effective service: people to staff the unstaffed and understaffed clinics and hospitals, the prisons, the

Armed Forces, the courts, the schools, and industry, all of which are crying out quite vocally for aid. But the problem is only in part one of numbers: inadequate numbers of trained psychiatrists, psychologists, and others; inadequate numbers of those motivated or exposed to the kinds of orientation that eventually makes workers in our field. Numbers have become a game, following the law of supply and demand.

Those in private practice, not unlike their colleagues but perhaps even more obviously, follow what may be called socio-physical laws and distribute themselves in relation to areas of high population. Thus, in the United States, mental health personnel are mostly concentrated in the northeast. And within each area in which they locate, the unequal distribution quickly becomes evident. Some socio-economic segments of our population find private services available; others, only the state hospitals. The upper socio-economic groups tend to get dynamic psychotherapy; the lower, organic treatments. A dismal picture.

What then? Will the patterns we see today remain? Some want only to go on doing as they have always done, and other people want them to. But on the horizon large changes are imminent. As they unfold, we must ask, "Is there logic in their development?" We see changes mentioned in the hospitals, in the emergency services, in family treatment; we see total community programs in which mental health is only one part of a range of health and welfare services. We see laws facilitating new programs, encouraging new ideas, and bringing new people into the field. We see not the numbers game of more and more psychiatrists, but psychiatrists facing problems in new ways, workers from a variety of disciplines, whether highly trained or minimally, awakening to the responsibility for the larger problems we face.

We find other workers equally concerned: teachers, ministers, social workers, nutritionists, agricultural and home extension workers; there are welfare and settlement houses and family care services, many of whom reach larger numbers of our population than we psychiatrists do.

And out of this massive array of programs and people, patterns are emerging. The over-all community structure, in all its complexity, teaches us the importance of an ecological understanding. Such understanding can aid us in the creation and the abatement of the problems and illness we see in our clinical work. It is the total community that must come under the microscope; from its laws, and political structure, to its economic problems and its geography. We are becoming increasingly aware of the changed world in which we live. We see the corporation (business, welfare, and governmental) play more important roles in our total lives. What will this do to us? What kinds of patients will it create? What about our changing culture? For example, we can look at adolescence not only as a period of psychosocial growth, but as an economic market to be catered to and developed, thus leading to tremendous pressures on the individual to conform. These developments, and many more, we have to understand.

Where the population patterning in our country is reflected in both diminished quality and quantity of all our personnel, we have looked to regional solutions. States band together, as in the Southern Regional Education Board and the Western Interstate Commission for Higher Education, to provide opportunities and services for strengthening mental health programs. Universities serve new functions and develop new roles. Universities and, most interestingly, the medical schools, are beginning to recognize responsibility not only for what we can call ivory towered education and research; they have left the walls of the campus and offered services and personnel, resources and direction, to the people who ask for them.

I would like to turn to a question that is foremost in my mind. If a psychiatrist is concerned with a total mental health program, does he direct his energies to therapeutic measures alone; or does he consider, as Virchow did, that disease is "life under changed conditions," and conclude that the "physician had to concern himself with the total environment of human beings and therefore could not avoid taking part in political action."

The psychiatrist, too, must look at the total ecology of man and decide where are the best points of intervention. He must be aware that any program geared to the prevention of mental disturbance and illness must be aware of the normal supports available for individuals in the community through unofficial agencies, institutions, and people not primarily concerned with psychiatry. These supports—a neighborhood fraternal organization, the corner cop, the friendly bartender or grocer—can often be lost to people by decisions of community government. Slum clearance and urban relocation projects, for instance, can pull the underpinnings from beneath a neighborhood and leave the individuals within it emotionally unsupported. A simple awareness of the impact of community decisions on people can often be the key to maintaining or replacing these supports. The psychiatrist must truly be a political personage in the best sense of the word. He must play a role in *controlling* the environment which man has created.

References

1. Weaver, W., "Science and Complexity," *Amer. Scientist,* 36:536-544, 1948.
2. Frank, L. K., "Research for What?" *J. Soc. Issues,* suppl. series 10: 20-21, 1957.

Bibliography

Albee, G. W., *Mental Health Manpower Trends,* New York: Basic Books, 1959.

Alinsky, S. D., *Reveille for Radicals,* Chicago: Univ. of Chicago Press, 1946.

Bauer, C., "Social Questions in Housing and Community Planning," *J. Soc. Issues,* 7:1-34, 1951.

Boulding, K., *The Skills of the Economist,* Cleveland: Howard Allen, 1958.

Buchanan, S., *The Corporation and the Republic,* New York: Fund for the Republic, 1958.

Caplan, G., *Concepts of Mental Health and Consultation,* Washington, D.C.: U.S. Department of Health, Education and Welfare, Pub. 373, 1959.

Committee on Nomenclature and Statistics, *Mental Disorder-Diagnostic and Statistical Manual,* Washington, D.C.: American Psychiatric Association, 1952.

Dahir, J., *Community for Better Living,* New York: Harper, 1952.

Dubos, R., *Mirage of Health,* New York: Harper, 1959.

———, "Medical Utopias," *Daedalus,* 87:410-424, 1959.

Duhl, L. J., "City Responsibility in Problems of Mental Health," *Proc. Amer. Municipal Assoc.,* Washington, D.C., 1957.

———, "Alcoholism: the Public Health Approach," *Quart. J. Studies on Alcohol,* 20:112-125, 1959.

Faris, R. E. L., and Dunham, H. W., *Mental Disorders in Urban Areas: an Ecological Study of Schizophrenia and Other Psychoses,* Chicago: Univ. of Chicago Press, 1939.

Farnsworth, D., *Mental Health in College and University*, Cambridge, Mass.: Harvard Univ. Press, 1957.

Galdston, I., *Social Medicine*, New York: Commonwealth Fund, 1949.

Gans, H. J., "Human Implications of Current Redevelopment and Relocation Planning," *J. Amer. Inst. Planners*, 25:15-25, 1959.

Glass, A. J., "Psychiatry in the Korean Campaign," *U.S. Armed Forces Med. J.*, 4:1563, 1963.

———, "Preventive Psychiatry in the Combat Zone," *U.S. Armed Forces Med. J.*, 4:683, 1953.

Greenblatt, M., Levinson, D., and Williams, R. H., eds., *The Patient and the Mental Hospital*, Glencoe, Ill.: The Free Press, 1957.

Gruenberg, E. M., "Application of Control Methods to Mental Illness," *Amer. J. Pub. Health*, 47:944-952, 1957.

———, "Prevention of Mental Disorders," *J. Chron. Dis.*, 9:189-198, 1959.

Haeckel, R., *Plant Communities*, 1895.

Halliday, J., *Psychosocial Medicine*, New York: Norton, 1948.

Heber, R., ed., "A Manual on Terminology and Classification in Mental Retardation," *Amer. J. Ment. Def.*, 64:2 (monograph suppl.), Sept. 1959.

Hollingshead, A. B., and Redlich, F. C., *Social Class and Mental Illness: A Community Study*, New York: Wiley, 1958.

Lindemann, E., *et al.*, "Mental Disorders as a Mass Phenomenon," *Arch. Neurol. and Psychiat.*, 66:648-650, 1951.

Lindemann, E., and Dawes, L. G., "Use of Psychoanalytic Constructs in Preventive Psychiatry," in *The Psychoanalytic Study of the Child*, Vol. VII, New York: International Univ. Press, 1952.

Macdonald, D., "Profiles: A Caste, A Culture, A Market," *The New Yorker*, Nov. 22 and 29, 1958.

Masland, R., Sarason, S., and Gladwin, T., *Mental Subnormality*, New York: Basic Books, 1958.

May, J., *The Ecology of Human Disease*, New York: M.D. Publications, 1958.

Milbank Memorial Fund, *An Approach to the Prevention of Disability from Chronic Psychoses—an Open Hospital Within the Community*, New York, 1958.

Nisbet, R. A., *The Quest for Community*, New York: Oxford Univ. Press, 1953.

Park, R., *Human Communities*, Glencoe, Ill.: The Free Press, 1952.

Pearse, I. H., and Crocker, L. H., *Peckham Experiment: A Study in the Living Structure of Society*, New Haven, Conn.: Yale Univ. Press, 1945.

Poston, R. W., "Public Health—Product of Community Action," *Amer. J. Pub. Health, 44*:303-308, 1954.

Stanton, A., and Schwartz, M., *The Mental Hospital,* New York: Basic Books, 1954.

Shaw, C. R., and McKay, H. D., *Social Factors in Juvenile Delinquency* (Wickersham Report), Washington, D.C.: U.S. Government Printing Office, 1931.

Sutter, J., "Population Genetics and the Study of Man, "*Impact of Science on Society, 6*:131-151, 1955.

Taylor, H., "The Unillusioned Generation," reprinted in *Best Articles and Stories, 3*:16-18, 1959.

Walter Reed Army Institute of Research, *Symposium on Preventive and Social Psychiatry,* Washington, D.C.: Walter Reed Army Center, 1957.

Wedge, B. M., ed., *Psychosocial Problems of College Men,* New Haven, Conn.: Yale Univ. Press, 1958.

Wirth, L., "Urban Society and Civilization," *Amer. J. Soc., 45*:743-755, 1940.

College as a New Environment

7

BENSON R. SNYDER

The university, with even more deliberateness than the city, consciously attempts to guide its destiny and control its environment. There are both dynamic forces and structured functions within the individual student which profoundly influence his interaction with his environment. These internal conditions have consequences for the educational planner. His control over the individual's reaction to the planned environment is relative. The range of effective actions available to him as planner is constrained. By describing how certain individuals within the university respond to that environment, I hope to give you a feeling for the quality of interactions that occur between the student and his school, and, by extension, the citizen and his city. The implications of this interaction for the planning process will also be explored.

Universities and colleges are profoundly influenced by rising enrollments, sputniks, lively consultations with the government, and, not least, the emergent generation which they teach. Neither the universities nor the cities of today are isolated from the surrounding land by moats or walls, like Carcassone. They are more like neighborhoods in a large metropolis, each with a distinctive ethnic character and architecture. Some are simply more provincial than others. Within this context, the university intends to affect the members of its academic community, their cognitive style, and their image of themselves. Obviously the affective and cognitive ties which bind the student to his university experience may be subtle and extensive.

Certain questions about the effects of the university environment may be the same as those about the effect of the environment of the city on its citizens. How does the university reach out and intervene in the lives of its students? What does the university leave untouched in its students' lives? The university imposes many restraints, and limits the students' choice for action. It defines certain tasks which the student must perform with at least a minimum of competence in order to earn his degree. Viewed from this perspective, the university constrains the students and clearly limits their freedom. This constraint, it can be argued, is in the service of developing another kind of freedom. The man who responds to impulse and acts at once to satisfy his immediate need has a limited freedom, profoundly different than the freedom that can come from a partial egosyntonic mastery of his drives. The ego, in this instance, may have a greater range of choice in coping both with his internal press and the demands of the environment. A limitation may thus become a net gain for the ego.

The limitations imposed by university environment on its students have a psychological dimension. The tasks which the university expects from its students limit the range of coping patterns which are adaptive for those tasks. A specific curriculum, for example, requires the development in the student of specific cognitive skills. Beyond this, the student must have a range of coping mechanisms and ego defenses in order to master the challenge of a course, or the anxiety of an exam. The student's image of himself will also be involved if the content of the course is even partially directed toward changing his intellectual climate of opinion.

Discussion of the environment and the individual's interaction with it necessarily deals with notions of reality sense, reality testing and climate of opinion. First, let me give you a brief clinical illustration of a student so bound by inner experience that he was able to react to external events only in extreme terms, primarily dictated by his intensely personal requirements. The therapist can view where he draws the line between his patients' inner and outer reality as a strategic decision with social consequences, based in part on where he expects to intervene, as well as on the data provided by the patient on how he thinks and feels. Our concepts of personality are useful here, since they can give us a logically consistent framework within which we can begin to make significant correlations between what is perceived, and those factors influencing that perception. This brief case will also serve to illustrate the clinical planning that precedes and goes along with an effort to alter the inner milieu.

A physics major was having difficulty completing his assignments.

During his consultation he spoke of his preoccupation with the fear that he would be exposed as worthless both in the therapy and in school. He was preoccupied with his fear that he was a mess and had an ineffective brain. He linked his feeling of being a mess with his messy room, and described his desk piled high with bits of paper and unfinished laboratory reports. When he felt most worthless and ashamed, he would withdraw from the painful reminders of the classroom and spend whole days playing bridge. This behavior clearly affected his work in school. In association with his sense of shame, he spoke repeatedly of feeling under tremendous pressures. He described these pressures as coming from outside himself; from professors, from his parents, from his classmates. Gradually, during therapy, he came to recognize these pressures as primarily an expression of his own expectations. He had to be the best physicist in at least the Western Hemisphere in order to feel worthwhile. Thinking for this young man was something to be proud of, yet using his mind was closely linked with his terror of being exposed as an intellectual featherweight. For him, thinking was not an uncomplicated, autonomous ego operation. It had become a highly charged process, subject to all the distortions of the neurotic symptom.

I will take a specific task that he was assigned in school and show you what he did with it. He was required to write a brief report for a theoretical seminar and could not get it done. Because of his own needs and expectations this brief paper was perceived as a demand for a doctoral treatise. The paper was never completed. Behind his feeling of being pressured by the paper lay his conviction that if he was not a genius, he was nothing. Here a profound sense of emptiness was apparent under his extreme defense. From other material in his treatment, this problem appeared to be related structurally to an ego that could not postpone his wish for total, immediate gratification. His ego was almost helpless in the face of his instinctual demands and surrendered to his fantasy. The new environment of school was effectively woven into the fabric of his constant and intensely personal nightmare. This is an extreme case in which the individual's inner climate and needs distorted his sense of reality and led him largely to ignore what in fact he did perceive.

The therapist intervened by repeatedly clarifying what the patient was expecting from his papers, i.e., proof of his infallibility rather than indication of his competence in physics. The professor was marking a paper from a brighter than average student, but when the patient received an A—, for example, this was not enough. His dream, his fantasy, had been punctured. It was in this context that his commitment to reality broke down. And it was toward this problem that the major therapeutic work was directed. There were other interventions. At one point the professor was told something of his student's sense of reality, and some of the reasons for his academic difficulty were reviewed. No manipulation of the environment, however, could have brought the university into line with the patient's demands or expectations. Thus the therapy was directed at the student's distorted perception. The major focus of the work was on the displacement of his ego's reality testing and reality sense. He responded to his sense of what he wanted, and not to what he saw.

You may well be saying this is indeed an extreme example, but the mechanisms and the dynamics are ubiquitous. The perceptual net functions like a sea anchor to windward, exerting a significant drag on the individual's response to the prevailing stimuli of his environment. It is only the case which is extreme. The social planner who ignores such phenomena is in for trouble—a grounding as it were, on the reef of the unconscious.

The therapy with the student avoided reference to causes. We focused rather on correlations. If he felt worthless then he would retreat from the attendant pain, with fantasies of greatness. Decisions on causes, as John Seeley points out, are primarily judicial and legislative acts. These decisions may be necessary and appropriate for educators and city planners who have to take legislative and judicial actions. In the therapy of this patient, and in psychoanalysis in general, we systematically investigate the impact of the psychoanalytic interpretation and focus then on the subsequent correlations that are evoked. In the most general sense, this changes the perceptual net, the basic data or information which is available to the patient and to the therapist. On the basis of this new data the patient then can make some decision, and judge for himself how he will behave.

The interventions and decisions of the city planner will effect the citizens of the city on various psychological levels. The planner could well consider whether his actions expand or constrict this perceptual net. They could question whether the sources of self-esteem, sanctioned by the community, are altered by their new environments. The planner, city administrator, or architect could theoretically drastically reduce or increase the number of decisions confronting the citizens each day—by changing his mode of transportation, his parks, the buildings that he sees or lives in, the pleasures or distractions easily at hand. An example of this occurred in 1953 when the residents of Le Corbusier's Unity House in Marseilles openly revolted against their architect. Lewis Mumford's summary of this episode serves as a verbal exclamation point:

> In designing Unity House, Le Corbusier betrayed the human contents to produce a monumental aesthetic effect. The result is an egocentric extravagance, as imposing as an Egyptian pyramid, which was meant to give immortality to a corpse, and—humanly speaking— as desolate.[1]

The university is a particular instance in a general class of situations where the individual is confronted with a new physical and emotional environment. And we are concerned here with the effects of that new environment on the individual. My more parochial concern is with education as an area in which the intellectual, social and more recently, the physical environment are consciously ordered to effect some significant change in its temporary inhabitants. I began with an illustration of how the individual can insulate himself to external influence. The new environment of the university became, for the physics student mentioned above, primarily a stage for acting out his inner conflicts. There is urgent need within the university for systematic knowledge of the effects of its environment on the inner world of its students. For example, the curriculum, living arrangements, grading practices, etc., could be examined to determine the extent to which they influenced specific adaptive patterns of the student. This knowledge can then be applied to planning, and to the formulation of educational decisions. This role of the planner, whether administrator or behavioral scientist, as a supplier of data for decisions, has been conceptualized in a variety of ways. He may be a model builder, a feed-back mechanism, or, as John Seeley has put it, a man with the art and intuition of the psychotherapist. As an illustration of what I mean, I will consider some of the effects of psychoanalytic theory on the way we conceptualize the environment of the university. The model of planner implicit in what follows is that of psychotherapist.

A major effect of psychoanalytic theory on education has been to shift the nature of the questions that are asked about both the student's emotional and academic development and his response to the new environment. There was a time when it was sufficient to inquire about the student's IQ, about the quality of his character, the cleanliness of his room, and of course his grade average. Now, one asks such questions as, How does the student psychologically integrate the new experience of college? Does a college or university education insure the student free, mature use of his intellect? What processes in the student interacting with the university milieu promote his creative and continued emotional growth? These questions imply a changed concept of the mind. The uses to which the student puts his education are thought of differently than before. A categorization of discrete traits has given way to a searching out of gross and subtle discrepancies between thought and act. This applies equally to the student and to the intended and the unintended consequences of the curriculum and of the college experience itself. Notions of cause have become conditional and are sought in dynamic processes located within the individual or between individuals. Not only the questions are changed, but the evidence we accept and the inferences we draw are profoundly altered. Our theory leads to a restless curiosity, not to closure. This, or any theory, certainly should not blind or restrict our vision. It should not be used as a psychological divining rod which points to the "bad mother" or the "distant angry father," and leave unexplored what the child did to cope with mother and/or with father. Our theory implies a method of procedure, a perspective, which is also clinical and directed openly toward intervention.

There is a more than superficial similarity, I think, between the analyst's relationship to his patient, and the educational planner's position with respect to the university, which is the object of this study, or the planner's position in the city. Our patients are asked to tell us in honest detail what happened, before we turn to tentative speculation on why it happened as it did. We constantly assess the meaning to the patient of our interventions, our questions, and our insights. The resistances of the patients are respected and are carefully noted. They are also thoroughly investigated. The patient and the physician are both committed to change but accept, as the major legitimate agent for change, insight and increase in self-awareness. Ideally, the number of cues to which the patient may respond are multiplied. His restrictions on both perception and response are minimized and subject eventually to an altered and increased conscious control. These same points are highly relevant for the participant investigator in a college or the participant planner in a larger social context. Such a theory, such a procedure does not provide a comfortable climate of opinion for the individual who rests with easy answers or fixed notions of cause and effect.

Several points, though obvious, warrant further emphasis. The concepts of ego psychology have a unique significance for teachers, for analysts, and indeed for all behavioral scientists with an interest in the effects of the environment on the individual. The city planner or architect will also find significance here if he is concerned with subtle, long-term effect of his act on a population.

The imagery that Freud used to describe the ego varied. Initially Freud saw man's control over the forces that move him as largely an illusion. The ego was compared to a man riding a spirited horse without a bridle. Several years later Freud introduced the analogy of a constitutional monarch with limited powers to describe the ego's operation. The ego is the observer of the unconscious and the conscious, the programmer for our perceptions from outer reality and from within. With this information, the ego orders action or delay, restrains the impulse, defends against anxiety. The ego makes an executive compromise with conflict, which, in the extreme, may be a studied and persistent failure to integrate certain kinds of information into consciousness, as illustrated in the opening case. The ego adapts to stress, responds to transition, and effects in time some new internal compromise.

My purpose is not to press for a unique position for these concepts in the hierarchy of a general theory. It does seem to me, however, that it is in such an area that education and psychoanalysis have common ground and joint commitment. A university education can be expected to extend the student's still adolescent image of himself and his concepts of the world about him, or, in Erikson's terms, define his ego identity. The curriculum and intellectual activity, though the primary functions of the college, are obviously not the only factors operating to effect such changes within the student's ego. Similar questions can be posed for the inhabitants of the metropolis. For example what aspects of the environment of the city influence self-image or ego function?

At most universities, the freshman is faced with a major transition in his life. The majority of students have left home for the first time and are confronted with an often rude and harsh reality here. They must choose a career, make a meaningful commitment to a radically new mode of thinking, learn new cognitive skills, and produce far more actual work per week than they have been accustomed to in the past. For the first time, the vast majority must deal with intense competition for grades with their peers, and at the same time make meaningful relationships with at least some members of this group. During their undergraduate years they must develop a clear and cogent image of the scientist, or the engineer, or whatever it is they want to become, and this image must have some emotional reality for them. They must in short come to some new decisions about who they are and what they are going to be. All of this occurs to late adolescents who are in the process of defining their own psychological and social identities.

The students' patterns for coping with stress, and their adaptive potential for change, play a significant, often decisive, role in their ability to do well academically. Many students respond to academic demands with effective study, others react with fear to this same experience, and isolate themselves from the competitive, demanding milieu by either an inner withdrawal or by actual flight. The institution can effect this outcome by the way it presents these "demands" and by the variety of supports or pressures which attend them.

Some of the goals of the educational environment can be put into the terms of ego psychology as follows: The total educational experience should so spur the student that he extends both the range of his available ego functions and his potential adaptation to stress, that he develops those ego operations and those cognitive functions uniquely meaningful for him and the life task he has set for himself. It should strengthen his commitment to an expanded reality without impoverishment of his inner life. The goals of the urban environment could be similarly described.

There are several questions that come to my mind as I make this formulation. What is the psychological cost to the student in maintaining a successful college adaptation? Does he pay a short-term debt at the expense of long-term growth? What coin does the college actually ask of its students for its approval and its degree?

A brief illustration will clarify this cost factor and also highlight the quality of change that can be anticipated as a consequence of college. A senior physics major, when asked when he began to feel commitment to his field, thought with surprise of talking to his professor in the laboratory the previous semester. His professor had been a close associate of Fermi and had been recalling Fermi's constant doubt about his competence in physics. With regret, but also with relief, the senior suddenly saw his ideal as a diminished man who wasn't certain. He went on to say that at about this time his indecision over physics as a career no longer held the urgency for him that it had before. He noticed that his concern for grades, for being best, had lessened. A chronic state of "sadness" also lifted at this time. Frequently now, fraternity brothers teased him because he wore bluejeans—easier for working in the lab—and because he spent weekends working problems that were not assigned.

During the transition from his previous to his new ideal, from prior to present identity, the student described a sense of sadness, of being lost. This is a normal in-between period for the student as far as his ego ideal and aims are concerned. Personality changes in the student also involve a gradually increased tolerance to frustration. There is a perceptible shift in the sources of the student's self-esteem. Our senior, for example, relied less on marks and more on an inner sense of mastery of certain concepts in solid state physics. Less energy was committed to immediate gratification—more energy was in the service of his ego. To call his sadness only clinical depression may obscure for us a central interaction between the college and the student. His course work, his relationship to his professor—against the background of a series of subtle changes in his capacity to handle challenge—provided him with the opportunity to sharpen his cognitive skill and redefine his image of himself. These changes that occur are overdetermined. The forming of a working relationship with his teacher served to trigger a response which had been building all through adolescence. It is possible, and often happens, that the student remains fixed on the grade, afraid to risk his self-esteem by experimenting with a difficult or ambiguous demand. There are many forces in the college which may push the student toward an easy compromise. There are even stronger forces in the student himself with which he must come to terms.

The point is clear. The college may restrict the areas of choice available to its students—or provide them with an overwhelming array of alternatives. It may reinforce or partially free the student from a previous, neurotic adaptation. If his immediate adjustment to the college setting is at the expense of a further entrenchment of a neurotic pattern—the use of denial or projection as defense, for example—then the cost is indeed a high one, when one looks at his eventual emotional development.

Becker, in his book *The Heavenly City of the Eighteenth Century Philosophers,* stresses the relevance of the utopian construction to its current climate of opinion—and he gives a word of caution to anyone who would attempt to plan a bold and fresh environment:

> The underlying preoccupations of the eighteenth-century thought were still—allowances made for certain important alterations in bias—essentially the same as those of the thirteenth century. . . . The *philosophe* demolished the Heavenly City of St. Augustine only to rebuild it with more up to date materials.[2]

In describing the course of the nineteenth century, Becker goes on to say:

> The vision of man and his world as a neat and efficient machine, designed by an intelligent author of the universe, gradually faded away. Professors of science ceased to speak with any assurance of the laws of nature and were content to pursue with unabated ardor, but without any teleological implications whatever, their proper business of observing and experimenting with the something which is the stuff of the universe, of measuring and mastering its stress and movement.

The knowledge that comes from the therapeutic enterprise is the result of an empathic involvement with the patient, different than the knowing of the nineteenth century professors of science referred to by Becker. For the physician it must be more than an abstract interest in why something works. Clearly the therapeutic involvement means caring whether the student manages successfully to deal with the stresses in his environment. Such caring, on the physician's part, alters his relationship with his patient and influences his understanding of the symptoms. The psychiatrist as a behavioral scientist should give constant and precise attention to the psychological cost of successful adaptation. Both educational planner and psychiatrist should be concerned with whether success in college spells closure to ambiguity at thirty or the continuation of change and growth.

References

1. Lewis Mumford, in the *New Yorker,* October 5, 1957.
2. Carl Lotus Becker, *The Heavenly City of the Eighteenth Century Philosophers,* New Haven, Conn.: Yale Univ. Press, 1932.

8 Cultural Innovation and Disaster in the American City

DONALD A. COOK

Many warnings are put before us, usually consisting of massively repeated but spurious correlations between "causes" and "trends," behind which our search for basic concepts must take us to find the truly basic combinations of conditions which can explain them—and their equally real exceptions.

I want to issue some more warnings, but also to season them with examples that suggest that we can grope our way to fresh insights. Each of my warnings will therefore be accompanied by some case material and a bit of prophetic conjecture.

The first dilemma I should like to present is that today's city is seen at once as the source of the most important values of our culture, and, at the same time, as the source of its most characteristic and pressing problems. What I am going to suggest is that the same basic structural conditions of the modern city may in fact be responsible for both outcomes.

People engaged in social therapy, at any level—to say nothing of other forms of therapy—often repeat to each other, and to their patients, that one should treat not the symptom but the cause. The warning I bring is that, in dealing with city problems, we had best be careful in treating even the cause. In removing some basic structural cause of disorder, we may also remove the very basic structural conditions which permit a high rate of important innovation.

How can certain conditions be equally responsible for innovation and disaster? Take "density," for example. I believe that in the quantification of density there may be a critical point at which important dependent variables turn over, stop ascending and begin descending; and that, aside from some highly artificial constructs, we know nothing yet about where these critical points occur. My warning, in short, is against the assumption that density *per se* is necessarily either good or bad. We frequently hear such terms as "overcrowding"; on the other hand, density allows people to interact with each other at a high rate, and to have a broad range of choices from which to select their preferred interactions. It is my belief that the distinction between overcrowding and productive density is not simply quantitative; it has to do with a wider qualitative context in which these aspects of density are seen.

A comparable condition of people in cities is that a large number of different kinds of groups come to jostle each other. People coming to the city tend to be bewildered by what seems to be a lack of consistent norms, or by the presence of conflicting sets of norm systems whose rules and expectations continually alter and contradict one another. Yet this is precisely the many faceted aspect of urban group life that permits all the specializations of interest, passion, character, commitment, to coexist in a manner that breeds variety and often a good deal of interest stimulation among differing groups.

In terms of classical sociology, you could say that the dense and multiplex city is an environment in which the "secondary" group that you join out of shared interests becomes in fact your *primary* group, the face-to-face group with which you have your most important contacts.

Take the "neighborhood." It is usually presented as a relatively stable semi-ethnic slum that gives a good deal of satisfaction to those who remain in it. I would say that what is most characteristically *urbane* about the city is *not* the neighborhood; one of the transformations we shall continue to witness is precisely the destruction of this comfortable, self-contained social entity. Indeed, I think that its loss may be a good thing, from the point of view of the more exciting prospects of city life.

The older pattern was to check delinquent tendencies by encouraging the neighborhood identification: "Get to know your grocer," or (addressed to the grocer) "Get to know the kids on your block." The programs I visited in Chicago took the other slant: the aim was to destroy, especially for the immigrant Southern Negro youth, the hold of the neighborhood on him, precisely because its resources were so few and so uncharacteristic of the city. We wanted to teach these youngsters how to move around the city in a more genuine, urbane, and sophisticated way. This is a great task, and one that takes great skill. The point, however, is that *urbanity* does carry with it both the threat and the promise of release from the bonds of the primary groups—characteristically, the familial one.

There is, of course, in this release from primary-orientation groups, a critical period of transition. Girls who run away from home to the city without any mechanism for handling this transition commonly get into a good deal of trouble. On the other hand, there are institutions that do provide such mechanisms: the university, for example. This too is a place where you go to get away from home; it offers a secondary group, associated through common interests; but it also offers a number of socializing functions. Similarly, in cities, once a mechanism of transition is provided, and the crises weathered, a new kind of associational life becomes possible.

Another feature often, and justly, listed as a cause of disorder in city life is the rapidity of change. I would simply like to point out that we haven't known how to plan for innovation; so it has characteristically appeared at places where a great deal of rapid change is taking place. Genetically, the analogy is to mutation.

Most mutations are, in fact, lethal, because a mutation represents a rearrangement of an already stable structure and this, particularly if it is random, is potentially dangerous. For new mutations to have adaptive value, the total of mutations must be very large, since the probability of an important and viable mutation is low. City life, I think, is analogous. You have a seething cauldron in which new combinations are constantly arising. A large percentage of them are not stable; but it is necessary to keep the cauldron boiling in order to get that relatively small percentage of important and stable cultural innovations. I think we may be moving into a time when the disaster rate necessary to produce a given probability of important innovations can be altered through social engineering. My present point, however, is this: under modern conditions of cosmopolitan life, the same basic set of structural conditions gives rise *at the same time* to the possibilities for innovation—and for disaster. There is a city famous for having the highest rates of alcoholism, divorce, and suicide in the United States—but famous also for its current cultural renaissance, which is making it a mecca for many kinds of people.

The next point I want to make is that the culture of the city offers to the disfranchised and the deviant a genuinely important role. We know that the city serves as a haven for them. Some are attracted there; some are created in the cauldron of the city itself; and some, probably the most pathological, are the residues or failures of groups that have used the city to gain mobility and momentum to move on, leaving these residual enclaves.

This last group is probably the most unproductive. But the first two —those produced by the city, and those attracted to it—often play a very important role in maintaining skills that are important to the culture, and even more in making innovations that will, I believe, become ever more important over the years. I am not suggesting any general law; but I would like to offer a few examples, illustrating very different types of process.

First, consider the contribution of a few people, second generation, from a small area on the lower East Side of Manhattan, during the 1920's and 1930's. I am thinking of George Gershwin, Irving Berlin, and their fellows. Consider that when our State Department engages in cultural exchange with other countries, it choses to export *Porgy and Bess* as one of the most genuinely indigenous American products Consider that the *Rhapsody in Blue* means "U.S.A." to whole generations of Americans—and then remember that the nutrient solution in which this was bred is a two-by-four strip in a tiny area of New York. I know you can argue that this was really the product of many factors, the Jewish emphasis on music, the family life, and so on. What I am pointing out is that a transformation did take place: in the process of assimilation to a new culture, a disfranchised group has to form a new identity. That identity is not formed on any single model, of either the old culture or the new; it is synthesized out of elements picked up here or there—out of pieces of models, so to speak. What emerges is a true synthesis: not unrelated fragments of copy-cat but a genuine cultural product which, because it represents the injection of new material in forms compatible with the old, may be a very important contribution to the culture.

Then there is a group of deviants who are attracted to the city, partly as a refuge, rather than created by it: the homosexuals.

The obvious advantage of the city to the homosexual is the anonymity it affords. The bonds of social constraint are loosened, secondary groups with shared interests can form, and may become primary groups for him—though he usually has a dual set of rather complicated role relations, half in avowedly homosexual communities and half in other roles in which his homosexuality is more or less masked.

The role of the homosexual in such fields as art, music, dance, theater, publishing, and kindred pursuits has been a matter of considerable controversy. No unassailable facts are available. The panicky reactionary talks about it with overtones of paranoid threat, the liberal remains discreetly silent and asks for evidence, which is not forthcoming. My own impression, however, from years of living in New York and Washington, is that homosexuals play an extremely important role in aspects of our culture concerned with the graphic, verbal, and other arts. In many cases, after the identity crisis is settled, probably in the early twenties, there follow very stable and productive careers, with very little pathology, though with relationship problems common to such a mobile group. Since this country has never had a tradition of aristocratic support of the leisured disciplines of writing, and the other arts, of style and taste, we may count ourselves fortunate that they have been sustained largely by deviant groups. If, as seems likely, our culture over the next decade or two begins to accord higher status to people who are not directly engaged in producing a hard product—i.e., as verbal skills and skills of style, taste, and appreciation become more important and more widespread—it seems likely that the importance of this role for deviant groups may decline.

There is another aspect to the role of deviant and disfranchised groups, an aspect which contains some rather nice historical irony. First, why is it that such groups play an important role in the introduction of innovations? It is not simply because they are relatively detached from the main culture, and not simply out of spite. I think it is primarily because they simply have less of a vested interest in the status quo, and thus are more responsive to opportunities of new kinds, at variance with the characterological and economic expectations by which the status quo is defined.

Consider the fact, for example, that the Negro rose to prominence relatively early in the fields of sports, music, and entertainment, when these were held in somewhat lower regard but still offered opportunities to achieve relatively high status, income, and respect within the fields themselves—and without the requirement of close personal intimacy, which would close the door on a career such as that of a family doctor for white families. But now, as we shift from a production- to a consumption-oriented culture, the status of these roles has steadily gained, carrying the performers with them to new levels of interest, respect, and reward. In other words, the disfranchised group moves into fields that are relatively unimportant at the time they are available; the group develops skills within these roles; and then as the culture changes these fields move toward its center, and the groups move with them. The motto goes from "To him that hath shall be given," to "The last shall be first."

I am not saying that these processes of identity and career choice are not heavily fraught with personal suffering. What I am saying is that the forces that produce this difficulty and suffering, and those that bring about changes in society and culture, may be closely related, even interwoven, with each other.

For another example, let me offer the interracial dating pattern in New York. The men are typically upwardly-mobile Negroes from situations of closed opportunity in Brooklyn, Harlem, or even the new middle-class areas in New Jersey. They are known collectively as "A trainers," because they take the A train down to Washington Square, where they pick up girls who are currently known as "Bronx Bagel Babies." Interestingly, for reasons I have not been able to fathom, these are, typically, Jewish girls fleeing from mother-dominated homes in the Bronx or Brooklyn.

These couples are extremely unstable, and the rate at which coupling crystallizes into marriage is quite low. They are subject to all the familiar perils, from insulting hoodlums to police and suspicious hotels; the arrival of a baby may send the girl back to her mother, in both plea and defiance; the partners themselves may turn on each other with accusations of entering the relation for all the wrong motives—which is frequently true. The whole scene is filled with suffering. Yet out of it have come some genuine mutations: marriages that are stable, productive, and evocative of a fantastic kind of talent and skill. These are what we should *store* so that they can serve as models to be used by others as this trend becomes more and more important.

Now let me make one more point. It is that public, i.e., officially recognized, "problems" have this same quality of containing important clues to innovations that the culture is groping for and which its future shape will require. For my example, I shall cite "urban youth in trouble"—the delinquents. Now, in terms of the public record, the typical delinquent is not the intrapsychologically disturbed family case that is studied by psychoanalysts. He is a sociological client: out of school, out of work, lower class, usually of a minority group, between the ages of fourteen and eighteen. This group is certainly not doing anything useful; and the customary effort is to pursuade businessmen, for example, to give them jobs despite their lack of the requisite skills. But the position of this class, it may well be, is simply that of a straw in the wind; automation and other familiar forces may throw wider and wider segments of America's working population into exactly the same situation. Rather than try to force businesses to open their creaky doors a little wider, for kids who don't like such jobs anyhow, we should be studying the emerging value systems that these groups are developing, to see what lessons can be learned that are applicable to America as a whole. Here again I am thinking of matters of skill in personal interaction, in style and taste: the hip vocabulary, the etiquette for handling situations, the skills of forming relationships, of making discriminations and assigning reality values. I believe that all of these are skills the rest of us could profit by studying, not just in their present state but in the forms into which they will be transformed as they spread into wider, perhaps higher, status areas.

No system of social organization has survival value which assumes or requires that every individual shall care continuously about the community as a whole. Wise men, theorists, leaders, councils of government, yes; but to ask that everyone be totally dedicated to the problems of a democracy would be to stifle just those specialties of skill, passion, character, and commitment that I have been talking about. Their diversity, their variety, are the heart of the important virtues of urbanity. The need is not for an entire *populus* of community organizers, but for new kinds of institutions that will relieve us of the need for such a grim prospect. This is a task as difficult as it is significant; but it is one which I commend to all of us.

PART TWO

Renewal and Relocation-Urbs and Suburbs

In this section, we tackle head-on the problems of urban renewal and of the processes of dislocation and relocation involved in it. The head of the United States Housing and Home Finance Agency takes a hard look at the difficulties built in to this national effort by local factors and cultural lags. A British visitor, who studied this program on a Ford Foundation grant, gives his views, not only on the failure of renewal to help people, but on the culture of the "slum" population that is thereby displaced.

Two papers, growing out of research into a specific city slum, give us a fresh look at it as a partial source of security and identity, and describe the sense of grief and loss felt by many of the inhabitants when they are evicted from it. The area is the "West End," a river edge section of Boston acquired by the city in 1958 for purposes of demolition and rebuilding. This is how the research arose.

In 1956, a partnership between the psychiatric department of Massachusetts General Hospital and the Professional Services Branch of the National Institute of Mental Health (i.e., between Lindemann and Duhl) led to the conception of a long-term study, in some psychosocial depth, of the residents of the area which was to be "renewed" (i.e., demolished and made into something else), both before and after their relocation. The aims were to study their "coping" patterns in both situations, the emotional resources on which they relied, and their use or non-use of available facilities for intervention or aid. The "Center for Community Studies" was created; and it was as members of its staff that two of our authors, Ryan and Fried, made the studies reported here. The entire undertaking was unique; it was on-the-spot research in a community confronted by a severe crisis of a kind becoming "normal" in today's rapidly changing cities. The study occupied five years, and its earlier findings have been reported in *The Urban Villagers,* a book by Herbert Gans.

Gans and a fellow social scientist, Robert Gutman, report in this section on a radically different sort of relocation: the movement of middle-class white families from city to suburbs. In doing so, the writers challenge many of the familiar "myths of suburbia" that have created anxiety among those who have made the move, whether to Suburbia or to Exurbia. Both studies are based on personal researches by the authors; they both succeed in looking at an old problem in a new way.

Here again, certain themes recur, and will be met again: the meaning of "identity" for working class and middle class, the growth of class- and color-segregated communities, and what this means for teen-agers living in them, the economic problems of a center city without taxpayers and of suburbs without central services, and the need for planning for people rather than for property. The author does, in short, discuss here the new varieties of "stress" that spring from environmental change. Dr. Judd Marmor chaired one of the sessions at which some of these papers were given, and said:

> The environmental stresses to which the individual may be called upon to adapt include not only psychological ones such as bereavements or loss of love, but also physiological ones, sociological ones, and economic ones. Heat and cold, noise and dirt, housing and food, illness and aging, socio-cultural restrictions and taboos, status strivings and frustrations, vocational vicissitudes and economic privations, are but a few of the threads in the complex fabric of adaptive challenges with which every human being must cope as he moves through the labyrinths of the modern metropolis.

Major Factors in Urban Planning

9

ROBERT C. WEAVER

In the broadest sense, the urban planning process represents the self-conscious attempt by men to order their environment so as to realize certain common goals and values. As such, it is concerned not merely with the rational allocation of resources but, more importantly, with the selection of the goals and values toward which those resources should be directed. Thus, urban planning is an important part of the process by which consensus is achieved in a democratic society.

Too often, we tend to think of urban planning problems in the narrow sense of the technical issues surrounding the physical form of the city, the spatial arrangement of urban functions and the control and allocation of land. At the end of the planning process, decisions about land use, the location of transportation and the provision of housing and community facilities must be made. But before these issues can be decided, before the planner's map can be drawn and colored, there must be debate and decision about the goals of urban life, and the values and ends toward which the urban environment is to be shaped.

It is heartening, therefore, that the problems resulting from the increasing urbanization of the United States are today receiving such widespread attention and discussion. This attention, I believe, represents more than a superficial annoyance with the more obvious disjunctions, costs, and inconvenience which have resulted from rapid growth. Increasingly, there is a recognition that both the form and spirit of urban life in America are changing, and that the problems we confront are both a challenge to traditional values and an opportunity to improve the quality of our common life.

In this paper, therefore, I would like to review some of these problems and discuss their significance for students of the urban environment as well as their importance for public policy.

Government and the Metropolitan Community

The increasing urbanization of the nation has imposed unprecedented demands upon the institutions of local government in metropolitan areas. The physical expansion of urban centers has proceeded without much regard for the traditional boundaries between city and country, while at the same time giving rise to extensive demands for new public facilities and services. The responsibility for meeting these demands, however, has been fragmented among a multiplicity of local governments.

Experience in most metropolitan areas has indicated that there is no "invisible hand" to guarantee that the separate and individual decisions of a variety of localized sovereignties can produce facilities and services which will adequately meet the needs of the metropolitan region as a whole. Nor can such fragmented action secure the economies of scale which could be realized if water and sewer systems, mass transportation, highways, and other public works were planned, executed, and administered on a metropolitan scale. And besides this problem of providing for current needs there is also the necessity of planning for the future environment. In most metropolitan areas today, there is *no* governmental institution with the responsibility and authority to plan for the emerging needs of the expanding metropolis and to implement comprehensive programs which embody such plans.

Proposals for creating one or another form of metropolitan government date back to the 1920's. Almost without exception, however, these and subsequent proposals have been rejected by the voters. Whether the plans called for outright consolidation of separate municipalities into one new governmental unit, or whether they merely proposed the creation of a federal unit of government with limited powers and functions, citizens in the United States have almost universally refused to modify the traditional autonomy enjoyed by local governments. In this refusal to temper the autonomy of local government in the interests of the metropolitan community, we find one of the major institutional problems of the current urban scene.

While it does not yet appear how we shall create a more perfect union in our metropolitan areas, it may be possible to suggest some of the conditions which must be met if we are to make progress in finding a solution to this problem. Let me suggest several.

First, it seems to me that we need to recognize frankly that the rational appeal of a comprehensive institutional "solution"—i.e., metropolitan government—is limited to professional students of urban problems. What has been called the "strong bias toward simplicity, uniformity and symmetry of structure" [1] which characterizes proposals for metropolitan organization arises from a professional consensus about an approach to metropolitan problem-solving which seems to have no popular counterpart among the citizens of such areas. In our attempts to find institutional means for coping with problems in metropolitan areas, therefore, it may be necessary to explore the possibilities for pragmatic and proximate adjustments rather than comprehensive remedies.

Second, a number of recent studies cast doubt on the likelihood that the first steps toward solving this institutional problem will be the result of any widespread, popular perception of metropolitan problems or any general consensus about ways of dealing with them. Recently, for example, Robert Dahl has reviewed the process of governmental decision-making in New Haven, where dramatic progress has been made in redeveloping the core area of the city. Most decisions concerned with problems such as this, Dahl notes, took place within a context of relatively complete indifference on the part of a majority of the citizens.[2] Participation in all types of activity related to public concerns was extremely limited, and a study of attitudes revealed that most citizens were primarily concerned with "personal matters, health, jobs, children, and the like . . ." [3]

Even if a majority of the residents of metropolitan areas are not regularly interested in the problems of the larger community, however, is it not likely that the functional problems of the environment will compel their attention? Will problems which impinge directly on individuals and their private interests—the problems of children and schools, the frustrations of the journey to work, the need for "shelter" —mobilize interest and action? On the whole, questions of this type need to be investigated by social psychologists and other students. Until we have more evidence about such matters, it may not be wise to put too much hope in strategies of action which assume some direct relationship between the severity of social problems and the degree of popular action. As Dahl has noted, "in a political culture where individual achievement and non-governmental techniques are assigned a high priority in problem-solving, men may be frustrated in their primary activities without ever turning to politics for solutions." Dahl concludes from this study that the "ancient myth about the concern of citizens with the life of the democratic *polis* is false in the case of New Haven. Whether or not the myth was a reality in Athens will probably never be known." [4]

Third, the structure and operation of metropolitan organizations will need to reflect the considerable differences which appear to exist in levels of popular awareness and participation in public affairs. If we reject traditional assumptions that everyone is interested in public problems and interested to the same degree, it would appear that unitary institutional solutions will probably be unworkable. While the alternatives may not be subject to detailed description, some observers have stressed the desirability of metropolitan organizations which incorporate a high degree of centralized authority with respect to certain functions and a considerable degree of decentralization with respect to others. In their study of Chicago, Meyerson and Banfield have observed that the city's government operates along such lines, and that this arrangement conforms rather closely to the varying expectations and demands which different groups have about government. As they have noted:

> Most of the matters that were decided locally were of local interest. Whether a street was to be paved, the zoning law for a block changed, and the traffic cop transferred were questions which had direct and clearly ascertainable consequences mainly for the locality. . . . Some matters were on the border between being of local and of city-wide interest. . . . In these matters there would be friction because of overlapping jurisdictions of the local and central power holders.[5]

In metropolitan areas, there may be even sharper distinctions which can be drawn between matters of general interest—such as the provision of transportation, public utilities, recreation, and open space—and the concerns of most citizens for the problems of suburb and neighborhood.

Fourth, whatever institutional methods we design for dealing with metropolitan problems, it seems likely that considerable leadership will be necessary to create and sustain them. It might be argued that consensus in our metropolitan areas will be achieved *within* the developing framework of various types of metropolitan organizations, rather than before their creation. Perhaps the history of the federal union of the states provides a useful model in this respect.

If this historic example has any validity, it also suggests among other things that resourceful leadership will be necessary to bring such organizations into existence. In this respect, the increasing discussion and debate about metropolitan problems is reassuring evidence that such leadership may be in the process of emerging in many localities. Perhaps more study should be directed toward ways of understanding this phenomenon. As Dahl has observed, "Instead of seeking to explain why citizens are not interested, concerned and active, the task is to explain why a few citizens *are*." [6]

Fifth, among the many tasks which an emerging metropolitan leadership must confront, perhaps none is more important than that of developing a more widespread and effective sense of *membership* in the metropolitan community than exists today. On the one hand, the task of this leadership will be concerned with defining values and assisting in the process of establishing the goals and aims of the community. On the other, it must be concerned with minimizing conflict and bridging the cleavages in race and class which increasingly challenge the values and goals of urban life in the United States.

Segregation and Social Cleavages

Beneath the patchwork of local governments that spreads across the metropolis, there has developed a more troubling pattern of racial segregation and socio-economic stratification. In many ways, the increasing urbanization of the nation seems to have involved a centrifugal process by which races and classes are being separated out in terms of residence within metropolitan areas. The pace at which this is occurring is suggested by the fact that in the decade 1950 to 1960, the percentages of the nation's white population resident in the suburbs jumped from 15 per cent to 23 per cent, while the proportion of the non-white population resident in central cities increased from 39 per cent to 51 per cent. Increasingly, central cities are tending to become ghettos for the racially and economically underprivileged, so that divisions between city and suburb are becoming ones of race and class.

In analyzing these developments, it is useful to note how they differ from earlier patterns of development in urban areas. As has been noted elsewhere, the middle classes in American cities in the nineteenth century also tended to move away from the newer immigrants. But while the densely concentrated cities of that era also evidenced stratification and segregation, an important point is that this pattern tended to be concentrated largely within the boundaries of one municipality. Thus, an escape from residential proximity to the newer immigrants did not involve an avoidance of the social welfare and other costs which resulted from providing municipal services for these minorities.[7]

The flight to the suburbs in recent years has also been motivated in part by similar desires on the part of today's middle classes, many of whom are the children or grandchildren of yesterday's ethnic newcomers. Because of the pattern of local government in metropolitan areas today, however, this flight often results in an escape from the problems—and their costs. Attempts at metropolitan organization which will require sharing these costs and pooling resources, therefore, are likely to encounter resistance which finds some of its origin in racial prejudice and socio-economic exclusiveness.

The operation of racial prejudice in housing and residence also must be distinguished, in its effects on the Negro, from the effects which prejudice had on earlier ethnic minorities. Whatever the romanticism which surrounded the melting pot theory, middle class status was generally conferred upon earlier minorities once they had demonstrated adherence to the dominant culture in behavior and appearance. Thus, the goals of better housing, improved neighborhood, and better schools seemed within the reach of earlier minorities once they could secure the economic rewards which resulted from conformity to the Calvinist virtues of thrift, ambition, and industry.

The non-white, however, is confronted with a different situation. The economic status of the Negro has risen considerably during the last twenty years, and a significant Negro middle class is emerging. In their aspirations, self-image, and tastes, this group has taken on most of the traditional characteristics of the American middle class. In contrast to earlier ethnic minorities, however, the Negro is "stuck with pigmentation which in our society is the badge of difference and inferiority." [8] Nowhere is this more apparent than in the matter of housing and residence. Racial prejudice continues to bar the Negro from the type of housing and place of residence for which his income, aspirations, and behavior qualify him.

If the existence of racial prejudice frustrates the attempts of Negroes to secure improved housing in better neighborhoods, it also operates to limit the effectiveness of public programs designed to increase the supply of housing and improve the physical environment of the city. Federal housing programs, for example, have originated in a national consensus on the need to insure that there is decent, safe, and sanitary housing for every American family. The contradiction between national purpose and local prejudice, however, has long been evident. In many cities, low-rent public housing programs are restricted to the crowded older areas, and have resulted in the construction of new housing in an environment of blight and segregation. The Federal Urban Renewal Program has provided the means by which local public agencies could eliminate blighted housing and deteriorated areas of the central cities; but the net gains of this program have been seriously affected in many cities because of the existence of racial prejudice and discrimination. Local attempts to relocate families displaced by urban renewal projects into decent housing and better neighborhoods have been unsuccessful in many instances. During the past year we have recognized these problems, and federal programs are increasingly emphasizing more effective relocation at the local level. But the basic problem still harasses us.

Frontal attacks on discrimination in housing and residence are already under way and can be expected to increase during the next few years. As a result of this struggle, there will be an appearance of less and less understanding between the majority and minority groups. As I have said elsewhere, however, such tensions are frequently evidence of progress.

This prospect of the racial integration of neighborhoods in our cities raises some interesting questions about the degree of social communication and sharing of values which we can expect as a result of such integration. Let me explore this question by examining an assumption which seems to me to underlie some of the thinking in this field.

Perhaps because the city planning movement was so strongly influenced in its infancy by the architectural and engineering professions, planners have put great stress on the influence which the physical environment can have on the attitudes and behavior of individuals. Later, I will want to discuss the ways in which such assumptions influenced the goals of the housing reformers, but here let me note evidence of these assumptions when planners discuss the design and function of the neighborhood.

As I listen to some planners, they seem to suggest that physical propinquity between people of differing attitudes and social characteristics in some way produces meaningful social interaction and results in mutual identity and a reduction in social tensions. Planners and others have therefore emphasized the need for "balanced" neighborhoods which include people with a diversity of economic and social characteristics; and have laid emphasis on the physical design or layout of neighborhoods as a way of increasing meaningful communication. More recently there has also been a recrudescence of nostalgia for the "diversity" and "heterogeneity" which characterized certain neighborhoods in the central city. Again, the implication seems to be that population density and diversity and the physical design of the city exercise some unique and desirable influence on attitudes and behavior.

Stated in another way, one wonders whether mere physical "togetherness" alone will bridge the cleavages which separate race and class in the modern city. Urban ecologists need to take a careful look at these assumptions; and research is needed into questions of how the physical form of the neighborhood, and the social characteristics of its residents influence behavior and attitudes. It is conceivable—and I strongly suspect it to be true—that such research would indicate that physical propinquity may be an important, and at times indispensable, element in creating understanding and mutual appreciation among certain elements in our society. However, it may well be that such proximity is only a physical setting in which *other* carefully selected activities are required, to yield maximum results.

Perhaps, indeed, had we not created these consciously homogeneous neighborhoods, we should have less cleavage. But are not the two developments part and parcel of the same forces and attitudes? In part, this is true. But also the drive to sell exclusiveness, so characteristic of the development of suburbia, introduced an element of prestige in single-class and single-race developments. The result is that such neighborhoods today are both the symbol and the embodiment of social distance between classes and ethnic groups. Destruction of this symbol is fundamental to changing class and racial attitudes and distance, but it is doubtful if it, of and in itself, will effect the change.[9]

Recent experience in the urban renewal process tends to magnify the importance which should be assigned to the function of voluntary groups in helping to bring the success of programs to change and improve the environment of the city. In too many communities, plans for the clearing of blighted and obsolete areas have been viewed as matters which can be decided by technicians in consultation with the local power elite. Where these plans have ignored the needs and desires of significant groups in the community, and where the programs have been implemented largely by government action without enlisting the support and advice of citizen groups, urban renewal programs have gotten into serious difficulties.

Elsewhere, the process has been so markedly different that two observers have concluded recently that:

> It seems likely that successful urban renewal in large cities—successful in the sense of widely accepted both within and without the neighborhoods under renewal—will come primarily either in neighborhoods that have indigenous successful community organization or in neighborhoods in which some outside agency manages to create one.[10]

Because of such experience, students of urban problems need to give careful attention to the ways in which voluntary groups can provide the means for stimulating a more widespread sense of interdependence and mutual responsibility in the metropolitan community. Lacking the formal institutions of government which might serve to unite the metropolitan community in action toward the solution of common problems, we need to explore the part which community organizations can play in bringing about the consensus necessary for comprehensive governmental institutions and action.

We are reminded by Oscar Handlin of the important part which such groups played in solving the new and unfamiliar problems of the large city of the nineteenth century. Handlin has observed that the social system in cities in that time was

> . . . loosely structured through a large number of autonomous and scarcely articulated associations. The disorder of that situation in some ways added to the problems of expansion. But it provided a viable means through which large populations could act together toward immediate goals under unfamiliar conditions.[11]

Students of urban problems need to investigate whether it is possible for some outside agency to "create" such organizations, as suggested in the quotation cited earlier, particularly in situations where social disorganization and anomie have resulted in a paucity of active voluntary groups. While one of the problems confronting us may be the need for creating a metropolitan community in fact as well as in name, our ability to do this may be seriously conditioned by the success with which we are able to encourage voluntary groups to emerge in response to these problems.

Before prescribing community organization as the sovereign remedy for the social ills of the metropolis, therefore, it might be useful to reflect on the cautionary note sounded by Handlin, a note whose implications need to be investigated by social psychologists and students of culture and personality. Handlin writes:

> The growth of the contemporary suburb has . . . been only symptomatic of broader social changes in the life of the city. Lacking firmly fixed personal or social goals—and swayed by the imprecise standards communicated through the mass media, large parts of its population have lost the capacity for acting meaningfully in groups, except when it comes to matters which touch immediately upon their family life. Outside these narrow personal concerns there has been a perceptible decline in the capacity for group action.[12]

Urban Migrants and Their Environment

As the third and final example of the problems confronting urban planning, I have chosen some of the issues which involve the newest immigrants to our cities. Southern Negroes, Appalachian Whites, Puerto Ricans, and American Indians have been migrating to the city in large numbers in recent decades. As in the past, they inhabit the worst slums and the most deteriorated neighborhoods of the central cities. While all this is in the classic pattern of earlier immigration, these new arrivals present some unique problems which challenge us to re-examine traditional answers to questions about the methods and goals of acculturation and adjustment to the urban environment.

Perhaps the most obvious of these traditional "answers" involves what John P. Dean has called the "myths of housing reform." [13] Dean and other observers have demonstrated that a great many of the arguments for clearing slums and providing improved housing for slum dwellers were premised upon specious evidence about the supposedly causal role of slums in crime, delinquency, and ill-health. Most of this evidence, which consisted of correlations between evidence about the physical condition of housing and rates of social disorder and disease within slum areas, has been characterized by Robert K. Merton as follows:

> In its early phase social and psychological research on housing was virtually confined to social bookkeeping. During this phase, it was conventionally assumed that research comprised periodic audits of the proportion of substandard dwellings, meticulously described in terms of defective plumbing, defective structures, and, consequently, defective residents. It was devoted to gross and uncritical correlations between something called "bad housing"—typically meaning either slum areas with a high frequency of substandard housing or household groups living in substandard housing—and a series of social morbidities. . . . Yet the long and still continuing series of reports showing uniformly that slum areas, with their defective housing, are characterized by these social morbidities have seldom shown the role played by specifiable aspects of substandard housing.[14]

As a result of the assumption that the physical conditions of housing and neighborhoods have a direct and baneful effect upon the personalities and morals of slum dwellers, it is not surprising that rehousing was justified in terms of the beneficial effects it would have upon their attitudes and behavior. As Dean observed:

> The reformers argued . . . that ill health, uncleanliness, and delinquency are not *innate* characteristics, but are the result of life in the slum environment. Their conception of the slum environment emphasized primarily the inadequate *physical* environment of the slums. It understressed the connection between the *social* environment of the slums and the disorders they want to cure. So it was easy to jump to the conclusion that slum clearance would remove the social ills. . . .[15]

While today few would contend that there is such a direct relationship between physical environment and social behavior, it may be useful to review past experience if only to remind ourselves of the complexity of the problem we confront in trying to discharge the responsibility which our cities have toward the urban immigrants upon whose labors their economies are so dependent. Clearly, new housing and new neighborhoods are not in and of themselves enough to accomplish the acculturation of the urban immigrant and the slum dweller.

A similar observation has been made recently by James B. Conant, who writes:

> Among the preoccupations of those concerned with underprivileged areas, one often encounters a great emphasis on the importance of adequate, decent housing. To be sure, the inhabitants in slums (Negro and white) may be living in shockingly bad and even dangerous dwellings. They may also be living in new housing which is the result of a slum clearance project. I am willing to assume that improving the physical environment improves the lives of the inhabitants. To the extent that increased housing facilities diminish the mobility of the population, they may even have a direct bearing on the problem of education. But I am sure new housing works no miracles. I offer the following hypothesis for professional social workers and sociologists to demolish—namely, that the correlation between desirable social attitudes (including attitudes of youths) and job opportunities is far higher than between the former and housing conditions, as measured by plumbing and heating facilities, and space per family.[16]

Yet in trying to do "more" than improve housing, we confront several major problems. The first, and more familiar, concerns the continuing vitality of certain traditional popular beliefs about individualism—"Any man worth his salt will improve himself"—the debilitating effects of "charity," and the moral requirements for such charity. In criticizing the housing reformers for their failure to perceive the necessity of combining rehousing with extensive programs of social welfare measures, we must remember that their basic claim about the social right of every American family to a decent house is still disputed by a number of people in our society. If the traditional ethics of individualism have seriously circumscribed even the limited intentions of the public housing program, these same beliefs continue to impede the development of improved programs based upon subsequent insights and broader intentions.

Whatever the content and methods of the programs we devise for assisting urban migrants and slum dwellers, our ability to implement those programs will depend upon the degree to which there is a growing acceptance and acknowledgment of the community's responsibilities to all people. In assessing these prospects we must not be too quick in our optimism about assured progress in this sphere. The ethnic tensions and class antagonisms which marked the urban scene of the nineteenth century may have abated. It remains to be seen, however, whether our urban society has made strides toward developing more widespread social integration.

The second problem concerns the choice of methods which we will make and the success which we can expect from them. I mention this because it has lately become fashionable to criticize the naivete which some have seen as a characteristic of reform movements in America. If we are to be fashionable and hard-headed, it seems to me that we must acknowledge that dramatic progress in motivating the new urban immigrants to acculturate to the dominant values of our society is not probable until we can substantially alter the institutional conditions in our society which result in low wages, high rates of unemployment, and racial discrimination.

We cannot expect impressive results, for example, in inculcating the economic virtues of thrift in unskilled urban laborers with little job security and few prospects for improvement. There will probably not be dramatic mass conversions to middle class values on the part of Negro immigrants from the South as long as they see their middle class brothers confined by racial prejudice to the same residential ghettos inhabited by the newest arrivals to the city.

Given these problems, it seems to me that our search for the means to assist the urban immigrant must be directed toward several goals and must involve a diversity of techniques.

Perhaps our first objective must be to find techniques for assisting the transition to middle class status of those who are obviously upwardly mobile. For non-whites, for example, this will mean intensified efforts to increase opportunities for training and education which will enable them to enter professional, technical, and managerial groups. It will mean a continued struggle against discrimination in employment. And, as I have mentioned earlier, it will require that racial bars in housing and residence be removed.

The second objective involves the more difficult task of finding ways to "accelerate the effective functioning in urban life of those who do not become middle class." [17] Accepting such an objective may be difficult because it will require us to modify some of our traditional optimistic assumptions, about both the availability of middle class rewards in our society and the ability of individuals whose experiences or expectations have been devoid of middle class rewards to respond quickly to them. Those who refuse to acknowledge any responsibility for the problems of the immigrant and slum dweller probably make some such assumptions, at least tacitly.

This will be more difficult for many of us who are concerned with these problems because it may appear to require compromising basic social goals. One of the results of adopting such an objective, however, may be a distinct improvement in our ability to communicate with those whom we seek to assist. Too often our attempts to motivate those of low status in our cities, I think we have seemed to strike a false note by suggesting that personal effort alone will bring reward. As one perceptive foreign observer has noted, "if society is less frustrating than the subculture prefers to believe, it is also less open than it claims." [18]

In seeking to implement this second objective, it will be necessary to develop a number of new techniques. How, for example, are we to communicate more effectively with cultural groups who attach very different worth to the values of ambition, competition, and consumption, than we do? What are the behavioral norms which are required for successful urban living, and how can they be obtained? What types of cultural conditioning will be most successful in broadening the horizons of those "who have given up trying to escape from the ghetto life"? [19] All of these types of questions will need to be answered if we are to be successful in efforts to assist the immigrant to adjust to urban life. In defining these questions and in developing the techniques which will be required, we will need to enlist a broad range of talents and insights from the many scholarly and professional disciplines concerned with people and society.

In my discussion of this problem of urban immigrants, I have attempted to stress some of our own assumptions, attitudes and "answers" which will require modification and change if we are to be successful in formulating the problems and the programs. It has seemed important to do this because I believe that if we are successful in the pursuit of our basic objective—assisting the immigrants to acculturate to urban life—we can make an important contribution to the quality of urban life in the process. In confronting the values and mores of the immigrants, we see evidence of that diversity of values, classes, and social groups which has always characterized the urban environment. Our efforts to assist these groups can provide a significant opportunity to develop a broader tolerance of these differences, and a deeper appreciation of the part which a diversity of values can contribute to enhancing the quality and spirit of life in the modern metropolis.

Conclusion

From this review of some of the problems of the current urban scene, there emerges the larger question of how we shall make the modern metropolis a community as well as merely the physical setting for social life. I believe that psychologists and students of personality can make significant contributions to attempts to answer this question.

As we look at many of the problems which confront the planner and public administrator, it is apparent that attempts to cope with these problems will require a more widespread sense of interdependence and common purpose than presently exists among the residents of most metropolitan areas. Formation of the new organizations which will be needed to deal with problems common to metropolitan areas as a whole, and to plan for the future environment, will require that local autonomy and parochialisms be submerged in the pursuit of larger goals. Cleavages of race and class must be bridged if urban areas are to emerge as coherent societies and not merely collections of hostile or indifferent groups and areas. The resources of rich suburbs and the poorer central cities must be pooled in programs to improve education, provide needed social services and public facilities.

How can we achieve that image of the larger community and that sense of identity with it which will make these programs possible? Many of the insights which are emerging from the study of personality hold promise, I believe, of useful application to this problem. Research and study in many fields shows that personality is shaped as a result of dynamic interaction with the environment of family and society. Newer techniques in psychiatry emphasize the therapeutic role which the environment can play in attempts to improve the mental health of individuals. All of these trends in research and therapy suggest that students of personality can make important contributions in current attempts to develop techniques for improving the urban environment and developing a broader conception of the metropolitan community.

As we confront the problems of an urban environment which appears to be changing even as we observe it, all of us who are concerned with urban problems, whether we be adminstrators and practitioners or researchers and students, are impressed by the enormity and complexity of the tasks with which we are charged. Perhaps our reactions are not greatly different than those which Dreiser tells us that Sister Carrie had on her first visit to Chicago's loop. "She wondered at the magnitude of this life and at the importance of knowing much in order to do anything at all."

References

1. Banfield, E. C., and Grodzins, M., *Government and Housing in Metropolitan Areas,* New York: McGraw-Hill, 1958, p. 155.
2. Dahl, R. A., *Who Governs? Democracy and Power in an American City,* New Haven, Conn.: Yale Univ. Press, 1961, pp. 270 ff.
3. *Ibid.,* p. 279.
4. *Ibid.,* pp. 280, 281.
5. Meyerson, M., and Banfield, E. C., *Politics, Planning and the Public Interest,* Glencoe, Ill.: The Free Press, 1955.
6. Dahl, *op. cit.,* 279.
7. Weaver, R. C., *Proc. Acad. Pol. Sci.,* 27:31, 1960.
8. ———, *J. Intergroup Rel.,* 2:13, Winter 1960-1961.
9. ———, *Land Economics,* 36:235, 1960.
10. Rossi, P., and Dentler, R. A., *The Politics of Urban Renewal,* New York: The Free Press of Glencoe, 1961, p. 292.
11. Handlin, O., "The Social System," in *The Future Metropolis,* L. Rodwin, ed., New York: Braziller, 1961, p. 40.
12. *Ibid.,* p. 31.
13. Dean, J. P., "The Myths of Housing Reform," in *Reader in Urban Sociology,* P. K. Hatt and A. J. Reiss, eds., Glencoe, Ill.: The Free Press, 1951, p. 664.
14. Merton, R. K., "The Social Psychology of Housing," in *Current Trends in Social Psychology,* W. Dennis, ed., Pittsburgh: Univ. of Pittsburgh Press, 1948.
15. Dean, *op. cit.,* p. 667.
16. Conant, J. B., *Slums and Suburbs,* New York: McGraw-Hill, 1961, p. 32.
17. Weaver, R. C., *Proc. Acad. Pol. Sci.,* 27:36, 1960.
18. Marris, P., "A Report on Urban Renewal in the United States," this volume, p. 128.
19. Weaver, R. C., *op. cit.*

A Report on Urban Renewal in the United States

10

PETER MARRIS

In the first twelve years after the Housing Act of 1949, urban renewal projects had displaced about eighty-five thousand families in just under two hundred American cities.[1] In scale, then, it is not a very large program; but in the range of problems to be resolved, it is one of the most searching issues of domestic policy, and reflects some of the most characteristic dilemmas of contemporary American society. Its principles are defended as an expression of the enlightened liberalism of the administration, while its practices are condemned as another sell-out to real estate speculators. A plan of action which was conceived as the replacement of dilapidated buildings has become deeply involved in fundamental social problems: the persistence of racial intolerance in an egalitarian democracy; the growing pressure on minorities to assimilate the values of the dominant culture; the refusal of a large-scale, highly integrated society to surrender its traditional attachment to local political autonomy, or to grant powers of government wide enough to defend the public interest against exploitation by private capital; the failure of the world's richest nation to deploy its resources effectively against squalor and deprivation. As the cranes swing their first punch at a slum wall, the problems tumble out to harass and perplex. But if these problems could be solved in the context of urban renewal, the solutions would have far-reaching implications; and this makes urban renewal a symbol of the aspiring but puzzled idealism of America in 1963.

Urban renewal, because it usually displaces the poorest of the city's population—the immigrants, the cultural and ethnic minorities—in a situation where public authorities cannot evade responsibility for their welfare, raises all the issues of the underprivileged in contemporary America. At the same time, the form of renewal cannot be determined without conceiving an ideal of what cities in future should be, and what influence they can have on national culture; and these questions, of course, are not peculiar to the United States. Urban renewal is therefore one of the most far-reaching, complex, and difficult policies on which to comment.

Visiting foreigners are notorious for the facility of their criticisms, and the glibness of their solutions. I am no exception, and the approach which seems most practical to someone from a society more tolerant of centralized government and public enterprise may not be acceptable in an American context. But it may be, too, that the problems of urban renewal cannot be solved unless Americans can reconcile themselves to these harbingers of socialism.

The Decline of the Central City

The central city includes, typically, a business district; a railway and bus station; a university; Skid Row; a "hill," which, though it may be flat, has remained socially elevated amidst the surrounding decay, an island of gracious town houses for the sophisticated and well-to-do; a museum, housing a superb collection of pictures from every age and country except that in which the museum itself was built; and a park. Around these features, and extending far beyond them, miles of seedy tenements and row houses peel and flake, amiable or grim in their degenerate old age. Here, waves of immigration have left behind the least buoyant of their numbers, as the mainstream moves on to flood the surrounding countryside with suburban tracts. Over, under, and through it all, the expressways loop, tunnel, and carve their way with the contemptuous indifference of a new order. The metropolis, of which the central city is the heart, grows continually, but in the city itself there are sinister portents of decline. Department stores stand empty; buildings are pulled down and turned into parking lots, waiting for better times; offices follow their employees to the suburb. On placards in Detroit buses a wide-eyed child reaches out exclaiming, "There is more of everything downtown"—but every year there is less.

This decay of the city center is not new, and seems indeed to be a characteristic consequence of its growth. As the center becomes congested, the more prosperous move further out, abandoning their town houses to successively more ruthless exploitation. In this they are eagerly encouraged by real estate interests, who hope to realize a handsome return on land acquired on the city's fringes, and at the same time make a killing in the older property, from which, subdivided and indifferently maintained, satisfactory profits can be squeezed long after it deserves to be pulled down. The poor, after all, must be housed, and if they cannot afford what is new, or even shabby, they have little choice but to pay disproportionately for what is scarcely fit for habitation. So long as those who have the money are persuaded that a better home requires a better neighborhood, there is little incentive to pull down the houses they leave behind, still less to refurbish them. The city's newcomers provide a ready market for them as they stand.

This pattern of expansion at the fringe, and decay at the center, would still recur even if suburban life held no particular appeal. When the social status of a neighborhood is threatened by the newcomers who impinge on its boundaries, the residents will usually take flight. And once the flight begins, the more hesitant follow, fearing for the value of their property, the safety of their daughters in the street, the manners of their children in school, and the effect on their social standing of an address no longer fashionable. Only occasionally, a neighborhood defies these pressures: if the residents are sufficiently upper class, they can isolate themselves more effectively from their surroundings—by sending their children to private schools, for instance—and their status is secure enough to withstand the imputation of undesirable neighbors. So the old Yankees still hold the top of Beacon Hill. But for the most part, the newcomers have pushed out all who can afford to escape, until, as in Detroit, the proportion of native-born residents increases directly with the distance from the city center. This tendency for a neighborhood to tip downward in the social scale does not seem to depend upon racial prejudice: the older parts of the city have been abandoned by turns to Irish, Jewish, and Italian immigrants before the colored citizens arrived. Nor does it presuppose a preference for the suburbs: there is simply nowhere to move but out. It can, however, go on only so long as the established residents grow in prosperity, and so long as there is a continuing influx of poor newcomers ready to take the older property off their hands.

Since the war, two influences in particular have accelerated this familiar cycle. First, the newcomers have been predominantly colored. In the twelve largest metropolitan areas, the non-white population has increased much more rapidly than the white, and now accounts for 20 per cent of the residents. Almost all this proportional increase has been in the central cities, and the trend appears to be accelerated. Between 1950 and 1960, these twelve central cities lost over two million whites and gained just under two million non-white residents. Meanwhile the suburbs have added only marginally to their very small colored populations.[2] So the social status of neighborhoods is now drawn more sharply than ever in terms of race, and, by playing on prejudice, city blocks change their character more quickly and completely.

At the same time, a rising standard of living has made suburban living possible to a growing proportion of the population. They can now afford the ranch house and the car to overcome its relative isolation, and they are being powerfully persuaded to accept this as the ideal pattern of American life. The movement out from the central city has been greater than the influx: those who leave are not everywhere replaced, especially as the newcomers live for the most part at a higher density.

This net loss of population from the central city has raised alarm, especially when set beside the natural increase of the population as a whole. The newcomers, too, have less to spend. But, for the first time, a new and more disturbing trend has been noticed: the central city is losing not merely its population but its functions. The suburban supermarkets now rival in range and quality the downtown stores; businesses have begun to relocate their offices away from the central district; art galleries and theaters are being established in the suburbs—Philadelphia has five downtown theaters in the winter, but thirty peripheral summer theaters. As fewer people enter the city center to work, shop, or be entertained, it could become merely another suburb of the metropolis, distinguished only by its greater poverty, dilapidation, and perhaps the color of its inhabitants. At the same time, the metropolis disintegrates, and the traditional conception of a centralized urban culture begins to seem obsolete.

The Aims of Urban Renewal

The decline of the central city concerns, most immediately, the political and commercial interests which cannot recoup their loss of revenue or custom. A city can seldom collect taxes from those who have overstepped its boundaries, even though it may still have to provide services for their use. The more it taxes those who remain, the sooner they too will place themselves under a less exacting excise: and so the city faces a losing battle to maintain its functions. Hotels, restaurants, shops, or theaters, which depend upon the appeal of downtown to draw more than a local custom, see themselves going out of business as the metropolis disintegrates into local communities. To meet the needs of city government and commerce, urban renewal has to attract back into the city those who will provide the highest revenue and the best custom, and revive the prestige of urban life. The most straightforward aim of urban renewal is the reconstruction of the tax-base.

Besides this economic incentive, the importance of the central city can be defended for the quality of its culture. Suburbs tend to segregate people into very homogeneous communities of similar age and income, since the houses in any tract are much alike. They also separate homes from workplaces. In the central city, by contrast, a much greater diversity of people live side by side, mingled with shops, offices, factories, restaurants, and theaters. The city dweller can derive a much more varied interest from his environment; hence he should know more of the society in which he lives, and tolerate it more understandingly than his suburban counterpart. There is not much evidence to show whether, in fact, most people of the city see or care about their surroundings as this argument assumes: it may be that only the sophisticated conceive of the city with such detachment from their everyday concerns. But it remains true that the vitality of modern culture has been centered in the largest cities, and smaller communities cannot afford facilities for the intellectual elite. From this point of view, it is the cultural amenity of the city center, both as a place to live and a place to visit, that urban renewal needs to preserve.

The central city could lose not only its cultural diversity but the diversity of its population. If present trends continue, the Negro residents of the central cities of the largest metropolitan areas will eventually predominate. If the suburbs continue to block the entry of Negro households, there could grow up a form of political and residential *apartheid*. The central city becomes an enormous ghetto: "a black neck in a white noose." The intermingling of races in the city center is a logical corollary of the campaign for integration in the suburbs. To this end, it is important that urban renewal should maintain a racially mixed population in the city.

Finally, urban renewal can be seen as an opportunity to tackle the social problems of slum areas. Insofar as mean housing demoralizes its inhabitants, and the spirit of the ghetto undermines ambition, relocation offers the chance to introduce people to a more hopeful environment. In the words of Robert Weaver:

> . . . it is just at the moment that a family has been uprooted, has been provided through relocation assistance with the means of establishing a new home, and has been brought into contact—some for the first time, and many for reacquaintance—with the social agencies of the community, that miracles can be accomplished.

These four arguments—economic, cultural, integrationist, and social—provide the main justifications for urban renewal and set its aims. But it is important to recognize at the outset that these aims are neither consistent nor necessarily compatible. For the reconstruction of the tax base, the fate of the people relocated is not important; while, for the social worker, their rehabilitation is the principal object of redevelopment. The most profitable use of cleared land may be tall blocks of luxury apartments, socially and culturally isolated from their surroundings and alien to the traditional spirit of urban culture; but the people moved are unlikely to enjoy any part of the brave new world erected over their former homes.

Rebuilding

As yet, urban renewal has pulled down more than it has rebuilt, and it is too soon to know whether the new buildings will establish the urban communities for which they are designed. In Detroit, a row of austere glass-fronted town houses huddles rather forlornly amidst acres of well-grown hay: they have not found a ready market, and the developer has hesitated to proceed. In Chicago, new apartment buildings for professional people have filled up, with reasonably representative proportions of Negro and white tenants; but the redevelopment is wearying to the eye. The private apartments march along the lake front, hogging the view, while behind them has been drawn up a long drab line of public housing. Southwest Washington is being built to a less intimidating scale, and offers the pleasures of a marina to those who can afford to live there. One trend is already apparent: the private developer prefers to build for the higher income groups, so that the new residential projects tend to the extremes—luxury apartments or low-rent public housing, with little in between. In either case, costs have encouraged mostly high-rise building, and the monotony of scale that results has made the idea of rehabilitating buildings seem more attractive. It remains to be seen whether, in the end, this is cheaper than demolition.

The success of present plans depends, above all, on attracting enough people from the suburbs who can afford the fairly high rents of the new apartments. How many travel-weary commuters are there, bored with suburban life, waiting to exchange their gardens and safe schools for a smart address downtown? Until they know, developers seem to be proceeding cautiously, building a few blocks at a time. Meanwhile, whatever new communities urban renewal creates, its consequences for the families displaced follow a fairly consistent pattern.

Relocation

The households cleared by urban renewal have included many of the poorest in the city, and they have been mostly Negro. Apart from the West End of Boston, a characteristically Italian neighborhood, the proportion of non-white families relocated varies from about 62 per cent in New York to nearly 100 per cent in Baltimore, Washington, and Chicago. As a whole, about 80 per cent of the families relocated are non-white, and the remainder include many families, such as immigrants from the Appalachian Mountains, who belong to a distinctive minority culture.[3] Few, if any, of the families relocated could afford the private housing planned to replace their old homes.

Information about families relocated is not complete, and sometimes conflicting. Relocation authorities publish reports, but a proportion of families, varying from a small percentage to as many as half, do not use the relocation services, and their fate is unknown. Estimates of the success of relocation vary according to the assumptions made about the group who have not reported their new circumstances: relocation authorities tend to be more optimistic than independent enquirers. Again, in assessing the improvement in housing standards, different criteria may be used. The law requires the authorities to ensure that "decent, safe, and sanitary" housing is available to the families relocated, at a reasonable rent. It does not stipulate that the housing should be in a decent, safe, and sanitary neighborhood, nor that the new housing need necessarily be better than the old. Some of the housing in the cleared area will have been up to standard. So a family moved from a decent, safe, and sanitary house in the cleared area to a similar house in a similar neighborhood, and perhaps paying a higher rent, could still be considered to have been satisfactorily relocated. But from their own point of view, they are worse off.

With these qualifications, the consequences of relocation are fairly well known. Most families moved to neighborhoods similar to those from which they were cleared, usually on the fringes of the renewal project. Between 15 per cent and 50 per cent (in Philadelphia, on some assumptions, the figure could be as high as 78 per cent) were still in substandard housing, and more than this were still in blighted areas. In most cities, less than 10 per cent were relocated in public housing. On average, contract rents went up by twelve to twenty dollars, and the proportion of income spent on rent probably increased from around 17 per cent to 25 per cent. The number of people to a room did not change or was slightly reduced, but the families do not seem on the whole to have been very overcrowded in the first place.

These estimates suggest that the relocated families often achieved only marginal improvement in their housing, at the cost of higher rents. Some are still living in slums, and many more have moved to nearby areas which may rapidly deteriorate into new slums. The director of one redevelopment agency, Justin Herman, has stated unequivocally:

> San Francisco need not be proud of its record on how it has rehoused its displaced families—four out of five of which are non-white. Look at the relocation map showing where these families have gone and you find the greatest concentration of them just over the borders of the project area, in the very slums that were designated as such by the Board of Supervisors as blighted—and they have not improved—a decade ago.[4]

He also affirmed that the housing to be erected in the renewal projects would be out of reach of many displaced families, who often could not afford any of the existing housing in San Francisco of minimum quality. Other cities have been no more successful.

It seems that many more families could have been satisfactorily rehoused if they had been willing to accept public housing. A report on relocation by the Philadelphia Housing Association estimates that, in sixteen cities, the proportion of relocated families eligible for public housing was seldom below 50 per cent and sometimes as high as 80 per cent or 90 per cent in the years 1955-1957. In Philadelphia itself,

> during the first two years of the central relocation service, almost 80% (1234) of the families studied appeared to be eligible for public housing; only 67% (1033) were referred to public housing, and less than 15% (244) actually moved to public housing during the period under study. No data are available on how many applied. During this same period, a total of 5772 moved into public housing projects. Relocation cases thus accounted for only 4.2% of new tenancies in public housing even though families dislocated through urban renewal activities had first preference and public housing was available.[5]

In San Francisco, a third of both white and Negro families have been estimated to be still living in slums because they refused public housing. There seems, then, to be a widespread prejudice against public housing among the families relocated.

Public housing apart, there has probably also been private housing of reasonable quality available for the relocated families which they did not take up. Many seem to have preferred worse housing at a lower rent: in both Chicago and Philadelphia, for instance, those who were still in substandard housing after relocation paid substantially lower rents than those in houses of better quality. Since standard housing could be found when the time came to relocate, it was presumably available before: families, had they wished, and been able to afford it, might have moved out of the slum areas without waiting for redevelopment. Hence the low rents they were paying in the slums, and their liking for the neighborhood, must have seemed more important to them than the shabbiness and inconvenience of their home. Forced to move, many chose a neighborhood similar to the one they had left, where rents were as low as they could find.

If all the families had been willing to accept the best that the relocation services could find, wherever it might be, in public or in private housing, the record would have been better. But there were some families for which the relocation services were unable to provide any decent place to live, especially the very large families and the socially unacceptable. In Pittsburgh, for instance, the authorities were unable to find anything adequate for seventy-four unmarried mothers. Relocation can also be especially hard on old people who owned their former homes: they are likely to be ineligible for a mortgage, and can be difficult to place as tenants with their special needs. In some cities, the difficulties will be greater in the future, because there will be less vacant housing available.

Besides households, urban renewal may require the relocation of businesses. On this, I was able to gather little information. A report by the Baltimore Urban Renewal Agency in 1959 shows that in one project, 17 per cent of small concerns went out of business, 4 per cent were branches of larger concerns which were not replaced, and 58 per cent were relocated. The fate of the remaining fifth of the businesses displaced was not known. Of retailers alone, a third went out of business. The concerns which failed were mostly run by widows and older men, who chose this moment to retire: relocation may only have prompted a decision they would soon have taken for other reasons. At the same time, since there was no provision to compensate for loss of good-will, it seems likely that those who wished to stay in business must have faced financial difficulties.

Lastly, has urban renewal used the opportunity to combine relocation with social welfare? How many "miracles" of rehabilitation have happened? Some families may well have been encouraged by a better house to face the world with more pride but, for the most part, relocation has probably made the major problems more difficult to tackle. It disrupts the work of established agencies of social welfare and, worse, destroys the informal pattern of mutual help and tolerance which had grown up in the old communities. Neurotics and psychotics whose eccentricities were harbored, if not loved, in the slum streets, find themselves rejected in primmer neighborhoods. Adolescents whose fear of the wider society was protected by the subculture of the slums become lost and unhappy. In the years after the West End of Boston was pulled down, teen-agers revisited nostalgically the rubble of their former homes. Skid Row has simply moved elsewhere. It may be that, in the long run, this exposure to a more demanding society will force the slum dwellers to assimilate its standards, but even if this were all to the good, it is harsh medicine. Meanwhile, urban renewal disperses people in need where they may be more difficult to reach.[6] This is not to deny the value of campaigns of social improvement stimulated by urban renewal, such as special help to schools in slum areas or the encouragement of neighborhood associations. But these do not depend upon relocation; they represent, rather, a very different conception of the whole problem, in which housing needs take second place to the needs of people.

On the whole then, it seems fair to say that relocation has provided only marginally better housing, in very similar neighborhoods, at higher rents, and has done as much to worsen as to solve the social problems of the families displaced. The crucial issue, in short, is the housing of the slum dwellers themselves.

The Culture of Slums

The slum dwellers are characteristically the most recent in-migrants to the city. They include Negroes from the south, country people from the Southern Appalachians, Puerto Ricans, Mexicans, American Indians, and a few French Canadians. Their labor is very valuable to the city, since they are ready to do the worst paid work, on which important industries depend. It has been estimated, for instance, that three million workers in New York depend, directly or indirectly, on the needle trades, which depend in turn on Puerto Rican labor.[7] In-migration tends to fluctuate with the jobs available: if the work is not there, fewer people come. The in-migrants, therefore, come to the city because the city needs them: it cannot repudiate responsibility for their welfare.

Once they reach the city, they seem to settle there as permanently as most Americans. It is sometimes suggested that they are transients, moving house annually and returning to country districts in bad times. Instances are cited of Negro schools where there has been a complete changeover of pupils in a year. Yet, though some may follow such a restless course, figures I collated do not suggest that the families displaced by urban renewal are especially migratory. In Philadelphia, 17 per cent of families had been living in the homes demolished less than a year, 40 per cent for more than ten years; half of these had lived in the city more than twenty years. In one cleared area of Baltimore, 18 per cent had been there less than a year, a third more than ten years; in a Chicago program, only 7 per cent had been less than a year in the houses from which they were cleared, and the median length of residence was eight years. Of a group of mostly single men cleared from a Skid Row in Minneapolis, 8 per cent had lived less than one year and two-thirds more than ten years at the same address.[8] Since about 17 per cent of American families move each year, these figures suggest that the slum dwellers are if anything less mobile than most people.

Since most of the slum dwellers are not, after all, such newcomers to the city, their failure to make good cannot altogether be explained by their unfamiliarity with urban society. The in-migrant from, say, the Appalachians, will certainly arrive with attitudes toward education derived from his rural background. In the Kentucky mountains, school teachers are among the worst paid in America, classes may have as many as a hundred pupils, and the standard of education is inevitably low. School learning is not very relevant to a life of subsistence farming, and the parents may decide that their children will be more usefully employed in the fields than at school. When a newcomer from Kentucky first arrives in the city, he may well treat the schools as he does at home. But since there is no longer any farm work to engage the children's time more urgently, it seems most likely that, within a year or two, he will adopt the same attitude to his children's schooling as his neighbors. If he remains indifferent, it may be that education is valued as little in his part of the city as at home.

It is, I think, a mistake to conceive the assimilation of in-migrants in terms of two cultures: the dominant culture of America, represented by city life, and the culture of the rural society from which they came. The city contains subcultures as stable and viable as the conventional norms, and it is to one of these subcultures that the newcomer is first introduced. The more successfully he becomes integrated in it, the more difficult it becomes to interest him in the values of the dominant culture.

These subcultures, of course, differ among themselves: each has grown out of the experience of an ethnic group with its own religious and family traditions. But they are likely to share common characteristics arising from their economic and social status. These in-migrants are generally the poorest, least educated, and lowest in status of the city's population. Society at large is competitive, and maintains (when convenient) that everyone enjoys an equal opportunity. Some in-migrants accept the challenge—especially Jewish newcomers—but for most the chances of success are remote, and now heavily weighted against them by racial discrimination. So they can only protect themselves against a sense of failure and inferiority by denying that the opportunity is open, and by decrying the rewards for which the more hopeful compete. The subculture repudiates the values of the wider society to escape its censure.

Characteristically, the subculture divides the world into "we" and "they." [9] "They" are all the agents of the dominant culture, official or unofficial, benevolent or persecutory—police, government, school, social workers, and indeed anyone who carries the stigmata of the successful middle class. All these are held to discriminate against the people of the subculture, and to exploit them: even the apparently benevolent must be getting something out of it, a personal advantage which is concealed by the hypocrisy of their avowed intentions. It is thus exceedingly difficult for anyone outside the subculture to be of help, since his motives are immediately suspect. It is barely possible even for anyone within it to exercise effective leadership: as soon as he establishes a position where he can act usefully in the wider society on behalf of his people, he is suspected of disloyalty. Herbert Gans, in his study of the West End of Boston, describes, for instance, the ambivalent attitudes towards local politicians: even though they came from the neighborhood, they were not trusted, fundamentally because to take part in political life was itself a damaging compromise with the outside world. This paranoid attitude to society at large is much encouraged by the many instances of corruption, discrimination, and exploitation which the people see around them.

But the subculture does not explain the poverty and low status of its people only in terms of discrimination. Not only does the pretense of a fair chance for them seem fraudulent, a cynical attempt to cloak the realities of power, but even in society at large, those who get on are assumed to have succeeded only by acting contemptibly. They suck up to the boss and kick their buddies in the teeth, exploit the weak, and buy their way to general esteem. Care-laden and corrupt, they feed parasitically on the useful work of other human hands. In the subculture, people see themselves as poor because they have not lost their pride and because they despise the mean rewards of a competitive society.

However, though they repudiate rewards which can only be won by compromise with the dominant norms, they may admire success achieved in defiance of them. Hence their attitude to crime can be ambivalent: the values of the subculture do not in themselves approve crime, but if the victims belong to the outside world, they may be at least indifferent to it. And quasi-illegal activities, such as gambling, are often more acceptable than conventional ways of making money. William Foote Whyte, speaking of one such subculture, writes:

> In effect, the society at large puts a premium on disloyalty to Cornerville and penalizes those who are best adjusted to the life of the district. At the same time the society holds out attractive rewards in terms of money and material possessions to the "successful" man. For most Cornerville people these rewards are available only through advancement in the world of rackets and politics.[10]

The entertainment industry is neutral ground: the careers of stars from the subculture will be judged by their loyalty to their origins. The people of the West End, for instance, admired Frank Sinatra, because they felt he still defied conventional society and remained faithful to the more or less disreputable friends who had given him his start: he had forced the world to accept him without compromise. To retain their approval, success, however achieved, must not threaten the rationalizations which protect their self-esteem: in a rotten society only the poor are honest, and anyway they never had a chance.

It follows that the subculture cannot tolerate conventional ambition. Any boy who works hard at school, and qualifies for a good job without losing his integrity, proves that society does not always discriminate against the members of the subculture, or exact debasement as the price of its rewards. Hence the ambitious will be discouraged, ridiculed, and finally ostracized: their example is by imputation humiliating to the rest. The subculture exacts close conformity and an overriding loyalty to the group: the deserter travels a lonely road, burdened with a sense of guilt.

If this were all, the subculture would be as dreary as it seems to many conventional observers—apathetic, conformist, leaderless, intolerant, frightened, and quasi-criminal. But its countervailing ethic is free, too, to emphasize the virtues most difficult to reconcile with American norms—it places loyalty above ambition, solidarity above competition, personal relationships above impersonal goals, openhandedness above thrift, and the enjoyment of the present above care for the future. And though it may not interpret the world more honestly than the dominant culture, it is honest about different things. Above all, while the wider society accepts that the interests of a career, even when narrowly conceived as money-making or the pursuit of status, may override obligations to family or friends, the subculture does not.[11]

The protective solidarity of the subculture helps to explain an apparent paradox. To the outsider, the community appears very tightly integrated, and yet it has no leaders, few community associations, no means of asserting a common purpose: it may not even be very neighborly, as neighborliness is understood in the suburbs. It is held together as a community only by its hostility to the world outside, and lacks any integrating organization. The functioning groups are much smaller—the circle of close relatives, the age grades who have grown up together. Hence when such a community is disrupted, people are bereft above all of moral support. They are likely to burrow back as fast as they can into the protective culture of the slums.

The Limitations of Social Welfare

This very general characterization of low-status groups leaves out of account many other distinctive qualities of their culture. They may differ from the majority in their attitude to children, in the interpretation of sexual relationships, patterns of family structure, or the enjoyment of leisure. But here subcultures may differ as much among themselves as with the conventional norms. It is as a reaction to the threat of humiliation that subcultures raise the most barriers to social reform.

In the first place, if I have understood their function aright, the resistance of subcultures to assimilation does not arise in the origins of the in-migrants. Though it is obviously sensible to forewarn newcomers of the problems they will encounter in the city, and to acquaint them with its institutions, this will not enable them to establish themselves in the city with high enough status. If they were able to acquire skills before they came to the city which would ensure them a promising job as soon as they arrived, their circumstances would be very different but, of course, it is just because they lack the opportunities to acquire such skills at home that they migrate to the city.

Secondly, programs of social welfare which plan to work by stimulating local leadership face the difficulty that leadership is suspect. Anyone who cooperates with the reformers will be accused of deserting his own people and probably of seeking a personal advantage. The "natural leaders" whom social workers seek to promote are usually those best able to perform personal services: they can give credit, find jobs, provide information. They are leaders with clients, not organizations, and they need not be disinterested. Their clients are willing to pay a price for their services. Such leadership easily degenerates into exploitation when it is given wider scope.

Thirdly, reformers who appeal to the dominant values of society are likely to drive the slum dwellers further into retreat. Unless slum children qualify for skilled jobs, they will remain poor: but to claim that they *can* qualify if only they take education more seriously is profoundly threatening. It suggests that they have only themselves to blame for their present poverty. A Negro child knows he is handicapped: rather than run the risk of failure, it is safer to cite discrimination to prove that success is out of reach. Even if the brighter children have the courage to attempt a career, they face the ostracism of their peers. Besides, the gap between the modest status of a steady job and the success which commands respect is still very wide: any slum child whose heart is set on two-toned convertibles and glamorous women has little choice but to steal the one and buy the other. Initiative will be more handsomely rewarded by a criminal or quasi-criminal career than by mugging lessons in school. Thus any appeal to legitimate ambition is likely to evoke a response only among the deviants in the subculture, who reject the values of their peers. They will need much moral support and hard practical work to ensure that the promises given them can be made good. For if society is less frustrating than the subculture prefers to believe, it is also less open than it claims.

Any social reform directed at the shortcomings of people, rather than of society, is handicapped by the humiliating imputations of its policy. If the remarks administrators make about social reform through urban renewal were addressed not to respected citizens but to the slum dwellers themselves, they would amount to something like this:

> Some of you are competent people who can look after yourselves, but we well realize that many of you are drunken, criminal, senile, immoral, or mad. We do not, of course, blame you: we are sorry for you. You are probably illiterate peasants from some rural slum, and cannot be expected to know any better. Now, however, eviction from your old homes will provide you with a healthy stimulus to pull yourselves together. And we are ready and eager to help. We are going to get together all the social workers we can find to teach you how to behave properly and keep yourselves clean. Of course, you can't expect respectable citizens to welcome you as neighbors until you have shown

that you have lost your nasty habits: it wouldn't be fair to them. So to begin with, quite rightly, you must be grateful for the second rate. This is how we are discharging our responsibility toward you, and it is an impressive record.

I have not invented the substance of this parody. It summarizes faithfully, if in very different language, an address by William Slayton, Commissioner of the Urban Renewal Administration Housing and Home Finance Agency. However, he was not talking to relocated families but at a Welfare Federation dinner in Cleveland.

Of all reformers, the social worker who carefully avoids an authoritarian manner is at bottom the most hurtful to pride. Armed with his theories of group therapy, he invites his patients—for he understands them in terms of maladjustment—to accept him as an equal. He does not command or exhort, but manipulates. Hence his pretense of joining a peer group is a deception, by which he hopes to exercise his curative skills. This technique involves the fundamentally arrogant assumption that social deprivation is an inadequacy of personality which he has a right to cure without consulting the wishes of the victims. They react by manipulating him in turn and, with a lifetime's experience of evading authority, often beat him at his own game.

It follows that social welfare agencies, though they provide many useful services, must meet profound resistance when they seek to enlarge their function to include social reform. People need to be very confident of themselves before they can admit their weaknesses as the price of being helped. Besides, the welfare agencies have no powers to reform the injustices and inequalities which have driven the slum dweller into retreat. Even the more comprehensive programs of community development now being worked out in association with urban renewal suffer from the limited resources of voluntary action. A thorough analysis of social needs, from which may be projected the schools, clinics, libraries, playgrounds, and housing that a community should have, remains only a theoretical exercise unless there are powers to implement the plan. Such planning in the abstract sometimes seems to serve as a substitute for action—a means of disguising the inadequacy of the resources available. There is no more respectable way of evading a problem than to conduct research into it. At the same time, there is no surer way to waste effort than to take action without preliminary study.

The Revision of Urban Renewal

This discussion has led to three conclusions which are, I think, crucial to the working out of renewal policies:

1. That relocation has achieved little over-all improvement in the circumstances of the people displaced.

2. Whether the interests of the people moved or the revitalization of the city are put first, urban renewal cannot achieve its ultimate purpose so long as slum communities are merely displaced or scattered.

3. Social welfare programs cannot succeed in integrating slum communities with the wider society. Faced with many handicaps, the slum dwellers retreat into a subculture which, though it increases these handicaps, protects them from humiliation.

If these conclusions are broadly true, the fundamental need is to dissolve the subculture as a self-frustrating defense against a sense of inferiority. This can be achieved only when the real disadvantages of racial discrimination, low wages, and high rates of unemployment are removed. But meanwhile, anything which raises the status of the community in the eyes of society at large helps to reduce its need to retreat.

Such a policy would require the rebuilding or rehabilitation of slum areas as homes for the slum dwellers themselves, not to a perfunctory minimum standard, but as places in which people can live with pride, and which will enhance the appearance of the city. This would not preclude the clearance of sites for other uses, provided that those displaced were rehoused together in a comprehensively developed community near their places of work. In other words, to get rid of slums, build something better for the slum dwellers—and the higher the standard of rebuilding, the more the city gains. But the rebuilding must be conceived in terms of the whole community, not merely of individual families.

Such a policy could only be implemented by the creation of new public funds, which would not be recoverable. The objections are readily foreseen; but are they insurmountable?

In the first place, real estate interests would certainly object to any increase in housing built with public money. But public building for low incomes only damages the real estate market by reducing the demand for *old* property, and this is probably all to the good: the exploitative slum landlord would be worst hit, and his case does not deserve consideration. The pressure of demand for cheap housing has made it much more difficult to condemn outworn buildings.

It is hard to see how greater government influence on housing can be avoided, whatever the policy. Since there is a gap between the cheapest new private housing which can be built, even with the support of the new regulations, and eligible public housing, there are people whose incomes are too high to admit them to a project, yet too low to afford anything decent for themselves. Some further public subsidy to assist this income group seems inevitable. Rather than continue the present practice in public housing, and create new facilities to meet this need, I am suggesting that the old public housing approach should be abandoned altogether, in favor of a comprehensive policy for all those cleared from slum areas. This would avoid the discrimination by income which does so much to damage the status of the public housing tenant.

Secondly, there will be objections to a policy which provides subsidized housing without a strict categorization of need. Why should a family which has had to take what it can afford on the open market pay taxes to enable another to live better more cheaply? At least, in public housing, the beneficiaries are made aware that their privilege depends upon their poverty. The protest is natural enough, but shortsighted. It is cheaper in the long run to be generous at the outset. Besides, urban renewal at present heavily subsidizes the building of luxury apartments by writing down the cost of land to the developer. If taxpayers are already subsidizing homes for the rich, why should they refuse to subsidize homes for the poor?

Luxury apartments would, of course, make a much better return in taxes to the city treasury. But should urban renewal be judged primarily by its contribution to the city's resources? Other fiscal reform could restore the city's revenue—metropolitan government apart, presumably the allocation of city, state, and federal funds could be revised in the city's favor. On present trends, it looks as if the federal government may, in any case, have to contribute increasingly to the maintenance of the central city. To treat urban renewal itself as a tax-raising device seems a perversion of its true purpose—especially if the building of a few blocks of high-rent apartments downtown is achieved at the cost of more rapid deterioration elsewhere in the city.

A policy of rebuilding slum areas for their present residents is open to the final objection that it perpetuates ghettos. Granted that the subculture gives psychological protection and attenuates the process of assimilation, a plan which recognizes the value of these functions also recognizes a form of segregation. It is therefore essential that any community built in place of slums should be designed for open occupancy, and that families from the slums pulled down should still be helped to relocate in an altogether different neighborhood if they prefer. For this reason alone, the community must be planned to a high standard, without restriction on the income of residents, so that it does not have built into it a social character ultimately harmful to integration. With these provisions, the policy does not involve compromise with discrimination.

These objections do not, then, rule out a policy for urban renewal much more closely related to the needs of the slum dwellers themselves. The areas cleared—or partly cleared, and partly restored—would be reconstructed to a comprehensive plan, including all the amenities the community will need—schools, clinics, playgrounds, libraries, shops, cinemas, restaurants, churches. As each neighborhood was built, tenancies would be offered to the residents of areas under clearance, at rents they could afford. This would require a subsidy, but any assessment of rent by income would have to be very tactfully handled, to avoid stigmatizing the neighborhood as reserved for objects of charity. It has been suggested in England that rents of council tenants might be assessed from their income tax code. The method does not require the tenant to disclose his income to the landlord, and avoids the humiliating inquisition of a means test, while it is fairer to the taxpayer than a flat rate. If a similar system were applicable in America, it could provide a basis of calculation. Provided the cost of acquiring the land were written off entirely, the economic rent might not be above the maximum payable in present public housing, and, at this price, vacancies not taken up by the families to be relocated might be offered on the market. But whatever the assessment of rent, it is essential that there should be no upper income limit.

Reconstruction on this scale offers a great deal of scope to architects and town planners, and could enhance the appearance of the city very greatly. It seems to me to offer the best hope of meeting the social and aesthetic aims of urban renewal. It is probably also the only way of arresting the further deterioration of the central city, and would, in the long run, do most to maintain the fiscal viability of the city as a governmental unit. And it would prove that a free-enterprise society is not inevitably inhibited from vigorous public action when it sees the need.

References

1. Urban Renewal Administration, "Relocation from Urban Renewal Project Areas, through June 1960," *Bulletin of Housing and Home Finance Agency,* Washington, D.C., 1960.
2. Sharp, H., "Race as a Factor in Metropolitan Growth, 1930-1960" (paper presented at the 1961 meetings of the Population Association of America), Ann Arbor: Univ. of Michigan Survey Research Center. Morton Grodzins, in *The Metropolitan Area as a Racial Problem* (Pittsburgh: Univ. of Pittsburgh Press, 1958), comments: "All evidence makes it highly probable that within thirty years Negroes will constitute from 25 to 50 per cent of the total population in at least ten of the fourteen largest central cities."
3. The percentages given in this section derive from the following reports and articles. They are not comprehensive or very recent, but discussions with relocation authorities suggest that the experiences they report are representative: *Relocation in Philadelphia,* Philadelphia: Philadelphia Housing Association, Nov. 1958 (some figures for sixteen cities are given on p. 79); *Rehousing Residents Displaced From Public Housing Clearance Sites in Chicago* 1957-1958, Chicago: special report to the Chicago Housing Authority from the Department of City Planning; *The Displacement of Small Businesses from a Slum Clearance Area* and *Ten Years of Relocation Experience in Baltimore,* Baltimore: Urban Renewal and Housing Agency, June 1959 and June 1961; Heltz, D., *Report on the Relocation of Residents and Certain Institutions from the Gateway Center Project Area,* Minneapolis: Housing and Development Authority, June 1961; Smith, W. F., *Relocation in San Francisco,* San Francisco: Bay Area Real Estate Report, fourth quarter, 1960; Lichfield, N., "Relocation—The Impact on Housing Welfare," *J. Amer. Inst. Planners,* 27:199-203, 1961.
4. Herman, M. J., "The Realities of Urban Renewal for Minority Groups," statement before the Council for Civic Unity of San Francisco, March 1960.
5. *Relocation in Philadelphia,* p. 29.
6. For the experience of one social welfare agency see Dale, J., "Fami-

lies and Children in Urban Development: a View from a Settlement House," *Children,* Dec. 1959.

7. Senior, C., *Strangers Then Neighbors,* New York: Freedom Books, 1961, pp. 64-65.
8. Figures derived from the references in note 3 above.
9. In the description of the slum culture which follows, I have emphasized those aspects of it which will tend to frustrate its assimilation into the wider society. An analysis of any particular slum culture would reveal a greater complexity of social patterns. For this description, I have relied much on the discussions in Herbert J. Gans's recent study of the West End of Boston, *The Urban Villagers* (New York: The Free Press of Glencoe, 1963), which he kindly lent me in draft. See also: Whyte, W. F., *Street Corner Society,* Chicago: Univ. of Chicago Press, 1955; Kerr, M., *The People of Ship Street,* New York: Humanities Press, 1958 (this describes a Liverpool slum community).
10. Whyte, *op. cit.,* p. 274.
11. For a defense of slum culture see Seeley, J., "The Slum: Its Nature, Use, and Users," *J. Amer. Inst. Planners,* 25:7-14, 1959.

Personal Identity in an Urban Slum

11

EDWARD J. RYAN

INTRODUCTION

One outcome of anthropological studies has been the demonstration of the variety of value systems and world views which man, in various cultures, uses in assessing his environment, in judging other men and their actions, and in evaluating his own self and his behavior. It is largely relative to these "ideal" elements that the individual determines to what extent he "measures up," i.e., whether he is moral or immoral, successful or not successful, adequate or lacking. It is in such a structure, with its component ethical and moral values and beliefs, that much of man's essential humanity has it locus. As elements of a culture or subculture to which commitment is given, ideal elements, in varying degrees, determine behavior, specify the particular attributes of social roles, define the goals of life, and provide a system of meanings and bases for interpreting experience.

To the extent that such a system is internalized, made a part of the self, it forms elements of the individual's ego identity: his sense of who and what he is, his sense of continuity with the past and with the future and its goals. Erikson has cogently and elegantly stressed the role of ideal structures in binding together the temporal vagaries of the sense of the self in terms of *particular* orientations to which the individual gives commitment. As he puts it:

> All ideologies ask for, as the prize for the promised possession of a future, uncompromising commitment to some absolute hierarchy of values and some rigid principle of conduct: be that principle total obedience to tradition, if the future is the eternalization of ancestry; total resignation, if the future is to be of another world; total martial discipline, if the future is to be reserved for some brand of armed super-

man; total inner reform, if the future is perceived as an advance edition of heaven on earth; or (to mention only one of the ideological ingredients of our time) complete pragmatic abandon to the processes of production and to human teamwork, if unceasing production seems to be the thread which holds present and future together.[1]

For present purposes, we will bypass issues concerning the processes of attaining a sense of the self and the modes of solution of successive identity crises related to various life stages. Rather, our principal interest is focused on problems of *maintenance* of the already formed identity in the presence of challenges to it which have their origin in the structure of the socio-cultural system in which the individual lives.

It is, at least *prima facie*, in the small, homogeneous, and relatively isolated society in which the natural or given truth of the propositions and orientations of the culture is unquestioned that their unambivalent integration and maintenance within the self is, *ceteris paribus*, least problematic for the individual. This is not only because of a lack of effective alternatives, but also because the conditions postulated imply a constant reassertion in social interaction of the content of the culture. Where alternative orientations are available and encountered, the maintenance of a secure sense of personal identity becomes more difficult.

In assessing an actual social system relative to these ideal elements, then, the critical points of interest are the degree of cultural differentiation in the system, the loci of these differences relative to the central interests or salient orientations of the socio-cultural subsystems created by the differentiation, and the availability and types of various possible mechanisms or strategies for handling the resultant strains experienced by the individual.

In terms of both empirical evidence and theoretical conception, of course, it is in the city that there is a meeting of different cultural traditions and systems of social relationships, and that alternative ideal structures and their differential evaluation are most immediately presented to the individual.

The city or urban area has been conceptualized in a number of ways, each appropriate to different fields of research. Investigators have, for instance, looked at the city as it appears, physically, to its residents; as a series of economically specialized areas; as an agglomerate of neighborhoods; and as a set of zones ecologically related to its physical growth and the movement of its population. It is equally possible to conceive of the city as composed of a set of social and cultural subsystems, connected by certain value relationships. Such a subsystem can be identified, and its borders specified, by the higher rate of social interaction among its component individuals as compared with their relationships with outsiders, and by the sharing of a common normative system of values and beliefs which forms the "moral order" within which interaction takes place. Such a system, when viewed as an abstract model, need not be geographically localized. Certainly the urbanites whose specialized wants and interests involve them in *non*-localized social networks (e. g., a profession) are members of such non-localized subcultural systems. Geographically localized subcultural systems are also indentifiable in our cities. A neighborhood, for example, may constitute such a subsystem.

With respect to such a localized subsystem, two additional general points must be made. First, not all of the roles which its members act are contained within the system itself. The majority of the men, for example, may pursue their occupations in a different section of the city from the one in which they live; the women, when shopping, may commonly use the central city shopping area; recreation may be partly sought away from the local residential area. Second, the members of such a subsystem are likely to be aware of its status in the value scheme of the larger society.

Our analysis is concerned with the West End of Boston, a lower and working class area of tenement residence lying in the belt adjoining the central business district, and an area undergoing the physical dilapidation characteristic of such belts. Our concern is with the role which the values of the West End subculture played in maintaining the identity of its members. Our particular emphasis is on the roles of *occupation,* salient in the dominant middle-class configuration of "identity," and of *friendship*, which was the salient feature in West End culture.

The value propositions which are set forth below are derived from ethnographic work in the West End. They stand independently as ethnographic formulations. The responses to questions from a survey-type interview (which was completed with a random sample of men living in the West End) are introduced only to provide evidence that those formulations have general validity in this subculture. The analysis, then, is suggestive and descriptive.

In Boston, the West End was known to the community in general as a slum. Historically, it was an area in which ethnic groups settled upon arrival in the United States. Some thirty or forty years ago, a large proportion of its population was composed of Eastern European Jews. In 1958, its population, including both immigrants and American-born generations, was about 47 per cent Italian, 10 per cent Jewish, and 10 per cent Polish. There was also a scattering of smaller groups of Albanians, Ukranians, Irish, French Canadians, Old Yankees, Russians, and others. In area it covered perhaps seventy acres. The buildings of the central forty-eight acres of this tract were destroyed in 1958-1960 as part of Boston's program of urban renewal. It is to this area that we apply the term "West End" as a geographical reference.

That geographical usage must be distinguished, however, from the concept of the West End as a socio-culture system. In making this distinction, we can estimate that something of the order of ninety per cent of the residents of this area identified themselves as West Enders. Parallel to this sharp *social* line between themselves and others, these West Enders perceived a sharp boundary demarcating the West End *as an area* from other parts of the city. When it was said, for instance, that a certain girl had "married outside [the West End]," the geographical component of this reference was significant primarily because of its social structural implications. The geographical outside was significant because it implied leaving (going outside) the West End social system. Conversely, this phrase was not used in reference to a West End girl who married a non-West Ender but continued to live in the West End after marriage. Residents who participated in this identity also participated in a system of social interaction clearly demarcated from non-West End interaction. Those social relationships were normatively governed by a distinctive and shared system of values upon which the identity of West Enders was based. The non-West Enders who lived in the area were mainly groups such as students or medical residents, nurses, and technical personnel from the nearby Massachusetts General Hospital. They did not identify as West Enders, nor did they participate in its normative structure. They lived in the area, but were not members of its socio-cultural system.

West End Culture

Turning to the analysis of West End culture, and its relation to the individual ego identity, the occupational role is a convenient starting point. In the American social system in general, the occupational role is generally considered to have a marked salience and, nominally, to be characterized by an *achievement* and *distant-future* orientation of action.

In contrast, life in the West End was focused upon more immediate events. And, in contrast to the nominal middle-class value system, there was no institutionalized achievement drive strongly obtruding in role expectations and definitions. In West End culture there thus appears to be a genuine difference from the dominant American pattern. In a sample of TAT protocols, only 27 per cent of the stories placed the goals of action in a distant future. The same proportion told stories in which the goals of action involved the hero in efforts to achievement through some transformation of the self (e.g., the boy with the violin becomes a musician, rather than, say, deciding to practice on the instrument). This time-achievement orientation, however, must not be taken to mean that West Enders were content with their lot. Nor does it imply that in this configuration there were not specific goals for improving that lot, or that there were not notable emphases on competence and competitiveness.

Before undertaking further discussion of this value configuration, it will be convenient to examine the way in which West Enders conceive of their environment. This element, the world view of the culture, underlies the value configuration thus far set forth: a relatively minor achievement theme and a dominant orientation to the present, together with significant components of values which we have referred to as competence and competitiveness. It can be noted that in response to a question which asks the respondent to choose between the idea that a "man's success is in the cards" and the belief that "there's nothing that a man can't be if he really wants to and works hard," only 12 per cent agreed with the former alternative. In contrast, 65 per cent agreed that effort alone determined success. While this might be interpreted as a reflection of the value of "activism-for-its-own-sake," in the dominant American pattern, the comments which accompany these responses indicate otherwise. For instance, we commonly find such statements as: "He should try because you can go ahead then," or, "A man should work himself up."

There is certainly no feeling in these data of the individual being in the grip of overpowering external forces. Neither do they imply, however, the orientation in the dominant American tradition which views the environment as something which can be molded and successfully bent to one's will. Little filters through to this population of the scientific premise that nature is controllable and to be manipulated to man's goals. Rather, in ethnographic data, there is the sense of the environment as an ethically and morally neutral field in which man can pursue his interests.

Complementary to this statement of the relationship of man to his environment is the proposition that man is responsible for the outcome of his own actions. When stated in this way, survey data appear to require a modification of the foregoing propositions. First, supporting these propositions, in TAT protocols 21 per cent of the outcomes of stories are determined by the hero's internal state: his ambition or lack of it, his affective upsets, his rebellions and his incapacity. In another 21 per cent, it is determined by the hero's own effort. However, in contrast to this major theme, in 27 per cent of the protocols, the outcome is determined by an external agent who is, with one exception, human. The dominant theme in these protocols is that the agent forces the protagonist to do something against his will. These actions, however, usually turn out well in the end; only rarely are they unsuccessful. This secondary theme, which was not anticipated in our analysis of ethnographic materials, appears to indicate a perception of constraint as one attribute of the social environment. This constraint, however, turns out to be in the ultimate interest of the individual. Hence, when the individual is not accountable for his own fate, the pattern tends to be one in which disruptive impulses are controlled by the environment so that goals are thereby achieved. (A second exception to the main West End theme that man is responsible for the outcome of his actions may be offered by the 12 per cent of our sample who are immigrant Italians, most of them of southern peasant origin. In various contexts I have been impressed that the idea of *destino* was of some significance in this group. However, *destino* should not, I think, be understood to emphasize the idea of "preordained," as the English translations of "fate" or "destiny" would imply. Rather, it appears to refer more to the south Italian peasant's profound pessimism about the possibility of taking effective action to alter his life circumstances. There is thus, for this group, a sense of an external determination of the course of the individual life, and an accompanying sense of helplessness in the face of seemingly inexorable forces in the universe.)

Value themes of competence and competition, formulated above, are consistent with this view of man in his environment. The theme of competence in the occupational role is supported by responses to the question. "What kind of personal satisfactions for yourself do you get out of work?" Fifty per cent of the men stated, in various ways, that they felt a pride in task accomplishment as their primary satisfaction. Another 16 per cent found that they derived a sense of pride and personal worth in working as their main satisfaction.

With regard to the theme of competitiveness in the occupational role, we asked the question, "What are you most likely to do when you feel someone else is better at something you're both doing?" Twenty per cent denied any concern or simply stated that they felt helpless to do anything if the other person was better. An additional 15 per cent responded that they would take pleasure in the other's accomplishment, congratulate him, and the like. Fifty-four per cent, however, indicated a competitive persistence or attempt to improve so as to surpass the other person.

A closely related item in the value structure, implying an orientation to striving in the occupational role, is indicated in the responses to the question, "What is the most important way in which you would like your children's future to be different from your own life?" Thirty-nine per cent stated that they wanted their children to have more education. Remarks concerning education which accompanied this choice clearly indicate that education was perceived principally as a source of occupational opportunity. Further, improved work status, stated directly, is the second most frequent response to the above question. The related response of an improved financial situation is third in importance. In total, this configuration of education, work status, and financial improvement was indicated in 76 per cent of the replies. Conversely, when asked in what ways they wanted their children's future to be exactly the same as their own, these categories received no mention at all. Rather, in these responses, emphasis was placed on factors concerned with marriage and the family.

However, in our data two additional points must be made, in order to comprehend the significance of this striving theme in West End culture. First, it does not reflect the classical "getting ahead" theme in American society. This is to be expected in terms of the minor achievement orientation in the West End. Thus, when asked what kind of a job they would like if they could have any job they wanted, only 9 per cent of the men's responses referred to increased opportunities or getting ahead. Similarly, when asked what they liked and what they disliked about their present jobs, in each case only 1 per cent mentioned opportunity for advancement. Dissatisfaction with a job focused on the difficulty, monotony, or other specific characteristics of the work situation, on financial recompense, and on authority relationships. Parallel to this, work satisfactions mainly concerned work conditions, satisfactions derived from doing the particular tasks involved, and the relative absence of an immediate authority relationship on the job.

One further question indicates the significance of occupational opportunity for West Enders relative to other values and institutions. Thus, when the respondents were asked to state which they would prefer to be, an auto mechanic who had many friends and who was contented, or a general manager who was to become a leading businessman but who had little time for fun, 64 per cent chose the auto mechanic.

Strongly implied by the modest satisfactions and goals of the occupational role, in conjunction with the more fundamental achievement and time orientation in this subculture, is the proposition that the occupational role does not have the same degree of salience as it nominally possesses in other parts of American society. Stated more positively, this subculture provided an alternative orientation in terms of which rewards were apportioned and satisfactions derived. It was impressive how infrequently the question of "what is his occupation?" was asked. It was also not common, in referring to another person, to specify his occupation. This information was not a critical element in placing another person. Consequently, the occupations of others were frequently not known. As a part of this pattern, talk about jobs and work was very uncommon in the bars, delicatessens, and on the corners. Rather, another person was more likely to be placed and talked about relative to his moral characteristics and his sociability.

In short, the linkage of the individual identity to its past, and to the promise of its future, was provided in West End culture not by the career line but by expressive interpersonal experience. We are referring, of course, to a symbolic past, reconstructed in imagination, and a symbolic future dictated by the ethico-cultural mandate out of which the individual fashions the continuity of his ego identity. In conversation with West Enders it was rare to learn of either past jobs or occupational aspirations. Rather, the meaningful past was a sequence of good times and memories of places where the gang got together and of events that happened there. Tales of the past enshrined feeling in relation to others. They were not a record of striving for goals. Equally, concern for the future was largely phrased in these same terms, not in terms of movement on the occupational-social ladder.

This expressive orientation had its fullest empirical expression in the focal value of *friendliness.* For example, when asked to identify the major components of good social standing, while education and occupation were usually named first (the West Ender, as has been said, was aware of his place in the general American scheme of things), it is striking that *having a lot of friends* ranked a high third, above income, influence, or ethnic group. The context in which the question was asked dealt explicitly with social status.

The full force of this focal value is, however, revealed in response to the question asked of West Enders after residential relocation: "What are the neighbors like, compared to the West End?" In spite of the wide variety of differing circumstances and problems which members of this population faced in their new locations, 73 per cent who found a difference in their new neighbors specified this to be a difference in relative friendliness.

Or again, when asked what made the area in which they lived in the West End seem like a neighborhood to them, 43 per cent mentioned only their feeling of attachment to people there, 17 per cent referred to the general atmosphere of friendliness without indicating specific ties, and another 20 per cent mentioned close personal ties and friendly people in conjunction with a reference to other attributes of the area. Eighty per cent of the responses, then, had reference to this focal value.

The critical dimension of the value of friendliness is the perception of the West End environment as hospitable, friendly, and succorant. This perception does not imply frequency or quality of interaction, or personality characteristics such as liking and being liked by people.

That residential contiguity accounted for only 17 per cent of close relationships does not reflect the significance of the West End for its residents. Neighborhood relations were characterized by a high rate of interaction, but tended to be casual, not marked by depth or intimacy. Yet, in them, the individual found fulfillment of the value of "friendliness."

A critical specific value, which serves to indicate more precisely the signification of the concept of friendliness, may be referred to by the term "commonness." A negative injunction related to it would be "Don't put on airs," or as West Enders say, "Like people for themselves," "Most people are just average," or, "Be honest with people, try to be yourself." There is the strong theme that the good man is the plain man, that the average citizen—which the West Ender considers himself to be—has in him the elements of strength and goodness. In short, there is virtue in being of the common clay.

In this patern, any attempt to mask or hide the self—reserve in social interaction, or control of interaction through appointments, and the like—was seen as a sign of unfriendliness. One "dropped in" on others for coffee in the kitchen or for a bottle of beer and talk without prior announcement or invitation. The pattern thus included a strong injunction to openness in human relationships, a quality which included both receptivity to the initiative of others and an active outgoingness to them. As a consequence, personal difficulties tended to be discussed with unusual openness. The basis of this openness may be given an alternative statement. First, West End ethics, as stated above, affirmed the responsibility of the individual for the outcome of his own actions. Secondly, man's nature was believed to contain faults —or, we might say, frailties—which were to be accepted. From this it may be deduced, correctly, that various forms of adversity were largely expected, and passively—in a cultural sense—accepted. Adversity, personal difficulty, and human failure—that is, as a consequence of human frailty—were expected, and formed the subject of much casual conversation.

This configuration was strongly institutionalized in the friend and neighbor roles. Illustration of these values in action may be found in quotations from field notes concerning the women's coffee klatsch. Indeed, the dominant theme of this institution in the West End was the airing of personal difficulties. Reward was obtained not only in the opportunity for catharsis which it afforded but also in the expressions of commiseration and agreement automatically forthcoming from the group caught up in the interchange. An observer comments:

> A great deal of the women's talk had to do with the West End being torn down. They talked about the hardships of all the people they knew . . . they also talked a great deal about their families. Jane especially kept talking about her ungrateful daughter. Then she talked about her ungrateful mother . . . she said her daughter wants her to marry again, but a few years ago the daughter wouldn't hear of it. Now she tells her mother to go out and get herself fixed up and get married. Gloria talks about her husband's ailments. He has all kinds of them. He fell on his head when he was young and since that time has had epileptic fits. She says they're not hereditary. . . . The anxiety they expressed was tremendous; this seems to be a theme of their interaction, a banding together to let off steam about their troubles.

The acceptance of the personal revelations of others with a minimum of punitive, devaluative, or derisive reactions is paralleled by a similar acceptance of the faults and difficulties of others, even when the other person is not present. Illustrative of this acceptance is the quality of interchange revealed in the following field note excerpt:

> The talk is about the corner bar and one of Ella's friends whom she had earlier mentioned as being very close but never seems to visit. They talk about her getting drunk all the time on muscatel wine. She drinks by herself and then goes over to her mother's house. She can't afford a good drink like V.O., they say, because she drinks a bottle a day. The talk continues about her not visiting Ella very much. . . . She changed the subject and said that she had been down in the West End Saturday. She went into Jim's bar and found Eddie there. "Him and Joe are hitting the bottle together," she remarked, "and I asked him when he was going to stop drinking." She continued that he replied that he had been playing the same number for days and the day he didn't play it, last Saturday, it came up. He was going to stop drinking, but was so disgusted he started again.

In brief, then, the West End subculture constituted an environment in which those elements of the West Ender's identity which defined him to be a common man, including acknowledgment of the faults and vulnerabilities included in that estate, did not run the risk of a reaction by others which constituted a threat to or denial of his particular, but nevertheless essential, humanity.

A third specific value, which further defines the focal value of friendliness, is "helping others." Thus, in response to the question, "What are the main things that you would expect of a friend that you wouldn't expect of someone else?" giving or receiving assistance is either the only response or a prominent theme in 60 per cent of the replies. Usually these data include a spontaneously related incident of help given or received. An illustration from materials from a Polish woman informant is an account of how she had taken the electric bill from a neighbor's mailbox and paid it for several months during a period when that family was out of work.

The point is not, of course, the extent to which this value was effective in action, important as that problem is. Rather, our concern is to illustrate how such values provided the individual with a meaningful framework within which life was organized, and also formed essential elements of a concept of the self as a worthy entity. However, sufficient incidents did occur, or came to be invented, to furnish a fund of accounts of such prodigies of morality. Thus, even if it is only a mythology, that mythology was founded on the perception of the West End as a friendly, succorant social environment. Similarly, the self was perceived as a participant in, if not a constituent of, that morality. This was an element of the West End identity which was consistently reiterated and reinforced by the culture. Indeed, this concatenation of elements—the focal value of friendliness, with its defining specific values of commonness, acceptance of others, and help giving—formed the central orientation in West End culture.

A second focal value in West End culture, *ethnic harmony,* in addition to being a value in itself, also serves as an apt illustration of the theme of acceptance of commonness. The value of ethnic harmony was a principal integrative focus of West End culture and is exemplified in the near universal and proud assertion, "We're a league of nations down here." The presence of this value, along with its strong investment with affect, also, of course, implies ethnic differentiation to be a fundamental dimension of the social structure of the area. Indeed, research personnel going into the area found that the basic question which West Enders asked in placing them socially was that of "nationality." Once so placed, finer elements of social identification could be made. Equally, other West Enders were basically categorized according to ethnicity, and informants themselves consistently and spontaneously identified ethnically. Indeed, when we asked our interview respondents to name the five people they felt closest to other than their wives, children, or parents, 57 per cent named persons mostly of their own ethnic group and only 5 per cent named mostly persons of other ethnic groups. In 68 per cent of the cases, the first named person was of the same ethnic group as the respondent.

The strength of the value of ethnic harmony is indicated by the fact that only 3 per cent of the population spoke of nationality group as being of any importance in determining the social standing of a person in the community. Fifty per cent, moreover, named it as the least important item in the list. West Enders were well aware of the fact that in American culture there is a strong invidious element in being ethnically identified. This was very clear in the material from informants as well as in interaction in bars and on street corners. The model of the immigrant generation was constantly present and perceived as a degrading example for the American born. Conversely, the immigrants were constantly presented with this image of themselves held by the American born. However, because of the insistent acceptance and high valuation placed on the fact of another's ethnicity, as enjoined in the value of ethnic harmony, these elements of possible conflict and strife were only rarely manifest in social interaction. Persons were openly ethnically identified, but possible accompanying invidious and pejorative connotations were submerged in the assertion that "We're a league of nations down here." In orienting in this manner, the individual was reaffirming the worth of his own identity. In the West End, of course, the reciprocal behavior of others also provided an external source of such reassurance.

Summary and Conclusions

Our analysis reveals that West End culture differs markedly in pattern and in emphasis from the nominal system sometimes referred to as the dominant American pattern. Two areas were salient: *integration,* the holding together of a markedly differentiated socio-cultural system, as exemplified in the value of ethnic harmony; and *expressiveness,* an orientation to the involvement in and enjoyment of human relationships. West End culture placed its highest valuation precisely in this latter area. In contrast, there was much less emphasis placed on instrumental striving. Thus occupational goals tended to be modest, relatively immediate, and subordinate in significance to human relations. This pattern is consistent with the West End orientation to time and achievement, the substantive variables with which the analysis was begun. The life of the West End man was primarily polarized in relation to two sources of identity: the family-kinship group, and the corner or friendship group—what the West Ender called the "hanging group" (in the sense of the group of guys who "hung [out]" on a corner, or in a bar, etc.). "Hanging," in the sense of the cluster of values which defined the social roles in which the members of these groups interacted, was extremely important in the institutional structure of the West End. Its importance can be defined relative to two dimensions: first, the overwhelming commitment to and involvement in the group by its members; and, second, the extensiveness of participation in such groups. In our sample of adult men of *all* ages, 56 per cent stated that their friendships included the hanging pattern. Loosely speaking, it was the male counterpart of the female coffee klatsch.

West Enders, then, were the bearers of a *sub*-socio-cultural system. That system was geographically localized and, in specific content and pattern emphasis, was at marked variance with the dominant American pattern in terms of the elements given salience. In consequence, West Enders in their everyday lives were confronted with alternative cultural orientations at variance with their own. It was, of course, especially in roles which were not carried out wholly within the West End social structure that these alternatives may be presumed to have had their greatest and most direct impact upon the West Ender. Thus, the men (or employed women) in their occupational roles, the women as shoppers, or both sexes in recreational activities, came face to face with expectations and actions which were contrary to, derisive of, or even punitive toward, their own orientations and modes of behavior based upon them. This encounter also occurred through intrusion of non-West End values into the West End through radio, television, newspapers, and, perhaps, professional personnel in various callings. Insofar as these alternatives were middle-class configurations, and thus more highly valued and closer to the central institutions of American society, they constituted an especially potent challenge to the orientations of West End culture. To the extent that West End culture formed elements of the ego identity of its bearers, a challenge to it was a challenge to that identity: to the certainty of the conception of the self and thereby to the individual's sense of continuity with the past and commitment to the future. Further, the individual's sense of his own personal worth was also directly involved, for implicit in such challenge was a devaluation of West End culture and a consequent devaluation of the West Ender himself.

However, in our observation a counterposed process was occurring in the West End—on the street corners, in the grocery stores, in the homes, in the coffee klatsch. Wherever West Enders got together, those elements of West End culture upon which the West End identity was founded were consistently reinforced, their value and rightness asserted, in interaction with others within the framework of the West End moral order. In that interaction, the demands for getting ahead, the orientations to middle-class culture, were effectively balanced and reduced in perspective. The salient West End expressive orientation was effective in providing the individual with an alternative structure upon which his sense of personal worth and certainty of identity could be maintained, even though challenged. Wealth, education, high status occupations, and social power, as it were, could be given their due recognition; but at the same time it was possible to affirm implicitly, and at times overtly, the superiority of West End morality. This basic value dilemma was commonly phrased in the West End in the form of the not unusual question, What had the person who achieved such goals sacrificed, in terms of either his relationships with others or his personal contentment? In group interaction in the West End the outcome of this moral choice was never in doubt. The West End participant's identification with and allocation of priority to expressive gratification was never allowed to come into question.

The values thus reaffirmed in the process of social interaction in West End culture were of significance in the individual's efforts to find coherence and meaning in the world, especially in those aspects of experience which were particularly anxiety-provoking. They functioned to sustain his concept of his value as a person, his particular organization of reality, and, finally, his sense of continuity of the self within that reality. Considerations of this order constitute a class of variables which must be taken account of if we are to comprehend the significance in the lives of the residents of areas too quickly dismissed with the pejorative term, "slum."

Reference

1. Erikson, E. H., "The Problem of Ego-Identity," in *Identity and Anxiety*, M. R. Stein, A. J. Vidich, and D. M. White, eds., Glencoe, Ill.: The Free Press, 1960, pp. 81-82.

Grieving for a Lost Home

12

MARC FRIED

INTRODUCTION

For some time we have known that the forced dislocation from an urban slum is a highly disruptive and disturbing experience. This is implicit in the strong, positive attachments to the former slum residential area—in the case of this study the West End of Boston—and in the continued attachment to the area among those who left before any imminent danger of eviction. Since we were observing people in the midst of a crisis, we were all too ready to modify our impressions and to conclude that these were likely to be transitory reactions. But the post-relocation experiences of a great many people have borne out their most pessimistic pre-relocation expectations. There are wide variations in the success of post-relocation adjustment and considerable variability in the depth and quality of the loss experience. But for the majority it seems quite precise to speak of their reactions as expressions of *grief*. These are manifest in the feelings of painful loss, the continued longing, the general depressive tone, frequent symptoms of psychological or social or somatic distress, the active work required in adapting to the altered situation, the sense of helplessness, the occasional expressions of both direct and displaced anger, and tendencies to idealize the lost place.[1]

At their most extreme, these reactions of grief are intense, deeply felt, and, at times, overwhelming. In response to a series of questions concerning the feelings of sadness and depression which people experienced *after* moving, many replies were unambiguous: "I felt as though I had lost everything," "I felt like my heart was taken out of me," "I felt like taking the gaspipe," "I lost all the friends I knew," "I always felt I had to go home to the West End and even now I feel like crying when I pass by," "Something of me went with the West End,"

"I felt cheated," "What's the use of thinking about it," "I threw up a lot," "I had a nervous breakdown." Certainly, some people were overjoyed with the change and many felt no sense of loss. Among 250 women, however, 26 per cent report that they still feel sad or depressed two years later, and another 20 per cent report a long period (six months to two years) of sadness or depression. Altogether, therefore, at least 46 per cent give evidence of a fairly severe grief reaction or worse. And among 316 men, the data show only a slightly smaller percentage (38 per cent) with long-term grief reactions. The true proportion of depressive reactions is undoubtedly higher since many women and men who report no feelings of sadness or depression indicate clearly depressive responses to other questions.

In answer to another question, "How did you feel when you saw or heard that the building you had lived in was torn down?" a similar finding emerges. As in the previous instance, the responses are often quite extreme and most frequently quite pathetic. They range from those who replied: "I was glad because the building had rats," to moderate responses such as "the building was bad but I felt sorry," and "I didn't want to see it go," to the most frequent group comprising such reactions as "it was like a piece being taken from me," "I felt terrible," "I used to stare at the spot where the building stood," "I was sick to my stomach." This question in particular, by its evocative quality, seemed to stir up sad memories even among many people who denied any feeling of sadness or depression. The difference from the previous result is indicated by the fact that 54 per cent of the women and 46 per cent of the men report severely depressed or disturbed reactions; 19 per cent of the women and about 31 per cent of the men report satisfaction or indifference; and 27 per cent of the women and 23 per cent of the men report moderately depressed or ambivalent feelings. Thus it is clear that, for the majority of those who were displaced from the West End, leaving their residential area involved a moderate or extreme sense of loss and an accompanying affective reaction of grief.

While these figures go beyond any expectation which we had or which is clearly implied in other studies, the realization that relocation was a crisis with potential danger to mental health for many people was one of the motivating factors for this investigation.* In study-

* This is implicit in the prior work on "crisis" and situational predicaments by Dr. Erich Lindemann under whose initiative the current work was undertaken and carried out.

ing the impact of relocation on the lives of a working-class population through a comparison of pre-relocation and post-relocation interview data, a number of issues arise concerning the psychology of urban living which have received little systematic attention. Yet, if we are to understand the effects of relocation and the significance of the loss of a residential environment, it is essential that we have a deeper appreciation of the psychological implications of both physical and social aspects of residential experience. Thus we are led to formulations which deal with the functions and meanings of the residential area in the lives of working class people.

The Nature of the Loss in Relocation: The Spatial Factor

Any severe loss may represent a disruption in one's relationship to the past, to the present, and to the future. Losses generally bring about fragmentation of routines, of relationships, and of expectations, and frequently imply an alteration in the world of physically available objects and spatially oriented action. It is a disruption in that sense of continuity which is ordinarily a taken-for-granted framework for functioning in a universe which has temporal, social, and spatial dimensions. From this point of view, the loss of an important place represents a change in a potentially significant component of the experience of continuity.

But why should the loss of a place, even a very important place, be so critical for the individual's sense of continuity; and why should grief at such loss be so widespread a phenomenon? In order to clarify this, it is necessary to consider the meaning which this area, the West End of Boston, had for the lives of its inhabitants. In an earlier paper we tried to assess this, and came to conclusions which corroborate, although they go further, the results from the few related studies.

> In studying the reasons for satisfaction that the majority of slum residents experience, two major components have emerged. On the one hand, the residential area is the region in which a vast and interlocking set of social networks is localized. And, on the other, the physical area has considerable meaning as an extension of home, in which various parts are delineated and structured on the basis of a sense of belonging. These two components provide the context in which the residential area may so easily be invested with considerable, multiply-determined meaning. . . . the greatest proportion of this

> working-class group . . . shows a fairly common experience and usage of the residential area . . . dominated by a conception of the local area beyond the dwelling unit as an integral part of home. This view of an area as home and the significance of local people and local places are so profoundly at variance with typical middle-class orientations that it is difficult to appreciate the intensity of meaning, the basic sense of identity involved in living in the particular area.[2]

Nor is the intense investment of a residential area, both as an important physical space and as the locus for meaningful interpersonal ties, limited to the West End.[3] What is common to a host of studies is the evidence for the integrity of the urban, working-class, slum community as a social and spatial unit. It is the sense of belonging someplace, in a particular place which is quite familiar and easily delineated, in a wide area in which one feels "at home." This is the core of meaning of the local area. And this applies for many people who have few close relationships within the area. Even familiar and expectable streets and houses, faces at the window and people walking by, personal greetings and impersonal sounds may serve to designate the concrete foci of a sense of belonging somewhere and may provide special kinds of interpersonal and social meaning to a region one defines as "home."

It would be impossible to understand the reactions both to dislocation and to relocation and, particularly, the depth and frequency of grief responses without taking account of working-class orientations to residential areas. One of our primary theses is that the strength of the grief reaction to the loss of the West End is largely a function of prior orientations to the area. Thus, we certainly expect to find that the greater a person's pre-relocation commitment to the area, the more likely he is to react with marked grief. This prediction is confirmed again and again by the data.* † For the women, among those

* The analysis involves a comparison of information from interviews administered *before* relocation with a depth of grief index derived from follow-up interviews approximately two years *after* relocation. The pre-relocation interviews were administered to a randomly selected sample of 473 women from households in this area at the time the land was taken by the city. The post-relocation interviews were completed with 92 per cent of the women who had given pre-relocation interviews and with 87 per cent of the men from those households in which there was a husband in the household. Primary emphasis will be given to the results with the women since we do not have as full a range of pre-relocation information for the men. However, since a split schedule was used for the post-relocation interviews, the depth of grief index is available for only 259 women.

† Dr. Jason Aronson was largely responsible for developing the series of questions on grief. The opening question of the series was: Many people have told

who had said they liked living in the West End *very much* during the pre-location interviews, 73 per cent evidence a severe post-relocation grief reaction; among those who had less extreme but positive feelings about living in the West End, 53 per cent show a similar order of grief; and among those who were ambivalent or negative about the West End, only 34 per cent show a severe grief reaction. Or, considering a more specific feature of our formulation, the pre-relocation view of the West End as "home" shows an even stronger relationship to the depth of post-relocation grief. Among those women who said they had no real home, only 20 per cent give evidence of severe grief; among those who claimed some other area as their real home, 34 per cent fall into the severe grief category; but among the women for whom the *West End* was the real home, 68 per cent report severe grief reactions. Although the data for the men are less complete, the results are substantially similar. It is also quite understandable that the length of West End residence should bear a strong relationship to the loss reaction, although it is less powerful than some of the other findings and almost certainly it is not the critical component.

More directly relevant to our emphasis on the importance of places, it is quite striking that the greater the area of the West End which was known, the more likely there is to be a severe grief response. Among the women who said they knew only their own block during the pre-relocation interview, only 13 per cent report marked grief; at the other extreme, among those who knew most of the West End, 64 per cent have a marked grief reaction. This relationship is maintained when a wide range of interrelated variables is held con-

us that just after they moved they felt sad or depressed. Did you feel this way? This was followed by the three specific questions on which the index was based: (1) Would you describe how you felt? (2) How long did these feelings last? (3) How did you feel when you saw or heard that the building you had lived in was torn down? Each person was given a score from 1 to 4 on the basis of the coded responses to these questions and the scores were summated. For purposes of analysis, we divided the final scores into three groups: minimal grief, moderate grief, and severe or marked grief. The phrasing of these questions appears to dispose the respondent to give a "grief" response. In fact, however, there is a tendency to reject the idea of "sadness" among many people who show other evidence of a grief response. In cross-tabulating the "grief" scores with a series of questions in which there is no suggestion of sadness, unhappiness, or dissatisfaction, it is clear that the grief index is the more severe criterion. Those who are classified in the severe grief category almost invariably show severe grief reactions by any of the other criteria; but many who are categorized as "minimal grief" on the index fall into the extremes of unhappiness or dissatisfaction on the other items.

stant. Only in one instance, when there is a generally negative orientation to the West End, does more extensive knowledge of the area lead to a somewhat smaller proportion of severe grief responses. Thus, the wider an individual's familiarity with the local area, the greater his commitment to the locality. This wider familiarity evidently signifies a greater sense of the wholeness and integrity of the entire West End and, we would suggest, a more expanded sense of being "at home" throughout the entire local region. It is striking, too, that while familiarity with, use of, and comfort in the spatial regions of the residential area are closely related to extensiveness of personal contact, the spatial patterns have independent significance and represent an additional basis for a feeling of commitment to that larger, local region which is "home."

The Sense of Spatial Identity

In stressing the importance of places and access to local facilities, we wish only to redress the almost total neglect of spatial dimensions in dealing with human behavior. We certainly do not mean thereby to give too little emphasis to the fundamental importance of interpersonal relationships and social organization in defining the meaning of the area. Nor do we wish to underestimate the significance of cultural orientations and social organization in defining the character and importance of spatial dimensions. However, the crisis of loss of a residential area brings to the fore the importance of the local spatial region and alerts us to the greater generality of spatial conceptions as determinants of behavior. In fact, we might say that a *sense of spatial identity* is fundamental to human functioning. It represents a phenomenal or ideational integration of important experiences concerning environmental arrangements and contacts in relation to the individual's conception of his own body in space.* It is based on spatial memories, spatial imagery, the spatial framework of current activity, and the implicit spatial components of ideals and aspirations.

* Erik Erikson (see Bibliography) includes spatial components in discussing the sense of ego identity and his work has influenced the discussion of spatial variables. In distinguishing the sense of spatial identity from the sense of ego identity, I am suggesting that variations in spatial identity do not correspond exactly to variations in ego identity. By separating these concepts, it becomes possible to study their interrelationships empirically.

It appears to us also that these feelings of being at home and of belonging are, in the working class, integrally tied to a *specific* place. We would not expect similar effects or, at least, effects of similar proportion in a middle-class area. Generally speaking, an integrated sense of spatial identity in the middle class is not as contingent on the external stability of place or as dependent on the localization of social patterns, interpersonal relationships, and daily routines. In these data, in fact, there is a marked relationship between class status and depth of grief; the higher the status, by any of several indices, the smaller the proportions of severe grief. It is primarily in the working class, and largely because of the importance of external stability, that dislocation from a familiar residential area has so great an effect on fragmenting the sense of spatial identity.

External stability is also extremely important in interpersonal patterns within the working class. And dislocation and relocation involve a fragmentation of the external bases for interpersonal relationships and group networks. Thus, relocation undermines the established interpersonal relationships and group ties of the people involved and, in effect, destroys the sense of group identity of a great many individuals. "Group identity," a concept originally formulated by Erik Erikson, refers to the individual's sense of belonging, of being a part of larger human and social entities. It may include belonging to organizations or interpersonal networks with which a person is directly involved; and it may refer to "membership" in social groups with whom an individual has little overt contact, whether it be a family, a social class, an ethnic collectivity, a profession, or a group of people sharing a common ideology. What is common to these various patterns of group identity is that they represent an integrated sense of shared human qualities, of some sense of communality with other people which is essential for meaningful social functioning. Since, most notably in the working class, effective relationships with others are dependent upon a continuing sense of common group identity, the experience of loss and disruption of these affiliations is intense and frequently irrevocable. On the grounds, therefore, of both spatial and interpersonal orientations and commitments, dislocation from the residential area represents a particularly marked disruption in the sense of continuity for the majority of this group.

The Nature of the Loss in Relocation: Social and Personal Factors

Previously we said that by emphasizing the spatial dimension of the orientation to the West End, we did not mean to diminish the importance of social patterns in the experience of the local area and their effects on post-relocation loss reactions. Nor do we wish to neglect personality factors involved in the widespread grief reactions. It is quite clear that pre-relocation social relationships and intrapsychic dispositions *do* affect the depth of grief in response to leaving the West End. The strongest of these patterns is based on the association between depth of grief and pre-relocation feelings about neighbors. Among those women who had very positive feelings about their neighbors, 76 per cent show severe grief reactions; among those who were positive but less extreme, 56 per cent show severe grief; and among those who were relatively negative, 38 per cent have marked grief responses. Similarly, among the women whose five closest friends lived in the West End, 67 per cent show marked grief; among those whose friends were mostly in the West End or equally distributed inside and outside the area, 55 per cent have severe grief reactions; and among those whose friends were mostly or all outside, 44 per cent show severe grief.

The fact that these differences, although great, are not as consistently powerful as the differences relating to spatial use patterns does not necessarily imply the *greater* importance of spatial factors. If we hold the effect of spatial variables constant and examine the relationship between depth of grief and the interpersonal variables, it becomes apparent that the effect of interpersonal contacts on depth of grief is consistent regardless of differences in spatial orientation; and, likewise, the effect of spatial orientations on depth of grief is consistent regardless of differences in interpersonal relationships. Thus, each set of factors contributes independently to the depth of grief in spite of some degree of internal relationship. In short, we suggest that *either* spatial identity or group identity may be a critical focus of loss of continuity and thereby lead to severe grief; but if *both* bases for the sense of continuity are localized *within the residential area* the disruption of continuity is greater, and the proportions of marked grief correspondingly higher.

It is noteworthy that, apart from local interpersonal and social relationships and local spatial orientations and use (and variables which are closely related to these), there are few other social or personal factors in the pre-relocation situation which are related to depth of grief. These negative findings are of particular importance in emphasizing that not all the variables which influence the grief reaction to dislocation are of equal importance. It should be added that a predisposition to depression markedly accentuates the depth of grief in response to the loss of one's residential area. But it is also clear that prior depressive orientations do not account for the entire relationship. The effects of the general depressive orientation and of the social, interpersonal, and spatial relationships within the West End are essentially additive; both sets of factors contribute markedly to the final result. Thus, among the women with a severe depressive orientation, an extremely large proportion (81 per cent) of those who regarded the West End as their real home show marked grief. But among the women without a depressive orientation, only a moderate proportion (58 per cent) of those who similarly viewed the West End as home show severe grief. On the other hand, when the West End is not seen as the person's real home, an increasing severity of general depressive orientation does *not* lead to an increased proportion of severe grief reactions.

The Nature of the Loss in Relocation: Case Analyses

The dependence of the sense of continuity on external resources in the working class, particularly on the availability and local presence of familiar places which have the character of "home," and of familiar people whose patterns of behavior and response are relatively predictable, does not account for all of the reaction of grief to dislocation. In addition to these factors, which may be accentuated by depressive predispositions, it is quite evident that the realities of *post*-relocation experience are bound to affect the perpetuation, quality, and depth of grief. And, in fact, our data show that there is a strong association between positive or negative experiences in the post-relocation situation and the proportions who show severe grief. But this issue is complicated by two factors: (1) the extent to which potentially meaningful post-relocation circumstances can be a satisfying experience is *affected* by the degree and tenaciousness of previous commitments to the West End, and (2) the post-relocation "reality" is, in part, *selected* by the people who move and thus is a function of many personality factors, including the ability to anticipate needs, demands, and environmental opportunities.

In trying to understand the effects of pre-relocation orientations and post-relocation experiences of grief, we must bear in mind that the grief reactions we have described and analyzed are based on responses given approximately two years after relocation. Most people manage to achieve some adaptation to their experiences of loss and grief, and learn to deal with new situations and new experiences on their own terms. A wide variety of adaptive methods can be employed to salvage fragments of the sense of continuity, or to try to re-establish it on new grounds. Nonetheless, it is the tenaciousness of the imagery and affect of grief, despite these efforts at dealing with the altered reality, which is so strikingly similar to mourning for a lost person.

In coping with the sense of loss, some families tried to remain physically close to the area they knew, even though most of their close interpersonal relationships remain disrupted; and by this method, they appear often to have modified their feelings of grief. Other families try to move among relatives and maintain a sense of continuity through some degree of constancy in the external bases for their group identity. Yet others respond to the loss of place and people by accentuating the importance of those role relationships which remain. Thus, a number of women report increased closeness to their husbands, which they often explicitly relate to the decrease in the availability of other social relationships for both partners and which, in turn, modifies the severity of grief. In order to clarify some of the complexities of pre-relocation orientations and of post-relocation adjustments most concretely, a review of several cases may prove to be instructive.

It is evident that a very strong positive pre-relocation orientation to the West End is relatively infrequently associated with a complete absence of grief; and that, likewise, a negative pre-relocation orientation to the area is infrequently associated with a strong grief response. The two types which are numerically dominant are, in terms of rational expectations, consistent: those with strong positive feelings about the West End and severe grief; and those with negative feelings about the West End and minimal or moderate grief. The two "deviant" types, by the same token, are both numerically smaller and inconsistent: those with strong positive pre-relocation orientations and little grief; and those with negative pre-relocation orientations and severe grief. A closer examination of those "deviant" cases with strong pre-relocation commitment to the West End and minimal post-relocation grief often reveals either important reservations in their prior involvement with the West End or, more frequently, the denial or rejection of feelings of grief rather than their total absence. And the association of minimal pre-relocation commitment to the West End with a severe grief response often proves on closer examination to be a function of a deep involvement in the West End which is modified by markedly ambivalent statements; or, more generally, the grief reaction itself is quite modest and tenuous or is even a pseudo-grief which masks the primacy of dissatisfaction with the current area.

Grief Patterns: Case Examples

In turning to case analysis, we shall concentrate on the specific factors which operate in families of all four types, those representing the two dominant and those representing the two deviant patterns.

1. The Figella family exemplifies the association of strong positive pre-relocation attachments to the West End and a severe grief reaction. This is the most frequent of all the patterns and, although the Figella family is only one "type" among those who show this pattern, they are prototypical of a familiar West End constellation.

Both Mr. and Mrs. Figella are second-generation Americans who were born and brought up in the West End. In her pre-relocation interview, Mrs. Figella described her feelings about living in the West End unambiguously: "It's a wonderful place, the people are friendly." She "loves everything about it" and anticipates missing her relatives above all. She is satisfied with her dwelling: "It's comfortable, clean and warm." And the marriage appears to be deeply satisfying for both husband and wife. They share many household activities and have a warm family life with their three children.

Both Mr. and Mrs. Figella feel that their lives have changed a great deal since relocation. They are clearly referring, however, to the pattern and conditions of their relationships with other people. Their home life has changed little except that Mr. Figella is home more. He continues to work at the same job as a manual laborer with a modest but sufficient income. While they have many economic insecurities, the relocation has not produced any serious financial difficulty for them.

In relocating, the Figella family bought a house. Both husband and wife are quite satisfied with the physical arrangements but, all in all, they are dissatisfied with the move. When asked what she dislikes about her present dwelling, Mrs. Figella replied simply and pathetically: "It's in Arlington and I want to be in the West End." Both Mr. and Mrs. Figella are outgoing, friendly people with a very wide circle of social contacts. Although they still see their relatives often, they both feel isolated from them and they regret the loss of their friends. As Mr. Figella puts it: "I come home from work and that's it. I just plant myself in the house."

The Figella family is, in many respects, typical of a well-adjusted working-class family. They have relatively few ambitions for themselves or for their children. They continue in close contact with many people; but they no longer have the same extensiveness of mutual cooperation in household activities, they cannot "drop in" as casually as before, they do not have the sense of being surrounded by a familiar area and familiar people. Thus, while their objective situation is not dramatically altered, the changes do involve important elements of stability and continuity in their lives. They manifest the importance of externally available resources for an integral sense of spatial and group identity. However, they have always maintained a very close marital relationship, and their family provides a substantial basis for a sense of continuity. They can evidently cope with difficulties on the strength of their many internal and external resources. Nonetheless, they have suffered from the move, and find it extremely difficult to reorganize their lives completely in adapting to a new geographical situation and new patterns of social affiliation. Their grief for a lost home seems to be one form of maintaining continuity on the basis of memories. While it prevents a more wholehearted adjustment to their altered lives, such adjustments would imply forsaking the remaining fragments of a continuity which was central to their conceptions of themselves and of the world.

2. There are many similarities between the Figella family and the Giuliano family. But Mrs. Giuliano shows relatively little pre-relocation commitment to the West End and little post-relocation grief. Mr.

Giuliano was somewhat more deeply involved in the West End and, although satisfied with the change, feels that relocation was "like having the rug pulled out from under you." Mr. and Mrs. Giuliano are also second-generation Americans, of similar background to the Figellas'. But Mrs. Giuliano only moved to the West End at her marriage. Mrs. Giuliano had many objections to the area: "For me it is too congested. I never did care for it . . . too many barrooms, on every corner, too many families in one building. . . . The sidewalks are too narrow and the kids can't play outside." But she does expect to miss the stores and many favorite places. Her housing ambitions go beyond West End standards and she wants more space inside and outside. She had no blood relatives in the West End but was close to her husband's family and had friends nearby.

Mr. Giuliano was born in the West End and he had many relatives in the area. He has a relatively high status manual job but only a modest income. His wife does not complain about this although she is only moderately satisfied with the marriage. In part she objected to the fact that they went out so little and that he spent too much time on the corner with his friends. His social networks in the West End were more extensive and involved than were Mrs. Giuliano's. And he missed the West End more than she did after the relocation. But even Mr. Giuliano says that, all in all, he is satisfied with the change.

Mrs. Guiliano feels the change is "wonderful." She missed her friends but got over it. And a few of Mr. Guiliano's hanging group live close by so they can continue to hang together. Both are satisfied with the house they bought although Mrs. Giuliano's ambitions have now gone beyond this. The post-relocation situation has led to an improved marital relationship: Mr. Guiliano is home more and they go out more together.

Mr. and Mrs. Guiliano exemplify a pattern which seems most likely to be associated with a beneficial experience from relocation. Unlike Mr. and Mrs. Figella, who completely accept their working-class status and are embedded in the social and cultural patterns of the working class, Mr. and Mrs. Giuliano show many evidences of social mobility. Mr. Giuliano's present job is, properly speaking, outside the working-class category because of its relatively high status and he himself does not "work with his hands." And Mrs. Giuliano's housing ambitions, preferences in social relationships, orientation to the class structure, and attitudes toward a variety of matters from shopping to child rearing are indications of a readiness to achieve middle-class status. Mr. Giuliano is prepared for and Mrs. Giuliano clearly desires "discontinuity" with some of the central bases for their former identity. Their present situation is, in fact, a transitional one which allows them to reintegrate their lives at a new and higher status level without too precipitate a change. And their marital relationship seems sufficiently meaningful to provide a significant core of continuity in the process of change in their patterns of social and cultural experience. The lack of grief in this case is quite understandable and appropriate to their patterns of social orientation and expectation.

3. Yet another pattern is introduced by the Borowski family, who had an intense pre-location commitment to the West End and relatively little post-relocation grief. The Borowski's are both second-generation and have four children.

Mrs. Borowski was brought up in the West End but her husband has lived there only since the marriage (fifteen years before). Her feelings about living in the West End were clear: "I love it—it's the only home I've even known." She had reservations about the dirt in the area but loved the people, the places, and the convenience and maintained an extremely wide circle of friends. They had some relatives nearby but were primarily oriented towards friends, both within and outside the West End. Mr. Borowski, a highly skilled manual worker with a moderately high income, was as deeply attached to the West End as his wife.

Mr. Borowski missed the West End very much but was quite satisfied with their new situation and could anticipate feeling thoroughly at home in the new neighborhood. Mrs. Borowski proclaims that "home is where you hang your hat; it's up to you to make the adjustments." But she also says, "If I knew the people were coming back to the West End, I would pick up this little house and put it back on my corner." She claims she was not sad after relocation but, when asked how she felt when the building she lived in was torn down, a strangely morbid association is aroused: "It's just like a plant . . . when you tear up its roots, it dies! I didn't die but I felt kind of bad. It was home . . . Don't look back, try to go ahead."

Despite evidences of underlying grief, both Mr. and Mrs. Borowski have already adjusted to the change with remarkable alacrity. They bought a one-family house and have many friends in the new area. They do not feel as close to their new neighbors as they did to their West End friends, and they still maintain extensive contact with the latter. They are comfortable and happy in their new surroundings and maintain the close, warm, and mutually appreciative marital relationship they formerly had.

Mr. and Mrs. Borowski, and particularly Mrs. Borowski, reveal a sense of loss which is largely submerged beneath active efforts to deal with the present. It was possible for them to do this both because of personality factors (that is, the ability to deny the intense affective meaning of the change and to detach themselves from highly "cathected" objects with relative ease) and because of prior social patterns and orientations. Not only is Mr. Borowski, by occupation, among the highest group of working-class status, but this family has been "transitional" for some time. Remaining in the West End was clearly a matter of preference for them. They could have moved out quite easily on the basis of income; and many of their friends were scattered throughout metropolitan Boston. But while they are less self-consciously mobile than the Giuliano's, they had already shifted to many patterns more typical of the middle class before leaving the West End. These ranged from their joint weekly shopping expeditions to their recreational patterns, which included such sports as boating and such regular plans as yearly vacations. They experienced a disruption in continuity by virtue of their former spatial and group identity. But the bases for maintaining this identity had undergone many changes over the years; and they had already established a feeling for places and people, for a potential redefinition of "home" which was less contingent on the immediate and local availability of familiar spaces and familiar friends. Despite their preparedness for the move by virtue of cultural orientation, social experience, and personal disposition, the change was a considerable wrench for them. But, to the extent that they can be categorized as "over-adjusters," the residue of their lives in the West End is primarily a matter of painful memories which are only occasionally reawakened.

4. The alternate deviant pattern, minimal pre-relocation commitment associated with severe post-relocation grief, is manifested by Mr. and Mrs. Pagliuca. As in the previous case, this classification applies more fully to Mrs. Pagliuca, since Mr. Pagliuca appears to have had stronger ties to the West End. Mr. Pagliuca is a second-

generation American but Mrs. Pagliuca is first-generation from an urban European background. For both of them, however, there is some evidence that the sadness and regret about the loss of the West End should perhaps be designated as pseudo-grief.

Mrs. Pagliuca had a difficult time in the West End. But she also had a difficult time before that. She moved into the West End when she got married. And she complains bitterly about her marriage, her husband's relatives, West Enders in general. She says of the West End: "I don't like it. The people . . . the buildings are full of rats. There are no places to play for the children." She liked the apartment but complained about the lady downstairs, the dirt, the repairs required, and the coldness during the winter. She also complains a great deal about lack of money. Her husband's wages are not too low but he seems to have periods of unemployment and often drinks his money away.

Mr. Pagliuca was attached to some of his friends and the bars in the West End. But he didn't like his housing situation there. And his reaction tends to be one of bitterness ("a rotten deal") rather than of sadness. Both Mr. and Mrs. Pagliuca are quite satisfied with their post-relocation apartment but are thoroughly dissatisfied with the area. They have had considerable difficulty with neighbors: ". . . I don't like this; people are mean here; my children get blamed for anything and everything; and there's no transportation near here." She now idealizes the West End and claims that she misses everything about it.

Mr. Pagliuca is an unskilled manual laborer. Financial problems create a constant focus for difficulty and arguments. But both Mr. and Mrs. Pagliuca appear more satisfied with one another than before relocation. They have four children, some of whom are in legal difficulty. There is also some evidence of past cruelty toward the children, at least on Mrs. Pagliuca's part.

It is evident from this summary that the Pagliuca family is deviant in a social as well as in a statistical sense. They show few signs of adjusting to the move or, for that matter, of any basic potential for successful adjustment to further moves (which they are now planning). It may be that families with such initial difficulties, with such a tenuous basis for maintaining a sense of continuity under any circumstances, suffer most acutely from disruption of these minimal ties. The Pagliuca family has few inner resources and, having lost the minimal external resources signified by a gross sense of belonging, of being tolerated if not accepted, they appear to be hopelessly at sea. Although we refer to their grief as "pseudo-grief" on the basis of the shift from pre-relocation to post-relocation statements, there is a sense in which it is quite real. Within the post-relocation interviews their responses are quite consistent; and a review of all the data suggests that, although their ties were quite modest, their current difficulties have revealed the importance of these meager involvements and the problems of re-establishing anew an equivalent basis for identity formation. Thus, even for Mr. and Mrs. Pagliuca, we can speak of the disruption in the sense of continuity, although this continuity was based on a very fragile experience of minimal comfort, with familiar places and relatively tolerant people. Their grief reaction, pseudo or real, may further influence (and be influenced by) dissatisfactions with any new residential situation. The fact that it is based on an idealized past accentuates rather than minimizes its effect on current expectations and behavior.

Conclusions

Grieving for a lost home is evidently a widespread and serious social phenomenon following in the wake of urban dislocation. It is likely to increase social and psychological "pathology" in a limited number of instances; and it is also likely to create new opportunities for some, and to increase the rate of social mobility for others. For the greatest number, dislocation is unlikely to have either effect but does lead to intense personal suffering despite moderately successful adaptation to the total situation of relocation. Under these circumstances, it becomes most critical that we face the realities of the effects of relocation on working-class residents of slums and, on the basis of knowledge and understanding, that we learn to deal more effectively with the problems engendered.

In evaluating these data on the effect of pre-location experiences on post-relocation reactions of grief, we have arrived at a number of conclusions:

1. The affective reaction to the loss of the West End can be quite precisely described as a grief response showing most of the characteristics of grief and mourning for a lost person.

2. One of the important components of the grief reaction is the

fragmentation of the sense of spatial identity. This is manifest, not only in the pre-location experience of the spatial area as an expanded "home," but in the varying degrees of grief following relocation, arising from variations in the pre-relocation orientation to and use of local spatial regions.

3. Another component, of equal importance, is the dependence of the sense of group identity on stable, social networks. Dislocation necessarily led to the fragmentation of this group identity which was based, to such a large extent, on the external availability and overt contact with familiar groups of people.

4. Associated with these "cognitive" components, described as the sense of spatial identity and the sense of group identity, are strong affective qualities. We have not tried to delineate them but they appear to fall into the realm of a feeling of security in and commitment to the external spatial and group patterns which are the tangible, visible aspects of these identity components. However, a predisposition to depressive reactions also markedly affects the depth of grief reaction.

5. Theoretically, we can speak of spatial and group identity as critical foci of the sense of continuity. This sense of continuity is not *necessarily* contingent on the external stability of place, people, and security or support. But for the working class these concrete, external resources and the experience of stability, availability, and familiarity which they provide are essential for a meaningful sense of continuity. Thus, dislocation and the loss of the residential area represent a fragmentation of some of the essential components of the sense of continuity in the working class.

It is in the light of these observations and conclusions that we must consider problems of social planning which are associated with the changes induced by physical planning for relocation. Urban planning cannot be limited to "bricks and mortar." While these data tell us little about the importance of housing or the aspects of housing which are important, they indicate that considerations of a non-housing nature are critical. There is evidence, for example, that the frequency of the grief response is not affected by such housing factors as increase or decrease in apartment size or home ownership. But physical factors may be of great importance when related to the subjective significance of different spatial and physical arrangements, or to their capacity for gratifying different socio-cultural groups. For the present, we can only stress the importance of local areas as *spatial and social* arrangements which are central to the lives of working-class people. And, in view of the enormous importance of such local areas, we are led to consider the convergence of familiar people and familiar places as a focal consideration in formulating planning decisions.

We can learn to deal with these problems only through research, through exploratory and imaginative service programs, and through a more careful consideration of the place of residential stability in salvaging the precarious thread of continuity. The outcomes of crises are always manifold and, just as there is an increase in strain and difficulty, so also there is an increase in opportunities for adapting at a more satisfying level of functioning. The judicious use of minimal resources of counseling and assistance may permit many working-class people to reorganize and integrate a meaningful sense of spatial and group identity under the challenge of social change. Only a relatively small group of those whose functioning has always been marginal and who cannot cope with the added strain of adjusting to wholly new problems are likely to require major forms of intervention.

In general, our results would imply the necessity for providing increased opportunities for maintaining a sense of continuity for those people, mainly from the working class, whose residential areas are being renewed. This may involve several factors: (1) diminishing the amount of drastic redevelopment and the consequent mass demolition of property and mass dislocation from homes; (2) providing more frequently for people to move within their former residential areas during and after the renewal; and (3) when dislocation and relocation are unavoidable, planning the relocation possibilities in order to provide new areas which can be assimilated to old objectives. A closer examination of slum areas may even provide some concrete information regarding specific physical variables, the physical and spatial arrangements typical of slum areas and slum housing, which offer considerable gratification to the residents. These may often be translated into effective modern architectural and areal design. And, in conjunction with planning decisions which take more careful account of the human consequences of urban physical change, it is possible to utilize social, psychological, and psychiatric services. The use of highly skilled resources, including opportunities for the education of professional and even lay personnel in largely unfamiliar problems and methods, can minimize some of the more destructive and widespread effects of relocation; and, for some families, can offer constructive experiences in dealing with new adaptational possibilities. The problem is large. But only by assuring the integrity of some of the external bases for the sense of continuity in the working class, and by maximizing the opportunities for meaningful adaptation, can we accomplish planned urban change without serious hazard to human welfare.

References

1. Abraham, K., "Notes on the Psycho-analytical Investigation and Treatment of Manic-Depressive Insanity and Allied Conditions" (1911), and "A Short Study of the Development of the Libido, Viewed in the Light of Mental Disorders" (1924), in *Selected Papers of Karl Abraham,* Vol. I, New York: Basic Books, 1953; Bibring, E., "The Mechanisms of Depression," in *Affective Disorders,* P. Greenacre, ed., New York: International Univ. Press, 1953; Bowlby, J., "Processes of Mourning," *Int. J. Psychoanal.,* 42:317-340, 1961; Freud, S., "Mourning and Melancholia" (1917), in *Collected Papers,* Vol. III, New York: Basic Books, 1959; Hoggart, R., *The Uses of Literacy: Changing Patterns in English Mass Culture,* New York: Oxford Univ. Press, 1957; Klein, M., "Mourning and Its Relations to Manic-Depressive States," *Int. J. Psychoanal., 21*:125-153, 1940; Lindemann, E., "Symptomatology and Management of Acute Grief," *Am. J. Psychiat., 101*:141-148, 1944; Marris, P., *Widows and Their Families,* London: Routledge and Kegan Paul, 1958; Rochlin, G., "The Dread of Abandonment," in *The Psychoanalytic Study of the Child,* Vol. XVI, New York: International Univ. Press, 1961; Volkart, E. H., with S. T. Michael, "Bereavement and Mental Health," in *Explorations in Social Psychiatry,* A. H. Leighton, J. A. Clausen, and R. N. Wilson, eds., New York: Basic Books, 1957.
2. Fried, M., and Gleicher, P., "Some Sources of Residential Satisfaction in an Urban Slum," *J. Amer. Inst. Planners,* 27:305-315, 1961.
3. Gans, H., *The Urban Villagers,* New York: The Free Press of Glencoe, 1963; Gans, H., "The Human Implications of Current Redevelopment and Relocation Planning," *J. Amer. Inst. Planners,* 25:15-25, 1959; Hoggart, R., *op. cit.;* Hole, V., "Social Effects of Planned Rehousing," *Town Planning Rev.,* 30:161-173, 1959; Marris, P., *Family and Social Change in an African City,* Evanston, Ill.: Northwestern Univ. Press, 1962; Mogey, J. M., *Family and Neighbourhood,* New York: Oxford

Univ. Press, 1956; Seeley, J., "The Slum: Its Nature, Use, and Users," *J. Amer. Inst. Planners,* 25:7-14, 1959; Vereker, C., and Mays, J. B., *Urban Redevelopment and Social Change,* New York: Lounz, 1960; Young, M., and Willmott, P., *Family and Kinship in East London,* Glencoe, Ill.: The Free Press, 1957.

Bibliography

Erikson, E., "Ego Development and Historical Change," in *The Psychoanalytic Study of the Child,* Vol. II, New York: International Univ. Press, 1946.

———, "The Problem of Ego Identity," *J. Amer. Psychoanal. Assoc.,* 4:56-121, 1956.

Firey, W., *Land Use in Central Boston,* Cambridge, Mass.: Harvard Univ. Press, 1947.

Population Mobility in the American Middle Class

13

ROBERT GUTMAN

The subject of population mobility has been of perennial interest in this country, attested to by the fact that as early as 1850 the decennial census of the federal government attempted to compare information regarding the state in which people lived at the census date with the state in which they were born.[1] It was considered important a century ago, and it still is considered significant today, to track the tendency of the American population to redistribute itself, to discover which areas of the nation were losing population and which states and regions would become the centers of population growth in the future.

In recent decades, the interest in internal migration has been mounting. Beginning in 1940, the census tried to improve the completeness of its information regarding the sources of population by asking not only where people were born but also where they had lived five years previously. More recently, in 1948 to be exact, the Current Population Survey of the Census Bureau initiated a practice, which it has maintained each year, of asking a sample of the population where they lived one year previous to the date of the survey.[2]

Numerous factors have contributed toward the mounting desire to have a greater amount of accurate and up-to-date information regarding the flow of people back and forth, north and south, from city to suburb and back again throughout the nation. Perhaps what is most significant about the specific reasons which have had the combined effect of improving our information about migration is that most of them reflect the emerging tendency to regard internal migration as a "problem"—as a phenomenon which not only presents an opportunity to people and to society, but also gives rise to difficulties and challenges which demand planned social action to meet them.

Two examples of the changing view of the migratory process have arisen recently. One is the widespread sentiment that the natural mobility of the population poses a serious threat to the ability of the great cities to remain responsible and effective political, social, and economic units. The populations involved in this issue are the lower-class, predominantly Negro groups coming into the city, and the middle-class, almost exclusively white families which are fleeing. The other example is the increasing interest and concern shown by scholars and practitioners in the field of mental health in the possibly morbid impact of the spread of population to the housing developments and real estate subdivisions located on the fringes of the metropolis.[3]

This paper is concerned with the migration experience of this latter group. In discussing their mobility, I will be trying to suggest answers to three questions: how suburban settlements react to middle-class whites after they have moved in; how the migrants respond to the settlements; and what the impact of mobility is on the migrants themselves.[4] My focus will be principally on the social and psychological dimensions of mobility. The suburbs studied have been either *established suburbs*—settlements with little vacant land, built up in terms of single-family, two-story dwellings, containing relatively heterogeneous populations, and usually located close to the core area of the metropolis; or they have been *developments*—new settlements of single-family dwellings, many of them "ranch" houses, in municipalities with considerable undeveloped land, with comparatively homogeneous populations, and usually situated farther out in the fringe area of the metropolitan region.

Some of the literature describing the experience of newcomers to housing developments has created an image of settlements desperate for additional personnel. It has been suggested that, in the settlements which spring up on the fringes of the metropolitan region, cliques, neighboring groups, and social networks begin to involve newcomers almost immediately after they take possession of their house. The familiar picture is that painted by Whyte in his study of Park Forest, Illinois.[5] In Park Forest, it seemed that every neighborhood was its own Welcome Wagon. When a new resident arrived, people in adjoining apartments or houses rushed to help them move in, lugging furniture, carrying boxes, providing casseroles for the first night's supper, "sitting" for the mother while she arranged the furniture and got the household underway.

Our studies of recent migrants to housing developments in central

New Jersey would indicate that their experience has been much more various than Whyte indicates. Some migrants did report intense interaction following their initial arrival similar to what seems to have been the case in Park Forest; but others reported a much different, almost impersonal initial encounter. At least four factors seemed to have played a part. Existing in one combination, they led toward the Park Forest pattern; but in another combination they resulted in a very different response from the community.

1. To borrow a conceptual distinction Gans has adopted in discussing suburban settlements,[6] some of the respondents intended to make the settlement their permanent home; these were the "permanents." Others regarded the settlement as a temporary domicile, either for the reason that they expected to be shifted to a different post, say in the case of Army personnel, or because they were looking forward to moving to still better housing in the immediate future. Gans dubs the former group "transients," and the latter he calls "upwardly mobiles." In our developments, it was the "transients" and the "upwardly mobiles" who were most likely to report the Park Forest pattern, whereas the "permanents" claimed to have had little social contact with their neighbors during the early days in the settlement.

2. Class differences seem also to have been responsible for variation in the initial experience. Working-class wives, or wives with only high school or less than high school education had more distant relationships with neighbors, at least in these early stages of living in the settlement, than did wives of middle-class husbands and wives with some college experience. The lack of socializing skill in members of the working classes who move to the suburbs has been noted before, in the case of both American and English working-class groups.[7] The psychological dynamics which underlie this incapacity have yet to be explored. In the case of respondents in one development, it seems to have been intensified by the tendency, which was marked among the working-class wives, to regard the majority of other newcomers to the settlement as belonging to a higher social class than themselves, though in fact the development was divided fairly evenly between blue-collar and white-collar groups.

3. Whether migrants confronted the Park Forest type of response or some other pattern depended, too, upon the presence or absence of social class homogeneity among their immediate neighbors. "Transient" and "upwardly mobile" families were often bitterly dis-

appointed by the settlement in the first days. If they found themselves hidden among families who were oriented to permanent residence, they quickly compensated for this dissatisfaction if the weather was warm and it was easy to meet other newcomers.

4. Indeed, the seasonal factor contributed independently to the pattern of social interaction that emerged in the settlement, with the winter arrivals least likely to encounter social hyperactivity.

As various as were the experiences of those families who moved to developments, they nevertheless shared a pattern of experience as newcomers which distinguished them as a group from families who moved to the established suburb. The families who moved to the established suburb usually moved into an older house on a block where most of the residents were relatively permanent, and where their dwelling might have been the only one to change hands during the year. The intense pattern of social interaction which Whyte reports, and which we found in some situations in the development, never emerged here. Instead, an enormous variety of patterns emerged, at least in the initial encounters and during the first few weeks. Respondents reported that the real estate agents introduced them to neighbors before they had taken possession. In some cases, wives were called on by other wives in the neighborhood, sometimes individually and sometimes in groups. Neighboring wives, or husbands, encountered each other casually, while out gardening and cleaning up the yard or in tending children. And, of course, there were the usual meetings brought about by the children, who themselves often were the first to establish contact with the human population of the new environment.

Perhaps what is most striking, however, is that, to a much greater degree than in the housing developments, the newcomers integrated themselves into the established communities not through the informal social networks of the immediate neighborhood but through the voluntary associations of the total settlement. In part, the difference can be attributed to the fact that the developments had few voluntary associations, since they were so new. Looked at from another perspective, however, it is clear that the newcomers to the established suburbs had to rely on the churches, the political parties, and the women's organizations just for the reason that the neighborhood failed to provide the primary group affiliations which the newcomers sought. Sometimes a neighbor would inform the newcomer about the existence of the voluntary association, and might even take the newcomer to his first meeting; but even in these cases it was up to the migrant himself to find his own primary group within the association.

Several aspects of this integrative process in the established suburbs are worth noting. The voluntary associations of the suburbs, even the established suburbs, are usually short of personnel. Although the shortage often diminishes the effectiveness of the association, it performs the very useful function of making the association anxious to incorporate the newcomer into its system of organizational roles, thus making the community appear to welcome the migrant.

The nature of the normal integrative process in the established suburb implies that unless a family is willing to affiliate with community organizations—unless it is willing to devote both time and energy to community activities—primary group membership in the settlement is hard to achieve. The most disappointed women we interviewed in the established suburb were often those without any ties to the voluntary associations, and for just the reason that they had not been able to learn to use them for satisfying primary group needs. Furthermore, this pattern of integration served the very positive function of relating the newcomer to a community-wide rather than a block-centered or neighborhood-oriented activity. Perhaps, therefore, it is not surprising that we found newcomers to the established suburb to be much more knowledgeable about community problems and political issues than were the recent migrants to the development. A final aspect of the assimilation process which deserves comment is that it helps to explain why established suburbs often offer an unpleasant prospect for social groups or personalities which do not easily achieve an institutional expression, or which have not yet acquired organizational form in a particular settlement. Intellectuals, for example, may find the established suburb uncongenial for this reason—as uncongenial, if not more so, than the development. Or if a new social group is entering a town—say, working-class people who migrate into a middle-class suburb—it will be more difficult for them to become integrated than it would be in the development, at least until such time as the typical working-class voluntary associations have been organized.

I have been discussing the way in which the settlement and its population respond to the newcomer. How does the newcomer react to the settlement? How does the newcomer behave in order to hasten or facilitate his assimilation and integration into the settlement?

Suburban migrants vary in the degree to which they define integration into the settlement as *their* responsibility. Working-class respondents are more likely than not to assume only limited initiative for meeting other people, striking up acquaintanceships and making friends. Insofar as working-class families do assume responsibility for integration, usually it will be the husband rather than the wife who undertakes the job. In the middle class, both spouses believe that it is up to them to inaugurate the encounter with the community. The wife in particular undertakes exploratory forays into the social activities which are going on in the settlement, or into the cliques and friendship groups which already have started to form on the block or in the neighborhood.

A problem which bothers many middle-class people is not *whether* to assume responsibility but rather *how much* responsibility they should assume. Many women reported that they felt considerable confusion in their first days in a settlement about the degree of initiative they could display without coming to be regarded as aggressive or overly forward. This concern was especially evident among women who moved into established suburbs where social networks were already established. In this type of settlement, the women were aware that cliques and groups already existed which they wanted to "break into," but they were concerned lest these groups close ranks and present a negative face toward them. The advantage of the housing development was that "groups" were less evident. Newcomers rarely were in the position of breaking into groups since "groups" had hardly begun to form or, at least, newcomers were not aware that groups had formed.

Both in the established suburbs and, to a lesser degree, in the housing developments certain people already in the settlement had the role of "integrators." They created the channels through which the newcomer first became acquainted with the networks already set up in the settlement. These integrators were themselves usually isolated and alienated from the existing networks, even though they had been living in the settlement for some time. Their psychological satisfaction consisted in providing the bridge for the newcomers, who often felt flattered that an "oldtimer" resident was willing to invite them to parties and other informal social gatherings. Newcomers who became successfully assimilated into the settlement soon recognized that the "integrators" themselves were isolates, and rapidly dissociated themselves from the social world of the integrator. Fortunately for the integrator, by the time he or she managed to introduce the newcomer to the community and the newcomer in turn had gone on to abandon the integrator, there were new arrivals in the settlement to whom the integrator could once again proffer the hand of friendship. In the established suburb in which we paid particular attention to the role of the integrator, it seemed that these people were most often divorced or older single women.

Although often the subject of derision, integrators provide an essential mechanism for getting newcomers involved in the social networks of the settlement. Not only do they offer the specific human contact through which social interaction between migrants and oldtimers is initiated, integrators also perform an important function by communicating to the newcomers the norms that prevail in the settlement. Indeed, the very fact that the integrators are not usually full members of the groups which dominate in the settlement allows them to define the norms explicitly—since, like most deviants and second-class citizens, they are more self-conscious about what is considered "proper" in the community than people who are deeply involved in its life. The activity of the integrators is especially crucial for the additional reason that the rules governing the relationships between newcomers and oldtimers in suburban settlements *are* ambiguous. The rules are sufficiently unclear for almost any hypothesis about how to behave to be better than none at all, and the integrators do provide at least a definition of proper behavior.

The lack of clarity about informal social norms in the suburbs is an interesting phenomenon in itself. I have already mentioned the apparent helplessness of working-class newcomers in initiating social interaction, and the confusion which middle-class families evidence about how much responsibility they should assume. One might believe that the uncertainty of middle-class newcomers about how to behave could have disastrous consequences—both for those who, in showing too little initiative, given the standards of their community, would fail in making acquaintances and friends; and for those who, in evidencing too much initiative, given the norms of their settlement, would be regarded as too aggressive and therefore might be rejected. But the fact of the matter is that newcomers' efforts at assimilation usually do not have disastrous consequences, for the reason that the lack of clear norms results in a wide range of tolerance. In our interviews we asked all sorts of people, both newcomers and those already established in settlements, how they thought newcomers ought to behave, and how oldtimers should behave toward newcomers. A large proportion of the respondents obviously had no certain notions about these questions. Those who did have such notions were usually aware that other people might have different ideas, but they did not feel impelled to argue with or condemn those who had notions other than their own. Perhaps this is what critics of American society have had in mind when they have contrasted ours with English society, and have said that American society lacks manners.[8] Indeed it does lack manners, if we regard as "mannerlessness" the absence of informal social norms which prescribe how newcomers and oldtimers should behave toward each other.

There seem to be consistent differences among newcomers in the way in which they seek to relate themselves to the settlement, but it is frankly difficult at this stage in our research to describe these differences. For example, the sources of variation, other than social class, in the initial encounters of people with new settlements is not readily apparent. One could say that some people feel more threatened by the role of newcomer than others do, but this may be no more than a restatement in other terms of the same thought. Variations in newcomers' responses probably bear some relationship, in the case of women, to whether they have children or not, and to how adequate their relationships are to their husbands. Women with children and women with happy marriages are better able to find emotional support during the transitional phases of moving to a new settlement than are women whose family life is unstable. Women who regard themselves as more different from most other women, with special tastes and interests which on the basis of previous experience they know are not easily matched, will experience greater anxiety and greater difficulty in the role of newcomers.

I have described a few of the economic, social, and psychological factors which influence the different ways in which settlements respond to newcomers; and I also have described what our studies reveal about differences in newcomers' responses to the experience of migration. What can we say about the total impact of mobility in the middle class? Does it have a morbid influence on the migrants themselves?

The overwhelming impression which emerges is that the experience of moving is not nearly so destructive as some commentators have imagined.[9] Like many other experiences which disrupt the continuity of life and which remove people from their association with old groups and involve them in the fate of new ones, mobility constitutes a psychological hazard. For the great majority of respondents, the hazard represented by residential mobility is not necessarily greater in magnitude than experiences which have a similar general structure, such as occupational mobility or the shift from high school to college.

There were a number of women, however, for whom the move to a new settlement was a very distressing experience. In the case of a few of them, the emotions they expressed toward neighbors and acquaintances in the new settlement bordered on the hysterical. But in talking further with these women, we received the definite impression that they were fragile personalities, and the distress which they exhibited in this new situation was comparable to the distress they felt in earlier encounters with new situations that did not involve shifts in the location of the home site.

In contrast to the women who found the experience of moving an almost unbearable strain, others positively appeared to flourish as a consequence of the move. I am thinking here not only of those who were overjoyed to contemplate the spaciousness of their house and the ease of raising children in the suburbs in comparison with the situation they had in the apartments of the central city. There were also women who seemed to thrive on the very fact of change in their physical and social environment. These were people who were almost manic in their enthusiasm for their new world and who were absurdly and naively convinced that the interpersonal problems which they had endured in their old settlement would almost miraculously disappear now that they had moved to the suburbs.

Four types of women whom we met seemed to have the most trouble in adjusting to their new settlement. In the first place, there were the migrants who were downwardly mobile. These were women who regarded their present settlement and way of life, including their husband's new job associated with this life, as socially less prestigeful and favorable than the situation associated with the house and settlement in which they lived just previously. It was not the fact of change which disturbed them, but rather that they defined the change as change for the worse. Not only did they view their present environment as less favorable than the old, but this view in turn prevented them from exploring ways of coping with change and discovering the opportunities to become assimilated to the settlement. They were rigid in their determination to hold on to an old way of behaving which they valued highly because of its association with a former existence that was more prestigeful, thus avoiding the recognition that the old way was inapplicable to the situation in which they now found themselves.

The existence of these individuals among the migrants reminds one of the importance of the experience of social mobility for the American character. Our society has so fully institutionalized the expectation of class mobility that the experience of mobility has become an essential coping trait for people buffeted by experiences that otherwise would be searing in their impact on mental health. As long as class mobility operates, the impact of residential mobility, divorce, job alienation, and a host of otherwise hazardous experiences is obscured and suppressed. Once class mobility is absent or disappears, however, the underlying strains on the personality are revealed and emerge in all their morbid complexity.

It is doubtful, however, that the absence of the mobility experience can account for the presence of the second type of individual who found migration difficult: the working-class wife. The fact of movement to the suburbs in itself constituted for these women an experience of moving upward in the social scale. Their problem in becoming adjusted to the new settlements probably bears more relationship to the inherent inexperience of this group in dealing with the sociability demands of different social environments.

Women who tended to be very expressive emotionally, from ethnic cultures such as the Italian and Polish, also seemed to have problems in relating to the new settlements. One could believe this response to have been a function of their largely working-class origins, and of the fact that they were usually a minority in the population, except for the fact that middle-class women who were expressive types also demonstrated similar difficulties. Regardless of ethnic or class affiliation, these individuals reported considerable strain in their relations with neighbors, usually revolving around the issue of reciprocity in social relationships. When we asked respondents whether they would like to have their most intimate friend as a next-door neighbor, the overwhelming majority of women said: "No!" These more expressive women, however, replied in the affirmative. If we inquired whether people thought that their neighbors should do more in the way of greeting newcomers, exchanging recipes, encouraging personal confidence, and so on, the great mass of respondents reported a negative opinion; but the expressive women said they wished their neighbors would engage in more of this kind of sociability. It was as if the expressive women had not learned that the neighbor relationship is of a special sort, demanding more responsibility than acquaintanceship, yet allowing for less intensity and intimacy than friendship. Because their neighbors did things for them, usually of an instrumental variety, the expressive women foolishly assumed that this fact betokened more scope for confidence and familiarity than the neighbors intended, with the consequence that they felt "jilted" by neighbors and became hostile and aggressive toward them.

I already have commented on the fourth type of individual who seemed to have most difficulty with mobility. These are the individuals, particularly women, whose tastes and interests are relatively sparsely distributed in the total population and who therefore inevitably find it difficult to discover other persons with similar tastes and interests among the residents of the housing developments and established suburbs on the metropolitan fringe.

A description of these types points the way toward an understanding of the reasons why Americans adjust as well as they do to the experience of population mobility. Mobility has been written into the American character. The ability to strike up satisfying conversations with people one has never met before, the willingness to concede the legitimacy of a wide range of behavior patterns, the focus on the family as the primary group which must provide the principal source of emotional satisfaction—these traits, often attributed to Americans by foreigners, indeed play a very positive role in easing the transition from one settlement to another. Individuals who find most people "boring," who have set convictions about child-rearing or cooking, who are unhappy with their husbands and children, or who look to their parents for emotional support, have failed to internalize the standard traits of the American; and they are people also who we found have had difficulty in adjusting to the role of the newcomer.

References

1. Smith, T. L., *Fundamentals of Population Study*, Philadelphia: Lippincott, 1960.
2. "Internal Migration in the United States: April, 1947 to April, 1948," *Current Population Reports: Population Characteristics*, Series P-20, No. 22, Washington: U.S. Bureau of the Census, Jan. 28, 1949.
3. This concern is illustrated by many of the contributors to a seminar discussion of the impact of population mobility. See Duhl, L., and Gutman R., eds., *Problems of Migration in the American Middle Classes*, New Brunswick, N.J.: Rutgers Urban Studies Center, 1961.
4. There is a small but interesting social science literature dealing with different aspects of the social psychology of population mobility. Much of this literature is summarized in Rossi, P. H., *Why Families Move*, Glencoe, Ill.: The Free Press, 1953; and in Foote, N., Abu-Lughod, J., *et al.*, *Housing Choices and Housing Constraints*, New York: McGraw-Hill, 1960 (especially Part 2).
5. Whyte, W. H., *The Organization Man*, New York: Simon and Schuster, 1956, Part 7.
6. Gans, H., "Types of Moves," in L. Duhl and R. Gutman, *op. cit.*
7. Young, M., and Willmott, P., *Family and Kinship in East London*, Glencoe, Ill.: The Free Press, 1957, Chapter 10.
8. Trilling, L., *The Liberal Imagination*, New York: Viking Press, 1950, pp. 205-222, *passim*.
9. Gordon, R. E., Gordon, K. K., and Gunther, M., *The Split-Level Trap*, New York: Dell, 1962, Chapter 1.

Effects of the Move from City to Suburb

14

HERBERT J. GANS

Of the many changes that have taken place in America since World War II, one of the most important, and certainly the most visible, has been the migration of the white middle class from the city to the suburbs. Every American city, large and small, is now ringed by suburban subdivisions of varying sizes and price levels, and where once farmers raised fruits and vegetables for city tables, young families are now raising children.

Much has been written about the suburban exodus, and much of that has been critical. Journalists, essayists, social workers, psychologists, and psychiatrists have argued that the departure from the city, and suburban life itself, have had undesirable effects on the people involved and on the larger society. The critics have suggested that suburbia is one of the slayers of traditional American individualism, that it has made people more conforming and other-directed. They have argued that there is too much socializing, useless hyperactivity in voluntary associations, competition, and conspicuous consumption. Many of these evils are thought to be the result of boredom produced by the demographic homogeneity of suburban life, and by the loss of the stimulation associated with city life. The critics have also described a matriarchy and child-dominated society, resulting from the lack of job opportunities within the average suburb and the husband's consequent absence from the home during the children's waking hours. More recently, a psychiatrist has argued that the suburban way of life is a product of excessive social mobility and is so full of stress that it increases psychosomatic illness, divorce, alcoholism, suicide attempts, and mental illness generally.[1] In short, suburbia is thought to be a source of negative effects in American life.

Although the concept of suburban pathology has entered our folklore, empirical studies of people who have moved from city to suburb suggests that the concept is false, that it is a myth rather than a fact. This paper attempts to describe the actual effects of the move, and to consider the implications these create for city planners, social planners, and the professions which Erich Lindemann has aptly described as caretakers.

Effects of the Move from City to Suburb

The effects of suburban life can best be determined through an investigation of behavior changes which people undergo after the move. A number of sociological studies have now been made of this topic.[2] My own analysis will be based primarily on preliminary conclusions from my own research among people who moved from Philadelphia and other nearby cities to a new suburban community of low-priced single-family homes.* My findings are similar to those of Berger's study of factory workers who moved from Richmond, California, to a suburban tract in Milpitas; and to Willmott's study of London slum dwellers who moved to Dagenham, a quasi-suburban municipal housing estate. These studies suggest the following conclusions:

1. For the vast majority of city dwellers, the move to the suburb results in relatively few, and for the most part, minor changes in the way of life. As one respondent explained: "I don't know how a new house changes your life. You have a pattern you go by, and that stays the same no matter where you live."

2. The most frequently reported changes that do take place are not caused by the move to the suburb, but are reasons for moving there in the first place. These reasons are based on aspirations for ownership of a single-family house that are today satisfied only in suburbia.

* This study is still in process. It includes a two-year participant observation analysis of the evolution of the new community, a mail questionnaire to determine population characteristics and aspirations before occupancy, and panel interviews with a sample of residents just after, and two to three years after the move to determine behavior changes. Interviews were also conducted with a special sample of fifty city dwellers two years after the move. The research is being supported by the Institute for Urban Studies, University of Pennsylvania. The mail questionnaire has been aided by grants from the National Institute of Mental Health (M-2866A) and the Social Science Research Council; the interviewing program, by a grant from the American Philosophical Society. Work on the manuscript has been supported by Penjerdel (Pennsylvania-New Jersey-Delaware Metropolitan Project, Inc.).

These aspirations have not been created by the suburbs, however, and are therefore not effects of the move.

3. A few changes in behavior can be traced to life in the suburb itself, independent from aspirations people held before they moved. Some of these can therefore be designated as effects of the move. Most of the changes are positive in nature, but a few result in problems that require solutions.

4. Most of the effects described by the myth of suburbia either can be traced to factors other than the move to suburbia, or do not take place at all.

Each of these conclusions will now be discussed in further detail. The studies I have cited are in agreement that people's lives are not changed drastically by the move to the suburb. Berger found, for example, that factory workers continued to maintain their working-class styles when they became homeowners, and showed no interest in adopting the patterns of social life, religious activity, voting behavior, status-striving, or class mobility predicted by the suburban myth. My own study reached the same conclusions about a more middle-class population. These two studies are based on interviews with people about two years after the move to the suburbs. The same results have been obtained by Willmott's study, however, which indicated that after twenty to forty years of life in Dagenham the residents maintained most of the working-class ways of life that they had pursued in the slums from which they came.

My own research asked people specifically what changes they had experienced as a result of the move. Although the analysis of these interviews is still in process, a preliminary review of the data suggests the following changes as most important: the satisfactions of a new home and of home ownership, the availability of more living space, increased social life, somewhat greater organizational participation, and the development of family and community financial problems. Adolescents and culturally deviant people experience some social isolation, and adaptation problems.

Most of these changes fall into the second category mentioned above: they are the results of pre-occupancy aspirations, rather than the effects of the suburb. Thus, the changes reported most often derive from owning a home, and having more space inside and outside the house. Home ownership gives people the feeling of having an equity—or sharing it with the bank—more privacy from neighbors than they had either in apartments or Philadelphia row-houses, and an opportunity to improve the house and yard in their own, individual way. This not only satisfies desires for self-expression and creativity, but for joint family activity around the house that brings the family closer together. The house is also a locale for the relaxation that many working- and lower middle-class Americans derive from "puttering" and "tinkering." The increased living space which people have obtained as a result of their move permits adults and children to get out of each other's way more easily than before, and this in turn reduces family conflict.

The crucial change here is that of house type, rather than community: from the rented apartment or row-house to the single-family house. Since the opportunity for home ownership is by and large available only in the suburb, at least for new houses in the low and medium price ranges, this is primarily why young families move from the city to the suburb. Even so, I suspect similar changes would be reported by people who move from an apartment to a house within the city limits, or within the suburbs.

Other frequently mentioned changes are an increase in social life and in organizational activity. These have been reported in many new suburbs, and can be traced to the newness of the communities, rather than to the fact that they are suburban. Moving into a new community creates an initial feeling of cohesion and universal friendliness, especially if there are shared problems. These feelings may disappear as people settle down, the novelty of the community wears off, and class and other cultural differences make themselves felt. Even so, there is probably more social life among suburbanites than among city dwellers of equal age and socio-economic level. There are several reasons for this difference. First, many people move to the suburbs with the hope of making new friends, and those that come with this purpose are able to do so. For example, the interviews I conducted six to nine months after the move show that 23 out of 55 couples wanted to do more visiting with other couples and 83 per cent achieved their wish. (These interviews were conducted among a random sample of *all* residents, not just ex-city dwellers, but among the 13 ex-city dwellers in this sample, the 5 who wanted to do more visiting in their new home all achieved their aim.) Also, there are many people of similar age and with similar interests, and many opportunities to meet them. And finally, a new house encourages entertaining, while the absence of movies and restaurants in a new community discourages other forms of diversion.

The increase in community activity can also be attributed to the newness of the community. A new suburb usually lacks the basic church and voluntary organizations which residents need. Consequently, even people who have never been active before and had no intention of becoming so find themselves helping to start organization in their new community. Once the organization is safely under way, they drop out, and eventually the typical pattern develops, in which a small number of people are active in many organizations and the large majority are inactive.

The remaining changes listed earlier can be attributed to the move itself, and are thus an effect of suburban life. Probably the most important one—at least in a low price suburb—is the development of family and community financial problems. Since a house is more expensive to keep up than the apartments from which most people come, suburban life adds new expenditures to the family budget. Many of them are unavoidable ones. If they coincide with the increasing expenditures of a growing family, as they usually do, the household budget is often under considerable strain. Since the preponderance of young families also creates new needs for classrooms and teachers, the tax rate is likely to rise at the same time, thus increasing the financial burden even further.

This in turn has a number of other effects, most of them undesirable. Financial problems are a prime cause of marital conflicts, or a new source of discord for couples already saddled with marital difficulties. Moreover, these problems have consequences for the entire community. In American society, private expenditures have traditionally had higher priority than public ones. As the former rise, people try to reduce their financial problems by demanding reductions in public expenditures. This hampers the provision of needed community services, and especially so in a new community. Moreover, political conflicts develop between those who want additional services, and can pay the taxes, and those who want services cut to the bone because they are unwilling or unable to pay for them. Since school expenditures constitute about three-fourths of the local public expenditures, this conflict often focuses around the school and may extend to curriculum questions as well. This problem is typically found in the low and medium price suburbs, especially those which lack industrial taxpayers.

The move to the suburbs also creates behavior changes of a largely negative type for the adolescents and for those who deviate culturally from the majority of their neighbors. Adolescents are perhaps the most enthusiastic city dwellers in our society, since they are frequent users of urban entertainment facilities. Many of them suffer in the move to the low density suburb. Unless they have cars, they cannot easily get to the nearby shopping centers; and if they do go there, the proprietors object because high shopping center rents make adolescent trade unprofitable. As a result, the teen-agers become bored, and may turn to vandalism and miscellaneous mischief to get even with the adults who have inflicted suburbia—or what some teenagers have called "endsville"—on them. Nevertheless, the actual delinquency rate remains low, mainly because the large majority of adolescents are middle-class ones whose life is taken up with school work and friends.

In the community I studied, the cultural minorities were not ethnic or religious groups, but cosmopolite middle- and upper middle-class families, and working-class people. The cosmopolites may move to suburbia because it is easier to raise their children there, but they miss the city's cultural facilities, as well as people with interests similar to their own. Although they become unhappy, their discontent has positive functions for the community. Quite often, they take more part in community activities than they would have in the city or in a more cosmopolite suburb because, like other minorities, they stream to organizations to find friends. Also, they set up civic groups which try to persuade the community to accept their ideas and high standards for education and municipal government. While the cosmopolites generally lack the votes to implement their standards, they are more influential than their numbers, and contribute organizational skill and knowledge to the community. Moreover, their ability to express themselves in the larger community adds to the total set of alternative policies under public discussion, thus improving the quality of the policy-making process.

A second group of cultural deviants is the working-class population from the city. Not only do they feel the economic pinch most severely, but some report that the distance from the city, and the lack of public transportation have cut them off from relatives and old friends. The ones who suffer most are the people who have come directly from neighborhoods in which they grew up, and especially those who cannot make friends in the new community. Since they may lack the social skills and the geographical mobility of the cosmopolites, they cannot defend themselves as easily against social isolation.

It should be noted that the problems of both the cosmopolites and the working-class people result from being in a numerical minority, rather than from suburban residence. They do not suffer from pressures to conform, but from a shortage of like-minded people in their surroundings. Were they to live in communities with more compatible people, many of their problems would disappear.

Most of the changes attributed to suburban life by the myth of suburbia are either insignificant, or not supported by the available evidence. For example, the increase in commuting time seemed, in my study, to be lower than is often thought. Fifty per cent of 400 people responding to a mail questionnaire indicated their journey to work was longer; 37 per cent, that it was now shorter. For the entire sample, the median journey was only thirty-three minutes each way. Among those interviewed, only about 10 per cent reported spending less time with their family, but about 40 per cent reported spending more time than they did in their previous residence. Moreover, 39 per cent of the respondents reported that the family did more things together than in their previous residence. Fifty-nine per cent reported no change, and only one person reported fewer joint activities.

As I noted earlier, most of the joint family activity is stimulated by the new house, and is likely to decrease as its novelty wears off. Nevertheless, two years of observation revealed no evidence that suburban life had any unilaterally harmful effect on either the quality or quantity of family life. The myth-makers' claim that suburbia is creating a new matriarchy in America is not justified either. Women may have greater equality and more influence in the home than their mothers and grandmothers, but this is a universal trend in American society, especially among working-class and lower middle-class people.

Maladies such as status-striving, competition, and conformity, which are prominent in the suburban myth, are less so in the actual suburb. My observations suggested that much of what is called competition or status-seeking is really an expression of normal class differences, as seen by those of lower status. Thus, lower income respondents described the way of life of their more affluent neighbors as "showing off," or "trying to keep up with the Joneses," an interpretation that minimized their resentment over income inequalities. Higher income people had similarly deprecating comments about those behavior patterns of lower income people which differed from their own. At the same time, they ascribed similarities in the ways of life of lower income neighbors to a desire for conformity.

Enforced conformity has often been described as the scourge of suburban life; yet in the community I studied, instances of this were rare. Most people are willing to tolerate differences of behavior that do not affect them personally. The vast majority of suburbanites are therefore free to live as they please, and their frequent reports of having more privacy in the suburbs than they had in the city is one illustration of this freedom. People do conform in such matters as lawn care—and demand it from their neighbors—largely because they share personally in the appearance of the entire street front. Suburbanites also conform by copying each other's ideas in home improvements, but only those which they consider desirable or useful. People who deliberately strive to maximize their prestige, show off status symbols, or resort to conspicuous consumption are usually socially marginal types who have difficulty in relating to other people. Their neighbors feel sorry for them even while they criticize them. Such strivers are few in number.

Finally, there is no reason to believe that the move from the city to suburb, or suburban life itself, has any effect on mental health, other than a positive one. Most interview respondents report improvements in health and disposition. The number of crimes, suicide attempts, serious delinquent acts, and cases of mental illness, as noticed by doctors and ministers, are comparatively few in the community I studied; and if translated into rates, far below those reported for city inhabitants. Since the suburbs lack the lower class populations which account for the majority of such pathologies, this is not surprising. I was able to get information about many of the people whose behavior suggested serious mental illness; and in almost every case, they had histories of similar disturbance in previous residences. Some of them moved to the suburb I studied in the false hope that the newness of the community and the change of environment would solve their problems.

Nor does the move to the suburbs lead to increased boredom and loneliness. Most people find that the house, the yard, and the increased social life leave them less time to be bored—in fact, less spare time generally—than life in a city apartment. For example, 40 per cent of fifty-five ex-Philadelphians interviewed on this question said they had never been bored, either in the city or in the suburb. Of the twenty-three who said they were sometimes bored, 9 reported no change, 8 were less bored in the suburb, and 6, more. These were mainly women, but the reasons for their boredom have little to do with the community. It was the result of the children growing up and needing them less, of husbands whose work kept them away from home too much, or of anxieties brought on by economic and marital problems.

This analysis may be summarized as follows. The move from city to suburb creates relatively few changes in behavior. Most of these, representing the achievement of aspirations held prior to the move, can be described as *intended* changes. They are effects not of suburban life, but of the larger cultural milieu in which people form their aspirations. This milieu has traditionally stressed the desirability of home ownership, and life in a single-family house. Since most of the intended changes stem from the change in house type, rather than the change in settlement type, the move to the suburb may be considered as the most recent form of a traditional aspiration.

A number of behavior changes which took place after people moved to the suburbs had nothing to do with pre-occupancy aspirations or contradicted them. They may be described as *unintended* changes. Some of them result from the newness of the community, but others can be traced to one or another aspect of suburban life. Economic problems, and the difficulties of the adolescents, are two examples. These, then, can be considered as effects of suburban life, although even they are not entirely caused by suburbia. But most of the effects which have been attributed to the suburb by the myth of suburbia are not supported by empirical evidence.

Why then, does the myth exist? By far the most important reason for its existence is the fact that, since World War II, many people have been able to raise their standards of living, and adopt styles of consumption previously available to the upper middle class only. One part of this change has been the move to the suburbs. Since the post-war subdivisions are a new phenomenon and a highly visible one, the ways of life which have been observed there have been attributed to the community, rather than to the age and class position of the people involved.

Most of the people who have written about suburbia come—like other writers—from the cosmopolite upper middle class. Their criticism of suburban life is actually directed at working- and lower middle-class, non-cosmopolite ways, which can be found in most city neighborhoods as well, but are not as visible there as they are in suburbia. For example, the suburbanites are criticized for turning their back on the city's cultural facilities, but what little evidence exists on the use of such facilities suggested that they are avoided by working- and lower middle-class people who live in the city as well. In short, the myth of suburbia is an implicit criticism of the non-cosmopolite nature of the working class and lower middle class, and is only a contemporary variation on a theme that has been prominent in American critical writing for many decades. The major innovation—and one that must be considered undesirable—is for the critic to invoke concepts of mental health and illness, and thus to identify as pathological what is in reality mainly a difference of class cultures between him and those he criticizes.

Implications for Physical and Social Planning

My analysis of the alleged and real effects of suburbia has a number of implications for social theory, for city or physical planning, for social planning, and for the caretaking professions.

With respect to social theory, the fact that people's lives are not changed drastically by the move from city to suburb suggests that the differences between these settlement types are either fewer, or, more likely, less relevant to the way people live than has been traditionally believed. In short, the community itself does not shape people's ways of life as significantly as has been proposed by ecological and planning theory. The major behavior patterns are determined, rather, by the period of the life-cycle, and the opportunities and aspirations associated with class position.

At one time in American history, the local community did shape the processes that determine ways of life. When the country was rural, income, education, and occupational opportunity were determined within a small area. Today, however, many patterns of life are determined by national economic and social structures, and given the ease of geographical mobility, the community has become less important.

Physical planners, especially those with architectural training, believe that the physical characteristics of the community have important influences on people's ways of living, and that changes in housing and site design, density of structures and amount of open space can change their behavior. The findings I have reported here, and other studies of the impact of physical features on behavior, suggest that this belief is open to serious question.[3] It fails to recognize some of the more important, but non-physical, causes of human behavior. For example, the planners who aim to eliminate urban sprawl—the discontinuous spreading of suburban subdivisions over the rural landscape—and who also wish people to make greater use of the city's downtown districts, have usually proposed that suburbanites move into urban elevator apartments, or into row-house neighborhoods closer to the edge of the city. It is not at all certain that this will solve the problem. Most of the suburbanites I interviewed have little interest in using downtown facilities, and would not move into the city or closer to it for the sake of shortening the journey to work and the wife's monthly or semi-monthly trip to the department store. Urban sprawl and the decline of the downtown can be halted only if more people want to make greater use of the city. These goals cannot be achieved solely by physical design, or even by mass transportation schemes; they require the development of cosmopolite interests among people. This in turn requires—among other things—changes in the education offered in public high schools and most colleges.

Ways of life are determined principally by economic and social conditions, not by architectural schemes. This means that future suburban planning must place greater emphasis on the problems of the suburban population, and this in turn requires the use of social planning methods that involve changes in the social, economic and political structure of our society, and in the programming of public services and caretaking functions.

Despite the generally positive effect of the suburban move, suburban residents have their share of problems. These problems are neither as sensational nor as distinctive to suburbia as the mythmakers have suggested, however. They are old and familiar ones that exist in the city as well, and have not yet been solved there—or wherever people may live.

Perhaps the most important problems are located in the family, both in the marital relationship and among the children. As I have already suggested, ex-city residents find family life improved after the move to the suburbs, but couples who had marital problems in the city have them in the suburbs too. These are familiar difficulties, brought about by sexual or cultural incompatibility, personality clashes, and emotional disturbances in one or both of the spouses. The children's problems are also familiar ones; for example, learning difficulties, serious emotional disturbances, conflicts over discipline with parents and teachers, as well as organic impairment and retardation.

One of the major causes of marital problems, in the suburbs as elsewhere, is economic. In many cases, it is not the lack of money per se which causes problems, since there is usually enough for the basic needs. The conflicts result from disagreement about the allocation of money for items other than food and shelter, and often reflect cultural differences and blocked communication between the spouses. Even so, there are also people for whom the problem is first and foremost financial; who could not really afford to move to the suburbs but have done so nevertheless. It would be arrogant—and useless—to recommend that they go back to the aging apartment buildings or crowded city neighborhoods from which they came. The only real solution is an economic one. Our society may be wealthy compared to others, but families who try to raise three children on $6000 a year are hardly affluent. In the short run, housing subsidies will help, but in the long run, further increases in real income are necessary. These—as well as changes in the tax structure—will subsequently reduce the financial difficulties of suburban municipalities.

My study supports previous findings that unhappy suburbanites are more likely to be women than men. For the latter, the suburb is a peaceful retreat from the city and the job. Most of the women are also content there. The wives of traveling salesmen, airplane pilots, and of other men whose work takes them out of the house for days or weeks on end are probably most unhappy. Many of the marital problems in the community I studied were found among such families. Their problem is not a suburban one, and indeed, the women seem to feel less isolated in the suburb than they did in their previous residence.

A less serious but numerically more important problem is that of the women who want to be more than housekeepers and mothers, especially among those who have gone to college. Some have solved this problem by taking part-time jobs, or by finding satisfying unpaid work in voluntary organizations and community service, meanwhile sending their children to nursery schools or day-care centers. Their problem is not unique to suburbia, and it is likely to become more widespread as larger numbers of women obtain college educations.

Adolescents, as I have already noted, face problems in suburbia, because they lack the after-school facilities that are available to them in the city. If these cannot be supplied commercially, they will have to be made available from public resources, with care being taken that they are programmed on the basis of adolescent needs, rather than by adult desires. This is more easily said than done. Adults have reacted quite negatively to the development of the adolescent youth culture that has developed in America, as elsewhere, over the past two decades. Many adults, especially in the working and lower middle classes, stereotype all teenagers as delinquents. As a result, community leaders are hesitant about providing them with recreational facilities for fear that gang fights, sexual episodes, and other forms of misbehavior will upset the voters and cause them to blame the public officials.

The problems of bored middle-class adolescents are much less serious than those of working-class and lower-class ones. As Paul Goodman and others have noted, our society provides no function for the teen-ager who does not want to remain in school. This problem, which has nothing to do with the suburbs, is exacerbated in middle-class suburbs by the fact that such teenagers are a hostile and unhappy minority in a predominantly middle-class environment.

Finally, another group who suffer in the suburbs—as they do everywhere—are people who differ too greatly from their neighbors and other residents, and are therefore socially isolated. As I noted earlier, in the community I studied, this affected primarily the cosmopolite minority, and working-class women. The former can fend for themselves, and eventually move to a community of more compatible people. In this process, however, the original community loses their participation in civic problem-solving activities. I am frankly uncertain whether or not this is a serious loss in a working-class or lower middle-class community. While upper middle-class people have the intellectual and administrative skills I described earlier, they also tend to see community problems—and their solutions—from an upper middle-class perspective, and they are often blind to the problems faced by the other classes. This question urgently requires empirical research.

Working-class women—as well as their families—who are in a minority in the neighborhood cannot solve their isolation problem as easily as others, especially those who have difficulty in entering into new roles. They might be better off if they remained in their old neighborhoods in the city, or if they moved into the modern dwellings being made available there by urban renewal projects in their price range.

I have tried to describe what appear to be the major problems of suburban residents, especially in low and medium priced communities. Few are distinctive to suburbia, and they bear little resemblance to those described in the myth of suburbia. The problems aired by the myth-makers are principally those of their suburban cosmopolite friends, and of the upper middle class generally.

Needless to say, most suburbanites are not cosmopolites; they are people who lived in the city more from necessity than from choice. Thanks to the FHA, the suburbs have made it possible for them to achieve much of what they want out of life, although the suburban exodus has in turn raised yet unsolved problems in metropolitan government, such as the financing of public services, which I have not discussed here.

Because suburbanites are above average in education, income, and many other characteristics—even in a lower middle-class suburb—their life is comparatively problem-free, and the problems I have listed are much less serious than those of less fortunate Americans. Indeed, the most critical problems in American society are to be found among the people who cannot move to the suburbs, who are doomed to a deprived existence in urban and rural slums because of low income, lack of occupational skill, and racial discrimination. Their needs take precedence over all of the problems I have described here.

References

1. Gordon, R. E., Gordon, K. K., and Gunther, M., *The Split-Level Trap*, New York: Dell, 1962.

2. See, for example, Berger, B. M., *Working Class Suburb*, Berkeley: Univ. of California Press, 1960, and Willmott, P., *Evolution of a Community*, London: Routledge and Kegan Paul, 1963. For some other studies of the move in England, see: Young, M., and Willmott, P., *Family and Kinship in East London*, Glencoe, Ill.: The Free Press, 1957; Willmott, P., and Young, M., *Family and Class in a London Suburb*, New York: Humanities Press, 1960; Mogey, J., *Family and Neighbourhood*, New York: Oxford Univ. Press, 1956; Mogey, J., and Morris, R., "Causes of Change in Family Role Patterns," *Bull. Res. Center on Fam. Devel.*, 1:1-9, 1960; and Hole, V., "Social Effects of Planned Rehousing," *Town Planning Rev.*, 30:161-173, 1959.
3. Rosow, I., "Social Effects of the Physical Environment," *J. Amer. Inst. Planners*, 27:127-133, 1961.

PART THREE

Social Action-and Reaction

This section continues, in depth, the exploration of slums, public housing, poverty, and mental ill-health. The first paper, by Robert Connery, illustrates dramatically, through a description of the administrative mazes of three types of metropolitan area, the tangled web of local government that makes so difficult a concerted onslaught on mental disease.

The next three papers are curiously interrelated. Two of them, those by Wilner and Hollingshead, present contrasting reports of attitudes toward slums and public housing, in Puerto Rico and in Baltimore; and the third, by Ellen Lurie, deals with problems of organization and action among residents of a slum-cum-public-housing district in New York City. It is apparent in all three that public housing itself creates resistances that reflect the unresolved conflict between the middle-class attitudes of the housing authorities and the culture of the slum dwellers themselves. In some ways, these three papers hark back to Ryan and Fried; and the East Harlem paper also points ahead to the position that Poston will state in the following section.

Another study by Bruce Dohrenwend shows the effects of ethnic and status environments on the perception of mental disturbance and on the judgment of its significance. This is followed by a discussion by Thomas Gladwin of lower-class delinquency with a suggestion for a change of strategy in relieving some of the pressures that produce it.

Harold Isaacs' powerful statement of the Negro's drive for a new identity continues the themes of poverty and social frustration, and of differences in ethnic cultures and values. The eruption of the new African states clearly complicates the Negro's choice of identities and his strategies for attaining "somebodiness."

In the final paper of this section, the levels and varieties of poverty, with their consequences and implications, are discussed in the light of the possibility of a total social attack on them: delinquency, minority attitudes, alcoholism, and others. A fresh look reveals that these are—as one of the boys says in *West Side Story*—"social" diseases, calling for a reappraisal of our society, our information, and ourselves.

15 Metropolitan Barriers to Mental Health Services

ROBERT H. CONNERY

Today we are witnessing a tremendous movement of population from the rural countryside into urban areas. This is not only true in the United States and Western Europe but also in Africa, Asia, and Latin America. To be sure, underdeveloped countries may have only 10 to 20 per cent of their population living in urban centers in contrast with almost two-thirds of the population in the United States. But from Moscow, Tokyo, and Johannesburg to Jakarta, Karachi, and Lagos, the world's rural population is on the move toward the bright lights, the excitement, and economic opportunities of the cities.

To understand the mental health implications of this movement in the United States, it is important to define what is meant by urban centers. Particularly a distinction should be drawn between a "city," which is a legal entity, and terms like urban center, urban sprawl, or urban complex. These are sociological terms which may mean a single city but more frequently identify a group of governmental units and even some unincorporated areas which are densely settled.

The term most frequently applied to these urban centers in the United States is the Census Bureau phrase "metropolitan area." In brief, this is a county which contains at least one city of 50,000 or more inhabitants. In addition, contiguous counties are included if they are essentially urban in character. There are some 200 such "metropolitan areas" in the United States. Unsatisfactory as this term sometimes is, because it uses counties as its basis, and thus may include rural as well as urban areas, it is difficult to find a better one. In the 1960 census the Census Bureau used a new term, "urbanized area," which can be characterized as the physical city as distinguished both from the legal city and the metropolitan community. Its boundaries are determined by the pattern of urban growth. It represents the thickly settled core of the metropolitan area.

Metropolitan communities are not legal entities as such, and thus have no recognized status in the governmental apparatus. In a single metropolitan community there may be hundreds of municipal corporations, cities, towns, and villages, but the community as a whole does not exist as a governmental unit. Though metropolitan communities are the pattern of American life, it is a pattern without legal recognition; and community problems of health, welfare, and recreation at the local level are fragmented among many units of government.

There is also a lack of personal identification with a metropolitan complex. In a real sense Gertrude Stein's line, "There is no there there," applies with startling directness to a metropolitan area. There usually is a certain degree of identification with one's own neighborhood—even of loyalty to an individual town or city in a metropolitan complex—but there is no loyalty to the metropolitan area as a whole. Thus the achievement of a solution to the problems of metropolitan areas is handicapped by the fact that these areas are not even symbols that attract men.

When one attempts to build a metropolitan model, one is faced immediately with the problem of great variation among metropolitan communities in size of land area, in population, and in number of government units. The largest is the New York-Northern New Jersey complex, covering parts of two states, with a population of some 15 million people, and including 1700 separate government jurisdictions.[1] The smallest is Meriden, Connecticut, with 51,000, and the next is San Angelo, Texas, with 64,000 population.

Nevertheless, metropolitan areas seem to fall into three groups. The first would be made up of isolated central cities of 50,000 or more inhabitants surrounded by unincorporated urban settlements. This is the oldest type, and is still common in much of the South and in the Plains and Mountain States. The second type consists of a central city surrounded by a number of suburbs incorporated as cities, towns, and villages. This type is common in the Midwest and far West, and for that matter it is fairly common throughout the country with the exception of the Northeast. The third and most recent type consists of clusters of great cities that form a continuous pattern of dense urban settlements, as on the Northeastern seaboard. These are the strip cities of the modern metropolis.

Many metropolitan communities extend beyond the jurisdiction of a single state. From New York and Philadelphia on the East coast to Chicago and Cincinnati in the Midwest, nearly fifty metropolitan communities extend across state boundary lines. About one American in every four lives in one of these interstate metropolitan communities.

There are also a number of metropolitan communities that lie athwart international boundaries. The Detroit-Windsor, the Buffalo, and the Seattle-Tacoma areas on the Canadian border are already well-developed international communities. The entire Rio Grande Valley, the San Diego area, and the Great Lakes-St. Lawrence River region all give promise of rapid urban development. Already sewage disposal, water supply, air pollution, and transportation have become problems demanding attention and solution. Neither the local communities themselves nor the individual states acting alone can deal adequately with these problems.

A pilot study, covering excellent examples of each of the three types of metropolitan area—the Philadelphia-Camden area, the New Orleans area, and the five metropolitan communities of the North Carolina Piedmont Crescent, was made last spring by the Institute of Public Administration in New York City under contract with the National Institute of Mental Health. It illustrates some of the impact upon mental health programs of fragmented government in these areas.[2]

The Philadelphia-Camden area, with a population of 4,342,897 and covering five counties in Pennsylvania and three in New Jersey, was selected because of its size and because it is a northern industrial area. It represents the urban strip community. Philadelphia, its center city, is one of the nation's oldest urban centers and has long been noted for its excellent medical facilities. The suburban counties include wealthy residential centers as well as industrial ones. And the area straddles an interstate boundary and thus includes parts of two states, Pennsylvania and New Jersey, a pattern common in many metropolitan areas. To be sure, the New York-New Jersey metropolitan area is larger, but its very size makes it unique and impairs its usefulness as a sample of a northern metropolitan area.

New Orleans, with a population of 868,480, was selected as a good example of a metropolitan area of moderate size, representing the single city with incorporated satellites. Located in the South, and within the single state of Louisiana, it includes three counties. The pattern of settlement there has been different from that of the Philadelphia-Camden area, and it offers a wide range of interesting problems—racial, industrial, social, and political.

While there seems to be considerable evidence that the administrative problems of mental health programs in the large metropolitan areas are more complicated than those in small ones, it is also true that a majority of the metropolitan areas reported in the 1960 census are much smaller in population than either Philadelphia-Camden or New Orleans. The median was an area with approximately a quarter of a million people. For this reason, five small metropolitan areas in the North Carolina Piedmont Crescent were studied, although in considerably less detail, and principally for the purpose of testing the findings in administrative relationships that had been made in the larger areas. They are single cities surrounded by unincorporated areas of settlement. These North Carolina metropolitan areas include Charlotte, with a population of 272,111; Greensboro-High Point, with a population of 246,520; Winston-Salem, with a population of 189,428; Raleigh, with a population of 169,082; and Durham, with a population of 111,995. All five are new industrial areas in the South with a substantial percentage of non-whites.

The Philadelphia-Camden Community

There are 726 units of government in the Philadelphia-Camden metropolitan area. These include 140 municipalities, 199 townships, 332 school districts, and 48 special districts. Some of these units are classified according to population as first, second, third, or fourth class, each with different powers of government. This classification can be important because it reflects the amount of power that can be wielded in the health field.

The population is composed primarily of native born whites, but in the last two decades there has been a significant increase in Negro population, particularly in the city of Philadelphia. In 1950 Negroes made up 18.2 per cent of the city's population, in 1960 they constituted 26.7 per cent, and in the next two decades may well increase to over 40 per cent. The 1960 figure of 26.7 per cent in Philadelphia compares with 14 per cent in New York, 22.9 per cent in Chicago,

28.9 per cent in Detroit, and 37.4 per cent in New Orleans. The Puerto Rican population, now estimated at 40,000, is increasing sharply. Except for Camden and Gloucester counties there are few Negroes in the suburban counties.

There has been an increase proportionately in the very young and older groups throughout the metropolitan community, due in part to the rising birth rates and lengthening life span. In the metropolitan area the percentage of the population over sixty-five years of age is 9.1 per cent, a higher percentage than that of New Orleans. Persons under eighteen years of age comprise 33.5 per cent of the population. There is some variation within the area; the city of Philadelphia has fewer young people than do the suburban counties.

The movement of population to the suburbs and the urbanization of the inner ring counties has been a conspicuous phenomenon. Delaware County, for example, has tripled its population in forty years. Philadelphia County—the city of Philadelphia—now has only 46.1 per cent of the metropolitan population, compared to two-thirds of it in 1920. Reliable estimates covering the next two decades indicate that the population in the suburban counties will continue to grow at a much more rapid rate than it will in the central city.

The movement of population towards the suburbs and the increasing number of non-whites in the central city have had certain social consequences. People moving to the suburbs generally belong to a higher income group than those who replace them in the central city. On the other hand, the newcomers in the central city are less well adjusted socially than those who have left. This has meant an increase in juvenile delinquency, increased demands for welfare services, and special educational and recreational programs. It has also meant an increased need for governmental services of all sorts—police, housing, and hospitals. Since the local tax base has changed little, these services can be provided only with increased state or federal aid.

There is also another result. The division between whites in the suburbs and non-whites in the central city has also had a disintegrating effect on the social structure of the whole metropolitan area. As the city becomes more identified with the Negroes and the suburbs more with the whites, the social bonds that unite the whole metropolitan area are strained. To be sure, there have always been economic divisions in the area, but this new division poses another challenge to community integration and to the possibility of cooperation.

Montgomery County is an excellent example of what is happening in a suburban area. The county had a population of 516,682, according to the 1960 census. Twenty years ago it had a population of 289,000. It is estimated that by 1985 there will be over 850,000 people in the county. Extending some forty miles northwest of the city of Philadelphia, it is a wealthy county, the residence of thousands of commuters. But it also has a considerable amount of light industry and scattered heavy industrial plants. The county seat is Norristown.

The most striking feature of the county's government is its fragmentation of functions. Although much of the county is urban, its government is for the most part still that of a rural farming community. In addition to the Montgomery County government, there are 129 other units: 38 townships, 24 boroughs, 62 school districts, and a number of special districts. (Incidentally, Chester County, with the smallest population of any of the five Pennsylvania counties in the Philadelphia area, has the largest number of governmental units. With a population of 210,000, it has 144 government units: 57 townships, 16 boroughs, and 70 school districts. Philadelphia County, with ten times the population of Chester, has a single combined city-county government and one school district.)

There are 33 public health jurisdictions in Montgomery County. Ten of the 12 first-class townships have their own boards of health. Twenty-six second-class townships have no boards of health but are served directly by the State Health Department. There are 24 boroughs, 22 of which have separate boards of health; 2 are served directly by the State Health Department. Thus 10 township health boards, 22 borough health boards, and the State Health Department operate within the same county.

None of these health boards has anything to do with mental health programs. They are concerned solely with sanitation, food inspection, and the prevention of nuisances. Each board appoints a health officer who is usually a part-time employee without professional training either in medicine or public health. The boards, however, are required to have a physician among their members. The health officer's only exposure to mental health problems is in a single short course given by the State Department of Health. A recent survey indicates that few of these local health officers in the state of Pennsylvania have any special qualifications. A majority had not gone beyond high school and the average salary was less than $500 per year. It is dubious whether this group can be educated on mental health problems to a significant extent.

Both Pennsylvania and New Jersey have state health departments, but neither one administers a mental health program. In Pennsylvania, mental health is a division of the Department of Welfare; in New Jersey, mental health is administered by the Department of Institutions and Agencies. In the city of Philadelphia itself, however, mental health is a division of the city health department.

There are a large number of public and private mental health programs under way in the Philadelphia-Camden area. This is probably what one would expect in the light of the long tradition of public service and the excellent medical facilities that exist there. With few exceptions, these programs are of the type that exist in other parts of the country.

In recognition of the need for preventive mental health services, and the trend toward extra-mural care, a substantial number of community mental health clinics have been established. The demand for clinical services is heavy, and there are long waiting lists at most of the clinics. The city of Philadelphia has recently established an alcoholic control center, but there is very little in the way of facilities for alcoholics in the suburban counties. The city of Philadelphia also has an active program for the aged. There are a number of public mental institutions operated by the state government, as well as some general hospitals and many small private hospitals that accept psychiatric patients. A reception center at the Philadelphia General Hospital operates as a screening facility.

The New Orleans Metropolitan Area

The New Orleans metropolitan area differs in a good many ways from the Philadelphia-Camden area, but there are also marked similarities. As defined in the 1960 census, the New Orleans metropolitan community embraced three parishes or counties: Orleans, Jefferson, and St. Bernard. A fourth parish, Plaquemines, stands to be included in the New Orleans metropolitan area in the next ten or twenty years. Each parish has its own governing body.

A great deal of this area is under water, and in much of the remainder water is close to the surface. The most important effect of both surface and subsurface water has been the constriction of the great bulk of the area's population within a relatively small area. Beginning as a small dot on the bend of the Mississippi in the early 1700's, the city spread slowly, following the highest land along the river edge and two high ridges between the river and Lake Pontchartrain. But land was drained very slowly, and even by the 1930's the city had not really reached the lake. Better pumping systems, extensive levees, and a sea wall on the south shore of the lake have facilitated suburban expansion in recent decades.

In Orleans Parish, the rate of population growth since the Civil War has been fairly constant as the city increased from 174,491 in 1860 to 627,525 in 1960. The nature of growth outside of the city has been quite different. Until 1920, population outside the city remained roughly 10 per cent of that within Orleans Parish. But in the decade from 1920 to 1930, population spurted in Jefferson Parish, leveled in the 1930's, and sky-rocketed after World War II. In the postwar period, the population of Jefferson Parish quadrupled from 50,427 in 1940 to 208,769 in 1960. The same pattern of growth occurred in St. Bernard Parish but on a smaller scale. In Plaquemines Parish, growth has been less spectacular. Suburbia is, then, a comparatively recent development in the New Orleans area.

Until recently the bulk of the population was concentrated in Orleans; and thus the metropolitan community problems were largely the problems of Orleans Parish. What was done in Orleans Parish reflected substantially the response of the entire community to its problems. With the growth of population in the surrounding parishes, this situation no longer obtains. Action in Orleans alone may be insufficient to meet a problem, or it may be frustrated by contrary action in an adjoining parish. The efforts of the community to handle gambling after World War II provide a good example; when Orleans "cleaned up," the gamblers simply moved to Jefferson Parish; in 1952 it required the efforts of a U. S. Senate committee to bring pressure in Jefferson to clean up gambling there. But the gamblers have returned. Some 275 federal gambling stamps were issued in Jefferson Parish in 1960.

In short, population growth has made an inter-governmental approach to many community problems imperative. Administrative cooperation between parishes has worked successfully in several areas. But the community has had much less success with political cooperation among the parishes, a point that may prove troublesome in the event a metropolitan approach to mental health problems is attempted.

Two critical age groups, as far as mental health is concerned, are the young and the old. Both are increasing in the metropolitan area, both numerically and proportionately. In Orleans Parish, however, the proportion under five years of age was exactly the same in 1950 as it was in 1900. In the suburbs it has increased rapidly. Conversely, the group over sixty-five has quadrupled in Orleans Parish in the past half century and at about half that rate in the Jefferson Parish. If the above trends persist, the aged will present a much greater mental health problem in Orleans Parish than in Jefferson; conversely, the youth group will become increasingly important in Jefferson.

As the pattern of settlement in the New Orleans metropolitan area becomes more spread out than it is at present, there will be greater commuter problems throughout the area. Population growth also may lessen the "salt and pepper checkerboard" residential pattern in New Orleans where there has been a surprising number of Negroes living next to whites. Industrial development, undoubtedly adversely affected by the school integration situation, will likely depend more and more on outside capital. Such capital, if it comes, may leaven the traditionally conservative business outlook of the community elite to some extent, and may offset a movement away from New Orleans of large corporation and federal government regional offices.

Today few, if any, political leaders in Louisiana are against good mental health *per se*. But mental health is a vague and general thing. In the political arena, mental health tends to get broken down into specific projects and proposals involving particular legal enactments and specified sums of public money. The mental health program then becomes one of selling a particular project to the community, to the legislature, and to the governor. Some types of mental health programs, for example alcoholism, have been difficult to "sell" in Louisiana. Often, as a result, persuasion entails educating public opinion to the necessity of the projects.

In the New Orleans area, with its limited local tax base and its conservative dislike of direct taxation, local public financial support for mental health programs is not easy to obtain. There is a tendency to go to the Legislature and the governor for action. Indeed, the governor has proved to be more important than the legislature, both as an initiator of mental health programs and as one who determines the amount of annual expenditures. Louisiana has an executive budget, and items that are not included in the governor's budget in the first instance stand little chance of adoption. This makes effective liaison with the governor's office essential. Even if a proposed appropriation is included in the executive budget, it will undoubtedly have to be defended against competing claims for funds for other purposes.

The metropolitan area must face another problem. Legislators may be willing to build the hospital or the clinic, but frequently, because of pressure from other parts of the state, not in the metropolitan area where it is most needed. Also, legislators would rather spend money to build nice edifices than to provide better services.

Metropolitan Communities of the North Carolina Crescent

The five metropolitan communities located in the North Carolina Piedmont—Charlotte, Greensboro-High Point, Winston-Salem, Durham, and Raleigh—are in many ways similar to metropolitan communities in other parts of the country. But they also are different in significant ways. In the past, Southern cities did not grow as fast as those in other parts of the country. Today, however, the process has been dramatically reversed. Southern cities are growing twice as fast as those of the nation as a whole. Moreover, the decline in rural population in the South since 1940, while part of a national tendency, is a much more definite trend than that of the nation as a whole. There have been radical changes in racial patterns. While both whites and Negroes have been moving away from the farms, more of the whites have been moving into Southern cities than have the Negroes. Thus for the region as a whole, the growing urban white population compensates for the rural white losses. On the other hand, a substantial percentage of Negroes are leaving the South for northern areas, shifting the nation's Negro population from the South to other regions at the rate of about 1 per cent per year. Thus the South, while continuing its traditional role of exporting people, has shifted the racial character of its export to such a degree that today the overwhelming portion of it is Negro.

Unlike the large metropolitan areas in other parts of the country, the five metropolitan areas in the North Carolina Crescent each comprise but a single county. These Piedmont areas also differ from larger metropolitan areas in that they have few incorporated suburbs. Indeed, the amount of urbanized area outside the central cities is quite limited. All of the urbanized area of Raleigh, for instance, is within the city's corporate limits. The Piedmont Crescent metropolitan areas are also distinctive in that they have few governmental units. Raleigh, with the largest number, has sixteen county, municipal, special districts, and school systems; while Durham, with the least, has only four. The Philadelphia area, in contrast, has 726 governmental units. Even when one allows for the difference in population, the Philadelphia-Camden area has four times as many units of government as does Durham.

The Impact of "Multiple Sovereignty" on Mental Health Service

Health officers, Mental Health Association personnel, and community leaders of all types in Philadelphia-Camden, New Orleans, and North Carolina agreed that there were serious unmet mental health needs in the metropolitan communities. Although these varied in specifics from one community to another, there was agreement upon major goals. Mental hospitals are too big and they have too many patients. Special facilities for children and young adults exist but are inadequate. Liaison between mental hospitals and community facilities is far from satisfactory. Halfway houses, night hospitals, day hospitals, and after-care clinics, where they do exist, are not integrated into hospital-community programs. School mental health programs frequently lack trained personnel. Family programs involving parents in group therapy concerning parent-child relationships are in their infancy. Programs for the aged are still too much on the individual rather than the community basis. Minority groups, such as the Negroes and the poor white mill workers, are not reached by community programs, nor are facilities available to these groups in proportion to their numbers or their needs. All of these are problems that most mental health administrators would admit are widely prevalent.

The question that concerns this paper, however, is the extent to which the political and administrative structure of metropolitan communities helps or handicaps mental health programs. Posing the question does not necessarily mean that an easy solution can be found. Indeed there is scant reason to suppose that one best method can be developed which will meet the needs of all metropolitan communities. It should be emphasized again that there are at least three broad patterns of metropolitan development and many individual variations.

One effect of local government jurisdictions which rest upon area, in a rigid pattern which has little relation to actual community units, is that adequate planning is difficult. Moreover, this fragmentation of government leads to units too small to make or carry out sound decisions upon mental health programs. On the other hand, the metropolitan area as a whole may be too big. Neighborhoods have a vital role to play in maintaining sound mental health. "State plans" covering a two-year period are submitted by the states to federal agencies each year. There seems to be no question that they constitute a good administrative plan of action within the terms of funds available, but one may question whether these plans are adequate in terms of broad community needs.

In interstate communities such as Philadelphia and Camden, the state boundary is an iron curtain which cuts through the middle of the metropolitan area. In one sense it is not too much to say that the two portions of the area lie back to back; Pennsylvania looks towards Harrisburg and New Jersey towards Trenton. Even voluntary agencies are organized along state lines. While this division, at the moment, may not be as important as the internal division within each state, it causes some difficulties.

Health and Welfare Councils have been the major community planning agencies. Concerned with health in all its aspects, these would seem to offer an excellent means of integrating government health programs with voluntary efforts. And to a certain extent these councils, where they exist, have been successful. For example, they have made a number of excellent county surveys in the Philadelphia area. But they are not continuous planning agencies, and they have not been able to break out of the limits imposed by rigid governmental units.

There is a statewide plan in Louisiana, but it is little more than a statement of goals for the state rather than for the metropolitan area. Lacking a comprehensive metropolitan plan, mental health groups focus their efforts on obtaining a specific facility such as a school in New Orleans for the mentally retarded. This one-step-at-a-time procedure, although tactically successful, does not provide any real measure of community needs.

Public health organization is tied to government organization. Public health programs in a large portion of the metropolitan areas studied are handled by elected boards, and services are provided by untrained health officers. Fully one-third of the population in the Philadelphia-Camden metropolitan area is served by these township or borough boards, the common administrative pattern throughout the state of Pennsylvania. There is no evidence whatsoever that these agencies could administer an effective mental health program. Another one-third have minimal public health services provided by the state. The remaining one-third of the population, who live in Bucks and Philadelphia counties, is served by professional county health departments. But in the whole state of Pennsylvania there are only four counties, Bucks, Philadelphia, Allegheny, and Erie, which have county health departments.

Organizing children's health programs around public school systems also reflects the fragmentation of local government. Not all the children in a metropolitan community attend public schools, but even more important, the level of services in small school districts leaves much to be desired. As a result, early identification of children needing treatment is spotty and inefficient.

Most states restrict the amount of taxes that can be levied by cities, counties, and other local units of government. This fact, taken together with the rising cost of ordinary governmental services, makes the financing of new programs difficult. Thus local pressure groups turn to the state for assistance not only in opening mental health clinics but in their continued support.

Transferring mental health activities from local units of government to the state simply opens up a new host of inter-governmental problems. If education, welfare, and public health are still administered locally, how can mental health activities under state direction best be integrated with them? If mental health is made primarily a state function, how can it be integrated with other state activities? Should it be established as a separate department of the state government, or joined with public health, the state university, or some other state department? All of these arrangements have been tried, but which is the most efficient?

Indeed one may well ask how *are* decisions about public undertakings made in metropolitan communities? Who determines the priorities between the competing claims of health, housing, and transportation programs for the limited resourses which are available? Far too little is known about how decisions are made in mental health programs, and even less in the context of metropolitan communities.

The metropolis potentially offers greater abundance, more residential space, and a fuller cultural life than any previous pattern of urban living; but it also presents a major challenge to man's ingenuity. Can he create a political organization flexible enough to adapt itself to metropolitan community needs? Can he reorganize the present fragmented political structure so that it will serve the needs of today's social structure? This is the challenge posed by the modern metropolis.

References

1. For a recent and exhaustive study of this area see Vernon, R., ed., *New York Metropolitan Region Study,* 9 vols., published under the names of individual authors, Cambridge, Mass.: Harvard Univ. Press, 1960. See also Gottmann, J., *Megalopolis: The Urbanized Northeastern Seaboard of the United States,* New York: Twentieth Century Fund, 1960.
2. Connery, R. H., Deener, D. R., and Swanson, B. E., *Mental Health in Metropolitan Areas: A Pilot Study,* New York: Institute of Public Administration, 1961.

Effects of Housing on Health and Performance 16

DANIEL M. WILNER
ROSABELLE PRICE WALKLEY

The first part of this paper presents a brief review of forty studies which have investigated the relationship that housing bears to physical and social pathology. This review serves as the backdrop for the second part of the paper, which is essentially a summary of a study of the effects of housing on physical and mental health, conducted at The Johns Hopkins University.*

Review of Forty Selected Studies

The researches reviewed constitute a sample of studies relating to housing quality, variously measured or defined, and various physical and social aberrations. The sample is not exhaustive. The main principle of selection was that the study should present first-hand analysis by the author(s), whether of field data or of previously collected census and health data. General speculative and hortatory works based on previously obtained analytic *results* were excluded. Most of the studies have been published since World War II.

Major Orientations Of the forty investigations reviewed,† sixteen were of European origin and twenty-four were of American origin. Of the European studies, fifteen dealt with housing in British cities‡ and one with housing in Copenhagen. The American studies dealt with housing in the United States and Hawaii.§

* The study staff members responsible for the research held appointments in the School of Hygiene and Public Health, The Johns Hopkins University, in the period 1954-1960. The investigation was supported by a research grant from the National Institutes of Health, Public Health Service, United States Department of Health, Education, and Welfare.

† See bibliography for the complete list of studies.

‡ British cities included London (3), the borough of Islington (6), towns in Hertfordshire (22) and Northamptonshire (23), Glasgow (24, 30 and 40), Oxford (26), Newcastle-upon-Tyne (38), Edinburgh (39), etc.

§ American cities in specific studies include New Haven (2), Cincinnati (4),

Twenty-four reports (fourteen European and ten American) were concerned with the relationship between housing and health. There was some concentration on the relationship between housing and tuberculosis, but a number of other topics also were covered in the various studies: general morbidity rates, death rates, birth rates, infant morbidity, respiratory disease, accident rates, etc. Sixteen reports (fourteen American and two European) dealt with social and psychological matters, with a clustering, in the American studies, on juvenile delinquency.

The forty studies used various discrete and non-discrete measures of housing quality. Approximately one-third relied solely on the criterion of crowding; another third introduced one or more additional variables such as dilapidation, toilet facilities, rental, etc.; the remainder used crude scales based on raters' judgments or contrasted public and slum housing without introducing specific measurements.

In a small number of the studies, housing itself was the variable of focus, and an attempt was made to relate housing to a fairly extensive range of dependent factors. However, a majority of the studies not only concentrated on a single dependent variable, but also, this variable constituted the primary focus of interest and its relationship to housing was sought as a possible etiological factor.

General Findings In all, twenty-six of the forty studies, both English and American, showed *positive* association between housing and health, or housing and social adjustment. In other words, poor housing tended to go with poor health and adjustment, better housing with better health and adjustment. Eleven seemed *ambiguous* as to outcome or showed *no relationship* between housing and the dependent variable. Only three studies showed actual *negative* findings. These were studies dealing with tuberculosis (23), with death rates (25), and with mental hospital admissions (22). (See Bibliography.)

Isolating the Effects of Housing, per se To say that two sets of measures are related is, of course, not the same as demonstrating the causal direction and strength of the effect. The problems of interpretation in such cases are well known, and have their counterpart in

---

Minneapolis (10), Hammond, East Chicago and Gary, Indiana (13), Birmingham, Alabama (16), Baltimore (18, 19), Boston (20), New York (21), Newark, New Jersey (31), Chicago (36), etc. Several studies presented data on a number of cities (35, 7, 8, 9).

a wide variety of cross-sectional epidemiologic studies relating diseases and their possible etiologic agents. In the instance of housing, a source of difficulty is the fact that housing itself is related to a number of personal characteristics of the inhabitants, e.g., education, income, cultural level, and the utilization of medical facilities.

The Possibilities of Statistical Control Where the study design permits, and when sufficient demographic information has been collected regarding persons and families, it is possible even in the cross-sectional study to pursue further the relative influence of housing and various non-housing factors known or suspected to be related to housing.

Only two of the studies reviewed, relying principally on census-type data, exploited to any extent the possibilities of further statistical control of a number of variables. In one, that of Benjamin (3) in London, multiple regression analysis showed that income and crowding were equally good guides to tuberculosis mortality. In the other, that of Lander (19) in Baltimore, investigating the causes of juvenile delinquency, high zero-order correlation of delinquency with several housing variables was found. However, further analysis, holding non-housing factors constant, produced partial correlation coefficients of essentially zero between delinquency and substandard housing or crowding.

The Possibilities of Experimental Control The alternative to the technique of statistical control in the cross-sectional study is the prospective study involving the introduction of some measure of experimental or quasi-experimental control. Ideally, the non-housing variables would be held constant, while housing quality alone was permitted to change. In the researches reviewed, five studies constituted the principal instances of this type of design, in the sense that they directly contrasted public and slum housing. These included studies by M'Gonigle (25) of rehoused families in the English midlands, by Mogey (26) of English workers in Oxford, by Barer (1) of tuberculosis in New Haven, by Rumney (31) of morbidity and delinquency in Newark, and by Chapin (10) of social variables in Minneapolis.

These five studies came closest to approximating research designs permitting unequivocal interpretation of effects. Dependent variables tested were diverse, however; samples were very small; matching on relevant characteristics unfortunately was not always successfully accomplished; and the effect of improved housing was not always determined.

THE JOHNS HOPKINS LONGITUDINAL STUDY

The instigation to undertake further research in this field arose from three principal considerations. First was the general scholarly interest in the effects on behavior of man's physical environment, an environment which in our epoch is, of course, largely of man's own devising. Second, in a more pragmatic vein, was the belief and conviction among social planners and officials in public agencies that improved housing leads to an improvement in health and the amelioration of social ills. A third consideration to some extent bridged the first two. This was the need to gain experience in the conduct of the sort of systematic research on complex social variables that may lead to relatively unequivocal assessment of effects.

In the spring of 1954, a study was undertaken in Baltimore, Maryland, with some of these considerations in mind. The research was stimulated by the Joint Committee on the Hygiene of Housing of the American Public Health Association and the National Association of Housing and Redevelopment Officials. It was conducted by a research group at the School of Hygiene and Public Health of The Johns Hopkins University.

In an effort to provide more conclusive findings than those reviewed above, a nearly classical study design was adopted in this research. It involved two samples, each surveyed eleven times in a period of approximately three years: a *test* group of 300 families (1,341 persons) who had originally lived in the slum but had subsequently moved to a new public housing project; and a *control* sample of 300 families (1,349 persons) who were slated to *remain* in the slum.* These two groups, of 300 each, constituted families

* Originally the test group consisted of approximately 400 families (2000 persons), and the control group of 600 families (3000 persons). Two problems arose which made necessary some adjustment of the two samples before the final analysis of the data began. The first problem was attrition in the samples over time. Such losses were not unexpected, and, in fact, unusually time-consuming measures were used to keep them to a minimum. In the course of ten waves of morbidity and adjustment surveys in the "after" period of the study, the sample loss was approximately 1.3 per cent per wave, or about 13 per cent of

who met two criteria: they missed at most only one or two survey-waves of interviewing, thus taking into account the problem of attrition, and they did not markedly change the quality of their housing during the study. Thus, the 300 test families consisted of those who remained in the public housing project throughout the study, and the 300 control families consisted of those who remained in essentially poorer, non-public housing. The two groups were well matched on a number of demographic, initial health, and initial adjustment characteristics. Both samples consisted of low-income Negro families. The housing development to which the test families moved consisted of both high-rise and low-rise buildings.

Through the cooperation of the Housing Authority, it was possible to survey both groups initially *before* the test sample moved to good housing. Subsequently, a total of ten "after" surveys were conducted with each family, in the home. Detailed assessment was made of housing quality, physical morbidity, and social-psychological adjustment. In addition, the performance of every child attending public school was assessed from school records.

Physical Health At the outset of the study, consideration of the ways in which the housing quality of test and control groups would differ led to a number of hypotheses and expectations regarding the role of housing in disease. Among important housing items considered were density and crowding, hot water and facilities for cleanliness, toilet, sharing of facilities, screening, rodent infestation, food storage, and refrigeration. It was anticipated, for example, that variation in the quality of these factors would affect introduction of infective organisms into the dwelling unit and their subsequent transmission among family members either by airborn or contact means.

There was basic confirmation of the morbidity hypotheses for persons under thirty-five years of age, and especially for children, but there was little confirmation of the hypotheses for persons thirty-five to fifty-nine. For persons under twenty years of age, the findings

the originally constituted matched groups. The second problem was totally unexpected. It was found that control families were in the passage of time moving to improved housing, a substantial proportion to public housing. This development undoubtedly was due to the increasing availability of adequate housing in the period 1955-58, while the study was being conducted. In order to adhere to the experimental conditions required by the study design, the original samples were adjusted to take these losses and moves into account, resulting in the two reduced effective samples of 300 test and 300 control families.

indicated *lower* incidence of illness and disability among test children than among controls in the last two years of the study.

Among boys, taking all conditions into account, test incidence rates were lower than control rates by approximately 48 episodes per 100 persons per year. This is a difference of about 20 per cent in the episodes of the test boys. Among girls, test rates were lower than control rates by about 23 episodes per 100 persons per year. This is a difference of about 10 per cent of the episodes of the test girls. Similar lower test than control rates held in general for more serious conditions, involving either medical attention or disability, and for the less serious conditions as well.

Disability findings for persons under twenty years of age tended generally to follow the direction and also the magnitude of the incidence data. Among males, test rates were lower than control rates by an average of about 122 days per 100 persons per year. This is a difference of about 25 per cent of test disability rates. Among females, the figures for comparable periods were about 41 days per 100 persons per pear, a difference of about 10 per cent.

Episodes were classified according to type of illness, using definitions of the *International Statistical Classification of Diseases, Injuries, and Causes of Death.* Five categories of conditions comprised 90 per cent of the episodes occurring among children. In the last two years of observation, test rates were regularly lower than control rates in three categories: infective and parasitic conditions, mainly the communicable diseases of childhood; digestive conditions; and accidents. The findings with respect to accidents are especially important and clear. Accidents were one-third lower in the housing project as contrasted with the slum. The data showed general confirmation of this fact among all age and sex groups under twenty. In at least one of the two years, test rates were also lower than control rates in respiratory conditions, and allergic and metabolic episodes.

The data for the "interim" period—about five months following the resettlement of test families into their new quarters—is of considerable interest to epidemiologists. In that period, test rates of illness and disability for almost every age-sex group under twenty were *higher* than control rates. Further examination of "interim" period data by classification of disease reveals that the higher test rates were entirely accounted for by three categories of conditions: infective and parasitic, respiratory, and digestive, all of which have communicability as a principal feature. The most likely explanation is that the test families, newly assembled into the housing project, were strangers to one another in more than just a social sense and lacked group immunity to common communicable diseases. A similar phenomenon has been observed in the rise of infectious disease in other newly assembled groups, as, for example, army recruits.

Morbidity data for young adults, aged twenty to thirty-four, showed, in general, similar but less marked effects than those described for children, and the effects observed were less related to the communicable diseases. Of particular interest was the observation that for adults, there were lower test than control episode and disability rates among young adult women of childbearing age, from twenty to thirty-four years. In this connection, there appeared a tendency to lower birth weights among infants born alive to control mothers than to test mothers, and also an attendant higher rate of prematurity. The background of this tendency has not yet been ascertained.

Social-Psychological Adjustment Test-control differences in housing quality were expected to play a role not only in physical health but also in matters of social-psychological adjustment. Of the specific elements that distinguished test from control housing, a few factors such as space in the dwelling unit were expected to be influential on both morbidity and social adjustment. However, several elements of housing quality that were thought to affect social attitudes and behavior differed from those believed to influence morbidity. Among these were aspects of the larger housing environment such as architecture and community facilities, as well as the esthetic qualities of the dwelling unit.

With the foregoing in mind, the expectation was that the slum environment offered inhibitions and restraints upon the development of wholesome family relationships, sociality and neighborliness, and good citizenship in the larger community. In addition, slum housing was considered from the point of view of personal psychological development as producing inhibitions and restraints upon realistic aspirations for self and family, upon morale, and upon appropriate solutions of, and points of view toward, life's problems. These considerations led to the delineation of six major social-psychological content areas, each based on its own specific set of hypotheses. The data were obtained by means of detailed interviews with the female head of the household.

The basic social adjustment findings indicated that a majority of the items in each area showed at least a directional trend confirming the expectations specified for the area. However, in most of the areas, by no means all of the test-control differences confirming the hypotheses reached acceptable levels of confidence. The detailed findings may be summarized briefly as follows:

1. Reactions to housing and space. A markedly larger proportion of test than control women liked their new housing circumstances, commented favorably on the safety of their children's play places, felt that they were getting their money's worth for the amount of the rental, indicated an increased likelihood for personal privacy, and reported reductions in friction and psychological discomfort directly related to space.

2. Relations with neighbors. The rehoused families, in contrast to the controls, underwent a marked increase in neighborly interaction of a mutually supportive variety, such as helping out with household activities, with children, and in time of illness. This heightened interaction was not viewed as infringing on privacy. The test women were more likely than controls to report both pleasant *and* unpleasant experiences with nearby women, but they were also more apt to have formed new, close friendships in the immediate neighborhood.

3. Personal and family relations. The data for this area showed directional trends confirming the hypotheses only in connection with common family activities and the mothers' reactions to, and discipline of, children. Other aspects of intra-familial activities, cooperation, and affect revealed findings that were mixed or counter to the hypotheses.

4. Attitudes and behavior toward neighborhood and community. Test respondents showed more pride in their immediate neighborhoods than did control respondents, reported more activities devoted to keeping up the neighborhood, and gave far more favorable views regarding the neighborhood as a place to live and to raise children. Other topics which pertained more to the "broader" neighborhood or community, such as satisfaction with proximity to various facilities, interest in "larger issues," and evaluation of Baltimore as a place to live, showed either no systematic test-control differences or only a slight advantage for the test group.

5. Social self-concept and aspirations. Test respondents, more than controls, were likely to indicate felt improvement in position in

life, and to report themselves as rising in the world. However, contrary to expectation, this perceived betterment was not, in general, accompanied by heightened aspirations for jobs, for their children, or for home ownership.

6. Psychological state. Findings for a series of ten psycho-social scales,* consisting of variables pertaining to the *self*, revealed directional trends confirming expectations on all the scales. Those topics dealing with general morale (Optimism-Pessimism, Satisfaction with Personal State of Affairs, and Potency) were more likely than the scales involving stressful, inner feeling states (Mood, Control of Temper, and Nervousness) to show test-control differences confirming the hypotheses.

School Performance of Children Consideration of several direct and indirect outcomes of differences in test-control housing quality suggested the possibility of differential scholastic achievement of the test and control children. The housing variable expected to be most directly related to school performance was that of dwelling unit density which, being lower for the test children, was expected to provide greater opportunity to study and to do homework unhampered by interruptions from other family members. In addition, there was the possibility of more indirect influences on the test group arising from expected advantages in morale and physical health.

To test these hypotheses, the records of 293 test and 287 control children attending Baltimore city public schools were examined. The data collected included scores on intelligence and achievement tests,† promotions, and attendance. Data on these measures for the "before" period indicated close initial comparability of the test and control groups. In the "after" period, the hypotheses regarding housing and *test performance* were not borne out: mean test scores (adjusted for grade level of children tested) were similar for the two groups of children. However, test children were considerably more likely to be *promoted* at a normal pace, control children being held back more often for one or more semesters. In connection with record of promotions, then, study hypotheses were confirmed.

* These scales were developed especially for the study population. The scaling method used was that devised by Louis Guttman, employing only the first, or direction, component.

† The intelligence tests were the Kuhlmann-Anderson and Otis. The achievement tests consisted of arithmetic achievement (Metropolitan and Stanford) and reading achievement (Iowa, Metropolitan, and Stanford).

One reason for the test-control promotion difference is suggested by the data on daily *attendance* at school. Corresponding to morbidity differences already described, mean daily attendance of test children was considerably higher than that of control children. Improved housing quality may thus play an indirect role in school performance of children in a way not completely anticipated by the original hypotheses, by lessening illness and in turn providing the opportunity through regular attendance for the kind of day-to-day school performance on which promotion from grade to grade is ultimately based.

Conclusions

Review of cross-sectional studies and the theoretical consideration of elements of housing probably related to health and social adjustment, had suggested that even in a three-year period a prospective, matched-group study would show marked effects of housing differences.

The basic conclusions of the study may be summarized as follows:

1. The adjustment findings, stressing the more moderate rather than the pathological manifestations of adjustment, were less dramatic than had been expected. In this connection it must be remembered that, for all the housing improvement, many other circumstances that would be expected to affect the way of life remained substantially the same. These were still families at the lowest end of the economic scale; practical family situations remained materially unimproved; in one-third of the families there was no husband present; and one-third were on public welfare.

2. The morbidity findings were considerably more substantial. Even in a three-year period, incidence of illness and disability was markedly reduced in better housing circumstances. This was true, as several of the cross-sectional researches reviewed had suggested, of younger persons and particularly of children.

3. The data concerning schools suggested an interweaving of social and physical variables. School promotions, while probably affected by intelligence and intellectual achievement, as in more general school samples, is apparently also related in a significant way to attendance at school. Attendance in turn is a function of

illness and health, in which housing circumstances seem to play an undoubted role.

Bibliography

1. Barer, N., "A Note on Tuberculosis Among Residents of a Housing Project," *J. Housing*, 2:133, 1945.
2. ———, "Delinquency Before, After Admission to New Haven Housing Development," *J. Housing*, 3:27, 1945.
3. Benjamin, B., "Tuberculosis and Social Conditions in the Metropolitan Boroughs of London," *Brit. J. Tuberc. and Dis. of Chest*, *47*:4-17, 1953.
4. Benjamin, J. E., Ruegsegger, J. W., and Senior, F. A., "The Influence of Overcrowding on the Incidence of Pneumonia," *Ohio State Med. J.*, *36*:1275-1281, 1940.
5. Bernstein, S. H., "Observations on the Effects of Housing on the Incidence and Spread of Common Respiratory Diseases Among Air Force Recruits," *Amer. J. Hyg.*, *65*:162-171, 1957.
6. Brett, G. Z., and Benjamin, B., "Housing and Tuberculosis in a Mass Radiography Survey," *Brit. J. Prev. and Soc. Med.*, *11*:7-9, 1957.
7. Britten, R. H., Brown, J. E., and Altman, I., "Certain Characteristics of Urban Housing and Their Relation to Illness and Accidents: Summary of Findings of the National Health Survey," *Milbank Mem. Fund Quart.*, *18*:91-113, 1940.
8. Britten, R. H., and Altman, I., "Illness and Accidents Among Persons Living Under Different Housing Conditions: Data Based on National Health Survey," *Pub. Health Rep.*, *56*:609-640, 1941.
9. Britten, R. H., "New Light on the Relation of Housing to Health," *Amer. J. Pub. Health*, *32*:193-199, 1942.
10. Chapin, F. S., "An Experiment on the Social Effects of Good Housing," *Amer. Soc. Rev.*, *5*:868-879, 1940.
11. Christensen, V., "Child Morbidity in a Good and a Bad Residential Area," *Danish Med. Bull.*, *3*:93-98, 1956.
12. Coulter, J. E., "Rheumatic Fever and Streptococcal Illness in Two Communities in New York State," *Milbank Mem. Fund Quart.* *30*:341-358, 1952.
13. Dirksen, C., *Economic Factors of Delinquency*, Milwaukee: Bruce, 1948.
14. Downes, J., and Simon, K., "Characteristics of Psychoneurotic Pa-

tients and Their Families as Revealed in a General Morbidity Study," *Milbank Mem. Fund Quart.*, 32:42-64, 1954.
15. Glueck, S., and Glueck, E., *One Thousand Juvenile Delinquents*, Cambridge, Mass.: Harvard Univ. Press, 1934.
16. Harlan, H., and Wherry, J., "Delinquency and Housing," *Soc. Forces*, 27:58-61, 1948.
17. Henzell, L. I., "Housing Conditions and Tuberculosis," *Med. Officer*, 62:200-201, 1939.
18. Keller, M., "Progress in School of Children in a Sample of Families in the Eastern Health District of Baltimore," *Milbank Mem. Fund Quart.*, 31:391-410, 1953.
19. Lander, B., *Towards an Understanding of Juvenile Delinquency*, New York: Columbia Univ. Press, 1954.
20. Loring, W. C., Jr., "Housing Characteristics and Social Disorganization," *Soc. Prob.*, 3:160-168, 1956.
21. Lowell, A. M., *Socio-economic Conditions and Tuberculosis Prevalence, New York City*, New York: New York Tuberculosis and Health Organization, 1956.
22. Martin, F. M., Brothersen, J. N. F., and Chave, S. P. W., "Incidence of Neurosis in a New Housing Estate," *Brit. J. Prev. and Soc. Med.*, 11:196-202, 1957.
23. Mackintosh, J. M., "Housing and Tuberculosis," *Brit. J. Tuberc.*, 28:67-70, 1934.
24. McMillan, J. S., "Examination of the Association Between Housing Conditions and Pulmonary Tuberculosis in Glasgow," *Brit. J. Prev. and Soc. Med.*, 11:142-151, 1957.
25. M'Gonigle, G. C. M., "Poverty, Nutrition and Public Health," *Proc. Royal Soc. Med.*, 26:677-687, 1933.
26. Mogey, J. M., "Changes in Family Life Experienced by English Workers Moving from Slums to Housing Estates," *Marriage and Fam. Liv.*, 17:123-128, 1955.
27. Murray, A. M. T., "The Growth and Nutrition of the Slum Child in Relation to Housing—One and Two-roomed House," *J. Hyg.*, 26:198-203, 1927.
28. Nelson, H., "Housing and Health," *Brit. Med. J.*, 2:395-397, 1945.
29. Ogburn, W. F., "Factors in the Variation of Crime Among Cities," *J. Amer. Stat. Assoc.*, 30:12-34, 1935.
30. Riley, I. D., "Housing Conditions and Children in Hospital," *Glasgow Med. J.*, 36:393-397, 1955.
31. Rumney, J., and Shuman, S., *A Study of the Social Effects of Public Housing in Newark, New Jersey*, Newark: Housing Authority of the City of Newark, 1946.

32. Savage, W. G., "Tuberculosis and Housing in Rural Districts," *Brit. J. Tuberc., 13*:160-162, 1919.

33. Schmitt, R. C., "Housing and Health on Oahu," *Amer. J. Pub. Health, 45*:1538-1540, 1955.

34. ———, "Density, Delinquency, and Crime in Honolulu," *Soc. and Soc. Research, 41*:274-276, 1957.

35. Schroeder, C., "Mental Disorders in Cities," *Amer. J. Soc., 48*:40-47, 1942.

36. Shaw, C. R., and McKay, H. D., "Social Factors in Juvenile Delinquency," *Report on the Causes of Crime,* Vol. 2, Washington, D.C.: U. S. Government Printing Office, 1931.

37. Slawson, J., *The Delinquent Boy,* Boston: Gorham Press, 1926.

38. Spence, J., Walton, W. S., Miller, F. J. W., and Court, S. D. M., *A Thousand Families in Newcastle-upon-Tyne,* London: Oxford Univ. Press, 1954.

39. Stein, L., "A Study of Respiratory Tuberculosis in Relation to Housing Conditions in Edinburgh," *Brit. J. Soc. Med., 4*:143-169, 1950.

40. ———, "Glasgow Tuberculosis and Housing," *Tubercle, 35*:195-203, 1954.

41. Wilner, D. M., Walkley, R. P., and Tayback, M., "How Does the Quality of Housing Affect Health and Family Adjustment?" *Amer. J. Pub. Health, 46*:736-744, 1956.

42. Wilner, D. M., and Walkley, R. P., "The Housing Environment and Public Health," in *Epidemiology of Mental Disorder,* B. Pasamanick, ed., New York: American Association for the Advancement of Science, 1959.

43. Wilner, D. M., and Walkley, R. P., abridgment of preceding title, *Pub. Health Rep., 72*:589-592, 1957.

44. Wilner, D. M., Walkley, R. P., Glasser, M., and Tayback, M., "The Effects of Housing Quality on Morbidity—Preliminary Findings," *Amer. J. Pub. Health, 48*:1607-1615, 1958.

45. Wilner, D. M., Walkley, R. P., Schram, J., Pinkerton, T., and Tayback, M., "Housing as an Environmental Factor in Mental Health: The Johns Hopkins Longitudinal Study," *Amer. J. Pub. Health, 50*:55-63, 1960.

46. Wilner, D. M., Walkley, R. P., Williams, H., and Tayback, M., "The Baltimore Study on the Effects of Housing on Health," *Baltimore Health News, 37*:45-50, 1960.

47. Wilner, D. M., Walkley, R. P., Pinkerton, T., and Tayback, M., "The Housing Environment and Family Life," working paper prepared for Expert Committee on Public Health Aspects of Housing, Geneva: World Health Organization, 1961.

48. Wilner, D. M., Walkley, R. P., Pinkerton, T., and Tayback, M., *The Housing Environment and Family Life: A Longitudinal Study of the Effects of Housing on Morbidity and Mental Health,* Baltimore: Johns Hopkins Press, 1962.

Attitudes Toward Slums and Public Housing in Puerto Rico

17

A. B. HOLLINGSHEAD

L. H. ROGLER

This paper reports selected aspects of an intensive study of lower-class families who reside in a rapidly changing metropolitan area.* For present purposes, we shall limit the discussion to three principal points: (1) a brief statement about the study; (2) a description of the neighborhoods where the families in our study live; and (3) some reactions of these families to the physical and human environments that enmesh their lives.

The locale of this research is the San Juan metropolitan area of Puerto Rico. Puerto Rico is of sociological interest for a number of reasons. Between 1500 and 1900, a relatively homogeneous culture developed. During the present century, selected American culture patterns have grown upon traditional Hispanic ones. Politically, this island experienced transition from a Spanish colony to a militarily-strategic possession of the United States; now it is an autonomous Commonwealth associated with the United States. Economically, it is changing from a predominantly rural, agricultural society to a highly urbanized, industrial one. Socially, it is developing classes that lie between an historic, small aristocratic segment of very rich families and the vast majority of poor people.

Today the impact of changes brought about by socio-cultural forces characteristic of our time is visible throughout the island, particularly in the metropolitan areas. New opportunities are being presented to persons in all segments of the social structure. Some aspects of the culture are changing rapidly; others are resistant to

* The research reported here is being done by the Social Science Research Center of The University of Puerto Rico. It is supported, in part, by a research grant from the National Institute of Mental Health, United States Public Health Service. August B. Hollingshead is Director, and Lloyd H. Rogler is Assistant Director.

change. In different degree, all socio-economic groups are affected by the admixture of the new cultural complexes with the old ones. The impact of the new, juxtaposed with the old, has created a confused social scene.

The Study Design

Schizophrenia in the Lower Class The study upon which this paper is based is focused upon schizophrenia in the lowest socio-economic class. We decided to study schizophrenia for a number of reasons. First, schizophrenia is a disabling disease. Second, in the psychiatric agencies of the Puerto Rican government, schizophrenia is the most frequently treated psychosis.* Third, the etiology of schizophrenia is a matter of debate.[1] Fourth, a number of studies have reported that schizophrenia is concentrated unduly in persons of lower socio-economic status.[2] A study of schizophrenia in the lowest socio-economic class in the San Juan metropolitan area appeared to be an intellectually-challenging venture.

The Study Group We decided to make an intensive study of families of procreation. The number had to be limited in order to collect the kinds of data we desired, but it had to be large enough to permit meaningful comparisons between groups. A minimum of forty families appeared to be necessary. Our research design required, first, that the families should fall into two categories—families with a schizophrenic spouse and families without a schizophrenic spouse; and, second, that the families should be as similar as possible in a number of other characteristics.

We established five criteria for families to be included in the study: (1) residence in the San Juan metropolitan area; (2) an age range from twenty to thirty-nine years; (3) spouses living in the same household; (4) low socio-economic status;[3] (5) no contact with a psychiatric agency prior to May 1, 1958.

The Field Phase Locating families who met our criteria was the first major field operation. We began with a list of persons who had

* A study of 500 out-patients in the State Psychiatric Hospital of Puerto Rico, receiving care during the fiscal year of 1956-1957, indicated that 53 per cent of the patients were schizophrenic. A study of 200 in-patients in the State Psychiatric Hospital of Puerto Rico, admitted during the fiscal year 1956-1957, indicated that 58 per cent were schizophrenic. These studies were done by the Department of Psychiatry, School of Medicine, The University of Puerto Rico. They have not been published.

either been referred to psychiatric clinics by a third party, or had come to the clinic themselves and solicited help. Most referrals were made by local officials in public health units, the police, physicians, and, of course, family members. As soon as the name of a disturbed person—either a referral or a solicitant—came to our attention, we visited his home to determine if he met the established criteria.

Persons who fulfilled our criteria were asked to cooperate with us. A minimal level of cooperation meant that the invited person and his, or her, spouse would submit themselves to a psychiatric examination. Each person was told, before he was taken to the psychiatrist's office, the kind of doctor he was to see, and the nature of the examination he would receive.

Each examination was made by a fully trained psychiatrist, who was himself a Puerto Rican. All examinations were made in the privacy of the psychiatrist's air-conditioned office. The psychiatric examination usually took about two hours. The spouses were given the same psychiatric examinations under the same conditions, at a different time and, usually, by a different psychiatrist. Persons who were diagnosed as schizophrenic were then asked, along with their spouses, to participate in the study.

Families with a schizophrenic spouse were matched by families drawn randomly from a pre-listed census of households taken in an earlier phase of the research. A family tentatively selected was visited by a field worker. The study was explained to the members of this family, and they were invited to participate in it. Husbands and wives were told that they would be taken to a psychiatrist and given a mental examination. We told them, also, that we would visit the home many times to gather information about the family. We believe it is worth noting that once people accepted our invitation to go to a psychiatrist, there were no refusals to participate in the study. This record we attribute to the quality and perseverance of the field staff and to the hospitality accorded to the field workers by these families. We may add that hospitality to comparative strangers is an important value in Puerto Rico.

The husband and the wife in the randomly selected families were taken separately to the office of a team psychiatrist. The psychiatrist gave the same mental-status examination used in the schizophrenic series, and under the same circumstances; that is, in private, in an air-conditioned office. If one spouse was diagnosed as suffering from an organic or functional psychosis, the family was eliminated. To be included in this study the spouses had to be diagnosed as mentally healthy, or at most showing only neurotic symptoms. The screening-in of persons suffering from schizophrenia in one group of families and the screening-out of psychotics in the other series of families was deliberate. It resulted in two groups of families with distinctly different psychiatric statuses. The two groups were equal in size; each was composed of twenty families.

These families may be viewed as a "sick" series and a "well" series. In technical terms, the sick series represented an experimental group, and the well series a control group. However, we did not perform any experiments on either the well or the sick families. We simply studied them in their homes and neighborhoods. During the twenty months of the field work, no person in the study was hospitalized for mental illness.

The Field Teams The field team was composed of professionally trained psychiatric social workers and social scientists, who were themselves Puerto Rican. We employed both men and women. Men were needed to interview males, and women to interview females. This was essential on certain topics, such as sex history. The field workers knew the culture, the local people, and how to interview. Nevertheless, Rogler maintained vigilant supervision over their daily work. To gather the data for the eight schedules used in the study required from 110 to 125 hours of face-to-face interviewing of the members of each family. The interviews for any given family spread over four to seven months. An average of forty interviews was necessary to complete the field work on the families with a schizophrenic member, and thirty-five with the families that did not have a schizophrenic in them. All of the interviews were conducted in Spanish.

Most of the interviews were carried out in the homes, but some were conducted in small corner coffee shops, bars, barber shops, beauty parlors, and the interviewers' cars, parks, and jails. We interviewed where we could and when we could. The field work was a give-and-take process. The male workers bought rum for some men, and some of the women field workers carried food to starving wives and children. Clothing was given to several families to cover the nakedness of children. In a few homes, interviewers sat on the floor, because this was the only place to sit. Unexpected tropical storms drenched the interviewers, and high tides caused homes over backed-up waters to sway precariously. In a number of instances, field workers walked thigh-deep in polluted water to and from humble homes on stilts. One interviewer was threatened with murder when she discovered a bootlegger surreptitiously plying his trade. Another interviewer received a friendly invitation to help castrate vicious dogs impounded by the mother of one of the wives in the schizophrenic group. With very minor and infrequent exceptions, the persons interviewed were cordial and cooperative.

Areas of Residence

The criterion of low socio-economic status resulted in the selection of families who live either in slums or in public housing projects known locally as *caserios*.

Slums The slums of San Juan have been built through the efforts of individuals and their families in search of a niche, where they may meet the necessities of life and death and store their meager possessions. Slums have grown on land too swampy to support commercial buildings and on hillsides so steep they have not been attractive for other uses. Any place where people can build a shelter from the rain and the sun may become a slum. The largest slums are built on low ground on the sides of both the Martin Pena Channel and the lagoons into which it leads. These low-lying slums stretch for several miles along the sides of the lagoons and backwaters of the meandering Channel.

The pressure for a place to build is so great that many homes are built on piles over tidal waters. The farther out in the water a house is built, the longer the piles. As one moves away from the Channel to higher ground, the piles become shorter. The houses are built on piles, even on the hillsides, to insure circulation of air, to minimize damage from termites, and to protect them from water. In the lower-lying areas, when the wind blows and the tides run high, the houses vibrate and sway. Several of our field workers reported getting seasick while interviewing in these homes. The longer the piles, the greater the amount of the movements from tidal action.

Each neighborhood within a slum has a name. One of the most delapidated and pestiferous neighborhoods is known as *Buenos Aires* —"good air." Another, surrounded by a slightly higher ground but whose center is an odoriferous pool of mud, is called "Black Ass." The most infamous slum, *La Perla*—"The Pearl"—is anchored on a steep hillside that descends to the Atlantic Ocean. The name of a slum is a sardonic indication of its inhabitant's attitude toward it.

Slums are adjacent to regularly established streets. Entrances from these streets enable the inhabitants to come and go. The "main street," or walkway, of a slum is interconnected with a network of narrow side alleys. The alleys branch into paths that end at someone's front door. In the main, the walkways meander from the entrance downhill to the edge of the lagoon, or uphill from a road. In hill slums, the walkways may be downhill from a highway.

Most walkways are simple dirt paths. Some walkways are covered with crushed rock that is dumped on the edge of the area by the city. Each householder hauls the rock to his house and spreads it on the walk, so that the walk in front of his house will not be a morass during rains. Some householders gather pieces of discarded linoleum from a dump, carry it to their home, lay it on the stones, and pound it down. Others use pieces of tar paper or discarded gunny bags to smooth the walkway. The hot tropical sun melts the linoleum and tar paper with the effect that it binds the underlying rocks into a solid mass. In low-lying slums, as the paths descend toward the water, the walkways are built out of wooden planks placed upon piles. These walkways often are washed away during storms and high waters.

The houses are not built at a uniform height above the ground or the water. Each builder sets the floor level of his house to suit his fancy and needs. The floors of homes built over the Channel and lagoons may be only a few inches above the water during high tide. When storms sweep over the area, these houses are flooded. The lack of uniformity in a house's height above the water line presents a stair-step effect from the walkways or the Channel.

Each house is built by a man who expects to live there as soon as possible, often while it is under construction. The builder is generally an unskilled worker who has a few simple tools—a hammer, a saw, and possibly a square and a plane. He selects a site, squats on it, and may assign his wife, or his child, to guard "his" property so that someone else does not claim it. He gathers pieces of wood for piles, joists, floors, walls, and rafters from a variety of sources. The incoming tide is scanned for floating lumber. Buildings being demolished are visited after, or before, regular working hours. Lumber, hardware, sheet iron, and other items are carted to the building site. New construction sites will be checked for possible materials. The watchman may be bribed to look the other way while the builder clandestinely selects something he wants. Gradually, the essential pieces are brought together and the house takes shape. The new house is likely to be very close to the next house, because of the scarcity of space and also because of the new neighbor's desire to have his house face a street, alley, path, or walkway. Frequently, not more than a foot or two separates one house from another.

These homes are rectangular in shape. The walls are made of wood, corrugated iron, opened and flattened five gallon kerosene tins, and old metal signs. The gable roofs are covered usually with corrugated iron. Apertures for the windows and doors are rough and often not trimmed. The doors and windows are made of rough boards, generally hinged to swing outward, to save inside space. The windows in adjacent houses often hit one another, unless the neighbors cooperate in opening and closing them.

When the family is at home during the day, the windows and doors are open. Otherwise, the heat is suffocating. At night the windows and doors are closed in order to keep out the night air, which is believed to be unhealthy. Then the family is away, the windows are secured from the inside and the door is locked from the outside with a steel hasp and a padlock.

Practically every house has a small front porch covered with a shed roof to protect the inhabitants from the sun's piercing rays. The more elaborate ones may have a back porch. Inside the house, the living space may be divided into rooms by partitions, which may or may not extend to the roof. Only the better slum homes have ceilings. Ceilings are expensive; besides, they impede the circulation of air.

Sanitation is provided by open ditches that run from the houses to the alleys and walkways. Feces, urine, washwater, coffee grounds, and other wastes are carried in the ditches to the lagoon. Toilet facilities vary from commercial earthenware stools to a hole cut in the floor. The toilet empties into the sewage trench. A person walking by a home on occasion may see a person urinating or defecating and hear the excrement hit the waters of the trench, or the lagoon.

Houses on high ground have outside latrines. The yard is usually so small that the latrine is immediately beside the house. It may block passage to the adjacent house.

The city has piped water into each slum. The water pipes are laid on top of the walks. At intervals there are public spigots beside the walkway. Some householders come to a spigot for their domestic water supply. The water is drawn into cans or jars which at one time contained kerosene, vegetables, or fruit. To avoid going to the public spigot, some householders run water lines to their houses. To do this, a hole is bored into the main. Then a copper tube is thrust into the hole and bound in place with an iron strap that encircles the main. The tube is run, in some instances, to a sink in the house and a spigot is attached. More commonly, the spigot is placed at the corner of the house. Periodically, officials from the Water Authority tear out these illicit private lines. Some homes are connected legitimately to the city's water mains.

A bathtub or a shower in the home is a rare luxury. Bathing is accomplished in a wash tub, basin, or gasoline can. Some men have built showers beside their houses. A neighborhood shower is common. It is made by tapping into the water main. A water pipe is run to a small vacant area and raised five or six feet above the ground; then a shower head is attached. A slat foot-rest is built to lay on the ground. A board wall with a door is built around the shower head; cracks from three-quarters to more than an inch wide separate one board from another.

Some homes are either legitimately or surreptitiously connected to the city's electrical system. Electricity is brought into the house on wires fastened to insulators in one or two places, so that the family can have light, a radio, and, desirably, a television set.

The slums, where most of our families live, are subject to the twice-daily flow and ebb of the tides. The incoming tide brings debris from the harbor (untreated sewage from the city, as well as the accumulation of sewage from the slums) into the network of house piles and walkways. To this accumulation is added the garbage from slum homes. Rubbish of many kinds—bottles, cans, cocoanut husks, grapefruit and orange rinds, gunny sacks, old automobile tires, rusted pieces of iron, paper boxes, newspapers, IBM cards, bones of chickens and pigs, old shoes, playing cards, condoms, and so on—is thrown under the houses and along the walkways. This mulch of rubbish and garbage is soaked periodically by the sudden rains which pass over the area. The hot, tropical sun helps decompose and dry the sodden debris. It also adds to the all-pervasive stench. Gradually, the rotting debris settles into the mud. The incoming tidal flow stirs up the sediment and floods the lower-lying areas. As the tide ebbs, a malodorous scum covers the lower portions of the walkways and the ground under the houses.

Caserios The public housing projects, *caserios*, which are planned, erected, and maintained by the Puerto Rican government, are in sharp contrast to the slums. The *caserios* embody established principles of good housing for low-income families. *Caserios* are built on solid and relatively dry land. They are surrounded by surveyed and paved streets. Each building is set apart from adjacent buildings. The foundations, walls, floors, stairs, and roofs are made of concrete. Sidewalks lead from each building to the street. The buildings are two, three, or four floors in height. High-rise buildings have not been erected.

Residential buildings in *caserios* are subdivided into one-family apartments. Each apartment has electricity, water, and sanitary facilities. The internal space is divided into a kitchen, bath, dining-living area, and one or more bedrooms. The more desirable apartments have a balcony with a wall approximately three feet high around it. In the older *caserios* windows are sometimes fitted with iron bars in order to keep thieves out of the apartments. The newer *caserios* have jalousie windows, which also provide protection and have the advantage of being easy to open and shut. The size of an assigned apartment is related to the number of persons in the family.

The construction of *caserios* to replace the slums is a major governmental objective. Although the government is building public housing as rapidly as possible, the slums are growing almost as fast as they are being replaced. This situation is traceable to the attraction that the San Juan area has for Puerto Ricans throughout the island. The vast majority of migrants to San Juan are unskilled, poorly educated, and without financial resources. The newly arrived migrant from another part of the island ordinarily drifts to the slums or a *caserio* apartment of some member of his kin group. As conditions become better for him, he moves from a room or sleeping space to a house or apartment. There is a chronic shortage of housing of any kind. Gradually, as the Housing Authority is able to carry out its program of building apartments, the worst slums are demolished. Before the debris can be hauled away, individuals in search of building materials carry off usable pieces. These raids are usually made at night or early in the morning. In this way the slums are replenished while the Housing Authority builds new apartments. Building goes on day and night—officially by day, unofficially by night.

Housing in Our Families The families in our study are divided unequally between slums and *caserios*. Sixty-five per cent live in slums, and 35 per cent live in *caserios*. The families living in *caserios* pay a mean rental of $14 per month. Families in the slums pay a mean rental of $22 per month. The 40 per cent of our families who own slum homes estimate their mean value as $1000. The slum dwellers are more crowded in their homes than the *caserio* dwellers are in their apartments. The *caserio* dwellers have 1.4 enclosed spaces per person in their apartments; the slum dwellers have only .9 enclosed spaces per person in their homes. The enclosed spaces in the *caserio* apartments are also larger than the enclosed spaces in slum homes. Hence, the living space per person is greater in *caserios* than in slum dwellings. By the criteria of "good" housing, *caserio* dwellers are "better" housed than the slum dwellers.

Reactions to Slums and Caserios

The third section of this paper describes some reactions of the husbands and wives in our families to their neighborhoods. The data we shall present are drawn from a series of questions we asked, which elicited information on each respondent's relations with his neighbors and his evaluation of the neighborhood where he lived. One of these questions asked the interviewee to tell us how he liked his present neighborhood. His answer is categorized on a four-point scale: "Like a lot"; "Like it a little"; "Dislike it a little"; "Dislike it a lot."

Responses to this question reveal dissimilar reactions to their neighborhoods by slum dwellers and *Caserio* dwellers. Sixty-five per cent of the men and women who live in slum homes like the slums, whereas 86 per cent of the men and 71 per cent of the women dislike *caserios*.

When the mental health of the person is taken into consideration, we find that in the *caserios* about the same proportion of sick persons and healthy persons dislike their neighborhoods. In the slums more well persons than sick persons like their neighborhoods, but the difference is not significant for either males or females.

The dislike of *caserios,* in comparison with slums, appeared in responses to other questions. These questions include relations with neighbors, persons the respondents would prefer not to have as neighbors, things the neighbors do that the husbands and wives in the study do not like, and the desire either to move to a different neighborhood or to stay in their present one. Responses to these questions show a consistent pattern of more slum dwellers than *caserio* dwellers liking their neighborhoods; this pattern is independent of the psychiatric distinction between sick and well.

The sharpest dissatisfaction with their present neighborhood, among both *caserios* and slum dwellers, is revealed in replies to the question: Do you think this is a good neighborhood in which to raise your children? This is an emotionally loaded subject to the parents in the study, because of the high hopes and aspirations they have for their children. The figures show that 38 per cent of the slum-dwelling husbands think the slum is a good place to raise their children, but only 7 per cent of the husbands in *caserios* believe a *caserio* is a good place to raise children. The wives are not as accepting of either slum or *caserios* conditions as the husbands. No wife in the *caserios* believes a *caserio* is a good place to raise children; only 15 per cent of the wives who live in the slums think that slums are a good place to raise children

The findings indicate that both *caserio* and slum dwellers are reacting against the physical, social, and cultural environments in which their class position has placed them. From their point of view, these environments are not conducive to the appropriate raising of children.

The Dilemma The basic findings we have presented pose two dilemmas. First, good housing—in accord with standards established by city planners and architects, and erected by an enlightened government—may result in the formation of social conditions people do not like. Second, when we control for the neighborhood factor, families who have one or both spouses afflicted with schizophrenia react to their neighborhoods in ways that are not essentially different from families where the spouses are mentally healthy. These findings call for an explanation. Why do *caserio* dwellers dislike their neighborhood significantly more than slum dwellers do theirs?

Caserio families, as well as slum families, are clear and articulate in describing the things they do not like. Persons in the slums resent the dampness and the filth most. *Caserio* dwellers object most vociferously to the restrictions imposed upon them by the Public Housing Authority. Complaints in these groups are registered, in a sense, against nature on the one hand, and government on the other.

Caserio dwellers have escaped from the water and mud, but the government has imposed a series of irritating regulations. Most of these rules run counter to lower-class folkways. For example, the Housing Authority rents an apartment to a single, nuclear family. Relatives and boarders are not supposed to be smuggled into the apartment by the authorized tenants. This restriction runs counter to obligations entailed by the kinship system. The kin tie places a personal obligation on a man or a woman to shelter and feed a relative by blood, marriage, or custom. The kin tie is rooted in the culture of Puerto Rico. The rule of the *Caserio* Authority is imposed by governmental agents; therefore, it may be violated without a feeling of guilt. The conflict here is between a personal obligation and an impersonal rule. To turn away a relative is reprehensible; to disregard a governmental regulation is not.

The rule on tenancy is violated frequently by *caserio* residents. However, when a tenant gives shelter to relatives, he or she knows that a neighbor could report this fact to the central office. When this happens, the central Authority may force the squatters to move. The legitimate tenant usually attempts to talk the Housing Authority into assigning an apartment in the same *caserio* to the relative. If possible, the housing official complies with the tenant's request. This results in kin-group clusters in a given building, or adjacent buildings.

Rules established by the Housing Authority to promote sanitation are another source or irritation. Housing Authority rules prohibit livestock in the apartments. This rule is breached by many families. Chickens, rabbits, pigs, and goats are smuggled into the *caserios*. Their owners house them in the bathroom, or on the walled-in balcony, until a neighbor reports the violation. Then the officials force them to dispose of the animal. The squeal of a dying hog, being sacrificed unwillingly to satisfy the orders of a petty bureaucrat, is not an unusual sound in and around a *caserio*. The neighbor who reported the animal's presence is known, or suspected. Interpersonal relations between the animal's owner and the real or alleged informer are impaired seriously. The two families may also have been enemies before, with one retaliating against the other.

Financial rules are also a source of discontent in *caserios*. The Housing Authority has a definite ceiling on the amount a family who lives in a *caserio* may earn. If a family's income exceeds the established limit and this becomes known, the family is forced to move into some other type of housing. This rule means that *caserio* dwellers have incomes below the maximum, or they attempt to make the authority believe they do. Families with incomes near or above the allowable maximum know that they must conceal the amount of their income or face the prospect of moving. If the neighbors become suspicious that their income is above the maximum, a report may be made to the Housing Authority. The less successful neighbor, who is envious of the prosperous family's good fortune, to even the score, gossips to the authorities. An investigation may follow, and the family may be evicted if the report is substantiated. *Caserio* dwellers hate neighbors who report them.

Each family is required to pay the monthly rental established for it by the Housing Authority. Ability to pay is determined by the size of the family and its income. The *caserio* officials are responsible for checking on a family's income, the number of persons living in an apartment, and the maintenance of the apartment. The rule of "pay or get out," coupled with the rule of maximum earnings, eliminates those who cannot pay rent, as well as those who can afford private housing. *Caserio* dwellers, therefore, are a selected segment of the population.

In sum, *caserio* dwellers dislike the social conditions imposed upon them by the Public Housing Authority. They have been uprooted, in the main, either by the destruction of their slum homes or by their having moved directly from rural portions of the island to *caserios* in San Juan. Slum dwellers and rural migrants, who have moved to *caserios*, find it difficult to adjust to the rules imposed by the Public Housing Authority. One of the most disturbing factors in *caserio* life is the potential power that one family has over another family. This power becomes effective when a family is reported by its neighbors to the *caserio* officials for an infraction of rules. In the slums, no immediate authority intervenes between neighbors. Social controls within a slum are a product of the values and expectations of the traditional culture. Within the *caserios*, the norms and expectancies of lower-class culture clash at many points with the rules and regulations imposed by the government—rules and regulations which derive from a different social class.

The Dream House Husbands and wives in *caserios* and slums are as clear in what they desire as they are in what they do not like. *Caserio* dwellers do not desire more and better *caserios;* they want a home of their own. Families in the slums know that they are living under the shadow of the bulldozer. Whether they own or rent their homes, it is only a matter of time until the government demolishes the slum where they live. These families, too, want a home of their own—but *not* in a *caserio.*

What kind of a home do slum and *caserio* dwellers desire? The interviewees are almost of one voice in describing the home they want to own. The house should be located on high ground, on a lot fifty by one hundred feet. The lot should be on a paved street with sidewalks, so members of the family will not be maimed or killed by trucks and automobiles. It should be near schools, stores, and a church. There should be easy access to public transportation, doctors, and a hospital. There should be playgrounds for the children nearby. The lot should be enclosed by a concrete wall sufficiently high to provide privacy for the family and protection for the children.

The house should be built of concrete, with the floor covered with glazed, ceramic tile. Corrugated iron roofs are not desired; preferably, the roof and ceiling should be made of reinforced concrete. The kitchen and bathroom should have glazed, ceramic tile on the walls. The interior should be divided into a kitchen, living and dining area, a bathroom, ample closet space, and two or three bedrooms. It should have a porch and a back patio.

These families want electricity properly installed in the home. They want city water in their homes, with sinks in the kitchen and in the bathroom. They also desire underground, sanitary sewers.

The neighborhood should be a quiet one. The neighbors should be people they can respect, and the neighbors should respect them. They want to be friendly with their neighbors, and they want their neighbors to reciprocate.

Summary and Conclusion

By way of summary, we shall say again: The materials we have presented are drawn from an intensive study of families who live in San Juan, Puerto Rico. The families have been matched for age, socio-economic status, marital union, and area of residence. The differentiating criterion between families is the mental status of one or both spouses. In one-half of the families, at least one spouse is suffering from schizophrenia. In the other half of the families, both spouses are mentally healthy or, at most, revealed neurotic symptoms to the examining psychiatrist. The study group, therefore, is composed of "sick" and "well" families. The well families are controls for the sick families.

All of the families studied live either in slums or public housing projects. The families who live in apartments in the public housing projects are housed more adequately than families who live in the slums. They pay far less rent per month for their apartments than the slum dwellers who rent do for their humble homes. There is less crowding in the apartments than in the slums.

The reactions of slum families to their physical and human environments are sharply different from the reactions of families in public housing apartments to their neighborhoods. Most slum dwellers like their neighborhoods; most dwellers in public housing dislike theirs. This finding poses a dilemma for social planners.

The slums have grown up naturally. They are overcrowded, malodorous, noisy, unsanitary, and under condemnation by "enlightened" segments of the society. Yet, their inhabitants are fonder of them than *caserio* dwellers are of their neighborhoods.

The caserios are a product of the planner's design. The buildings are architecturally sound, and the apartments are dry and larger than the slum homes. Modern plumbing, electricity, and other conveniences are provided. *Caserios* are organized as community centers. Yet the people in our study who live in them do not like them. They look forward to the time when they can escape both the bureaucratic apparatus of the *caserio* and the tensions between families, which this apparatus creates. The rules of the *caserios* are imposed by a bureaucracy with a different set of subcultural values and norms from those who are expected to abide by them. *Caserios* rules stem from middle-class, professional values. These values are not part of the class culture of the people who are expected to abide by them. These people are uprooted slum dwellers or rural migrants who have little understanding of the norms of the social engineers who are trying to help them and their children overcome the wretchedness of lower-class living conditions. Slum dwellers are not subject to the annoying penetration of an alien subculture. This is one of the dilemmas that confront people who must cope with ways of life that are changing rapidly.

References

1. Bellak, L., and Benedict, P. K., eds., *Schizophrenia: A Review of the Syndrome,* New York: Logos Press, 1958; Arieti, S., *Interpretation of Schizophrenia,* New York: Brunner, 1955; Jackson, D. D., ed., *The Etiology of Schizophrenia,* New York: Basic Books, 1960; Hollingshead, A. B., "Some Issues in the Epidemiology of Schizophrenia," *Amer. Soc. Rev., 26:*5-13, 1961.
2. Clausen, J. A., "The Sociology of Mental Illness," in *Sociology Today, Problems and Prospects,* R. K. Merton, L. Broom, and L. S. Cottrell, Jr., eds., New York: Basic Books, 1959, pp. 485-509; Faris, R. E. L., and Dunham, H. W., *Mental Disorders in Urban Areas,* Chicago: Univ. of Chicago Press, 1939; Schroeder, C. W., "Mental Disorders in Cities," *Amer. J. Soc., 48:*40-48, 1942; Clark, R. E., "Psychoses, Income, and Occupations Prestige," *Amer. J. Soc.,* 54:433-440, 1949; Hollingshead, A. B., and Redlich, F. C., "Social Stratification and Psychiatric Disorders," *Amer. Soc. Rev., 18:*163-169, 1953; Hollingshead, A. B., and Redlich, F. C., *Social Class and Mental Illness: A Community Study,* New York: Wiley, 1958.
3. Each family was stratified by the use of Hollingshead, A. B., *Two Factor Index of Social Position,* New Haven, Conn., 1957, privately printed.

Bibliography

For other aspects of Rogler's and Hollingshead's study, see the following:

Rogler, L. H., and Hollingshead, A. B., "Class and Disordered Speech in the Mentally Ill," *J. Health and Human Behavior,* 2:178-185, 1961.

———, "The Puerto Rican Spiritualist as a Psychiatrist," *Amer. J. Soc.,* 67:17-21, 1961.

———, "Alqunas Observaciones Sobre el Espiritismo y las Enfermedades Mentales Entre Puertorriquenos de Clase Baja," *Revista de Ciencias Sociales,* 4:141-150, Univ. of Puerto Rico, 1960.

Rogler, L. H., Hollingshead, A. B., and Torres, Aguiar, M. A., "Las Clases Sociales y la Comunicacion de Ideas de los Enfermas Mentales," *Revista de Ciencas Sociales,* 3:119-131, 1959.

There have been a large number of sociological and anthropological studies done in Puerto Rico, among which are the following:

Hatt, P. K., *Background of Human Fertility in Puerto Rico,* Princeton, N.J.: Princeton Univ. Press, 1952.

Hill, R., Stycos, J. M., and Back, C. W., *The Family and Population Control: A Puerto Rico Experiment in Social Change,* Chapel Hill: Univ. of North Carolina Press, 1959.

Landy, D., *Tropical Childhood, Cultural Transmission and Learning in a Rural Puerto Rican Village,* Chapel Hill: Univ. of North Carolina Press, 1959.

Mintz, S. W., *Worker in the Cane: A Puerto Rican Life History,* New Haven, Conn.: Yale Univ. Press, 1960.

Rogler, C. C., *Comerio, A Study of a Puerto Rican Town,* Lawrence: Univ. of Kansas Press, 1940.

Stewart, J. H., ed., *People of Puerto Rico,* Urbana: Univ. of Illinois Press, 1956.

Stycos, J. M., *Family and Fertility in Puerto Rico: A Study of the Lower Income Group,* New York: Columbia Univ. Press, 1955.

Tumin, M. M., and Feldman, A., *Social Class and Social Change in Puerto Rico,* Princeton, N.J.: Princeton Univ. Press, 1961.

Community Action in East Harlem

18

ELLEN LURIE

I am sure that the name East Harlem immediately evokes images for all of you: slums, dirt, deprivation, crime, illness, density, minority problems. My own image, after so many years there, is naturally quite different; like most settlement house workers, I am not the least bit objective in my attitude. Subjectively, sentimentally, I would rather recall for you the intimate, touching, poignant vignettes that are so much more happily remembered than the sordid stories of hopelessness. But, though I want to challenge the popular image of my community, I am chagrined to find an imp on the point of my pen who insists that I challenge my own point of view first. If you cannot leap to your conclusions, neither can I to mine.

Let me start with a factual description. East Harlem is located between Central Park and the East River, immediately north of one of the wealthiest residential sections in the world. Its area is from twenty to twenty-five blocks long, and about seven blocks wide. But, although its geographic outlines are fairly distinct, it also comprises two different school districts, two different police precincts, two different postal zones, one health district, two welfare districts, one planning district, one City Council district, three Assembly districts, one State Senate district, and one Congressional district—*none* of whose boundaries coincide! Many of these include blocks further to the south or west; fortunately the boundaries on the east and north are contained by a river.

The population of East Harlem is 180,000—one-fourth of them under nine years of age. Ethnically, they are about a third white (mostly Italian), a third Negro, and a third Puerto Rican. In economic terms, 95 per cent of all families earn less than $5,000. One-fifth live in public housing; most of the rest, in old-law tenements built before

1910. No banks have loaned mortgage money in East Harlem since before 1940. Only one new, privately constructed apartment house has been built in thirty years. There has been sporadic "modernization," to escape state rent controls. In rent-controlled buildings, the average cost of a four-room, walk-up, "railroad" flat is $35.00 a month; in decontrolled buildings, a single room of the same standard may cost $35.00 a week.

Waves of public spending have inundated the area since 1945. They have produced, in housing, eleven low-income projects for 12,000 families; one middle-income project for 400 families; and one middle-income, public-private cooperative project for 1600 families. They have also renovated the schools. The area has 27,000 children in public elementary and high schools, and another third of the children in eight parochial schools. Six public schools have been built since 1955, with four more under construction; five have been, and two are being modernized.

The area also has a new city hospital and three large private hospitals, which serve the entire city; a Public Health Center and four Child Health clinics, three public libraries, one new but on the boundary and serving other areas as well, two police stations, old and crowded, two fire stations, a Welfare Department office, four settlement houses, privately financed and operated, a Center for the Aged, and nine Day Care centers for small children of working mothers. There are eighteen official parks and playgrounds (eight attached to schools and four to housing projects), with access to two large city parks; and an outdoor swimming pool. The Post Office is new; our Congressman serves on the Post Office Committee of the House.

East Harlem ranks among the highest areas in the city in the rate of morbidity and mortality, the rate of crime, and the rate of mobility; in population density and numbers; and in the number and proportion of non-English speaking children. It also receives among the highest allotments of the city budget for police, sanitation, welfare, youth services, education, housing, parks, hospitals, and whatever else is correlated with these.

Now the imp has let go of the pen. I am free to interject my side of the statistics—if only to add to the confusion. The question is, what has happened to the people of East Harlem under the impact of all this change, growth, public spending, increased service and attention?

The settlement houses had, of course, been in the forefront of the fight for good housing and for slum clearance. I and my co-workers in the Project had been told, and we believed, that this would solve everyone's problems. Now, after ten years of relocation and rebuilding, we pulled our heads out of the sands of overwork—we took some time away from housing clinics and gang wars and day-care fights and mental health budgets and board meetings—and looked around us. Our neighbors didn't seem to be accepting all this beneficence with the right spirit of grace.

The huge modern housing projects had not only displaced many of the old familiar landmarks, but had caused the relocation of many of our old-time neighborhood residents. The very impressiveness of these solid, institutional, gigantic buildings seemed to be imbuing their new tenants with a sense of their own *un*impressiveness. Their size and public quality—which permitted both the long-awaited and highly touted attributes of sunshine, fresh air, and modern plumbing, as well as ardently hoped-for economic rents—the very factors which brought us what we had always envisioned as an absolute good, were also bringing increased anonymity and apathy.

Now we remembered nostalgically the old Italian band concerts, the colorful street fairs, the rowdy political rallies. With slightly sentimental fuzziness, we longed for the "cop on the beat who called us all by name," "the friendly game of stoop ball where everyone knew everyone else," "the neighborhood grocer" who combined cheap advice with not-so-cheap but always available credit.

And our neighbors? How did they feel? The remaining oldtimers would come and reminisce with us. Bemoaning all the changes, they remembered only the color and gaiety and vitality of the slum blocks, and easily forgot the concomitant misery, noise, and squalor. And our new neighbors? Some hated it so much that they almost never came outside, wouldn't unpack, kept their shades drawn. But many others sought us out. As they brought their children to our programs, they would tell us how overcrowded and old the schools were, how inadequate the police protection was, how quickly the new projects were being defaced by vandalism, how afraid they were to walk the streets at night.

They were looking to us for help, and we were longing for the good old days. For *then* we could blame everything on the bad housing.

Then we always knew exactly what to do: "press for better housing—that is the solution."

We began to see that our thinking had been too wishful. We were no longer certain what the answers were. However, it is not the settlement tradition to stay confused or inactive for long. We had always developed our best programs when we took our cue from the people who lived around us. This is what we would do now. Why wasn't all the new housing working better? If so many improvements were being made, why was East Harlem still a mess?

We thought it had something to do with the fact that the money which had been poured into our area had come from "downtown." Our East Harlem residents had had almost nothing to say about where or how it should be spent. As a result, our community leadership had been forced to relocate, or was left standing in the midst of such overwhelmingly complex newness that they didn't have the faintest notion what to do. Even the old line "club house politicians" had been unable to stop the deluge. Everyone was saying, "What's the use? You can't fight City Hall."

We had to start somewhere, and we decided to rely on our basic faith that the people around us had good sound sense—if we only had the sense to listen to them. We believed that the people living in East Harlem had the right and the responsibility to have a voice in decisions which involved their own future. Our faith in them, however, was not enough. They had to develop self-confidence, faith in their own worth, before they would dare to speak out and become involved in their own community.

Developing Leadership Our basic objective was to ferret out leadership within the community and to help that leadership take on a responsible role. At first we were not worried by the huge complexities, because we had no long-range planning goal in mind. We would make the most of each problem, each crisis, and learn together as we tried to work them out.

From 1955 to 1957, we experimented with this approach in a rather sketchy fashion, stealing staff away from other duties, slowly testing out the premise. Late in 1957, a private foundation gave the two settlement houses a rather extensive grant, and for four years a relatively intensive community organization program was carried on.

At first, the most glaring need in the community was for new schools. Only two new schools had been built since 1925, and eleven schools were more than fifty years old. All of them were on double session. It was inconceivable to the parents that the city could have built ten new housing projects, and not one new school. And no one knew what to do. The parents whom we knew told us about it, and we made some inquiries at the City Planning Commission. What we learned was even more startling. School needs all over the city were so great that, since there was not possibly enough money to go around, it was only where parents pressured and yelled that schools were built! Yet in East Harlem, with perhaps one exception, we didn't have any real Parent Associations in our schools. The area had been torn up, and new roots had not had any time to grow. However, each school did have two or three outspoken parent "leaders." They didn't have any organized following, but they were angry enough to want to do something if only they could be shown what to do. Twenty schools gave us fifty or sixty such parents, and this became the East Harlem Citizens School Committee. Together we studied the construction needs of all our schools; we set up our own priority, and then began to yell. We held rallies, and testified at City Hall—all sixty of us wearing large red badges saying "East Harlem." The city fathers were so surprised at this vocal assault from such a long dormant quarter—and the needs were so demonstrably critical—that we got new schools and new schools and more new schools. In the past five years more new school construction has taken place in East Harlem than in any other section of the city.

The first blow was struck. With this simple, easily understood objective, we stirred up interest and participation. But what then? We realized that leadership had been pulled together for this one most important purpose; but no solid foundation for ongoing participation had been laid. The "leaders" had been reacting to us and to each other. But leaders are no good without a membership behind them. Together we had to find ways to develop *real* Parent Associations which would learn to work together without us. Furthermore, we had to weave a new social fabric which would knit this "half-renewed-half-slum" community together. We were seeking a modern equivalent for the social clubs and church societies which had once flourished in store fronts all over East Harlem.

We dug in—and not just on crises now. Parents wanted to raise funds so their kids could have a party. Together we learned how to organize cake sales. Winter clothing was expensive, so our Parent Associations sponsored boot exchanges. We didn't know each other; our parents persuaded principals to give them a parents' room in the schools, where we held coffee hours, sewing classes, knitting clubs. We planned trips together, and monthly programs. We helped to choose sites, worried about the relocation problem; and, when the new schools were finally opened, our Parent Associations had grown in strength and self-confidence and experience, and were ready to face some very hard problems. For the new schools, like the new housing, weren't oozing milk and honey. Our children were just as far behind in reading. Our shortage of experienced teachers was just as shocking. And the school population was just as segregated.

But now we had built up around us an aggressive, enthusiastic group of parents—leaders *and* followers. The new schools were concrete evidence of what an alert group of citizens could do. Looking at next steps, they were expectant, surely a bit naive in their hopefulness. And we, too, were overly impressed with our own strength.

This time we chose several new avenues:

First, we had a beautiful neighborhood academic high school for boys—an older gift to our community from a beloved ex-alumnus, Mayor Fiorello LaGuardia. Although the high school could hold 2,500 children, only 600 boys were actually going. In New York City, on the high school level, children may choose from many high schools; but, for a number of reasons, they weren't choosing ours. Interestingly enough, it was not a segregated school at all. It was in the heart of the old Italian community, and mostly Italian boys were going there. Negro and Puerto Rican youngsters went to high schools outside of East Harlem. The result was an under-utilized school in an over-utilized area. The Board of Education decided to close the high school and convert it into a junior high school (and incidentally, spend no less than $10,000,000 to build another high school only fifteen blocks south!). With this announcement, all the latent community pride burst forth. Groups on all sides began to take a good look at the school. The details are too numerous for retelling here. The city only knew the school wasn't filled; therefore, close it. The community said the school was not used because it wasn't any good. "Make it a good school, a great school, then children from all over the city will want to go there, and our children will, too."

What is most fascinating to me about this story is this: many *city-*

wide civic and educational groups endorsed the position of our East Harlem parents. Basic concepts in secondary school education were questioned. Our parents wanted, for example, language courses geared not only to the college-bound but to the commercial student, or to the student who graduates into the armed services. "If our kids can speak Spanish and English on the streets, why can't the schools teach them to speak them right so that they can use them?" Columbia University, New York University, even the United Nations' Education Division, were fascinated, supportive, excited. But the New York City Board of Education tabled any such action. The professional educators on their staff resented lay people questioning their "expert judgment" about "professional" matters. Two "liberal" Board members contended that integration in East Harlem was impossible in the long run; that such a program was exciting, but not for our area. The result: we succeeded in keeping the high school open; it was made co-educational (we had asked for that); but none of the curriculum changes were made. Today, because of the tremendous population push at the high school level, the school *is* filled—it is segregated, and it is second rate.

Later I shall want to refer again to this lag or "wobble" between the ideas of professional experts and those of average, unspecialized citizens. I'm certain, though, that when a mechanical engineer invents a new kind of power tool, he asks the factory worker who is using the machine whether it actually is working as it had been planned. Surely we ought to be as wise, or simply as practical, when it comes to finding out whether the courses we are offering in our schools achieve their objectives for the students?

We experimented in another direction in our attempt to improve public education. Directly to the south of East Harlem is the so-called Silk Stocking District of Manhattan—rich, becoming richer. Most of the new luxury housing going up there is not meant for families with children. Therefore, the six or seven elementary schools in that area have become increasingly under-utilized—300 or 400 children (all white) in schools with 800 or 1200 seats. *Our* schools, ten and fifteen blocks to the north, were crowded and segregated. Our parents pressured for relief; and in 1959 a bus program was initiated by the Board of Education. Children whose parents so wished could ride a school bus to another school. This program, called Open Enrollment, has now been expanded, and more than 6000 youngsters are taking advantage of it in all sections of our city. Now, in the early stages of this program, some of our parents were also fighting to rezone a school located on the borderline between these two very different areas, so that a more natural form of integration could take place in this so-called "fringe" situation. Their struggle was half won, with some integration (25 per cent white). But about 200 Negro children had to be zoned out of the school (then 15 per cent white) to enable 200 white children to come in (to make it 25 per cent white). These Negro children were then required to go to an entirely segregated school. At first, the Negro parents fought this decision with all their might—and lost. They were assigned to the new but segregated East Harlem school; and, swallowing their disappointment, began in earnest to organize a Parent Association. We were privileged to staff this group. Six months later, the Board of Education announced they had changed their minds: the parents could, if they chose, bus their children out. Almost none of the leadership group took up the option! They had become so intrigued with the battle of improving their own school, they had seen other East Harlem schools so depleted of leadership and good students because of open enrollment, that they made the hard decision to stay—to fight for improvements in their own school and neighborhood, which they felt would have more enduring value.

What I have tried to show is how we moved from superficial levels to deeper ones. New schools were needed, and now we have almost, though not quite, enough. We can't blame our poor education on the quality of the buildings any longer. Integration? We've tested it—with varied results—but we do know that integration *alone* won't solve our educational problems. Our community has elected one Parent Association president a female district leader. Two others have been appointed to local school boards. But the end is nowhere in sight. We now begin to see that quality education is costly—and, even then, since we have learned from painful experience that there is no automatic virtue in large expenditures of public money—we do see that we must have high-quality people teaching and administering our schools. What we will do next as a community—or as a nation, for that matter—to achieve this, I don't know.

Growing Self-Responsibility Perhaps it would be helpful, because I want to be precise, to insert some statistics here. In 1955-1956 I conducted a study of families living in Washington Houses: 14 buildings, 1400 low-income families, 5000 people, mostly Negro and Puerto Rican; very few whites. We found what has subsequently been described by several other more highly documented but similar studies: many people were unhappy in the project; they were almost "mourning" for their slum life; they hated the public quality of life, they didn't want to participate in the community at all. There was anomie all over the place. It was in this fairly negative atmosphere that we started to organize a tenant association in 1957. We organized around a crisis. There had been an *attempted* rape on a Puerto Rican child. The Puerto Ricans, immediately, without knowing who did it, blamed the Negroes; the Negroes immediately got furious. Everybody wanted to put in an application to move; the Housing Authority was blamed for the whole thing. The only solution the tenants could come up with was, "Let's go see the Mayor."

Then we began to work with the families. After the immediate crisis was resolved, we started with a very simple thing—Christmas. Everyone loves to celebrate Christmas. That first year their Christmas celebration was planned almost entirely by our staff; mostly children came to the tree-lighting ceremony; and within a week the tree was stolen and all the lights were pulled apart.

During the next two years, we worked with tenants almost on a day-to-day, building-by-building basis, and on many levels of activity: police protection, social activities, register-to-vote campaigns, etc.

In 1959 ten buildings decided that they wanted to have their own Christmas celebrations—ten out of the fourteen. This time our staff took no role at all. If they wanted to have community celebrations, it was up to them, and ten of the buildings wanted a "public Christmas." An average of nine persons in each building, representing 10 per cent of the families, took leadership roles; they planned the parties, decided what to do, how much money would be needed, and enlisted their neighbors to help. They formed committees. An average of thirty-nine people per building (40 per cent) took what we call secondary leadership roles. They collected money, went together to purchase the food and decorations. Six hundred and ten (of 1000 families in the ten buildings) contributed an average of 36 cents each. This gives you a sense of the "followership"—the tenants trusted the people who collected the money. Nine hundred and seventeen children went to the ten different parties which 153 adults helped to conduct. All ten trees (which were jointly purchased at a discount price) stayed up all ten days with not a single instance of vandalism. All ten trees were down on the ground, not, as the Housing Authority had done in the past, up on rooftops where people could watch them but not touch them.

In 1961 there was an *actual* rape of a Puerto Rican child in the same project. I want to show you how differently *this* crisis was handled—four years later. The building chairman immediately called a meeting of all the adults in the building. What was the first item on their agenda? How would they help the child when she came back from the hospital? How were they, as her neighbors, going to receive her? What would they tell the other children so nobody would "make fun" of what had happened? How were they going to help the parents help their child? (We had nothing to do with staffing this meeting. We were not even there; this was reported to us afterward.)

The second item on their agenda was, what social controls should they have—they didn't use these words—to make sure such a thing didn't happen again. They agreed that different fathers would take turns at various times of the day or night, depending on their shifts, to help patrol this building over the next month of this critical period, so similar instances wouldn't happen, and so everyone would feel less anxious.

The third item was to ask the Housing Authority for increased police protection, and for bars to be installed on the lower windows. Both things were done. I don't know what better illustrates the sense of growth this group has achieved.

The East Harlem Project has moved in several other significant areas. We have worked with tenant associations and merchant associations toward improving housing and shopping conditions—in much the same way and with similar kinds of learning as described above with parent groups. (By *we*, I mean our neighbors and my co-workers in the East Harlem Project.)

Together we have been effective in many surface matters. If we have not been able to redesign all public housing, we have been able to make significant changes in the use and design of the open land surrounding those buildings. We have pushed successfully for stores in housing projects. We pressured for, and won, legislation to convert one public housing project into a community-sponsored, middle-income cooperative, which is being sold now. We pushed for stronger legislation in the field of credit buying; and at our request and with our help, Columbia University has just completed a thorough study of the implications of credit buying practices in our community.

Planning—and Planners At last, and in summary, I can get to that word "planning." We have been shouting it for seven years now —without much idea of what we meant, except we knew that at least schools should be built at the same time as the new housing. And now we face the second inundation.

From 1945 to 1955, unplanned bulldozing characterized East Harlem. In the next ten years, urban renewal and community renewal and conservation and other high-sounding programs are on their way. And this time we can't yell "Wait—ask us—plan with us!" For public hearings have been held on all of these programs, and we have participated in strong numbers. We are not at all certain how much our participation matters—whether we will really be listened to, or whether we will merely be a useful group to talk *at*.

What bothers me is that I am not sure we settlements have yet built a really independent foundation of community leadership. Have we merely substituted our form of forcing change for the city's less subtle, more obviously irrational methods?

I wonder increasingly when we—and our neighbors—will start making some hard decisions. In the past, the city had money to clear slums. They found some poor, needy, inarticulate area, and dumped the project there. Now we have become articulate—and so have many other communities. We're all experts at saying, "No, go away." But we must go beyond this. If we—and everyone else—say, "Don't clear my block—go renew some other place," somebody must stop and say painfully, "Yes, we must tear down, but let's plan it together."

Certainly, then, we have learned to organize; but where do we go next? We want to raise the level of participation; but how far can we really raise it?

I can't say, though perhaps many of you would want to, "Look, there is no such thing as government by the people; it is government by experts. Let the experts take over."

I don't believe this; I can't believe it. It is my religion that democracy must be a government of the people—of *all* the people. But I do understand now how difficult it is to make this happen. There are so many of us, and even in this one country, even in one city, although we all speak English, we are all speaking different languages. We see the city, each in our own way: as parents, as children, as teachers, lawyers, artists, laborers, scientists, sociologists, politicians, dreamers. Many of us say we love the city. We know the city has problems. We have got to find a way to share the burden of problem solving. And yet, we sit in separate rooms, and we keep our individual insight almost to ourselves.

What has happened, I think, is that the professionals who are studying city life, "urban growth," "social stress," etc., do so with a wonderful sense of objectivity. Their studies describing the effects of deprivation or mobility or renewal are all filled with a passion for truth; but with very little sense of *compassion* for what they have found. Our agencies and universities set up great research projects, and the problems of leadership and power structure in our urban society today are clearly, precisely, exhaustively examined.

But so what? What sense of pressure and obligation to these same agencies and universities feel toward moving into action on these fronts? Are they going to move in and face the community, or merely be satisfied with writing up the results?

We hear more and more about government agencies underwriting citizen action. But, do you know what this is? They are establishing company unions. Government cannot organize citizen participation, because the very nature of *real* citizen participation implies a threat to government agencies—for true citizen action breeds change and reform. Thus, if the money and staff stimulating such participation comes from government, what honest good can it actually be?

Some universities have set up "urban extension services," which are aimed at promoting citizen action around vital issues. But, in the last analysis, universities are deeply committed only to *research* in these areas. "Centers of urban study" are cropping up everywhere. Sociologists, psychologists, economists, and even philosophers, spend extensive time observing and analyzing problems of our urban society. I would like to see much more of this kind of research result in university-sponsored experiments in direct community action which would put their valuable knowledge to work.

During the past few years, for example, Columbia University's Medical Center has assigned a large research staff to study the Washington Heights Community under a grant from the National Institute of Mental Health. Certainly the center sees its obligation in the health service field and, I'm sure, as a result of its findings, it will make many policy changes and innovations in its current programs. But the hospital owns a great deal of property in this "changing" area, which is slowly but decidedly deteriorating physically and spiritually. How wonderful it would be if the center would see its own role in the community in broader terms. Its power and prestige and knowledge could be vitally significant ingredients, if they were harnessed to a joint citizen-community development program aimed at a revitalization of housing, and education, and all the other facets of life around it.

What I am trying to say is that none of us is outside of the society; none of us is independent of what the next person is learning. The experts on urban life have learned to listen to the bells in our society; they carefully and precisely record the quality of their tone, the frequency of their vibration, their implication for the future. But do they truly understand for whom those bells are tolling?

We in East Harlem have had many, many fascinating experiences in community action. But I, for one, feel no sense of exhilaration. I can't say with confidence, "The tools are there—we need only use them to turn chaos into order." I'm not sure the tools are all that reliable. I'm not even sure that we would recognize "order" when we achieved it. But we must not stop or withdraw. The vitality and excitement of East Harlem throbs through us all, and forces us to uncover paths we don't yet know are there, leading to shores beyond still uncharted waters.

19 Urban Leadership and the Appraisal of Abnormal Behavior

BRUCE P. DOHRENWEND

The setting is a section of New York City. It might be described from various administrative points of view as a health district, two school districts, most of two police precincts, the greater part of three New York State Assembly districts, or the larger portion of two United States Congressional districts. Like other sections of the city, this urban area has a name and is geographically quite distinct from its surroundings. Referred to as a "bedroom community" for the city's commercial and industrial center, the district has a population of about 270,000 persons.

Census materials, and data gathered in a sample survey, describe a population which is now mostly lower middle and working class. The four main ethnic groups (there are others of lesser size) are Jewish, Irish, Negro, and Puerto Rican, with both Jews and Negroes considerably more numerous than the other two groups.

Research on the social history of the area shows that this picture of today is quite different from that of yesterday. In 1920, this metropolitan community was evenly populated by three major ethnoreligious groups: Anglo-Saxon, Dutch, or German Protestants; Irish Catholics; and East European Jews. Throughout the thirties and forties, there continued to be a steady influx of Irish and Jews, with corresponding decreases in the original Protestant population. During this period up until World War II, the area was predominantly middle class in character, inhabited wholly by whites of European ancestry. With the war came great changes which are continuing into the present.

As in the city as a whole, there has been much movement out of the area on the part of higher income families who have been resettling in suburbs. There has also been heavy in-migration by Negroes from the South and, since about 1950, by Puerto Ricans. Today, these two ethnic groups make up the large majority of the families living in the southeastern quarter of the area, in the older, more deteriorated housing. This section, now inhabited for the most part by low-income families, is rapidly taking on the character of a slum. The change has been described as "slum invasion," ". . . a downgrading stage in which old housing . . . is rapidly being adapted to greater-density use than it was originally designed for." [1]

"Slum invasion" of the southeastern portion of the district is accompanied by symptoms of what the French sociologist Emile Durkheim[2] has described as *anomie,* a social state of "deregulation" and "declassification" in which common rules of conduct fail to govern behavior. Clues to the existence of anomic conditions are contained in police reports that prostitution, narcotic violation, street fights, and juvenile delinquency are heavily concentrated in this southeastern quarter. These may be taken as the more dramatic forms of anger, discontent, disillusionment, and irritated disgust with life that Durkheim describes as the more prevalent responses to anomie.[3]

The Problem

The aim in this paper is to trace certain influences of the differing socio-cultural environments within this urban area on the perceptions of a special group of its citizens—namely, its community leaders. More specifically, concern is with effects on aspects of these leaders' appraisals of various types of abnormal behavior. The term "appraisal" is being used here in the sense of Hollingshead and Redlich, as the lay counterpart to clinical diagnosis.[4]

In this study, leaders are drawn primarily from the four main subcultures in this urban area: Jewish, Irish, Negro, and Puerto Rican. The first two subcultures are relatively advantaged socially and economically; the last two, located for the most part in the slum environment of the southeastern quarter, are relatively disadvantaged. The question is: What is the impact of the different subcultural backgrounds of these leaders on their appraisals of abnormal behavior?

Selection of Leaders

The first step was to decide what would be meant by "leader" for purposes of this study. In a recent critical analysis of research on community leadership, Rossi states the problem in the following way: Study of power, influence, or leadership can center on (1) the "potential" for power inherent in positions of formal authority; (2) the definition of influence in terms of reputation in the community; and/or (3) actual processes of influence exerted around particular issues.[5] There are serious difficulties in following the last procedure: for example, in securing a meaningful sample of issues and time to study them. In the present research, therefore, reliance is placed on formal position and reputation.

Leaders were selected from five main orders of activity: Political-legal, economic, educational, religious, and, for the Puerto Ricans, social-recreational. Details of the selection procedures are set forth elsewhere.[6] The resulting list included state senators, assemblymen, municipal court justices, police captains, businessmen, school principals, clergymen, and heads of such organizations as the Chamber of Commerce, League of Women Voters, and Puerto Rican hometown clubs.

In all, ninety-one persons were designated for inclusion in the study. Interviews were obtained with eighty-seven of these, all but eight of whom come from one of the four main subcultures: thirty-eight Jewish leaders, ten Irish, nineteen Negro, and twelve Puerto Rican. On the whole, the leaders are highly educated and economically successful. Almost three-fourths are college graduates and, as a rule, have gone on to professional or graduate training as well. About two-thirds have incomes of $10,000 a year or more. Except in the educational order, in which the leaders are predominantly female, most are male. Nearly three-fourths are between forty and fifty-nine years old. Most of the Puerto Rican leaders were born outside the continental United States, while most of the Jewish and Irish leaders are children of immigrant parents. Of the leaders from the main ethnic groups, only the Negroes, by and large, have parents born in the States. Regardless of ethnic background, however, the large majority of the leaders have lived the greater part of their lives in the New York metropolitan region.

Reflections of Anomie

Three chief factors differentiate the leaders from these subcultures. The first is ethnic background, which is naturally different for all four. The second is religion, which contrasts the Catholic Irish and Puerto Rican leaders with the Jews and Negro Protestants. As was mentioned earlier, the Negro and Puerto Rican populations inhabit, for the most part, the slum and near-slum areas of the district. Thus a third factor of relative social and economic deprivation contrasts the status of the Negro and Puerto Rican groups with that of the relatively advantaged Jewish and Irish groups from which these leaders come.

How are these factors related to these leaders' appraisals of abnormal behavior? The main results are contained in the reactions of the leaders to brief case descriptions of six fictitious persons, each illustrating a particular type of psychiatric disorder. The cases portray paranoid schizophrenia, simple schizophrenia, anxiety neurosis, alcoholism, compulsive-phobic behavior, and juvenile character disorder. Developed by Shirley Star with psychiatric consultation, all six have been used in a number of other studies.[7]

Each leader was questioned about each of the six cases. For example, the case describing paranoid schizophrenia was read to the leader by the interviewer in the following manner:

> "Now I'd like to describe a certain kind of person and ask you a few questions about him . . . I'm thinking of a man—let's call him Frank Jones—who is very suspicious; he doesn't trust anybody and he's sure that everybody is against him. Sometimes he thinks that people he sees on the street are talking about him or following him around. A couple of times now, he has beaten up men who didn't even know him, because he thought that they were plotting against him. The other night, he began to curse his wife terribly; then he hit her and threatened to kill her, because, he said, she was working against him, too, just like everyone else."

The leader was asked first whether he thought there was anything wrong with this man. If he said "Yes," he was then asked whether he thought that Frank Jones had some kind of mental illness. Then *regardless of whether or not* he thought that Frank Jones was mentally ill, he was asked whether he thought that what was wrong was serious. A number of additional questions were asked, and then the entire procedure was repeated for each of the remaining five case descriptions.

In general, the leaders saw all six cases as examples of abnormal behavior. Thus, only 2 per cent said that there was nothing wrong in as many as three of the cases; an additional 8 per cent judged nothing wrong in two of the six cases; 17 per cent saw nothing wrong in one of the cases. Only in the case of the compulsive-phobic did as many as one-fifth of the leaders say that there was nothing wrong.

There is much more variability in their judgments of whether the abnormal behavior in each case is mental illness or not, and of whether it is serious or not.

These two sets of judgments conform closely to the pattern required for Guttman scales.[8] Each meets the major criterion, reproducibility of .90 or better, and enough of the remaining criteria to warrant treating them as two distinct scales, with the scale order of the items somewhat different in each.[6] Of special interest is the scale order of the cases on the dimension of seriousness. Here, according to the scale, the three cases which threaten others—paranoid, alcoholic, and juvenile character disorder—are more likely to be regarded as serious than the simple schizophrenic, anxiety neurotic, and compulsive-phobic problems which show little or no sociopathy, and appear to be of danger primarily to the individual concerned.

Given the high tendency of the group as a whole to judge that something is wrong in each of the six cases, it is no surprise that the leaders from all four subcultures are similar in this regard. But what about their tendencies to judge the cases as mentally ill, and to see the problems as "serious"—as measured by the two Guttman scales? Surprisingly, there are no differences in tendency to regard the cases as mentally ill, according to any of the three factors of interest in the present analysis: ethnic background, religion, or advantaged vs. disadvantaged group status. There is, however, a marked contrast in tendency to regard the disorders as serious which differentiates the leaders from the relatively advantaged Jewish and Irish groups, on the one hand, from the leaders from the relatively disadvantaged Negro and Puerto Rican groups on the other.

The leaders from the *advantaged* groups are much more likly to extend their judgments about what they regard as serious beyond the three cases which appear to threaten others. The leaders from the *disadvantaged* groups tend to concentrate their concern on the disorders with a strong sociopathic component.

This contrast holds when differences in the educational level and in orders of leadership activity between the leaders from the advantaged and disadvantaged groups are controlled by omitting those who are not college graduates, and by removing educational leaders (most of whom are Jewish) and social recreational leaders (all of whom are Puerto Rican). Consider the following difference: among the college graduate leaders from the political-legal, religious, and economic orders, 64 per cent from the advantaged groups, in contrast to only 31 per cent from the disadvantaged groups, regard at least four of the six cases as serious. Thus, to a much greater extent than the leaders from the disadvantaged groups, the leaders from the advantaged groups tend to extend their judgment of what is serious to the types of disorder which primarily harm the sufferer himself. In contrast, 62 per cent from the disadvantaged groups regard as serious either two or *all three* of the cases in which anti-social behaviors appear to threaten others, and *none* of the cases which appear of harm primarily to the individual concerned; the corresponding figure for the leaders from the advantaged groups is only 23 per cent. The probability is less than one in a hundred that such differential concentration on disorders which threaten others could have occurred by chance. Leaders from the disadvantaged groups would appear to give higher priority to sociopathy in their judgments about what is and what is not a serious problem. Their appraisals of abnormal behavior, in short, seem to reflect anomic conditions in the groups from which they come.

Is their further evidence for this interpretation? The answer is yes. For example, the first question to each leader in the interview was, "What does the term 'mental illness' mean to you?" This open-ended query was followed by two more, asking which were the more and which were the less serious kinds. In response, 62 per cent of the leaders from the disadvantaged groups, in contrast to only 36 per cent from the advantaged groups, used terms describing types of sociopathic behavior: "rebellion against society," "delinquency," "drinking," "drug addiction," "irresponsible behavior," and so on. Following his responses to the six case descriptions, each leader was asked two other general open-ended questions: "What do you think are the main causes of the most serious problems?" and "What do you think are the main causes of the less serious problems?" Forty-six per cent of the leaders from the disadvantaged groups mentioned slum conditions and poverty as against only 14 per cent of the leaders from the advantaged groups. Moreover, 38 per cent of the leaders from the disadvantaged groups attributed a causal role to prejudice, discrimination, and acculturative factors, as opposed to 9 per cent of the leaders from the advantaged groups. Consider what the responses of Jewish and Irish leaders from the now relatively advantaged groups might have been at the turn of the century! In this regard, there is an additional small, but rather interesting, difference in the ideas about cause. Almost a quarter of these leaders from the advantaged groups mention status worries such as "business failure," "keeping up socially," and so on; while only 7 per cent of the leaders from the disadvantaged groups mentioned such problems.

Conclusion

What, then, can be concluded from these results? Conant notes that educators concerned with the problems of slum schools do not get very excited about the need to include foreign languages in the curriculum when half the seventh and eighth grade pupils read English at fourth grade level or below.[9] In a study of soldiers' reactions to their living conditions, Naomi Rothwell found that there were few complaints about privacy if the barracks were cold.[10] And Gurin, Veroff, and Feld conclude, on the basis of their nationwide survey, that "interpersonal and personal sources of satisfaction assume prominence only when the basic material requisites of living are no longer in doubt . . ."[11] These are examples of the effect of situational imperatives on judgments about priorities. So also is the tendency of the leaders from the disadvantaged groups to reflect their concern with anomic social conditions by giving high priority to problems of aggressive anti-social behavior, and hence to forms of psychiatric disorder in which such behavior is implicated.

References

1. Hoover, E. M., and Vernon, R., *Anatomy of a Metropolis,* Cambridge, Mass.: Harvard Univ. Press, 1959.
2. Durkheim, E., *Suicide,* tr. J. A. Spaulding and G. Simpson, Glencoe, Ill.: The Free Press, 1951.
3. Dohrenwend, B. P., "Egoism, Altruism, Anomie, and Fatalism: A Conceptual Analysis of Durkheim's Types," *Amer. Soc. Rev.,* 24:466-473, 1959.
4. Hollingshead, A. B., and Redlich, F. C., *Social Class and Mental Illness: A Community Study,* New York: Wiley, 1958.

5. Rossi, P. H., "Community Decision-Making," in *Approaches to the Study of Politics,* ed. R. Young, Evanston, Ill.: Northwestern Univ. Press, 1958.
6. Dohrenwend, B. P., "Some Aspects of the Appraisal of Abnormal Behavior by Leaders in an Urban Area," *Amer. Psych., 117*:190-198, 1962; Dohrenwend, B. P., Bernard, V. W., and Kolb, L. C., "The Orientations of Leaders in an Urban Area towards Problems of Mental Illness," *Amer. J. Psychiat., 118*:683-691, 1962.
7. Star, S. A., *The Public's Ideas About Mental Illness,* Chicago: National Opinion Research Center, 1955, mimeographed; Cumming, E., and Cumming, J., *Closed Ranks,* Cambridge, Mass.: Harvard Univ. Press, 1957.
8. Guttman, L., "The Basis for Scalogram Analysis," in Stouffer, S. A., Guttman, L., Suchman, E. A., Lazarsfeld, P. F., Star, S. A., and Clausen, J. A., *Measurement and Prediction,* Princeton, N.J.: Princeton Univ. Press, 1950.
9. Conant, J. B., *Slums and Suburbs,* New York: McGraw-Hill, 1961.
10. Rothwell, N. D., *What Soldiers Think About Housing,* Troop Information and Education Division, Troop Attitude Research Branch, U.S. Army, 1958, mimeographed.
11. Gurin, G., Veroff, J., and Feld, Sheila, *Americans View Their Mental Health,* New York: Basic Books, 1960.

20 Strategies in Delinquency Prevention

THOMAS GLADWIN

Alarm over increases in juvenile delinquency is reaching acute proportions, and has created inescapable pressure on schools, police, social agencies, and governments to do something about delinquency. In particular, the alarm, and therefore the pressure, focuses on delinquency in lower-class urban populations. Presumably this is because delinquency is more prevalent in these populations, and also because lower-class delinquents display more of the physical violence which so distresses middle-class people. The question, then, is posed with increasing insistence: What can or should be done about delinquency in big city slums?

Current theoretical formulations on juvenile delinquency in the United States are phrased in largely sociological terms, emphasizing the interplay between personality structure and social institutions. Action programs based on these formulations select one or more strategic points around the circle of causality at which to intervene, and thereby hopefully to break the circle. Most commonly, manipulation is attempted with respect to the psychological links in the chain. Programs of this sort have largely been directed by social workers, with the assistance of psychiatrists and psychologists. The aim is to alter self-defeating attitudes and perceptions, and to redirect social energy toward more constructive goals which will hopefully prove more satisfying and less frustrating. However, in actual practice the relationship of a worker with lower-class clients is usually structured in terms of the psychoanalytically-oriented clinical training of the worker, and the goal of the relationship becomes one of draining off or deflecting acute psychological and social tensions. In essence, the worker tries to make conformity tolerable.

This strategy of psychological manipulation of individuals or groups has come under increasing criticism, especially with respect to lower-class delinquency. It has been pointed out that professional intervention based on a psychotherapeutic model has little impact on the basic social and cultural conditions which channel psychological needs in troublesome directions. This criticism states in effect that lower-class people develop self-defeating attitudes because they are in fact defeated by their society.

An additional argument against this kind of psychological intervention is provided by Walter B. Miller's findings in working with lower-class gangs, that while it was possible to change many psychological attributes—attitudes toward authority, adults, education, and to some extent general middle-class values—in a desirable direction, no significant reduction was achieved in the rate of delinquent acts.[1]

However, the dilemma of the social agencies has recently led to experiments with massive assaults on the social environment. These generally propose saturation of a lower-class neighborhood with multiple and varied services intended to alleviate simultaneously all of the various social limitations which the proponent of the plan views as serious. There are numerous obvious criticisms which can be leveled at the strategies of this sort thus far proposed. Most are so expensive in both money and professional requirements that they offer little hope of providing in themselves a strategic model of subsequent usefulness elsewhere.

The answer to this objection is that new insights and ideas will be found and proven effective, and that these can then be applied selectively and less expensively in other areas. However, the proposed programs are so global that their evaluation also tends to be global, and it becomes very unlikely that the specific impact of any single program component can be isolated and measured. Therefore even if these programs are demonstrably successful, their benefits will be largely limited to the affected area or community.

Perhaps we must recognize that juvenile delinquency *as such* is not directly amenable to programs of prevention or amelioration. If we accept this, we can contemplate programs which will achieve a more critical and economical focus upon selected components of the problem of the lower-class adolescent, with the expectation that in the long run delinquency rates will drop proportionately as one after another of the forces pressuring these adolescents is relieved. Juvenile delinquency is not a distinct social disease or syndrome. It encompasses a number of different kinds of behaviors. Furthermore, the behaviors defined as delinquent are by no means the only ways in which adolescents can or do respond to their many-faceted dilemmas. Juvenile delinquents are simply those individuals or groups who happen to react to a situation in ways which the larger society views as threatening. In contrast, the youth who enters military service, for example, may thereby achieve temporary relief from his difficulties, but his behavior is not considered delinquent.

Equally we must recognize that the pressures and the blockages are by no means perceived and experienced in the same way by everyone. One adolescent may feel frustrated and discriminated against because he cannot go to college or because he is unable to get a white-collar job, and therefore feel he must somehow vent his frustration, or at least escape from his dilemma. But another may have set his heart on being a long-haul truck driver and feel no frustration whatever.

The challenge, then, is to identify those attributes of the social environment which are perceived by the largest number of lower-class adolescents as unfair limitations upon them. If we can find realistic ways to relieve these limitations (which are usually very real) we may hope to reduce progressively a succession of those social pressures which cause some youths to react with behaviors we call delinquent.

However, any strategic alternative to a direct attack on delinquency must meet at least two conditions. One is that the alternatives be realistically feasible and within reach of available financial and professional resources. The second is that the goal of any new program must be high enough in the hierarchy of middle-class values so that the self-evident worth of the new program will justify its substitution for the original aim of simply preventing delinquency as such.

One goal meeting these requirements would be a substantial increase in the number of lower-class adolescents who complete high school and attain a regular and educationally respectable diploma. A diploma is not the cure for all the problems of any lower-class youth, and at best would be unattainable for many, but a substantial proportion of the population of our concern have the ability and would unquestionably be much better off if they could complete high school satisfactorily. It is therefore worth examining with some care the potential value and feasibility of starting the attack on the lower-class dilemma with a focus on the academic achievement of lower-class youths in high school.

Middle-class values link education not only to occupational opportunity but also to the formation of good character. High school dropouts are related in the popular view directly with delinquency—even though many adolescents leave school for the respectable purpose of entering productive employment. Similarly, the first question likely to be asked by enforcement officers or judges if a boy gets in trouble is, "How is he doing in school?" Clearly, a program goal of improving school performance and participation meets the criterion of self-evident worth as a substitute for, or an indirect approach to, delinquency prevention as such.

From what we as social scientists know of the lower-class dilemma, a valid high school diploma is clearly of ever increasing importance to an adolescent for at least two closely related reasons. It is in the first place a testimonial to "good character," and in fact during its acquisition many middle-class behaviors and attitudes are necessarily acquired. It reflects a willingness to conform.

It is also an essential, even though not in itself sufficient, key to the middle-class opportunity structure. This results from the continued dwindling of the skilled labor market and the increasing requirement of a high school diploma for consideration for even a semi-skilled job. And of course without a diploma from high school, college is also out of the question.

The difficulty is that lower-class children are lacking not so much in educational opportunities as in the capability or readiness to utilize these opportunities. Schools are available. In lower-class areas the teachers may not be quite as good but they at least meet minimum requirements. To some degree, the inability to capitalize on opportunities is recognized in planning for lower-class students. However, the response is usually an attempt to adapt the school to the child, rather than the reverse.

Thus it is frequently stated that schools demand middle-class behaviors, and that this handicaps the lower-class child. This is undoubtedly true, but the answer is not necessarily to relax the demands. If we recognize that a high school diploma acts as a badge of middle-class respectability, the schools must continue to demand middle-class behaviors. At the risk of appearing cynical, when I see a negligible relationship between the content of the average high school curriculum on the one hand, and the abilities required in the jobs for which a high school diploma is demanded on the other, I believe we are forced to conclude that the *primary* value of the diploma is as a certificate of socialization. It certifies that the holder of a diploma will respond in predictable ways to the expectations of middle-class employers.

There is real danger in pressuring schools to meet the lower-class child at his own level. Successful school participation requires above all working fairly hard and steadily at tasks which at best are often dull, in order to achieve a very distant reward, the diploma. In other words, in order that academic learning itself be achieved, the student must accept the necessity of hard work and delay in reward and gratification—behaviors which lie at the heart of middle-class values. Equipped to work within these values, lower-class youths can and do move upward. Without them they are more than likely to fail in school and to spend their lives in underprivileged poverty.

The problem therefore is not primarily one of making the schools more accepting of lower-class adolescents and their behaviors (although certain unnecessary rigidities could be relieved), but rather of preparing lower-class children to accept and fit into middle-class society. Part of this, of course, consists in effecting changes in elementary school curricula which will develop thinking styles better adapted to the requirements of curriculum in the higher grades, but this is a separate and complex problem. Even more important, for many lower-class children, is the development of more positive values and attitudes toward schooling and teachers such that they will be willing to modify their behaviors to conform to teachers' expectations, and yet will not in the process suffer a disastrous loss of status in the eyes of their peers.

It is hard to believe that the massive reality of the meaning of a high school diploma is unknown to lower-class youth. They must all know slightly older boys, in particular, who have found the doors to good jobs permanently closed to them for lack of a diploma. The reality is constantly restated in the mass media, in recruiting and employment offices, and in a thousand other ways. Yet equally constant is the expression of negative attitudes toward schools among lower-class adolescents.

The contrast between the perceived value, even necessity, of schooling, set against consistent attitudinal devaluation of the school, almost certainly reflects a thinly veiled rationalization. The need for rationalization emerges from a belief, based on long experience and shared by many lower-class adolescents, that sooner or later their academic careers will inevitably end in failure. Their school performance has been unsatisfactory and subject to criticism. As a social experience, school has been so humiliating that there is no realistic basis for expecting personal acceptance by teachers. In other words, the lower-class student sees the cards stacked against him.

Here it is useful also to bear in mind that an increasing number of studies have pointed out the quite limited future-time orientation which obtains in much of the lower class. The inability to implement plans or hopes discourages realistic thinking about one's status in the years to come. It is more comfortable, and often psychologically essential, to live from day to day. Only by stripping the future of reality can life appear tolerable. Yet I am convinced that any program which offered some measure of meaningful help and encouragement in school, and which could demonstrate some achievement or reward in return for the expenditure of energy or the demonstration of willingness, would find acceptance among large numbers of lower-class children from junior high school onward. I also believe—despite the hostility and rejection of school by these adolescents, which we see every day—that the relief from a perhaps unconscious sense of defeat would improve their outlook and behavior in school and out. They would, in effect, become less likely to undertake the acts we call delinquent. A few examples can be cited which point tentatively in this direction.

In a primarily lower-class Negro enclave known as Ken-Gar in a middle-class white area of Montgomery County, Maryland, school achievement was revealed as conspicuously poor when the schools were integrated, and delinquency was fairly high. A group of white adults from the surrounding area organized a program on a voluntary basis to tutor and encourage the Ken-Gar children in all grades. School achievement rose rapidly, high school drop-outs decreased, adults developed more interest in the schooling of their children, and there appears to have been some decrease in juvenile delinquency. Recently the success of this venture led to the county board of education hiring a full-time program director for Ken-Gar, and another person who is developing similar programs among other underprivileged groups in the county.

Neighborhood House, in a very depressed and apathetic Negro

slum area of Richmond, California, instituted a Study Hall Project. They set up a center for evening study, organized as a social center but with supervision and some tutorial help with homework. Although it is not yet clear what effect this has had on academic achievement, it has resulted in a striking change among neighborhood youths with respect to homework. Whereas in the past anyone who brought books home from school was obviously a square, now one has to account for oneself if books are not brought home. It is fashionable to study, or to seem to study, and with this half the battle is won. At the same time school personnel are aware of this project and are pleased by it. This undoubtedly affects favorably the response of teachers toward these students and increases the possibility of their social acceptance by the teachers, quite aside from objective academic achievement.

Another example is provided by the Work-Study Program of the University of Southern California Youth Studies Center, conducted in the Santa Monica schools. This is a program which combines a half day of study with a half day of (often subsidized) employment and vocational counseling. This program has apparently had some success in keeping students, who were selected as imminent drop-outs, in school. But the really interesting development is that in its second year the students began complaining that the academic part of the program was not sufficiently rich.

The most ambitious undertaking of this sort to date is the Higher Horizons program in New York City schools in underprivileged neighborhoods. With its exploratory predecessor, "Project 43," this has been evolving and expanding since 1956. It has included help with school work, counseling with parents and with teachers, class trips and cultural activities, and a variety of other approaches to helping students do better in school and feel better about schooling. There has been an explicit attempt to develop in the students the idea of planning for their futures, and the recognition that education is not only a necessary but also a possible part of such planning. Starting with two high schools it has expanded into elementary schools and into additional junior high and high schools. Careful evaluation demonstrates striking gains in almost all areas of school achievement and a reduction in school misbehavior, truancy, and drop-outs. Although out-of-school behavior, including delinquency, has not been evaluated, it is hard to believe that this has not been improved also.

These examples are only straws in the wind. They certainly do not exhaust the possibilities for ingenious programs. They encourage the belief, however, that very rewarding possibilities exist for programs which will actively focus on the negative attitudes toward education which pervade and infect the lower-class adolescent subculture in most cities. Opening up the possibilities for academic success at least to the point of getting through high school, with the change in values and behavior which this implies, will certainly not solve all the problems of lower-class youth, nor even touch some of the causes of juvenile delinquency. But it does offer a real hope for increasing access to the opportunity structure of our society for substantial numbers of lower-class persons, with a very modest social agency investment. As such, it is a strategy which should receive serious attention.

Reference

1. Miller, W. B., "The Impact of a 'Total Community' Delinquency Control Project," *Soc. Prob.*, *10*:168-191, 1962.

The Changing Identity of the Negro American

21

HAROLD R. ISAACS

It is very striking that this group of papers should afford us such a vivid picture of our stratified society, and the strange game of musical chairs that goes on within it—whether in space or in social status. Robert Gutman's discussion of migration movement to the suburbs had to be entirely a discussion of the white middle class, because Negroes still represent only a microscopic proportion of that migration. Marc Fried's mourners for the West End of Boston are a sort of residual segment of the working class, sufficiently rooted in their space to have developed a certain solid attachment to it, not to say affection for it. Their grief—if that is what it is—seems to arise only from being shaken out of a way of life that, if not a good way of life, had at least become a secure one that they were used to and did not want to leave.

I doubt whether one could say the same about the uprooted millions of Negroes who have been moving within our own society, moving in response to tremendous drives to seek something better, both in space and in way of life. If there is any "grieving" for a lost home, it would have to be interpreted quite differently. Negroes, like other segments of our society, have been stirred up to new demands, and have had to leave behind them all the kinds of "security" that went with the old hated order of things. There is discomfort, not to say wrenching pain, in having to cope with a whole new set of demands, upon oneself as well as upon the total environment.

And I must say, in response to Dr. Gutman's observation of unease in his white suburban audiences, that few things can produce more quivering uneasiness in almost any American audience than raising

The subject of this paper is the basis of the author's forthcoming book, *The New World of Negro Americans,* to be published by The John Day Co., New York.

the whole subject of race, of relations between peoples who go marked by these different labels and colors in our society. Yet we are today forced to consider these matters, and in some intimate and painful detail.

Negroes are the newest of the newcomers in all the major settlements of our country—from the trickle making its way to the edges of the suburbs to the millions pouring into our cities. The problems they have to cope with, and that our society belatedly has to cope with in relation to their newcoming, are of an infinitely larger, more intense order, a more critical order, than those that attend the adjustment of the middle class moving into the suburbs.

In 1910, 81 per cent of all Negroes lived in the eleven ex-Confederate states, most of them in rural areas. Drawn by great and grave circumstances—two world wars—and driven by a great need, the urge of people to escape suffocation and seek a better life elsewhere, great masses of people have been stirred into motion during the last fifty years. Between 1910 and 1920, the Negro population of four major Northern cities (New York, Chicago, Philadelphia, and Detroit) grew by some 750,000. During the 1940's, more than a million Negroes moved from South to North, and more than a million went into the armed forces and moved out to all corners of the world. In the 1950's, nearly a million and a half more left the rural South. The great bulk of this movement was into New York, California, Illinois, Michigan, Ohio, Pennsylvania, and New Jersey. Practically all of it, including the additional movement within the South itself to Texas and Florida, was into the cities. During the latter decades of this same period, we have had the shift of white middle-class millions from inner city to suburb. The result has been a sharp increase in the proportion of Negroes in our major city populations. In four of our twenty-five largest cities, Negroes make up more than one-third of the total population; in Washington, D.C., just over half. In these twenty-five cities there are now over six million Negroes, five million of them in the ten largest.

Plainly, then, Negroes have a large place and a large stake in the whole great mesh of problems in which our urban society is now caught. Many things follow from this, but at least one is that all who are concerned with the environment of the metropolis have to be aware of more than the obvious aspects of Negro states of mind, for Negroes are not only experiencing a massive shift in their physical and economic locations in the society; they are undergoing a much more massive change in their conceptions of their place in the world and in this society. Most profoundly of all, they are being compelled to change their conceptions of themselves.

I speak to this subject as a student of world politics and its effects. I trust it is clear that what is happening to Negroes is part of what is happening to everyone. The essential proposition here is that American democracy, having failed to extend the common rights of citizens to Negroes on its own initiative, is now being forced to do so by much larger events in the world, events that directly affect its own position and security in the world. The ending of the system of white supremacy in Asia and Africa is finally forcing the breakdown of the system of white supremacy in the United States. We are all participating in this great intercontinental rearrangement of power and relationships; whites are being compelled to abandon the habits of mastery, and non-whites the habits of subjection. With the collapse of its underpinning power, the whole vast and intricate superstructure wavers and begins to fall; it is like watching a slow-motion film of a building that has been dynamited. Slowly it falls out into the air, parts of it retaining form and structure even as it sinks and is gradually obscured by the great cloud of dust and rubble into which it falls. There they go, all the assumptions we all made about each other, about our own and other groups, "races," peoples, cultures, all the myths of white superiority and non-white inferiority, all the deeply imbedded notions and emotions, all the patterns of long-practiced behavior. All the habits and ideas we grew up on are obsolete. The system of Western white dominance they justified no longer exists. To the extent that these ideas still exist in our minds, we are threatened with departure from reality; we would hold suspended forever in the air those great slabs of the past which in fact already lie in ruins at our feet. All of it is being displaced and has to be replaced. All that was given, in a word, is now being taken away. We are already deep in this experience of change. There is hardly a corner of national or international life now that is not touched by it, and hardly anyone, white or black or whatever, who is not now faced by its demands.

In Asia and Africa where the colonies have become nation-states, this process of revision in relationship and mutual image can at least begin with a transfer of political power, and thus throw around the new confusions a screen of formal new status relationships. The white man pulls back from his position of power, in a few cases putting up a rear-guard fight but more often simply running pellmell from it, the basis of his position having evaporated with the willingness of his subjects to submit to it. Now, in the new situation, a new flag, a new government, a new "power," is established, and here at least the externals of behavior are governed by the protocol of diplomacy and the needs of policy. Hence, almost in a twinkling, yellow and brown and black men, only yesterday despised and relegated to the orders of inferiority, now take *their* places in the seats of the mighty, walk the red carpets of privilege, enjoy all the perquisites of sovereignty, are wooed instead of dominated (or are at least dominated in new and less offensive ways), and, wherever they can, begin to do a little dominating themselves. The Queen now dances with the black Prime Minister, and the Duke with the Prime Minister's black wife. To be sure, the new situation is a jumble of old rancors and old guilts, old shames and new needs. The shedding of colonial power does not at a stroke relieve the old colonial master of the whole burden of his beliefs about himself, nor Western white people generally of the legacy of what their whole culture taught them about these matters. That will take either more time or new and harder blows. By the same token, political independence obviously does not at a stroke free either the new nation or its people from *their* legacy of dependence and self-rejection. But at least the yielding now is to rulers of one's "own," and the most egregious forms of subordination to foreign rulers and foreign images of oneself are forced to disappear. The new national power can at least put a prohibitive tariff on their return, and under protection try to produce (to resurrect, recreate, or create as the case may be) a new national, cultural, or even "racial" identity on which indigenous self-respect can begin to thrive.

In American society, on the other hand, the end of white supremacy has to be signaled not by *separation* but by *integration*. Here there is no simple initial solution like changing the signs at a boundary line and raising a new flag. Here the issue remains locked in the society's unfulfilled promise of democratic pluralism. This promise is perhaps our greatest and most unique virtue; and our inability to realize it more rapidly may be our costliest and most profound failure. We have now been overtaken by it, at last. The gulf between our profession and our practice has become an abyss to whose edge the world has pushed us. Thus only in the 1950's do our courts begin to try to enforce what the Constitution has provided for nearly a century, and a combination of the safeguards of our federal system and the enormous drag of the past on the minds of all make this enforcement painfully slow and still only marginally effective. Thus now, when the new needs of protocol and world politics press upon the surviving old attitudes and practices, our government has to stumble through the embarrassment of trying to open to African diplomats the restaurants along Route 40 in Maryland or the housing in Washington and New York or the elite clubs not yet open to Negro Americans. Apologies, explanations, and a few "corrections" are made. Such episodes may be only embarrassing to whites suddenly caught with their hypocrisies showing, but it should require no high order of sensitivity to know what a galling thing it is to the Negro Americans from whom the society still largely withholds in most such places the grant of ordinary rights and decencies, and for most of whom, on a far larger scale, the needed apologies, explanations, and corrections have not yet been made.

Now it is obvious that much has changed in these matters in American life during the last twenty-five years or so. The change is not great enough to justify the glow of self-congratulation that lights up some white quarters, but it is greater than a great many Negroes can yet clearly see. The mass of Negroes suffers most acutely and in the largest proportionate numbers all the tensions and conflicts arising out of poverty. They have generally benefited last and least from social and economic improvements. They have still to fight their way in larger numbers into the more skilled and more lucrative occupations, into many unions, into spheres of employment and ways of life long closed to them simply because of their color. But Negroes of every class—both those who have most successfully pushed beyond the falling barriers and those still caught behind them—also feel all the tensions and conflicts arising out of their rejection by the white world in which they seek to "integrate," that is, to live.

These are and long have been the familiar facts of American life. Until quite recently this was the "expected" and "accepted" condition, producing its own forms of defense within the group and in every individual—the whole ghetto syndrome, religious refuges, the Uncle Tom and Sambo personalities, the protesters and the rebels, self-hate and counter-racist chauvinism, and much more. Today this condition carries over and persists even in the midst of great changes affecting every aspect of life for every Negro individual. Negroes feel the big wind at their backs and it blows on them from all corners of the world where, they know, the white man's rule and the white man's system is falling apart. Somehow all the big facts of life and history are at last working *for* them and not, as always before, against them. The barriers come down more and more, like the boundaries of the old ghettos in our cities. More and more Negroes move out over them, out of their physical and mental ghettos into new territory that is still inhospitable or even hostile, pocked, marked, and often heavily mined against them. They have to keep all their old caution and all their old guards up, but they also need a new scheme of life to cope with the new conditions. They have to bear with the change itself and its pace; the more things change, the more intolerable is the survival of the unchanged, the "faster" things move, the greater the frustration because never do they move fast enough.

So the tensions among Negroes have become less and less the tensions of submission and endurance, and more and more the tensions of change and self-reassertion. These two sets of responses, the old form of submission and the new form of aggression, co-exist now in almost every Negro individual. Perhaps "co-exist" is not the word; they jostle each other in a constant and bruising inward turmoil as each person seeks to discover the new terms of life. The older person fights both to hold on to and to throw off the older habits of mind and outlook; the younger person tries to find new ground to stand on, amid all the tangled fears and angers and despairs and exhilarations. Negroes are today still suffering most of the disabilities of second classness even as they are becoming aware that they need no longer submit to it, that times have changed, are changing, and will change a lot more. Neither old Southern college president nor boy on the streets of Harlem can remain as he was. All have to cut their way through the fabric of outlook and personality inherited from the past, in order to live in environments where they have to see others and to see themselves and to become aware of being seen by others in ways they never did before. Negroes of every estate are feeling this immense pressure upon them to see, not only the world about them, but themselves also anew.

All the powerful assumptions and circumstances that until the day before yesterday largely shaped Negro personalities are now disappearing. The old group identity—and I mean by this what Erik Erikson recently called a "shared sameness"—no longer fits the new social reality. The samenesses are ceasing to be the same. Like everyone else,

Negroes are having to rearrange the truths and falsities of how they see others and how they see themselves. New images are flashing back at them off the surfaces of today's new experiences. Habits of a lifetime, of a whole group past, have to be broken. All of it, rudely or exhilaratingly, comes up for disposal, renovation, replacement. Twenty-five years ago the late great Kelly Miller of Howard sardonically summed up the group identity of Negroes in a single phrase: "A Negro is anybody who'd be jimcrowed in Virginia." A "Negro" was and is, of course, a lot more than this, and now has to become someone quite else; the reshaping of the Negro group identity is already an unfolding part of our present experience.

I have been engaged in an effort to glimpse some aspects of this extremely complex matter, primarily by interviewing individuals who are directly involved in it. These individuals have been in the main persons who play a key role in the communication process; writers, scholars, editors, church leaders, and public figures. These interviews led me to begin to sort out certain intimately interrelated aspects of the Negro group identity. I will confine myself here to describing only two of these, simply by way of illustrating some of the complexities involved in this experience of group identity coming under pressure for change. I cite these, I hope it is clear, not because I think these particular elements tell the whole story, but because they illuminate some of its important parts. The first is the problem of the name to go by and the second is the flight from blackness.

A Name to Go By

The entire history of Negroes in America has conspired to give them a group identity that was negative or blurred or both. When James Baldwin titles his book *Nobody Knows My Name*, he is referring to the fact that a Negro's individuality as a particular person is lost in the white world behind the identifying external mask he wears as a "Negro." This mask was fashioned out of all that went into the struggle for survival in a hostile white society. It was shaped mainly out of the myths and stereotypes created by whites for their self-appeasement and so largely accepted by blacks for their self-defense. Hence the Uncle Tom, the Sambo, the Stepin Fetchit, and all the other figures in this particular wax museum. But the problem of the Negro group identity is much more than the problem of this synthetic group personality. Nobody may know "who" the "Negro" is, but this is at least partly because the person who is Negro has also been kept by these circumstances from knowing himself. Hardly anything illustrates this more dramatically than the fact that even as "Negro" he has had enormous difficulty in deciding what to call himself, what group name to go by.

When you begin to trace the matter back in time—and it goes back nearly 200 years—you find that the usages have varied and that preferences and arguments have swelled and swirled around a whole collection of labels: blacks, Africans, negroes (with the small "n"), Negroes (with the capitalization which became general usage only after a long struggle that ended only some thirty years ago and has still not ended in much of the South), Coloreds, Colored People, Colored Americans, People of Color, Ethiopians, Racemen, Negrosaxons, African Americans, Africo-Americans, Afro-Americans, Aframericans, American Negroes, Negro Americans. Even a brief look into these differences is the beginning of discovery of some of the real inwardness of the Negro identity problem.

During the last twenty years or so, the widest common practice has settled on "Negro," an embattled word which has held its own against almost constant assault. Differences, however, persist, both in opinions and usage. The term "colored" is still used almost as widely and not always interchangeably. The term "Negro" is still subject to challenge from various directions and the argument about it, kept alive by its inner essence and re-kindled by all our current events, still goes on. Black nationalists whose identification with Africa is more passionate now than ever since Africa became emergent, keep insisting on "Afro-American" or just plain "African." The push of this issue to the extremes of non-identity is illustrated at one end of the spectrum by the common use of the term "group" or "group man" (in which context whites would be "the majority group" or simply "the other group"), and at the other by the Black Muslims, who reject "Negro" and insist on "black" or "black men" but carry the Negro individual's identity problem to the ultimate dramatic extreme by requiring all their followers to abandon their family names (because they all come from white origins) and to substitute the most literal symbol of non-being—the Black Muslim calls himself by a first name followed simply by "X." There is a long history of such Islamic-type cults among Negroes; the predecessor of the present movement, founded in 1913, required its followers to "refuse longer to be called Negroes, black folk, colored people, or Ethiopians" but to be called "Asiatics" or "Moors" or "Moorish Americans."

The slave traders called their African cargo "negroes" or simply "blacks." Early in the slave trade, the word "negro" apparently came to be used more or less synonymously with "slave." Indeed, a South Carolina court held in 1819 that the word "negro" had the fixed meaning of "a slave." This has been a frequent reason given for objection to use of the word "Negro." It has been seen as "a badge of shame" hopelessly freighted with its "slave origin and its consequent degradation." Closely associated with this idea and even more commonly given as a reason for not liking the word is the slippage of "Negro" into "nigger," the term that carries in it all the obloquy and contempt and rejection which whites have inflicted on blacks in all this time. It has been suggested that this was, perhaps, "the clue to the whole business."

But it becomes clear from even a brief look that there are many other clues, much else to the business than this. Even on the basis of limited scrutiny, it becomes clear that for Negroes the issue of the name to go by has been deeply entwined with all the deepest and unresolved issues of the flight-from-self imposed upon them by their whole history in this society, of color—that is, of relative lightness and relative darkness, of the ways in which they have related to their African origins, of all the ways in which they have striven to be both in and of the white society from which they were so consistently and so completely excluded. I think that this emerges even from the simplest summary that it is possible to make of some of the complicated sequences and circumstances of this matter as it has appeared over time.

The record begins with the free Negroes who had come up out of the slave system by various means and had begun to group and to assert themselves at the time of the American Revolution and the establishment of the American Republic. The 1790 census noted 59,000 free Negroes in the population and although still called "Negroes" by whites, they had begun to distinguish themselves from the slaves by using the adjective "African." This was the name they attached to the new institutions they created for themselves at this time, e.g., the "African Baptist Church," formed in Savannah in 1779, the first African Lodge of Masons (1787), the Free African Society (1787), the African Methodist Episcopal Church (1796) and others. The first schools established for their children were called "Free African Schools" in New York and elsewhere.

By 1830, when free Negroes met together in their urgent common interest, the adjective "African" had been replaced by "Colored." In Philadelphia that year they formed the Convention of Colored Citizens of America, and in general had come to refer to themselves as "colored people" or "people of color." At least two sets of circumstances seem to me to be essential parts of the explanation for this change in terminology, though I must stress that I offer these not out of any detailed study of the historic materials but as an interpretation of the bare facts as I have gleaned them.

The first is that in the intervening time a concerted movement had been started to get free Negroes to migrate back to Africa. The overwhelming majority of free Negroes, especially in the Northern cities, wanted no part of any such migration. There were some free Negroes who despaired of ever being able to live decently in America and who looked back to Africa as an alternative, but these remained a small minority. It seems reasonable to suggest that the label "African" was abandoned, at least by Northern free Negroes, because they were intent upon remaining Americans and rejected the schemes to send them as "Africans" back to Africa.

But the choice of the term "people of color" or "colored people" to replace "African" suggests the second set of circumstances clearly involved in this change. The term "African" had been used mainly by free Negroes in the North, most of whom had gained their freedom in the early years of the Republic. The clusters of free Negroes in the South, especially those in Charleston, South Carolina and New Orleans, came out of a much older process. The first differentiation among the slaves was that made between the field hands and the house servants, and from among the latter came the issue of unions between white masters and slave women, often treated as a second family, given their freedom, means, and education. It was the descendants of such groups who developed their own special caste position (which included slaveholding of their own) and whose most visible mark of caste was their lighter color. This community in Charleston in 1790 formed not an "African" association, but the "Brown" Fellowship Society "which admitted only brown men of good character who paid an admission fee of fifty dollars." In New Orleans the even older and more aristocratic mixed descendants of the older

French and Spanish settlers became a distinct group in the population and were called the *gens de couleur*. It is from this term and from this group, carrying with it all the connotations of higher caste associated with non-blackness and mixed ancestry, that the vague and essentially non-descriptive term "colored" or "people of color" was derived. With its adoption by the Northern free Negroes in place of "African" during the decade before 1830, it became the general term of preferred and polite usage.

Although this term became one of general use and has persisted down through time until now, it has never stood alone or uncontradicted. At the very beginning, in the 1840's and 1850's, when some of the most militant free leaders, despairing of ever gaining a decent status in America, became advocates of migration to Africa, there was some effort made to revive the use of the term "African." In 1880, T. Thomas Fortune, editor of the *New York Age*, proposed the term "Afro-American" as a way of getting away from "Negro" and its vulgar equivalents. He argued that a new term was needed to describe the "new" race which was "much nearer the American than the African type." But although this term was adopted as the name of the Baltimore *Afro-American*, it never gained wide usage. It has survived, however, as the preferred usage of strongly nationalist or chauvinist-minded groups or individuals.

But the argument, largely centering on the continued use of "Negro," went on and on, acquiring peculiar force around the years of the turn of the century. Booker T. Washington advocated the use of "Negro" and opponents of the word charged this against his general posture of submission. But along came W. E. B. Du Bois, no submitter, who not only espoused "Negro" but used "black" and stressed color almost obsessively in his own special struggle for the reassertion of Negro identity. It did not matter, he pointed out, whether they were called "African" or "Ethiopian" or "colored" but what mattered was who and what you were and where you stood in the society. This was the view advocated by many other leaders over the years, although the N.A.A.C.P., founded in 1909 by Du Bois and others, followed the preferred usage among the middle- and upper-class Negroes and used "colored."

Most of the present generation of Negro adults grew up simply accepting these confused and divided usages without questioning what they might mean. Among those I interviewed, I noticed a fairly typical cleavage: members of what one might call the more traditional middle or upper class among Negroes almost invariably used "colored" and a few had strong views on the subject ("I never class myself as 'Negro,'" said an ex-college president. "I had to cease to be a 'Negro' in order to be a man.") The stronger "race man" types had opposite views. ("My father always believed we should use 'Negro' meaning black," said a noted labor leader. "As a term it has more strength than 'colored.'") More generally the younger and more sophisticated either used "Negro" alone or used it interchangeably with "colored." When asked, most of them said they were aware of the disputes over the matter but did not think them important. Most commonly, they said they thought the objection to "Negro" was its closeness to "nigger." Only a few thought there might be layers to the matter deeper than this, and then only when asked. "I hadn't thought," said a noted educator, "that any matter of color was involved in this, but it is quite possible. Some four or five years ago there was a motel sign up somewhere near here [Atlanta] which said 'for Negroes.' A taxi driver sneered as we went by it one day, 'He ought to know he won't get colored people's business with that sign.' And the fact is that the sign was changed sometime after that to 'for Colored.'" Said another well-known scholar: "I am sure there is something about color in the use of 'Negro' and 'Colored,' though it is not always at the tip of people's consciousness."

The fact is that just below the level of that more common consciousness, the issue of name-confusion is intimately locked with all the central issues of Negro identity-confusion: the flight from blackness, the flight from Negro-ness, itself, the yearning for whiteness. In its most extreme forms, this involved the total acceptance of the white man's estimate of the black man, the total rejection of self.

Color Caste: The Yearning to Be White

The flight from blackness and the yearning to be white have had a major part in the shaping of the Negro group identity down through the generations. This is, of course, a familiar phenomenon which has also been called "identification with the aggressor." In wanting to become like those who have dominated, despised, and rejected them, Negroes have been behaving like members of many other dominated, despised and rejected groups. All our various cultures and subcultures are filled with examples. It became part of the common experience of certain sections of the colonized peoples during the Western imperial epoch; it was even shared for quite a while by certain kinds of Chinese. In our own American culture, many of the patterns of this process have been plainly visible in the experience of successive immigrant groups relating themselves to the dominant group in the society. Jews, who have been despised and rejected for a longer time than anybody, have a number of chapters of this kind in their long history. Bruno Bettelheim's interpretation of what happened to some Jews in the Nazi extermination camps suggests a recent and extreme example. More familiar and more common has been the behavior attached to the idea of "assimilation," the effort to shed all vestiges of the Jewish identity by disappearing entirely into the dominant group. The equivalent among Negroes is, of course, "passing" into the white population. But to "pass" is possible only for a few; although a fair amount of it has taken place, our knowledge of the matter is limited. More generally people must find other ways of assimilating the majority view of themselves and of expressing the self-rejection and self-hatred that follows from this. Among Negroes the forms and modes of this process are endlessly varied. One of the most pervasive of these has been the institution of color caste which raised "whiteness" to the highest value in all aspects of life. This meant everything pertaining to civilization, culture, religion and human worth. It became among Negroes an intricate system of social, group, and personal relationships based directly on degrees of relative lightness and relative darkness and other degrees of physical Negro-ness, the shape and kinds of features, hair, lips, and nose which were "good" if they resembled the white's, "bad" if they did not. This was carried to the point of using artificial means—hair-straighteners and skin-whiteners—in the effort to close the gap between the two.

In coming to terms with himself, every Negro individual has had in one way or another to cope with the infinity of ways in which "white" is elevated above "black" in our society. The association of white and black with light and dark and the translation of these quantities of light into polarities of "good" and "evil" and "beauty" and "ugliness" has taken place in the conventions and languages of many cultures, but in few has this conversion of physical facts into religious and aesthetic values been worked harder than in our own. These concepts and usages of black evil and white goodness, of beautiful fairness and hideous blackness are deeply imbedded in the Bible, are folded into language of Milton and Shakespeare, indeed form part of almost every entwining strand of art and literature in which our history is clothed. "I am black but comely," sang the Shulamite maiden to the daughters of Jerusalem, and on that "but" hangs a whole great skein of our culture. This raising of "white" and debasement of "black" has been marked deep on the minds of all through time, every "white" person more or less unconsciously imbibing it as nourishment for his self-esteem, every "black" person finding himself forced either to resist this identification under conditions of total psychological disarmament—which some miraculously managed somehow to do in every successive generation—or else to yield to it, as the greater numbers inevitably did.

The imprint of this experience on Negroes over all this time has been seen and experienced by many, described, scrutinized, and studied by very few. The first really forthright and frank scrutiny it ever received from scholars was in a series of inquiries made in the late 1930's by a group of distinguished Negro and white social scientists and published in 1940 and 1941 for the American Youth Commission, especially E. Franklin Frazier's *Negro Youth at the Crossways* (Frazier probably dealt more frequently and more boldly with this matter in his works than anyone else), Charles Johnson's *Growing Up in the Black Belt,* Warner, Junker, and Adams', *Color and Human Nature,* and Allison Davis and John Dollard's, *Children of Bondage.* Until these studies appeared, very little had ever been said in print about this pervasive fact of Negro life. "Its existence," wrote James Weldon Johnson in 1912, in his *Autobiography of an Ex-Coloured Man,* "is rarely admitted and hardly ever mentioned; it may not be too strong a statement to say that the greater portion of the race is unconscious of its influence; yet this influence, though silent, is constant."

Apparently its first appearance as the central theme of a novel was in Wallace Thurman's *The Blacker the Berry* (1929) which brought out into the open what Langston Hughes called "a subject little dwelt upon in Negro fiction." The title comes from a folk saying often defensively on the lips of the darker-skinned, especially the women: "The blacker the berry, the sweeter the juice." Thurman's heroine is a dark girl whom he takes through every kind of Negro milieu, mercilessly depicting the hurts and the cruelties inflicted upon her. These begin when she is still in her cradle with the scorn and derision of relatives, "Try some lye," they would joke viciously to her mother, "it may eat it [the blackness] out. She can't look any worse!" When, in her young womanhood, a "yaller nigger" shows interest, she is flattered "that a man as light as he should find himself attracted to her," but then she finds she despises him for this very reason. She is drawn back to the man who has most brutally misused her, but even he, at the bottom of the pit of misfortune from which she tries vainly to lift him, feels free to step on her at will, and this finally forces her to look squarely at herself and her life. Thurman, an angry, gifted young writer who died very young, brings his dark heroine at the end to a positive affirmation of strength: "What she needed to do now was to accept her black skin as being real and unchangeable, to realize that certain things were, had been and would be, and with this in mind to begin life anew, always fighting, not so much for acceptance by other people, but for acceptance of herself and by herself." She can do this, but only at the price of achieving a terrible hardness of spirit.

Not many other writers even yet have chosen to deal explicitly and at length with these themes of lightness and darkness in Negro life. It is deeply enfolded—indeed, often hidden—in the writing of Langston Hughes. Saunders Redding comes back to it again and again in his work, but almost always glancingly or in brief episodes through which he still manages to show how enormously important it is to him. In a small part of the first chapter of his *No Day Of Triumph,* for example, he writes of his two grandmothers between whom there lay a deep abyss—"one was yellow, the other was black." He tells how, as a small boy who already knew there was "a stigma attached to blackness," he realized that for his Grandma Conway blackness was not merely a blemish but a *taint.* Another is his poignant account of a girl, a distant relative, who never overcame the handicap of her darker color, and ended up by dissolving as a human being.

In *The Third Generation* (1954) Chester Himes writes about a woman who is the product, three generations removed, of a union between a plantation lord and a slave. She is white in appearance and is wedded to this whiteness with an intensity that is a sickness. This is the way in which the sins of her forebears are visited upon her, for her obsession drags her, her husband, and her children into various kinds of self-destruction.

In *Proud Shoes* (1956) Pauli Murray gives us a portrait of her grandmother who was actually just such a woman, herself the daughter of a plantation owner and a slave who was mostly Cherokee Indian. She built her entire identity around these facts of her origin and her first loyalty was not only to her "whiteness" but to her "Southern aristocratic whiteness." Thus when a neighbor thinks to insult her by calling her "a half-white bastard," she retorts:

> "Hmph! You think I'm insulted? I'll tell anybody I'm a white man's child. A fine white man at that. A Southern aristocrat. If you want to know what I am, I'm an octoroon, that's what I am—seven-eighths white. The other eighth is Cherokee Indian. I don't have one drop of colored blood in me and I don't have to mix in with good-for-nothing niggers if I don't want to."

"Anyone who has been part of a family of mixed bloods in the United States or the West Indies," writes Miss Murray, "has lived intimately with the unremitting search for whiteness. To deny that it is part of one's heritage would be like saying one had no parents."

The "unremitting search for whiteness" of course had its counterpart in the aggressive reassertion of blackness. This too has taken many different forms. In rising to the most elementary kind of self-defense, Negro writers and scholars and poets have again and again over the years strongly proclaimed the virtues of their blackness. For a long time this kind of self-defense was held out at the edges of Negro life; black nationalism was the stuff of extremism, as in the case of Marcus Garvey whose appeal in the 1920's was made precisely to the dark and the poor against the better-off and the lighter skinned. It was, in fact, Garvey's brutal exposure of this deep cleavage which made many thoughtful Negroes realize how costly color caste had become. The beginning of the end of its most egregious forms dates from that time. W. E. B. Du Bois, who had helped crush Garvey, carried on a ceaseless campaign in all his writings, referring caressingly always to "golden brown," "warm ebony," and "satin black." As an expression of persistent color caste values, darker men of improved status more and more married lighter-skinned women, but the increasing frequency of such marriages had a taming effect on the overt expression of color caste and likewise began to shade a substantial segment of the population into an increasingly common brown. It began to be bad form to express color caste prejudices openly, although its practice continued in many more overt ways—much like the practice of anti-

Semitism in large sections of the American middle class. The 1940 studies of Frazier, Warner, Johnson, and others showed how deeply rooted both the offensive and defensive forms of this caste system were in the population, and although there is little clinical material, what little there is testifies to the critical importance of color caste in the lives of individuals who finally break down under the accumulated pressures of the Negro life experience. By the overwhelming testimony of my own interview material, color caste is both "on its way out" and "still very much with us." Both statements of course are true. One individual told me amusedly of standing at a reception for Kwame Nkrumah next to a nearly white Negro woman who breathed, "I am so proud I'm black!" Yet it is still not uncommon to find dark girls whose experiences even now differ hardly at all from those of Wallace Thurman's heroine of more than a generation ago.

Color caste has been breaking down for decades, but this process has been dramatically quickened in the last few years by the African emergence. The appearance of black Africans in positions of power and the establishment of African nations has not only begun to spur a more common respect for blackness but has created for American Negroes for the first time the basis of a prideful association with the continent of their remoter origins. This brings on new complexities and conflicts and—just as the establishment Israel does for Jews—raises in new and sharpened form the old problems of defining nationality, culture, and the mystiques of ethnic kinship. But these are problems on a new level of self-examination and self-respect. For Negroes this involves not only re-examining and profoundly revising their view of their place in America but also discovering all over again what they are to Africa and what Africa is to them, and how these parts of their identity fit together.

Africa has been central in the shaping of the Negro group identity. Its role in this process has until now been deeply and damagingly negative. Over the generations, some Negroes who despaired of ever achieving a decent manhood status in the white American society reached for an alternative identity in the form of a countering black nationalism and the impulse or the effort to go "back to Africa." But Africa was submerged under the domination of other white men and the only migration that actually took place produced no great source of pride or attraction. For most Negroes, however, Africa was the very opposite of a refuge. It remained the source of the blackness and the Negro-ness from which they wanted most of all to escape, the very last place in which to seek emotional or physical asylum.

Thus whether Negroes looked inward for support or outward for escape, they found no satisfactory way of coming to terms with themselves or of accepting a tolerable sense of who and what they were. Hence the ghetto dead-endedness, the nobodiness, the nothingness to which the life path led so many for so long. This appears poignantly stated by Richard Wright in his last-published novel, *The Long Dream,* in which Wright winds up a conversation among four boys in Mississippi in the middle 1950's with this exchange:

> "Okay . . . Nobody wants to go to Africa. Awright. Who wants to go to America?"
>
> "We awready in America, you fool!"
>
> "Aw, naw you ain't . . . You niggers ain't *nowhere.* You ain't in Africa 'cause the white man took you out. And you ain't in America . . . You can't live like no American 'cause you ain't no American. And you ain't African either. So what is you? Nothing! Just nothing!"

This linkage of identity, nationality, the relation to Africa summed up in the sense of *nobodiness* is part of the central design of the fabric of the Negro experience in America. These themes are repeated again and again in the words of strong-and-militant or strong-and-despairing men in every generation. They appear in what Arthur Davis of Howard University has called "the alien and exile theme" in writing by Negroes, whether in the poems of Countee Cullen a generation ago or in the essays of James Baldwin now. The struggle of Negroes for existences has meant the struggle to assert their *somebodiness* by somehow expressing and resolving these blurred confusions. Against all the denials and all the exclusions, Negroes have persisted in their struggle to achieve a decent status and a self-accepting identity as members of the American society. This has been an epic struggle, filled with some of the greatest agonies and greatest ironies of our history—indeed, of the whole human story.

Now this struggle comes finally to a time of great climaxes. Under the great pressure of world change, America changes and the Negro at last stands on the threshold of integration, that is of gaining at last the right to enjoy the rights enjoyed by all other members of the American society. But this victory comes late and it comes with agonizing slowness. This slowness produces a great and angry impatience that is expressed in the new militancy of Negroes, especially young Negroes, in asserting and demanding their rights. But it is also producing a new despair which reflects itself in increasing alienation. Signs of this abound at the outer fringes: in the growth of a movement like the Black Muslims who seek total separation from the white society; in the deep disaffection reflected in the attacks on policemen in the ghetto slums; in the appearance of a new fringe of more sophisticated alienates who find in the African emergence the prospect of some alternate solution to their problems of identity and even of nationality, and in the Castros and the Mao Tse-tungs of the new world the surrogates who will deal for them the avenging blows and perhaps even inflict on this white society the final doom they feel it has earned for itself by the sins of its past. Whether these new alienates are the last casualties of the fight or the harbingers of a gloomy future is a question that will only be decided by the speed with which the American society moves to accommodate itself to the new demands and the new state of affairs.

For the Negro, it is a time of coming out of limbo. He has had to locate himself somewhere between the white society's rejection of him and his rejection of himself. He did not know who he was, and although he did not want to be what the world said he was, he was brought to believe or fear that what the white world said about him was the truth. He coped with this, whether by fighting or submitting, or seeking some tolerable refuge, by burying deep his worst travails, and making some kind of life out of answerlessness. He endured, even found ways of laughing in sad or brittle derision. Yet all these things were stamped hard upon him by all the circumstances of his existence and found form and expression in each individual in endlessly varied ways, making up all together some of the elements of the personality that was shared in common by all.

Today's events and today's pressures are forcing all these issues up to the surface of life, raising again for answers all the unanswered questions, indeed for many individuals forcing themselves upon the conscious awareness for the first time. What I have described here only suggests some small part of the turmoil now beginning as Negroes in greater and greater numbers shed the burdens of *nobodiness* and begin to take on the new demands of *somebodiness*. All the issues

—name, nationality, color, origins—will acquire new shape and content. All the choices—alienation, assimilation, integration—will have to be redefined. Out of the recombining of all these elements, a new Negro group identity will have to be formed.

Planning and Poverty

22

LEONARD J. DUHL

Why are we concerned with poverty now? What is it? Are we concerned only with its economic aspects? What constellations of factors are related to it? What do we mean by wanting to eliminate it? Do we really want to? Is there perhaps a *need* for poverty? Are we talking of different kinds of "poverties," and of the complexities surrounding them? Are we prepared to think in new ways about these complexities? And who are the "we" who are to do all this? Are we thinking of poverty in the United States as separate from poverty in the rest of the world? And finally, why is all this a concern of mental health workers?

Following a period of great prosperity, in the most prosperous country in the world, we are faced with a crisis. Not since Franklin Roosevelt has a President reminded us that we are, in part, poverty-stricken. The poverty we see in 1961 is not the poverty of the thirties. We see pockets of poverty in specific geographic areas; we see poverty in some groups and not in others; and we see large segments of the population unemployed due to shifting patterns of industrial activity, and to automation. It was the President's decision to point to poverty as a critical problem; and he has done so quite ably, indicating its relationship to other problems that face the nation.

Never before in the history of man's development, in the heightening of his aspirations and in the attainment of the high levels of living by the many, have we had the potentiality for the application of resources, skills, and knowledge to the attack on poverty. Never before have we had such widespread manifestations of man's aspirations for

Presented at the Annual Forum of the National Conference on Social Welfare, Minneapolis, 1961, and published in *Social Welfare Forum, 1961* (New York: Columbia Univ. Press). Reprinted here in modified form.

a better life. We are at a point where poverty is no longer necessary; nor will it be tolerated, either by individuals or by the decision-makers of human society. We are at the point where individuals demand that we reach levels below which none shall fall. This means not only economic prosperity, but psychological, medical, and educational. In America, especially, this is potentially available for all. On the other hand, unachieved aspirations can occur more frequently as potentialities increase. The poverties of the future may indeed be more difficult to deal with unless we avoid the trap of equating prosperity with happiness.

The problem is acutely visible now, precisely because we *are* prosperous. As we face more and more of the concrete challenge of technology and science, we are brought face to face with other challenges which have been bypassed in our technological hurry. We undertake large-scale attacks on problems of health; and health and disease remind us of poverty. We attempt a nation-wide resolution of the problems of education; and poverty smacks us in the face. When we look at social security, health costs, housing, mental illness, and juvenile delinquency, poverty is still with us. We are looking anew at poverty in 1963 because of our success and prosperity.

Every one of us has had a personal look at poverty. Some of us have come from poverty-stricken homes, and have made our way into the professional world. Others of us, as professionals, have looked at other people's poverty. My own experience is not only that of an outsider looking at the poor of a big city, but also that of a person constantly exposed to the problem of giving help to a variety of people in poverty-stricken areas.

When, as observers, we rub shoulders with the poverty-stricken, we see them; we hear them; we smell the smells of their communities, their homes, and even of their bodies. Some of these things—the grime, the dirt, and the meanness of life—repel us. On the other hand, there are many ways in which the ways of the poor—the vitality, the interactions of the people, the color and excitement—are stimulating and exciting. The smells from the kitchens of the varied ethnic communities are enticing. The free-and-easy interpersonal contact, the close interplay, have attractions. It is mainly when, as professionals, we have to *do* something, to show proof of our humanitarian desires and skills, that the frustrations really build up.

Looking back in time, one sees a variety of views about poverty: the poor exist; they are part of life; they are useless, unworthy, not God-fearing, unproductive, unwilling; they are a menace. The poor who climb out of this morass are in the great American tradition of becoming middle class; they are not our problem. We are more concerned with the casualties—those who do not make the ascent or do not try; the hard-core poor. In times fortunately past, we were quite sure that genetic and hereditary factors were the cause of poverty and all that went with it. Produced by a circular sort of reasoning were action programs such as sterilization, isolation, and removal of the offspring from social opportunities. In fact, in some areas, there were attempts to isolate the poor in compounds for the "asocial." Thus, by keeping them segregated, it was hoped to control and diminish the chances of "infecting" the rest of society. More recently, we have looked at the symptomatology of poverty—disease, mental illness, delinquency, lack of employment, lack of funds, etc.—and treated the symptom with money, care, "welfare," but in many cases hardly adequately.

In recent years, a large number of basically complex and interrelated social problems have been redefined by political decision-makers as "mental health" problems. An issue such as delinquency associated with poverty, which has many implications for our total society, is so designated. What has in effect happened is that by treating the symptomatology we have brushed the problem under the rug. Giving money to solve a problem, or calling the problem one of mental health and treating the symptom, is equally ineffective. Whether in the guise of charity, with its implied contempt, or from the high-and-mighty position of the understanding psychiatrist or social worker who sees everything as a psychological problem inherent in the individual, the way we give affects both our perception of the problem and our ability to do something truly helpful.

Really to deal with delinquency, we would have to concern ourselves with many of the basic structures of our total society. None would be immune, since our political structure, our social organizations, our business ethics, values, and practices, as well as our communications media, physical environment, child raising, and many other factors would have to be examined. Too often our attitudes toward the poor, or poverty, are equated with our attitudes toward the lower class and all that is associated with it. Similarly, our attitudes toward minorities—toward atypical, non-characteristic Americans—are related to our concerns with poverty. By labeling the symptom (e.g., juvenile delinquency) as the disease, we avoid the responsibilities of re-evaluating our own attitudes toward poverty, minorities, or any other social problem.

One can look at the problem of alcoholism in the same way. At one level this can be seen as a medical problem. On other levels, it involves questions of availability, cost, location and numbers of bars and package stores, the level of taxes, the time of drinking, the habits, customs, culture, advertising, social services, education, societal values, politicians, criminals, and other agencies. The list can be endless. The problem is complex. To solve it, we need not only more work in the medico-psychiatric field, but in all other areas as well. For example, architecture and city planning are part of the solution to the problem of alcoholism, if we consider the effect of neighborhoods, ethnic groups, new communities, education, recreation, space, mobility, and so forth. The kind of communities we build, the way they are built, who is involved in the planning stages, the way in which the decision-makers are convinced of the value of certain decisions—not just to beautify the city or with the tax base in mind, but also for the prevention or even resolution of problems such as alcoholism—is central to the total community's responsibility.

I suggest that, as individuals and as a nation, we must step back and take a fresh look at the problems of poverty. We must go beyond "humanitarianism" for the required daring, for an imaginative new look at the problem, and for the action so desperately needed.

We need also a fresh look at the available information, skills, and technical tools. What are the major attempts now being made to reconceptualize these complex problems and to develop the needed social mechanisms for their control? I believe we do not as yet have the necessary political mechanisms. More importantly, we do not have the sense of commitment which comes only from a conscious reappraisal of ourselves, of our society, and of our day-by-day values.

In our mental hospitals, our prime interest has been to help the individual patient gain enough strength so that he will resume his place in his family and community. Many times, however, individual treatment does not succeed.

Within the past ten years, there has been a major breakthrough in understanding the patient in the mental hospital. What we have found out is that both the patient and the total hospital environment influence the patient's chances of getting well and being discharged.

It is this understanding of the total institution, with its complex interrelationship between staff and patient, that gives us insight into how we might rehabilitate individuals.

When these hospital studies are extended to look into the community from which the patients come and to which they are discharged, the same phenomenon is evident. When the community is unable to deal with the problems posed by the individual, it defines the individual as a health problem and turns the responsibility for dealing with him over to the hospital. Thus, we can suggest that if, ideally, we could deal with the total environment, a large number of persons could be prevented from *becoming* mental patients.

Implicit in this view is the notion that the obvious manifestations of the illness do not reside completely within the patient. Rather, they are effects of the community or its institutions on the individual. The individual *learns* how to be sick; our communities teach him by many techniques—in fact, a large part of what we know as illness is indeed iatrogenic.

Similarly, poverty, as we have seen it, is also associated with a constellation of factors. Its causes lie not only within the individual, but in his group and in our whole society.

Let me pose a few more questions. Is there intellectual poverty? Is there biological poverty? Cultural? A poverty of values, standards, beliefs, conceptualizations, goals, dreams, emotions? Is poverty ever single? Or is there really a constellation of poverties? And do we not all share some of them? I submit that when we are asked to look at economic poverty, we must look at all poverties, and all that is around and related to them.

Our prime concern as social workers and psychiatrists has been with the client or individual. He comes to us when he breaks down. We then are concerned with the way he has broken down, the problems leading to the breakdown, and the factors within him and his environment that will help to resolve the difficulties.

I have stated quite categorically that when we look at poverty, we most often have been concerned with symptoms. We are concerned there too, with symptomatology. It is a truism that we should not treat the disease but rather the patient. I would extend that further and say that to deal most adequately with human behavior we should deal with the individual, his family, his social and cultural groups, his varied geographic and functional communities, his nation, or even the community of nations. For until we are oriented to the complex interplay of all these systems, we will not know much even about disease or, what is more important, about man. With this understanding, specific interventions become more meaningful.

Rather than looking, as we have for almost a century, at the "cause-and-effect" disease model which has been very successful in many ways, I ask that we shift to a developmental model of man in an ecological framework. The individual is born with a basic genetic pattern already laid down, which plays a large role in all his subsequent development. As he grows, he is fed and nurtured with food, love, attention, and much more. This nurture is vital to his basic normal growth and development.

Parallel to this nurture is the development and adaptation of the human organism to the complex stresses, strains, and crises—good and bad, minimal or overwhelming—that face the individual. Early in life, the human organism can react to crisis by a variety of biological means; with brain damage, for example. His patterns of response tend to lay the groundwork for a whole system of related responses later in life. In fact, the earlier the response, the more general the long-term reaction may be. Mental retardation for life may be the result of early brain damage to the fetus. The adaptive response may thus make such changes in the individual that all subsequent reactions are influenced. Soon after birth, the adaptive responses open to the individual are broadened to include interpersonal influences. It is here that we see developed what we call personality and character.

In all the adaptive responses of the organism, the range of opportunities open to the individual (and here I do not refer only to conscious choice) are based primarily upon historical precedent. Thus, the hereditary framework plays a large role in determining this reaction, as do previous adaptive experiences and the general state of nurture and development.

Despite the importance of the historical, it is important to underline the fact that between the time of crisis and the response, the individual organism is open to the impact of the specific total situation at the moment. And it is at such moments that intervention from outside sources is most important. It is at this time that the mother has the greatest impact on the child; and that we as the official intervenors of society can play the most important role in aiding the individual to find a better response to the crisis situation than the one previously used. It is here that others who offer help have their impact, whether for good or bad. Excluding conscious professional outside intervention, the environment usually tends to remain stable, and thus there occurs repetition of the pattern by constant feedback and reinforcement. This reinforcement of old patterns is of such a nature that observers can predict patterns of behavior.

To return to the problems of the poverty-stricken, what we see as poverty is due to this constant feedback and reinforcement which lead to our stereotyped view of the "poverty-stricken." Contrary to this stereotyping, there are many varieties of such people, from many kinds of cultural backgrounds. Though there are similarities in these groups of the poor, there are also great differences.

We need to know much more about how people learn the behavior that we associate with poverty. Surely the behavior-patterns of their peers play an important role in determining this. At the same time, the patterns and behavior of the non-poverty-stricken—our tremendous middle class—play a large role in constantly reinforcing the behavior patterns of the individual concerned. This reinforcement from outside the group occurs at all times and at all levels of the communities we live in; for example, in the ways that the poor are dealt with when applying for jobs, in the variety of jobs open, in the use of credit, in educational and cultural opportunities, in the courts, in the attitudes of the press and the mass media, in the communication of values, norms, and restrictions, and so on. Clearly, if one is to deal with poverty, one must deal with all of these. Yet this is almost impossible; for to deal with multiple levels in a coordinated way requires social institutions unlike any of those we now possess.

Let us look now at what sort of actions are open to us. But first, let us look at our tools. New sources of data about these multiple problems in our society are required. In fact, some of these data are now available; however, they are available in many different organizations, in many different forms, and are geared for many different uses. A way must be found to cross-index and put them into a useful form within which total, integrated planning can take place. We have the technical tools, the computers, and even the models to do this.

More important is the need for *more* data. The need for research is so great that unless much more of it is done on all our social problems, and on all levels, we will remain impotent. The research need is so varied that it includes work in all the behavioral sciences from biology to psychology, sociology, economics, political science, and even philosophy.

Second, there is the need for ways to use the data intelligently: I repeat, for integrated planning. The word "planning" is likely to bring forth negative images, such as "totalitarianism"; nevertheless, if we look carefully at our American society, we find that much planning is indeed taking place. Business corporations, the Department of Defense, the Space Agency, Puerto Rico, all are involved in systematic analyses of the problems involved in their enterprises. From these analyses and the available data, logical plans evolve. To *plan* is to gather our knowledge of our collective resources and to exploit our capabilities for change, thus modifying ourselves in order to meet more adequately the needs of the present and the future. Unfortunately, most of the planning now taking place does not adequately consider the *behavioral* experience of man. However, the mechanics certainly are present and can be used.

What we need is the development of comprehensive social planning that will integrate our efforts for health, welfare, and education. At the same time, our knowledge of human behavior must be integrated into decision-making in areas beyond our prior experience, especially when they affect human behavior: in housing, urban design, health, recreation, education, social welfare, foreign affairs, technical assistance, and so forth. Work in all these areas will do much to forward our aspirations for man in our society. Though the ultimate decisions are political and not scientific, there is real need to recognize that the science of human behavior can play as important a role as the physical sciences in dealing with some of the important problems of our society—perhaps as important as missiles, space, and defense.

Crises are extremely important in living, both because of the danger involved and because of the opportunities. What is imperative, as many of these papers have shown, is that we find ways to help individuals to use the *opportunity* of crisis for growth.

We have both the knowledge and the ability to do so. Not only are psychiatrists, psychologists, and social workers important to people in crises; but *all* who deal with people in these problem times are important. We have a responsibility, perhaps direct, perhaps consultative, or perhaps one of communication, to see that more knowledge gets to the people who play important non-professional roles in these problem areas.

To utilize crisis for growth rather than decay; to teach and encourage adaptive mechanisms suitable to the complex problems facing individuals and society; to change the repetitive patterns of reaction seen in the poverty-stricken, it is necessary to emphasize the organizations in our society which exist, or could be created, to deal with these problems. We have seen schools face the crisis of integration, and the influx of migrants, by taking responsibility for the reorientation of the individual and his family to the urban and desegregated world. We have seen the army face similar problems. Hospitals can do the same. Our colleges and our technical training institutions potentially can play the same role. But, as we have seen in the schools, to assume such a responsibility means putting a tremendous stress upon the organization, and demands a re-evaluation of its goals, functions, and structure. Similarly, in urban relocation and new housing we can, with a completely new orientation and responsibility, face such human problems. Heretofore, the concern has primarily been money, bricks, and mortar. But, on the other hand, even apparently correct solutions to crises can lead to regression rather than advance. The long-range impact of policies, for example, may encourage dependency although the true goal is independence.

I could mention many organizations in our society with potential for positive use of crisis; however, I shall limit myself to listing briefly some new ones which show promise. The new "urbanization schools" proposed for such cities as Washington, D. C., if they can deal with the complexities of new ways of living in an adequate manner, may indeed be able to make an impact on the population moving to the cities. The idea of utilizing youth corps, Peace Corps, or work camps for a variety of activities useful to our society offers similar opportunities to the recipients and to the participants for growth, development, and change. It is no accident that in Israel the army is utilized as one of the country's main acculturating and "Israeli-orienting" organizations. It is through this experience that young people learn how to be soldiers. They also learn what patterns of behavior are expected of the new Israeli.

When society is stable, the kin, the family, and friends give support and aid during crisis. But in a mobile, changing, continually disruptive society, kin are no longer dependably present, even though the need for human ties is still strong. Whether we wish it or not, kinship will more and more be replaced by welfare services, by health services, adult education, church membership, and so forth. People need ties with others close by, geographically or functionally, in order both to exist and to grow. We ought to take a new look at all our services in this light, modifying, omitting, expanding, or creating new ones as needed—even if this means changes in our laws, regulations, business practices, and, ultimately, in some of the basic values of our society.

Central to planning is the question of who plans. Fortunately, one basic aspect of the American character is the ability to participate in voluntary co-operative endeavors. Since the early days of the Republic, however, America has become more complex; the groups and organizations in which we participate have become so big that direct voluntary involvement in significant planning has become relatively unavailable to the majority of our people. We must find new mechanisms to involve people in planning, or they will find new ways to deal with problems—whether those ways are good or evil.

To involve people in planning requires a basic respect for their values and beliefs, despite the fact that, without prior training, they may be unable to participate fully. What is required, then, is education, involvement, and participation; for unless people are involved, they cannot learn to participate.

The problems of poverty we face in the United States are not different from those we face in the rest of the world. It is extremely difficult to remake the poor in our own image. It is important to work slowly, to help them change, and *to change ourselves* so that new over-all patterns can evolve. This may be the only way to deal with the many crises that are facing us today. The crisis of poverty in our own country has important ties to the poverty of the world. To deal with either may require a complete reallocation of our efforts, our resources, and our values; it may, in fact, demand such innovation and change as only the most mature and creative can envision. New and expanded programs in social welfare, education, physical and mental health are important, but they are only part of our national responsibility.

One of the salient characteristics of the American has been his ability to respond to crises. In our history, crises have provided both major strides in our national development and major innovations in our culture. The challenge of poverty, I am certain, will not find us lacking the daring of the ingenuity that it demands.

PART FOUR

The Strategy of Intervention

The five papers in this section deal in one way or another with philosophies of social planning and social action. The first by Striner and Holmquist asserts that social scientists and action planners must learn to work in close partnership—a theme that has been implicit in many of the papers. The statement grows out of an experiment, not reported in the excerpt we present, in finding out how to bring these disparate and somewhat exclusive teams together. The second deplores the gap that separates the professionals from the people for whom they are planning. The remainder are concerned with the broad strategies of planning.

The binding theme is the question of how to look at the complexity of urban life, how to select and use the information needed to improve the metropolitan environment. The apparent diversity of views conceals a common concern with ecological relationships and levels of strategic intervention within a community. Poston, speaking for the very small urban center, shows that the information needed to implement change can be gathered by the community development experts working with local people. As the community becomes larger, the information must be gathered and pulled together in more sophisticated ways, suggesting critical points of intervention. Webber points to the lack of "market" information that makes the official's task difficult, and reminds us that quick and narrow-minded decisions are often irreversible. Perloff proposes a type of total information-seeking centered on the relationship between the lifetime earning power of a household and the personal development of its members.

Richard Meier's paper on the "simulation" of cities goes still further in discussing the abstractions needed for dealing with a complexity so great that we must use mathematical models and computers to demonstrate the crucial relationships.

To quote another of the session chairmen, Dr. Thomas Gladwin on the NIMH:

> Planning is a process of continuous prediction from a present condition to one or of possible future conditions. . . . What can social science contribute to metropolitan planning? . . . I believe there is a . . . gain to be sought from social science research . . . in the ability of the world of design and research to isolate from the bewildering complexity . . . certain key variables, or dimensions of behavior and of the environment . . . and to predict the outcome and perhaps the cost of alternative courses of action.
>
> Granted, . . . the social scientist is selective in what he looks at, I think social scientists tend to look at precisely those variables which constitute the working assumptions of present-day planners. They are testing the validity of those assumptions. Furthermore, although social science may not be as "hard" or "scientific" as natural science, every social scientist who has attempted rigorous research knows that his initial hypothesis about some aspects of human behavior is not a perfect prophecy, and therefore demonstrably not a self-fulfilling prophecy . . . the flow of human life, and the cost of creating roads or sewage systems can be estimated with far greater accuracy than can the cost of creating more satisfying styles of living. The highway planner can identify with some precision all the variables which lie within the universe of his concern, and predict with considerable accuracy the costs and outcome of any plan. He cannot predict the impact on a community of being divided down the middle with a ribbon of concrete . . . We who deal with human beings and society . . . do not know in many cases which of thousands of interrelated variables are likely to prove most crucial. Our first task, then, is to separate the relevant from the irrelevant.

This is also the task of these papers.

Social Science and Community Problems

23

HERBERT E. STRINER
HENRY E. HOLMQUIST

"We must indeed all hang together, or assuredly we shall all hang separately." This remark of Benjamin Franklin's, reportedly made at the signing of the Declaration of Independence, could well be directed at social scientists and planners who are concerned with the sound development of our urban areas. Here on the one hand are the specialists in economics, political science, psychology, sociology, and geography, all disciplines which are concerned with specific facets of a highly complicated "system" called an urban or metropolitan area. Standing off in another group are the planners, who are also concerned with the problems of urbanization. Instances are rare indeed of these two groups getting together to pool their information, experience, and interests in order to develop more effective means for dealing with the increasingly complex problems of metropolitan areas. As a matter of fact, the abysmal ignorance of each group's need for the other is most surprising. Just two years ago, during a lecture, a respected city planner from a major east coast city used the terms "social worker" and "social scientist" interchangeably. When queried from the audience, he indicated that he didn't see where there was any meaningful difference. Such luxury of ignorance, or lack of concern, on the part of planners and social scientists can no longer be permitted; the price to society is too high. Planners must increasingly use the social sciences for the development of more effective and rational metropolitan programs, and cease to duck the tough problems by substituting their visceral criteria for data, research, and analysis. Smart, clipped pronouncements that *sound* like immutable facts must give way to an honest *seeking* after facts.

Social scientists as well must undergo a painful metamorphosis. Pretensions to objective, non-human-oriented research for its own sake had better begin to be directed to a social product. This is not to say that basic research should not be done; of course, it must and should be. But, as Alfred North Whitehead, a fair authority in this matter, has stated, ". . . the notion of intelligence in pure abstraction from things understood is a myth. . . . We are finite beings; and such a grasp is denied to us."

Given the extremely intricate and complex series of relationships which go to make up the physical, social, economic, and political potpourri which we call a metropolitan environment, if we are to make a beginning in developing rational programs we must begin to understand what our available resources are, where our areas of ignorance may be, and what we must begin to do about them. Both planners and social scientists would do well to think about Socrates' chat with a supposedly very wise politician: "Probably neither of us knows anything very much worthwhile; but he thinks that he knows, when in reality he does not; I neither know nor think I know. On this small point at any rate I seem to have the better of him."

The major thesis of this paper is that the social sciences can contribute to the development of a better metropolitan environment. The word *can* is used for several reasons. To begin with, the social sciences must first see the ways in which they *could* contribute. There are of course problems of communication; the current inventory of methodologies and studies may not be suited to the specific metropolitan problems which have to be dealt with. But, above all, the social scientists and the metropolitan planners and policy-makers must become aware of each other's existence, and *reasons* for existing. If we remember that, in a relatively few years, close to 80 per cent of the population of this country will dwell in urban areas, and that the current outlook in these areas is one of racial friction, transportation chaos, and economic strangulation, then the necessity for planners and social scientists to recognize the critical reasons for each other's existence is paramount. The scientists—in the "natural" and physical as well as the social sciences—must produce the knowledge and techniques by means of which the planners and policy makers can arrive at good solutions to metropolitan problems.

The word "good," rather than "optimal" or "best," is also deliberately chosen. The scientist may not have the time, ability, tools of analysis, or data to provide what he may feel is an optimal solution. Nonetheless, a good solution may be of tremendous value for two important reasons. The first is that the problems are serious, and getting worse. Social conflict may never be susceptible to a 100 per cent cure; 50, 60, or 70 per cent cures can, however, change the course of history. This may have to be enough to salve the wounded egos of those doomed to something short of perfection. We live in a world of men, not of angels.

Second, social scientists must begin to effect *some* cures if they are to build a better ground for mutual trust and understanding, not only between themselves and planners, but also among themselves. An important feedback of success is the possibility of convincing policy-makers and planners of the potentials for further work, the need and value of more data, and the necessity for allocating funds and personnel for the fundamental research which must be the basis for developing new, and improving old, techniques.

Therefore, what we should aim for is a means of obtaining a significant rate of improvement which would not have occurred if we had used the "old" methods, whatever they were. Modern medicine cannot cure everything, and cannot even prevent the "common cold," but it certainly beats witchcraft.

Luckily for those who are interested in developing a systematic relationship between scientists and metropolitan planners and policy-makers, there are important precedents which can provide some guidance and presumably much hope. In a large number of instances the Army, Navy, and Air Force, as well as industrial firms, have dealt with "big system" problems with considerable success by the application of operations research or systems analysis. What is really involved is a team effort to use everything, *including* the kitchen sink, in order to deal with complex questions. Such questions range from, "Can and should there be integration in the armed forces?" to, "How do we design an aircraft instrument panel which will be least likely to induce error as a result of its being part of a man-machine system?" Such experiences provide (1) *precedents* which could guide us in the development of an approach which may be tailored to metropolitan problems; (2) *methodologies* which have been developed for problems which may be quite close to types which exist in urban areas (e.g., development of logistic support systems which could foreshadow the development of an urban transportation system); (3) *communication techniques* which have succeeded in providing a basis for research and action between military decision-makers and social scientists who are not necessarily atypical. The social sciences, however, can have an impact on planning and practice only if the practitioners and policy-makers are willing to expose themselves to social scientists over a fairly long and continuous period. But even this is useless unless the scientists, on their side, are willing to do their homework seriously, to try to understand the nature of the community's problems, and to work out ways in which both data and methodology from the sciences can be adapted for local application. The plight of our urban areas no longer permits the luxury of mutual indifference. But the effort to bring the two groups into a close working relationship must be made over and over, and most often by agencies outside of either. It requires faith, and it requires work.

24 Comparative Community Organization

RICHARD W. POSTON

In the newly developing countries of the world, such as these in Latin America and Asia, the great majority of the people live in villages of a few hundred to a few thousand population in which there is no institution of local government. Government in these countries is a highly centralized institution in which the nation's citizenry has no voice, and which, from a helpful or public service point of view, is remote and unreal to the majority of the people. From another point of view government is looked upon as an agent of exploitation, an authority to be feared, avoided, and regarded with suspicion. At the local level, there is also no established network of voluntary civic organization, and in the absence of either governmental or voluntary civic organization there is no social mechanism through which the people can participate in the formation of public decisions, or through which they can engage in organized efforts for the solution of social, political, and economic problems by peaceful means. There is virtually no civic machinery, formal or informal, through which the people may band together to study, to learn, to plan, to work, and take action to improve their environment. Planning and the determination of policy, the allocation of resources and the formation of programs designed to change the lives of the people, is a business which is limited to the ruling class and is a matter in which the majority of the people have no way of becoming involved or of knowing anything about. The people constitute little more than a mass target, mute and inert, toward which national plans and programs are directed.

This lack of civic organization at the local base of the society, in the villages, the towns, and the neighborhoods of the cities, which would make it possible for the people to engage in learnings, decisions, and actions aimed at improving their social and physical environment, has resulted in a great void between government and people, between the planners of change and those whose lives are to be changed. As a consequence of this void it is now commonplace to see in these countries programs being planned and large sums of money being spent, but achieving relatively little improvement because there is virtually no channel of communications between the givers and the receivers.

This void between government and people, or between the professional elite and the masses, is one of the important reasons why there is so much mass discontent, instability, and violence in the emergent countries of the world, and is one of the major reasons why it is possible for the agents of international communism to operate so effectively in these countries. Thus far little attention has been given to the development of viable democratic institutions at the local level which would make it possible to close the void between government and people and thereby enable the masses and the professional elite to mount an effective joint effort in accordance with the concept of freedom. It is largely because of these factors that billions of dollars of American foreign aid have thus far failed to bring about an environment of peace, order, and social progress in the far corners of the globe.

I mention this state of affairs in the international scene because I think it will help to make clear some of the reasons why there is so much waste of time, money, and manpower in the current efforts to improve the environment of our American cities. Here also we are finding it extremely difficult to make appropriate connections between the professional planners and the people. Here also we are experiencing great difficulty in organizing and motivating our communities in a way that will make it possible for the mass of the population to participate intelligently and effectively in the formation of decisions and actions that will harness the resources which we have available for changing and improving the environment in our cities.

In America we have a long established tradition of local democratic institutions which have been among the chief contributing factors to the national stability that we enjoy, but we are finding it increasingly difficult to maintain the civic muscle of these institutions. Probably there is no country in the world in which more people are engaged in voluntary civic activity than in the United States. We have men's and women's service clubs, youth organizations, chambers of commerce, PTA's—an almost endless list of citizens' associations in virtually every segment of human interest. Probably there has never been a time when we have had more people holding more memberships in more organizations for more worthwhile purposes than today. Beyond this we have the numerous official boards and commissions that have been appointed in the several states for the purpose of bringing about improvements of one kind or another in the American city, and we have the many agencies of the federal government which have been created for that purpose. Throughout the country municipalities have their own planning bodies, and private industry has made heavy investments in a multiplicity of projects and programs designed to bring about various community improvements. Many millions of dollars have gone into technical and scholarly surveys concerned with traffic congestion, housing, smog, delinquency, old people, young people, the arts, and virtually every other aspect of city life. Tons of illustrated brochures have been published to point up the problems, and the fields of public relations, city planning, industrial promotion, and similar endeavors have grown into lucrative business enterprises. Vast new outlays are needed for urban research, but millions of dollars have already been spent for reports that have been left to gather dust, and for plans that have yet to receive serious attention. In the American city of today a wide assortment of organizations, official and unofficial, vie with each other for credit and for public acceptance, but the volume of unsolved problems rising out of the urban environment continues to grow. The tens of millions of our citizens who remain untouched, uninterested, and unmoved continue to increase. The lack of coordinated effort between local jurisdictions within the sprawling metropolitan area remains unchanged, and the accumulation of technical knowledge continues to increase at a rate which is far greater than the willingness of the people to act.

Despite the wide assortment of efforts to improve the environment of the American city, we have demonstrated the same lack of appreciation for the importance of comprehensive community organization and community action at home that we have so dramatically demonstrated in our attempts to aid the newly developing countries of the world.

Community organization for civic action may take the form of an activity which is focused upon the construction of schools, the collection of funds for a social service, or the achievement of some other limited goal in a specialized area of interest. This is the type of community organization which today characterizes most of the civic effort that is being promoted in the American city. Much of this kind of community organization is motivated not by an earnest desire for the satisfaction which comes from the exercise of civic responsibility for the building of a better community, but is motivated by a desire to attain status or certain personal or professional advantages in business or politics.

Then there is another type of community organization which is more talked about in certain circles, but which in practice is given little emphasis. This is a kind of community organization to which I refer as community development—a much deeper and broader type of civic activity which is from time to time also focused upon specific limited projects, but which sees each of these projects as simply a part of the fuel that is used for the purpose of gaining the interest of the whole community in a continuous process of growth in the quality of community life, in the basic civic strength and the problem-solving capacity of the people as a civic body. In this kind of community organization, or community development, the community is looked upon as a social organism or as a human organization which in itself constitutes a major aspect of the environment of its residents, and which therefore exerts a powerful influence upon their habits, their attitudes, their values, their interests, and their patterns of behavior.

Implicit in community development is the assumption that most community problems are an outgrowth of the environment which in itself *is* the community: even most of those problems which result from external forces may continue to exist only because the inner nature of the community and its relationships to other communities are such as to block appropriate actions which would have the effect of altering or minimizing the adverse influence of these external forces. Thus, in community development, the community itself is looked upon as the problem toward which efforts of improvement should be aimed, and each item of deficiency is viewed as only symptomatic of the environment as a whole. In this kind of community organization the acquisition of a new community facility is not in itself considered as important as the civic energy and the methods by which that facility was attained, and the effect of the process of attaining it on strengthening the community's problem-solving capacity. It is these intangible qualities that are of supreme importance to the community development practitioner—the community's ability to accomplish things for itself, to make appropriate use of outside resources, to recognize and take effective steps to meet its needs, and to make democratic action and civic initiative integral parts of the community's inner character or environment. Only in a community which has these characteristics can a workable linkage be made between people and government, between the population mass and the professional planners, that will make it possible to realize the full potential of a free society for the well-being of man.

The disregard for this kind of community organization has been due to many factors, one of the most important of which has been the technological transition we have undergone in the change from a rural to an urban society. In the process of making this change there has been a tendency to assume that community problem-solving is something which can be accomplished by government experts or by professional planners and scholars without the active participation of the general citizenry. The people have tended to adopt attitudes of local helplessness and dependency. The professionals, particularly in government bureaus, have tended to act as though the people are largely incapable of knowing what is good for them, and there has been a tendency to dismiss self-help and democratic action as undependable, ineffectual, or out of date.

The common mode of operations of the professional elite in government agencies and in many other institutions, including universities, has become such as to *replace* community effort instead of supplementing and assisting it. The need for professionals and for government aid in the solution of community problems cannot be questioned, but unless this assistance is planned and applied in a way that will stimulate and awaken increased civic energy in our communities instead of putting them even more deeply to sleep, we can have every reason to expect that the environment of our cities will become less and less favorable to civic vitality and to a free, self-reliant problem-solving society.

A further reason why the need for community development has been so widely neglected is the emphasis that has come to be placed upon specialization, and the splinter approach to the solution of community problems. As a result of the emphasis on specialization it is now normal and customary for Americans to think not in terms of the community, but in terms of various specialized fields of knowledge that have become established in this country. Each of these fields is in turn broken into many finer specializations, and in hundreds of institutions of higher learning it is possible for a person to devote a lifetime to becoming an authority on the most minute particle of human knowledge. Around these specializations, university departments, private businesses, sections of the government bureaucracy, and individual careers are organized, and one of the chief measures of social prestige is the status a person attains in one of these accepted fields of specialization.

This emphasis has made it normal for Americans, particularly highly educated Americans, to think of community problems not in terms of the environment out of which the problems arise, but in terms of one of the recognized fields of specialized knowledge into which American scholars have divided and classified life.

It is therefore difficult for opinion leaders in government, in education, or in industry to think of the community as a social unit which in itself constitutes a problem. They have been taught to see it in terms of recreation, delinquency control, industrial development, traffic engineering, housing, municipal administration, school construction, library service, or as a problem in one of the health sciences. Inasmuch as community development does not fit neatly into any one of these established fields, but is concerned with the community as a whole, whose development calls for a broad integrated approach cutting across many fields, community development is a concept foreign to many Americans. Moreover, each professional division or section of the governing body has a budget allocation to worry about, along with matters of salaries, power, and other factors that make for status and influence. The concept of community development is too broad for these specialized interests. It represents a way of dealing with problems that is strange and unnatural.

This difficulty is particularly evidenced in the foreign aid program. When the President of the United States says that America is going to share her storehouse of knowledge with the newly developing countries of the world, the agriculturalist immediately and automatically translates that into manure piles, compost pits, and irrigation ditches. The home economist translates it into nutrition and child care. The educator translates it into school buildings and blackboards. The construction engineer translates it into public works. And the public health doctor translates it into latrines, mosquito abatement, and water wells. Almost nobody translates it in terms of unified, active, responsible, civic-minded, problem-solving communities.

Specialists in each discipline proceed as rapidly as possible to build up divisions, sections, and budgets around each of the splintered translations they have made, and go out to start work on projects in their respective fields, all operating separately and independently from each other. Each project becomes an end in itself, each designed to improve something which is considered important in terms of the professional values of the specialized field into which the project falls. The project that is eventually judged to be the most important, and which consequently gets the most money, depends primarily upon which division or section of the bureaucracy has been able to marshal the most pressure.

In our efforts to solve the problems which are growing out of the American city, we see this same influence reflected on an even larger scale. Here there is an even larger number of specialized agencies and sections of the bureaucracy, each stirring up projects, each enlisting its own set of followers, and each moving ahead as rapidly as possible to spend its budget with no more reference to the others than the law requires. In each case the project is the goal. Little or no thought is given to the impact the project could make for the purpose of generating a unified community effort to enrich the environment as a whole, and in most cases it would be either illegal or regarded as inefficient to manage the project in such a way as to motivate increased civic responsibility and self-reliance. The project itself is accomplished. But increased dependency, less civic spirit, greater fragmentation of effort, and new schemes to shift more responsibility onto higher levels of government become increasingly outstanding characteristics of the city. Civic paralysis takes deeper hold on the population, democracy becomes increasingly an unscientific cliché, and the problems of the city continue to multiply.

One of the most urgent problems to be faced by those who wish to enrich the environment of the American city, who wish to see increased national performance, and who wish to see democracy strengthened in America, is the need to build a more vital sense of community in each of the metropolitan areas in which our people live. The need is for a more active and meaningful pattern of interpersonal and intergroup relationships. It is for a deeper and more widespread feeling of local responsibility. It is a need for true community effort as contrasted with the splinter efforts of an assortment of specialized groups. These are some of the implications of the type of community organization to which I refer as community development.

It is an art in which emphasis is continuously placed upon the overall quality of community life instead of on any particular specialization or project. It is an operation in which all improvements are viewed and carried out in such a way as to make each one of them instrumental in developing an environment in which better problem solving habits, enriched human relations, and vigorous civic action are dominant characteristics.

The launching of such a program will require institutions dedicated to that purpose. It will require a clear recognition and acceptance of the concept of community development in the top levels of leadership in government, in education, in business, and in the professions. And until that recognition and acceptance come, regardless of what else we may do to improve our cities, significant headway will not be made toward reducing the backlog of unsolved social, political, and economic problems in the American city.

25 The Prospects for Policies Planning

MELVIN M. WEBBER

The idea of planning has become very fashionable since the war. Although the essence of the idea is very old, stemming back at least to the beginnings of early social science during the last century and to the formulation of the philosophy of pragmatism at the turn of the century, it is only quite recently that a large and diverse range of professional groups seems to have been attracted to it. Now we frequently hear of new efforts at planning being made in large corporations, local social welfare councils, public health establishments, university administrations, and in local governmental departments, as well as in such traditional places as military organizations and city planning agencies.

Something very important seems to be happening here, although it is seldom clear what it is, since one can never be sure what any given group means when it adopts the planning label. This uncertainty persists because the term has been applied to a wide range of concepts and hence to a wide variety of activities. More than that, it is because we continue to lack a *theory* of planning and hence a basis for consensus. Whatever it is that we so-called planners are doing, we do it in the absence of an explanation of the essence of what we do, or of a rationale that might guide us in doing it.

I will not pretend to present such an explanation or rationale here. But I do want to identify some of the subsidiary ideas that lie implicit in the notion of planning. Then I should like briefly to describe what it is that city planners have been doing so that, in turn, we can look at some of the potential relationships between city planning and some of the emerging planning activity in social welfare circles that is substantively related to city planning.

Planning as a Problem-Solving Method

I should make it clear, first, that I understand planning to be *a method for reaching decisions,* not a body of specific substantive goals. Applied within a fairly stable and widely shared general value framework, planning is a rather special way of deciding which specific goals are to be pursued and which specific actions are to be taken. Seen in this way, it is directly antithetical to the more popular view among some practitioners, who are also called planners, in which planning is a social movement aimed at accomplishing certain predetermined specific goals shared by members of the professional group or by other groups.

Having said this, it should also be apparent that the method is largely independent of the phenomena to be planned. Thus, essentially the same processes may be applied in deciding how to deploy a military force, in guiding the activities of a corporation, in determining which social services are to be provided, or in deciding about the city's physical structure.

Although in its essential characteristics the planning approach to problem-solving is largely neutral with respect to subject matter, and although it cannot work with specific goals predetermined, it is intrinsically normative. By its very nature, the planning task is oriented to choosing among alternative values—to evaluating alternative multi-goal sets, as these goals appear in a hierarchical and temporal continuum of ends-means.

In a one-sentence definition, I suggest that planning is that process of making rational decisions about future goals and future courses of action which relies upon explicit tracings of the repercussions and of the value implications associated with alternative courses of actions, and, in turn, requires explicit evaluation and choice among the alternative matching goal-action sets.

So pat a definition may not be readily acceptable to those whose professional experience has made them aware of the multiplicity of end-systems that mark heterogeneous populations. Among the various subpublics within a given urban population, there is a wide diversity of interests, life styles, and values. The preferences of any one group may be in direct conflict with those of other groups; indeed, the diverse values held by members of any given group may also be internally incompatible. Hence, governmental programs that might satisfy one group within the community might harm another; or if they satisfy some wants of a given group, they may simultaneously deprive the same group of others of its wants.

This value-pluralism makes the planning of governmental services an extremely complex undertaking, since democratic governments are obligated to foster the welfare of all members of the community. The task is all the more difficult in that it becomes necessary *explicitly* to identify the value sets of the various subpublics. As every psychiatrist knows, no individual, much less group, is consciously aware of all his (or its) wants. He therefore cannot rank his preferences for various goods and services; and we would certainly be hard pressed to say what combination of goods and services he would prefer at some date in the distant future, especially since his preferences are likely to change over time. And, yet, long-term public commitments must be made for educational, medical, housing, transportation, and other services that will intimately affect future levels of social welfare. We therefore cannot avoid an attempt consciously and explicitly to identify social goals, if the actions we take are to have reasonable probabilities of inducing the consequences that are desired.

This need for deliberate expression of public goals is peculiar to governments and to other organizations that distribute their services without direct charges. Private business enterprises are able to appraise people's relative preferences by offering goods and services on the open market, where people can select or reject them as they choose. By attaching prices to the items offered for sale, the business firm is able to appraise the relative valuations that consumers place on the various items. And since business management's own motivations (which include profits, relative advantage, prestige, and corporate survival) are predominantly self-centered, it is sufficient for it to test the market and then to produce those items that will further its own ends.

Governments must handle their accounting in a quite different way. The returns from a governmental enterprise—such as a public school system—are realized not only as "tax profits" to the enterprise but also as benefits that accrue directly to the customers and then to the other members of the community, as customers' benefits generate secondary returns. In the absence of a pricing system attached to the goods and services that governments provide, and in the face of plural values, it is therefore difficult to know what it is that customers prefer and, hence, what combination of services and facilities would benefit them and the community most.

How can we know the relative value of better elementary school instruction versus a better swimming pool, or of a public health clinic versus an improved system of traffic signals? Without a statement of consumers' preferences in the open market, we have had to rely instead on the political expressions of preference voiced by various interest groups in the community, and only sometimes by submitting the questions directly to the consumers in a bond-issue referendum. Our normal process, though, is to rely upon the value hypotheses of politicians and their professional staff assistants. By and large, this system works very well in the short run, for sensitive politicians and informed professionals are able to make reasonably good judgments about the *current* preferences of the various publics and about the actions that would satisfy them. But it works well *in the long run*—if it does—only through the intervention of Providence.

It is in the nature of things that actions taken now cannot influence events in the past. Actions taken today have significance for us only as they work to affect conditions in the future. Planning, which is an action-oriented activity, is by nature, therefore, also future-oriented.

It is also in the nature of things that events that have not yet happened cannot be "known." Although continuing improvements in our sciences are continually improving our predictive capabilities, there is a large part of the future that cannot be predicted—that is both unknown and unknowable. There is also a large part of the future that is uncontrollable—even in an absolutely totalitarian regime. This is because evolutionary processes in technology and in social institutions seem to have imperatives of their own, which refuse to yield before the deliberate efforts of men. It is also because our understanding of these processes is always inadequate, and we simply do not know which levers to pull to redirect the course of change. At any given moment in time, therefore, decision-makers (and their planner assistants) operate within limited ranges-of-choice whose boundaries are uncertain and which, at the very best, can be predicted only as gross probabilities.

Local governments thus confront some serious built-in dilemmas in trying to carry out the assignments that the communities have charged them with. They face an uncertain future which they can only partially control; they cannot know what their constituents really want; and, given the inevitable limitations on knowledge of the complex social systems they deal with, they cannot possibly trace out the full maze of consequences of their actions, much less understand the full maze of value implications of what they do. Yet they are called upon to offer a large array of services, to construct a large array of public works, and to police certain activities of individuals and organizations. And, to top it all, they are expected to do all these things in some rational way—to offer at least an approximation to an optimal combination of the various services, public works, and controls that would yield a high ratio of welfare returns to resources expended.

If the concerns of a municipality were solely with the short-run future, these problems would not be as severe; for, it could adjust its course readily, as errors in decisions come to light. This is the way the typical private corporation operates—feeling its way from month to month and year to year, testing its market, testing its competitors and suppliers, accommodating its course as its information radar feeds intelligence back into the management circuits. The established corporation can get by with relatively small, incremental decisions. Indeed it must, for it seldom can afford the risks that tie to big decisions calling for big changes.

Again, governments, including city governments, are peculiar. Although in many of their activities their behavior is quite like the corporation's, governments are forced to make some big, high-risk decisions that are not divisible into small incremental steps. These are of the yes-no rather than the more-or-less type of commitment, and they are typically made—of necessity—in the absence of adequate understanding of their probable impacts. Here in California the $175 billion water plan is a good example of what I point to, or the San Francisco area's proposed billion dollar transit system, or the University of California's intention to build several new replicas of its Berkeley campus. Other major long-range commitments could be cited at length—the large port development projects, the river valley development schemes, and above all, the tremendous investments in public education, health services, highways, and housing throughout the nation.

Inputs to projects of this magnitude cannot be modulated from month to month and year to year as readily as can those feeding into a corporation's operations—even if the Congress and the city councils remain reluctant to commit money beyond a two-year horizon. Once a decision has been made to support suburban housing construction, for example, a decision has thereby also been made to support the construction of highways, school houses, sewer and water lines, and the whole complex of related facilities. Governments, unlike private corporations, cannot simply decide to step out of a given line of activity once the investment has been amortized on the cost accounting books. Local government, as the corporate community, is the natural heir to all the local public and private developmental decisions that have already been made, however foolish or however wise. Much as we might wish to avoid it, as rational decision-makers we therefore cannot get away from the long-run future. During every today, we are confronted with problems we inherited from the long-run past—decisions that failed to take adequate account of the long-run consequences. And we know that the benefits (and the costs) of some of the things *we* do will not be realized until our distant future arrives—that the pay-off on some investments won't accrue until years after.

In addition to the welfare benefits that derive, the importance that a decision has for the long-run future depends upon (1) the ease with which it can be revised or reversed (which, in turn, depends upon the divisibility of decision units) and (2) the half-life of the consequences it generates. Contraposing these two characteristics as continua along the dimensions of a square field, we can then distinguish among certain of the decisions that local governments are called upon to make.

Looking only at the extremes, we can identify decisions, such as those relating to traffic-signal timing or garbage collection schedules, that have only short-range consequences and are readily adjusted; and we identify others, such as a city's annual report whose consequences are short-lived but once made cannot be easily changed. At the right-hand side of the chart fall matters such as school curricula and public health programs (in the federal government, foreign policy is the outstanding example). These are readily revised from time to time but, at any given moment in time, they generate long-range consequences. These, in turn, must be distinguished from decisions concerned with major public works and other physical structures that are both inherently resistant to change, and that continue to exert their influences throughout their lives.

In general it is the municipality's decisions on operating programs

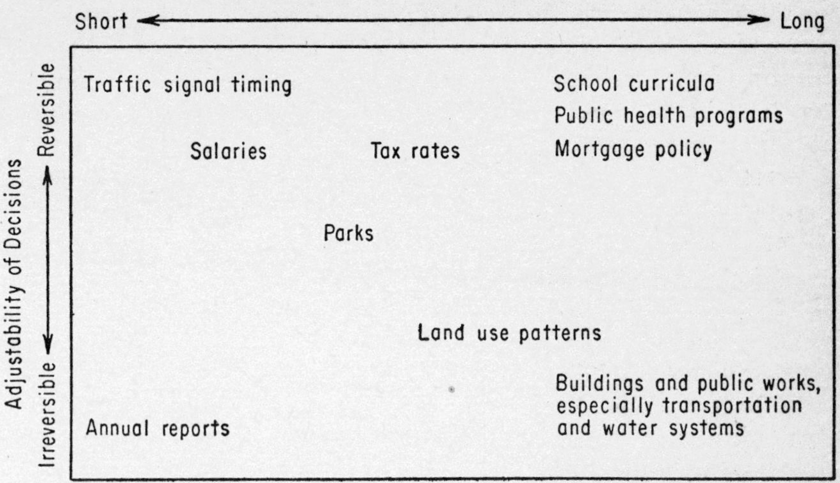

that can be modulated from time to time, and it is the decisions on physical facilities that are irreversible. This is the main rationale for the division between the so-called operating and capital budgets, of course. But the operating programs and the physical facilities both generate consequences having extended longevities.

The Functions of City Planning

It is partly because physical facilities are durable on both these dimensions that city planning has come to focus its attention on the physical city, rather than on the processes of the social-economic-political city. By tradition and by the profession's choice, city planning is primarily concerned with the physical plant within the muncipal territory and with the locations at which people conduct the various types of activities in which they engage. The typical city planning agency is only tangentially concerned with the non-locational aspects of the population's activities, and is scarcely concerned with the operating programs of the various service agencies in local government.

There are a number of other reasons for this partial approach to the urban system, in addition to those attached to the longevity of buildings and their consequences. The locational patterns in which activities are distributed bear directly upon the costs of living and upon the costs of doing business. More, since distance between places operates as a barrier to communication, locational patterns have meaning for us as they serve to open or foreclose opportunities for fruitful interaction with others; for participation in the community's social, economic, and political life; and for sharing in the cultural wealth of the urban society. Too, the physical shapes of cities have important symbolic and aesthetic meanings; and we are confident that, by applying intelligence in guiding the evolution of city forms, we can bring about important improvements over the results that atomistic decisions would otherwise bring. The need for intellectual specialization in complex fields reinforces the locational-physical focus of city planning, especially now when knowledge in this specific field is expanding so rapidly.

But it is unlikely that this partial approach to planning in local government was so deliberately designed when the professional activity was first institutionalized. Although a very diverse group of professionals contributed to the earliest formulations—they included economists, lawyers, engineers, social workers, political reformers, housers, conservationists, architects, landscape architects, and probably others—it was the conservationists, architects, landscape architects, and engineers who really led the way by themselves moving into city planning practice. They brought with them great sensitivities and skills in designing physical facilities and they also brought the thoughtways and the postulates of their mother professions.

I think these professional origins of city planning account for our persisting fundamentalist belief in land, our overriding attention to locational and physical aspects of the city, our intense attention to visual qualities, and our conception of the city as a closed mechanical system. These, and the wave of social reform on which they rode, probably also account for the biggest idea that drives the city planning movement. This is the proposition that the locational and physical environments are major determinants of behavior and of social welfare.

As David Riesman suggests, city planning may be the last stronghold of utopianism; certainly city planning has always attracted the idealist and the ideologue. Whatever else it has or has not been, city planning has traditionally been a movement of social reform.

It is surprising, then, that its approach has been so indirect—that it has relied so heavily upon efforts to manipulate the physical environmental influences on behavior, rather than seeking to deal with social behavior more directly. It is all the more surprising because the evidence that might support physical environmental determinism has been so sparse, because so little is even hypothesized about the effects of the physical environment, and because only a handful of (inconclusive) systematic tests of the resulting effects of planned developments has even been attempted.

But the most surprising paradox is this: Those city planners who believe most firmly that the physical environment is a powerful determinant of social behavior (and who thus justify physical planning as a socially useful enterprise) are the first to deny the proposition that city planners are thereby operating in the province of social planning. They are also the first to decry the efforts of those who would try explicitly to integrate the physical and the social planning efforts.

City Planning and Social Welfare Planning

There are certain explicit fiscal and mechanical criteria that must guide the physical planning of cities. The costs of various types of public works must be carefully weighed against the community's financial resources. Highway and school capacities must match the demands that future populations will impose. In most communities there is consensus on minimum standards for certain governmentally provided facilities, and city plans must fit these facilities into the budgetary and spatial designs. But city planning is clearly more than citywide engineering and cost accounting. It is an endeavor that seeks to improve the qualities of life for the city's residents.

City governments do have considerable power to shape the way the locational-physical city grows. If the locational-physical city does exert significant influences upon the important qualities of city life, controls exerted here could indeed serve as important means for generating welfare benefits. But decisions concerned with locational and physical development are not likely to yield the welfare benefits that are desired unless we understand something about the causal relationships so that we can then pursue courses of action that are directed to explicitly stated and specific social objectives.

If the doctrine of physical environmental determinism has some validity and changes in the physical environment do indeed exert important influence upon social behavior, it becomes imperative that plans for physical development be treated as instrumental to the accomplishment of specific social goals. Currently the city planner, who is poorly equipped to do so, is forced to hypothesize which goals are to be pursued; for there is no other professional staff agency having this responsibility He can't escape it, of course; for the long-term consequences of the facilities he recommends are generated whether they are deliberate or not.

The doctrine of physical environmental determinism, which is the main rationale for the large investments being made in city planning, is therefore also a doctrine that requires a parallel enterprise in social welfare planning.

Except for the visual qualities of the physical environment and for the mechanical and financial considerations I just mentioned, the artifactual city holds meaning for its inhabitants only as it serves to open or foreclose social and economic opportunities. In only special and limited ways is the artifact an end in itself. Its value lies in its instrumental capacities to serve as a means to accomplish certain social purposes. A plan for the physical city has utility, therefore, only as a step in a means-ends continuum that causally relates the artifactual city to the social-economic-political city.

We are only just beginning to ask the right questions about these relationships, and the papers in this symposium reflect a number of as yet disparate approaches to a few of them. The research that will expose such significant relationships as may pertain has only recently been started, and the papers presented here by Fried, Gans, Gutman, and Wilner report on some pioneering work in this new middle field. Current explorations in social welfare planning may soon begin to yield some value hypotheses that might guide the physical city planners, and Dr. Perloff's paper points to promising new directions. I think it is fair to say that city planning and the social and behavioral sciences are only now beginning to find each other, and I think the prospects are now getting bright for the development of some new theory that might permit city planning to adopt the planning method.

Without a body of theory relating the artifact to social goals, we cannot have confidence that our plans for the physical city will be compatible with our goals for the social city. And we cannot have confidence that our plans for the social city will conform to our various social goals, unless we trace through the repercussions of all we do in an effort to search out the value consequences.

It is clear, of course, that we will never have perfect information or perfect theory. Any evaluation of alternative goal-action sets must be partial and, in some large degree, inadequate. But, whatever the state of our arts and our sciences, this kind of repercussions analysis and valuation is always possible. If what each of us does is as important as we must believe it to be, and if our professional motivations are as selfless as we all contend, then we have no choice but to apply whatever knowledge is available to us in an effort to trace out the consequences of our actions and to weigh them on the welfare scale.

To do anything less is to cast doubt on the significance of our professional activities and on our private motivations. For unless we try to find our way through the complex web that ties us all one to the other, we can never be confident that what each of us does with one hand is not undone by his other, or that what one of us does is not unwittingly countered by the actions of his colleague.

As we increase our capacities to relate the plans and programs formulated within the various professional groups, and especially among groups within municipal government, the responsible political leaders will thereby be better able to make rational decisions about each of them. Now they are forced to make all sorts of decisions blindly, for lack of the analyses that would permit them to apply the planning method. If we could learn to talk to each other and then to trace the implications of our alternative plans and programs, the responsible political leaders would have better bases for making rational choices. If the consequences of proposals for various educational, recreational, public health, social service, and other programs could be fitted with proposals for redevelopment, public works, housing, industrial developments, and the like, then city governments would be in a better position to pursue integrated "policies plans." Such mutually reinforcing bundles of policies, dealing with all the aspects of development for which municipal governments have been given some responsibility, would offer better assurance than we now have that actions taken will contribute to the various objectives sought.

The current fascination with the idea of planning and the growing frequency of symposia, such as this one, suggest that the possibilities for policy planning are rapidly improving. With increasing knowledge, linking the various disciplines and the various welfare professions, we are fast moving into a position from which we can design rational courses of action—sequential series of goals. And if we really can learn to apply the planning method, the odds would be considerably greater that each of our professional endeavors would more effectively contribute to our mutual purposes.

Social Planning in the Metropolis 26

HARVEY S. PERLOFF

There is deep concern in urban communities throughout the United States about the social and human resources problems—problems of mental illness, crime and juvenile delinquency, chronic unemployment and continuing relief support, racial discrimination, family desertion and illegitimacy, and a failure to provide for the fulfillment of the potential of many members of the community. This concern has been translated into an ever increasing number of governmental, voluntary, and private efforts to cope with the problems. Projects in health, education, law enforcement, employment, recreation, and welfare have been proliferating.

On the positive side, there has been a healthy pragmatism in the development of action programs, and in some fields—as in mental health—an appropriately experimental approach in the face of many unknowns. There is, however, another side to the same coin. These urban services tend to be so unorganized that it is impossible for anyone in the community to know just what is going on, how much is being spent for different purposes and for various kinds of activities, who is gaining and who bears the load, or how well any particular set of programs is achieving the ends for which it was designed.

Also, action seems to outrun knowledge. Many things are being done even when no one is quite sure they are paying off in any significant sense. The drive is to get action under way no matter how little is understood about basic causes. It is difficult to get any sense of coherence or appropriateness in the human services taken as a whole. On inspection it seems that big guns are being trained on little problems and little guns on big problems. Obvious gaps are permitted to continue in some fields while others tend to become crowded with layers of projects.

Two examples might help to illustrate some of the difficulties and to highlight why it is likely that quite significant improvements could be achieved by the application of planning ideas and techniques to the field of social policy and human services.

Take the question of jobs and income. Persistent unemployment and inadequate income underlie many of the most difficult welfare problems, as well as some of the thorniest issues in the other human services. Yet programs touching on jobs and income are typically the concern of chambers of commerce and "area development" groups—with their own special (and generally, limited) points of view—and are only peripherally related to the human services. Training and vocational guidance, relief support, human relations, or anti-discrimination efforts, and "area development" tend to remain in operationally separate realms even though they are closely interrelated in fact and in impact. No one is responsible for "metering" on a continuous basis what is happening to the economy of the region within the context of national developments, nor for probing in depth the best possibilities for broadening the income base of the community. Amazingly little guidance on changing job market and new skill requirements is provided to those who have to make decisions about training and vocational counseling. Also, the efforts expended to strengthen the job-getting and income-increasing capacity of minority and disadvantaged groups are puny compared with the efforts directed at supporting such groups through welfare programs.

The need for a coordinated and priority-conscious approach to jobs and human services arises from a number of powerful forces at work in our economy. The rate of change of industrial structure and technology is accelerating, and, with it, changes in job characteristics and skill requirements. At the same time, there is an underlying shift toward tasks which require higher levels of training than in the past. Thus, increasingly, a person can become largely unemployable because of either inadequate training or obsolescence of skills. The ability to cope effectively with problems of maintaining youths in school, of training and retraining, of vocational guidance, of job adequacy, and of job restrictions will increasingly depend on community foresight and capability to adjust human services to powerful underlying trends.

The field of mental health provides another useful illustration. Impressive progress has yielded a host of programs, from extensive treatment services to citizen efforts to strengthen public support. We have been less successful in getting mental health approaches built into school, hospital, and social service procedures so that early diagnosis, continuing elements of "caretaker" support for individuals (particularly at times of crisis), and post-treatment assistance become normal parts of a widespread system to strengthen mental health. Also, because there is no regularized reporting covering all mental health efforts, including the amounts spent for various types of programs, evaluation tends to be inadequate. The community has no way of knowing the relative attention given to preventive as compared to curative efforts, and whether or not new findings are being sufficiently considered in the continued support of programs already under way. The mental health field poses enough inherent difficulties, especially in its community relations, without being handicapped by inadequate ties to the other human services, and without functioning in an informational vacuum.

Social Planning: Existing Inadequacies

The application of planning to human services and social policy mobilizes ideas and techniques which are already widely used in physical city planning, in natural resources development, in business activities, and in many other fields of endeavor. Essentially what is involved is an organized process which aims to clarify objectives, to point up alternative approaches to the solution of problems (with the relative advantages and disadvantages of each made explicit) so that the community can make open choices, and to evaluate results as a way of constantly improving strategy and programs.

Social welfare planning by voluntary agencies (e.g., community chests) has demonstrated the actual value—and even more, the potential value—of coordinated support and administration of social services. The idea of a research-based approach to community problems has been introduced. Finally, an outstanding achievement of the social welfare planning groups has been the tremendous amount of community involvement which has been generated.

But social planning to date has covered only a part of the total. It has not encompassed the governmental services nor many relevant private activities in health, education, employment, recreation, and welfare. This has made the coordination aspects of the planning, as well as the metering and reporting aspects, so partial that some of the most important objectives of the planning tend to get lost. Without looking at the total spectrum of human services, it is impossible to determine the appropriate balance and system of priorities, or to spot the gaps and duplication, or to achieve full organizational effectiveness for the community efforts taken as a whole.

Also, social planning to date has not actually had the strength to build a genuine research base for social policy and programs.

Where behavioral science knowledge cannot be applied *directly* in the solution of difficult social problems—as, say, in the case of juvenile delinquency—a well-developed scheme of broad-scale planning can serve as a *knowledge organizing mechanism,* providing feedbacks from the problems to research. The comprehensive, continuous metering over a wide area of linked problems can provide the type of informational framework which makes research both more sharply focused and more additive in nature.

Against this background, I would like to offer a proposition, namely, that both the good points and the weaknesses of social planning to date suggest that an effort to broaden, deepen, and strengthen planning for the human services promises a handsome pay-off in both individual and community terms, and so would be a sensible investment for any large modern metropolitan community.

General Community Objectives

Public planning of any type requires objectives which are generally accepted and understood ("You can't follow a map unless you know where you are going"). Thus, for example, economic policy in the United States before and during the 1930's floundered because the nation had not yet decided the extent of the federal government's responsibility for unemployment and business cycle control. Once it became widely accepted that the federal government should assume responsibility for seeking to maintain economic stabilization and full employment, then economic planning—with the assistance of specially designed agencies such as the Council of Economic Advisors—became feasible and effective.

In the same way, when we look at city planning, it is evident that it is only in those areas where there is widespread agreement on objectives that both planning and focused action become feasible. American city dwellers do not want traffic congestion, slums, or unpleasant productive activities (e.g., tanneries) mixed in with homes. Thus it is precisely in the realm of highway planning and construction, urban redevelopment, and zoning that physical city planning provides the most powerful levers.

With regard to planning for human services, on the other hand, it is often assumed that general community objectives cannot be formulated and, therefore, that social planning cannot help but be piecemeal and essentially ineffective. However, it is not so much a matter of the *non-existence* of community objectives as a matter of *operational non-recognition.*

Actually, I believe that widespread agreement exists in our larger metropolitan regions on certain social objectives, with both enough agreement and enough focus to provide a firm basis for broad-scale social planning. The following objectives, it seems to me, are high on almost every community agenda:

1. To maximize the proportion of families in the region who are self-supporting, and thus reduce dependency.

2. To increase the lifetime earning power of individuals—e.g., by cutting down our mortality and morbidity, by preventing mental illness, by providing useful work for the handicapped and the aged, and by the encouragement of individual entrepreneurship.

3. To provide at least minimum support—in monetary, consumption, and/or psychological terms—for those individuals and households who cannot provide it for themselves.

4. To seek to make the human services as effective and as economical as possible.

5. To enlarge the scope for individual and small-group decision and action. We have a strong belief that individuals and local groups are in the best position to determine what contributes most to their own welfare.

It is well to note that the first three objectives are measurable in statistical terms, and the last two in specific, even if qualitative, procedural terms, and thereby provide criteria against which diverse policies and programs can be judged. Thus, as far as the availability of common objectives is concerned, a firm base for effective social planning can be provided.

Specific Activities

It would be useful to try to project what a broad-based, well-supported social planning effort would cover. The following major activities would seem to me to be needed:

1. Metering and reporting. A first requirement is a highly informative, comprehensive annual report on the "state-of-the-region." Such a report would spell out progress (or lack of it) in both general and specific terms. It would show the number of families self-supporting, partially supported, and fully supported, with the major characteristics of each group, as well as the income of various groups and changes in the lifetime earning power of individuals. Also detailed would be the economic and social conditions of the community, analyzing the changing employment and manpower situation, and the major social and human resources problems facing the region. Finally, it would indicate what is being done to solve the problems of the community, providing, among other things, data on the public service expenditures and capital investment (showing groups gaining, where identifiable) and revenue receipts. Wherever possible, the information should be shown by political jurisdictions within the metropolis and by districts or neighborhoods. Behind such a report there would of course have to be a continuing information effort, building up a bank of basic data which makes analysis in depth possible.

2. Developing common strategies for human services activities. Undoubtedly substantial gains can be achieved by extending the "coordinating" umbrella of social planning to encompass governmental *and* private activities in a broad range of human services, including health, education, welfare, employment, law enforcement, and recreation. The organization of the social planning effort must involve not only representation of all the major decision-making groups but representatives who can make the important strategy and priority decisions. One of the key staff activities would be the preparation of "position" papers which draw on analyses of problems, evaluations of past performance, and research findings.

Projections can play a useful role, if properly employed. Valuable insight could be gained by projecting certain key data which reveal the evolving socio-economic situation, including population, job, and income changes, as well as the elements which make for changes in the public service requirements.

3. Integrating social planning with physical planning activities. What we have been discussing can be usefully conceived of as a planning effort parallel to the well-established physical planning activities of our urban communities. Such a view immediately suggests the need for integrating the two. Thus, social planning should provide for the preparation of analyses of the human aspects of proposed physical development programs in the region, such as housing and urban renewal. (This supposedly is being done, but in reality the orientation of physical planners has generally been such that only lip service has been paid to this important activity.) On the other side, careful study needs to be made of the physical and spatial dimensions of human services, so that facilities are designed to help advance the social objectives and not just to "house" the service activities. In general, there is need for joint consideration, wherever appropriate, of the economic, social, behavioral, and physical aspects of development programs in the region.

4. Strengthening the research base of human services. All the uncertainties and unknowns in this field make it mandatory for a very broad concept of research to be an integral aspect of the social planning effort. As in the planning itself, the main focus should be on understanding the larger forces which impinge on the individual and on ways of directing them into desired channels. Certain of these broader elements are discussed in the latter part of this paper. A sensitive informational funnel from research to policy and action is needed. The planning effort must evolve techniques for creatively "translating" research findings into increasingly effective programs. Since research is carried out mainly on a decentralized basis, an important type of activity of the central planning organ is assistance to community agencies in the design of research projects related to their operations, in the establishment of adequate techniques of evaluation, and in encouragement of the broadest possible applicability. In addition, continuing study of the community problems is almost certain to reveal areas of urgently needed information and insight, so that an important central function would be the encouragement of needed new research (carried out by those individuals and groups, wherever they may be located, who are best equipped to do so). An-

other function would be to stimulate demonstration projects to develop deeper understanding of key social, economic, and human resources problems and to improve methods and action strategies.

5. Long-range programming of human services activities. Assuming the establishment of coherent strategies and policies, it becomes possible to develop long-range general policies which can be employed in programming specific human services activities of governmental, voluntary, and private agencies. Such a "policies plan" would be based on common general objectives, common projections of situations and requirements, and an agreed-upon system of priorities. It would enable individual agencies to prepare both long-range and short-range programs and to guide their activities within the context of consistent community policy, rather than entirely within the specialized set of reference points of the agency itself (as tends to be the situation today).

One example will suggest the interconnections of the various planning activities. The information on the job market and on economic conditions generally, projections of labor force (manpower) supply and demand, and related information would provide a basis for high-level policy decisions about changes called for in training programs, vocational guidance, special aids to youth, welfare assistance, and other services, as well as "area development" efforts. The policies plan documents would show, among other things, how much money is likely to be available for the various broad service areas during the next year and several following, so that individual agencies might well be encouraged to change priority emphasis *within* their over-all programs and to undertake new or different measures called for by the changing situation. Thus, for example, the vocational agencies might make arrangements for more training in computers for Negro students as large firms greatly expand their computer facilities. Also a special effort might be made to arrange for tests to determine aptitude and motivation for this type of work among a broad range of older as well as young persons.

Effective programming requires careful estimates of the relative costs and benefits of alternative action programs, so that not simply the "useful things" are done but the *most* useful things *at a given level of expenditure* of time and money are done. Sound programming involves hard choices among good alternatives. Few tasks for social planning are as significant as that of strengthening and guiding the long-range programming of activities by the many individual agencies that have service responsibilities.

6. Enlisting grass roots participation. Effective planning is done in collaboration with the groups that are influenced by it. This calls for widespread participation in the preparation and carrying out of community plans. Determination of priorities of service and the general nature of programs to meet them is best done through the cooperation of the planning units with citizen organizations and neighborhood groups. A possible instrumentality to achieve genuine neighborhood participation in planning would be preparation of neighborhood "programs of improvement" by neighborhood organizations aided substantially by the physical and social planning units and by the governmental departments and voluntary agencies.

In general, by putting social problems in a broad context of metropolitan-change, by providing a longer chronological framework in which to develop programs and to estimate the costs and benefits of human services, and by the coordinating effect of program juxtaposition, broad social planning can be expected to contribute significantly to the achievement of the community objectives.

A Social Planning Framework

Given the difficulties and complexities with which social planning must deal, it is essential that its activities be sharply focused. This calls for a conceptual framework which can provide guidance and direction to all major planning activities, including data collection, reporting, projections, design of study and research, and the design of general and specific plans, programs, and projects. It will undoubtedly take a good bit of experience and experimentation to arrive at a conceptual framework that is suited to the social planning task in the large modern metropolis. However, a start has to be made somewhere, and I would like to suggest a general model which at least suggests the type of focus which is needed in planning for human services.

If the model is to provide a framework for bringing together the needed information, as well as for policy and program decisions, its components must literally be "accounted for"—that is, they must lend themselves to measurement in either quantitative terms or in meaningful and consistent qualitative terms. Also, the relationships among the elements must be identified in terms which can be described, if not directly measured.

There are three kinds of "elements" with which we are concerned in these models: (1) those reflecting directly the major community objectives, (2) those reflecting socio-economic forces or arrangements which influence the achievement of the objectives, and (3) the policies and programs required to influence the various forces in desired directions or to achieve the objectives more directly (as in health care).

A Social Planning Framework

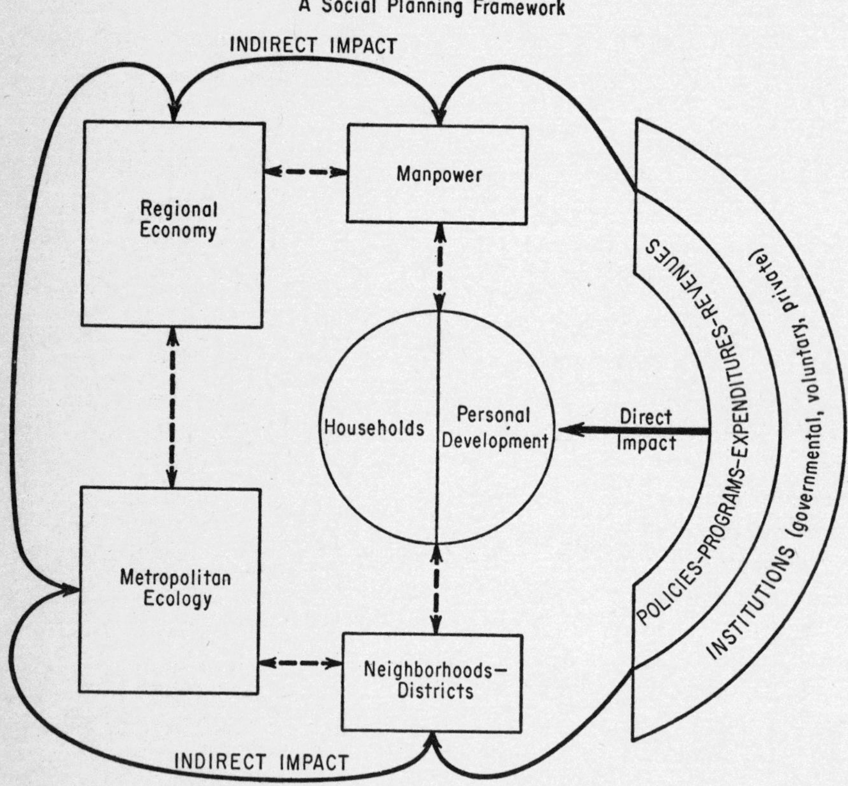

The Households

The central element of the model should logically reflect the main focus of the community objectives, and of social planning generally, on family welfare and individual development. Thus, the "core" items in the proposed planning model are *Households* and *Personal Development* submodels.

The household is chosen as the unit best reflecting the key decision-making, income-sharing, home-sharing, child-rearing functions. In most instances, the household is, of course, simply the immediate family, or the single individual when living alone; but there are many cases when it includes members of the joint family living together, and is a significant unit particularly among Negroes and first-generation immigrants.

The households submodel would generate information about the "production" (job holding and income earning) and "consumption" functions. Thus, it would provide a direct measure of the extent to which the community objectives (of self-support, high income, and the provision of a support floor) were being realized from year to year, as well as in comparison with other metropolitan communities.

The households submodel on the production side should provide *a full account* of the number of families who are financially self-supporting, partially self-supporting, and totally supported. In addition, it should provide an estimate of the number who are *potentially* self-supporting (totally or partially), as against those who will always have to be supported. It should show the numbers actually receiving aid as against those needing aid, given agreed-upon income standards. These data should be shown in terms of population characteristics, such as race, existence of a male head of household, age of head of household, educational level, and the like, so that at least the general relationships touching on self-support can be traced. The job-holding position of the households would also be recorded, including the extent of multiple breadwinners, moonlighting (the holding of two or more jobs), steady as against periodic employment, and other significant characteristics.

The major breakdown of households might well be in terms of the age of the head of the household, so that the tie to the personal development information would readily emerge. Thus, for example, the changing economic position of the aged would be highlighted, as would the position of every other age group. Household income information would be a natural corollary of job data. In addition, an estimated lifetime earning power index for each major group (by age, race, etc.) would provide a significant test over time of social progress, including the effectiveness of human services programs. If to the income earned by the households within any given year is added the income transfers, from pensions, payments in kind, and from relief grants, a figure for the total "pool of income" is provided (a figure, it might be mentioned, of significance to the business community and to local government finance officers, as well as to the human services agencies).

On the consumption side, the way in which income is used by the various groups would provide important information on a host of matters, including those relating to decisions on housing, education, health, recreation, and many other areas of interest to social planning. A full-bodied view of the consumption side would reveal where the strain on household budgets comes from. It would highlight the role of such matters as the number of children (and the potential effect of changes in the birth rate), and the effects of interest payments in consumer credit arrangements. This information in turn might direct attention to the possible desirability of more direct controls of consumer credit. A measure of this type could conceivably have as great an over-all effect on welfare as an increase in relief payments. In general, there would be a continuing evaluation of collective protection and regulation of private purchases and consumption (as in housing and drugs), of aid in money transactions, and of direct provision of public goods and services (e.g., public housing).

Wherever possible, the consumption data should follow the same age groupings as the job and income data, revealing not only the significant connection between income and consumption patterns but also the special consumption gaps or strains for each group.

Personal Development

A companion submodel and two associated "components" are needed to provide an adequate view of the human resources picture.

Information on personal development is clearly of great significance not only in making the households data meaningful, but also *directly* in designing and carrying out human services programs. The focus here would be on the "developmental" or life-cycle problems of the individuals in the community, literally from birth to death. At each stage of the life cycle, there are specific needs, many of which are socio-psychological in nature, such as socialization, development of motivation, skill learning, and outlets for creative urges—in general, involving cognitive, emotional, adaptational, and social development.

Group and Institutional "Support"

At each stage of life, certain groups and institutions play roles of support, guidance, and standard-setting which are critical to the development of the individual. These cover a wide range, from the family and informal neighborhood groups to the highly organized public and voluntary institutions, such as the schools, hospitals, courts, religious organizations, and welfare agencies. A key feature of social planning should be to identify these, to evaluate their adequacy, and to suggest ways of strengthening them or of devising substitute arrangements where the existing institutions are inadequate. In strengthening existing "support" institutions and devising new ones where needed, particular attention needs to be given to the fullest utilization of the "natural" points of contact, such as the family, the school, and the neighborhood. The job for social planning is to determine which approaches and arrangements are likely to yield the greatest returns in personal development and adaptation (at various cost levels) by drawing on research, pilot experiments, and the continuing evaluation of community efforts.

The Manpower Component

Given the central importance of jobs and of healthy and creative work situations, specific attention needs to be focused on manpower. The metropolitan region is a single labor market and the welfare of families in the region is closely tied to the character of that market. The manpower component would provide information on occupations and skills and the need for a continuing effort to balance supply and demand.

It can be seen that the four elements in the *direct* human resources focus—the household (income and consumption) patterns, the personal development situation, the institutional "support" component, and the manpower component—are interlocked. Their interconnections would emerge sharply in a continuing review of the type proposed here and would provide a very much firmer basis for social action than normally exists at present.

However, all the significant interconnections are not yet fully represented. To have the necessary manpower information, and to be in a position to guide manpower training and retraining as well as to open up increasing job opportunities, a great deal must be known about the regional economy. An instrument to strengthen and guide the "area development" work (the attraction of productive enterprises to the community) is needed also. Thus, there is need for another key submodel providing a picture in depth of the evolving regional economy, and an associated "component" focusing on the area development effort.

The Regional Economy Submodel

Data on the regional economy, properly organized, can provide the background information needed for sensible estimates of manpower requirements and household jobs and income which, in turn, can serve as a basis for program design and evaluation. Such data would reveal the changing industrial pattern of the region and highlight the factors behind such changes, particularly the relative advantages and disadvantages of the given region in attracting and holding various kinds of industries.

Techniques for handling information of this type in a meaningful way have been devised. They involve economic accounts showing for each major industry purchases and sales (the ties to other industries), production values, taxes paid, income paid out to capital and labor, and similar key information, adding up to a rounded picture of the regional economy. As such data are brought together year by year, the economic problems and the opportunities for expansion and improvement begin to emerge, and provide the knowledge needed to guide "area development" (or job and income attraction) efforts. Among other things, the ties between the economic and the social developments become evident and a more understanding approach to human service activities can be expected.

The Locational and Ecological Focus

Almost everything has to take place in space. Both the physical environment and the geographical relations among various activities and structures tend to play a significant role in the welfare of the people of the community.

From the standpoint of family (or household) welfare, the "micro-environment" of the neighborhood is particularly important. It is here that the youth receives much of his developmental "support" in terms of his schooling, his playmates, and the adult standards provided. Here the family receives (or does not receive) certain of the important human services and the help and companionship of friends, neighbors, and informal "caretakers." Thus, personal development supports and human services both need to be evaluated within the neighborhood context, as well as across the board.

This calls for a detailed examination of (1) the situation within each neighborhood, in terms of the characteristics of the people and their problems; (2) the characteristics and problems of the physical environment (including such considerations as adequacy of play space); and (3) the requirements for and adequacy of the human services.

Social planning can make a particularly significant contribution to community welfare if it were to join forces with physical city planning in helping to establish a continuous process of *neighborhood improvement.* Situations rarely if ever remain exactly the same. They either get worse or better. Once a process of neighborhood betterment is initiated, increased individual pride and motivation can, under favorable conditions, follow suit. The probabilities of such an impact are particularly great if the improvement is the product mainly of a neighborhood effort.

Specifically, the social and physical planning activities might well focus a fair share of their attention on helping neighborhood groups to devise "improvement programs" which look to a gradual upgrading of both the physical environment and the adequacy and effectiveness of the human services. This would involve "technical assistance" in neighborhood planning by the planning bodies as well as the more co-ordinated provision of the public, voluntary, and private services. This might well provide the kind of powerful organizing focus that a successful "community development" movement requires.

Policies and Programs

The information outlined above would make it possible to evaluate the adequacy of the existing policies and programs with regard to human services. Once the gaps and inadequacies are revealed, the basis is laid for the design of improved policies and programs, or at least a rechanneling of expenditure—assuming also a flow of information from pilot projects probing new program possibilities. Social planning must also provide a continuing overview of existing programs and expenditures, as a basis for the design of policy and plans for the future.

The policy and program submodel thus should cover all human services (public, voluntary, and private) throughout the metropolitan region and should set forth the needed information within the framework of total public and voluntary expenditures, as well as estimates of total private expenditures (from the households submodel). The information might be broken down by the key functions (education, health, recreation, welfare, etc.), and should provide program objectives and work units as well as financial outlays (coming as close as possible to the information that is called for in a comprehensive program budget). Of course, the revenue picture also needs to be provided as a key element in program decisions. For example, the nature of the drain on family personal budgets imposed by an increase in taxes to raise service levels should be considered. As far as possible an attempt should also be made to distinguish between the true "investment" element in human services as compared to the "expenditure" element.

A summary institutional "component" of this submodel is also called for. What the human services agencies are doing, what they are equipped to do, what their limitations and potentialities are (the probability of effective "delivery"), all need consideration. An informative view would require an analysis within the framework of the broader power structure, but even a more limited continuing analysis of agency effectiveness and institutional performance could provide invaluable insights for effective social planning.

All this adds up to a complicated framework. However, there doesn't seem to me to be any gain in oversimplifying the complex human-socio-economic-political matrix with which planning for the public services must deal. The important requirement is to get the necessary information for the development of effective policy and programs.

As noted earlier, a framework such as this can be applied for all the major functions involved in social planning, including data collection, metering, reporting, the preparation of projections, the design of studies, the setting of targets, and the preparation of plans, programs, and projects. As a matter of fact, a large part of its usefulness stems from the consistent pattern which it would bring to the forefront as a basis for decision making and action.

The establishment of broadly based social planning in our metropolitan areas is a challenge of large proportions. It is a challenge as to whether or not our urban communities can organize themselves to quite consciously look toward creating the conditions in which all persons can achieve their fullest potentialities and have productive and creative lives.

"Game" Procedure in the Simulation of Cities

27

RICHARD L. MEIER

Everyone who takes a continuing interest in the functioning of his own community, or a professional interest in other communities, has already synthesized for himself a mental image of the way a community works. He believes he can predict many of the consequences of actions undertaken by the community, and can estimate the effects of disturbances that originate from outside it. In most urban places, anywhere from 5 per cent to 20 per cent of the adult population has developed images of this degree of elaborateness, and the leadership of the community is normally drawn from this stratum.

Yet any investigator who interviews members of this leading set is immediately impressed with the frequency of grossly defective and warped images of "community." It is not necessary to quote any studies; these observations are universal. If community development programs do nothing else, they can at least be credited with improving the quality of the respective images of community, and with creating a body of concepts necessary to the extension of an understanding of community organization to a new circle of individuals. Community development programs are therefore educational, even when not successful in achieving local goals. However, the price, as measured in terms of human time and other resources such as special skills, is often very high. Other important welfare responsibilities, outside the orbit of community action, tend to be neglected. We need other, more economical, means for conveying an image of community organization than those which now exist. In particular, the perceptions of the political, economic, social, cultural, esthetic, and physical features of large communities need to be integrated, because the gravest difficulties lie in visualizing how action in any one of these aspects has consequences in others.

Recently, some new techniques have appeared on the scene which enable investigators to formulate a model of a complex system and allow them to trace, much more completely than before, the *conditions preceding* decision as well as the consequences. These techniques focus upon methods of *simulation*. The results are more applicable to the real world than those which are deduced from the geometric diagrams of the economists, or even from the maps of the geographers, because the time factor is incorporated. Simulations are also more understandable to the layman.

Normally a simulation takes the form of a small-scale working model upon which various strategies for action are tested. Some models use people to make routine decisions within prescribed roles; others use random subsidiary decisions in a program of calculations. Often a computer is introduced to speed up the process. The model may extract competitive elements from the situation (in our case it is the urban community), and potential decision makers may then be asked to carry on the simulation as a "game," making a series of decisions that affect the structure of the "community" as they proceed in much the same manner as they would in the "real world."

Although this approach has not yet been applied to cities (except for specialized purposes such as vehicular traffic, disasters, or elections), closely related studies have been carried out for corporations, markets, and military organizations.[1] When executives, managers, operators, and military officers are allowed to try out their own strategies, as well as those for which they have little sympathy, they improve their image of the organization—most often by filling in huge gaps and correcting gross misconceptions. (The most common statement by participants in present game-type simulations is, "I never realized before that the [x] factor was so important!"). To my knowledge, at least a half-dozen investigators have proposed that simulations of cities be prepared; but with the possible exception of one heroic case (the Penn-Jersey model of the Philadelphia metropolitan area), no one has made any significant progress.

Perhaps one reason cities have not been simulated, while work has proceeded a long way in that direction for other large institutions, is that the organization of a city is loosely coupled, and as a result there is a wider range of significant variables. One way of restating this argument is to assert that the computers are still far from being large enough to simulate a city in the same level of detail that is demanded for the serious business games. Other investigators will point out that crucial data are still not being provided in cities, particularly those concerning rates of change. It might be pointed out also that until recently there has been relatively little concerted demand for improved management and planning of cities, or the requisite support for research and development.

The Design of a Simulation

The real challenge is to reproduce the essential features of a city in a tiny comprehensible package. A set of maps is not enough. Years must be compressed into hours or even minutes, the number of actors must be reduced to the handful that can be accommodated in a laboratory or classroom, the physical structure must be reproduced on a table top, the historical background and law must be synopsized so that it can become familiar within days or weeks, and the interaction must remain simple enough so that it can be comprehended by a single brain. This last feature is the most difficult challenge of all.

The reason this task is difficult is that no body of unified theory is available which tells us how the variables in the urban social system are to be fitted together. At least a dozen different overlapping models exist in literature that have been illuminated by case studies and have been put into some form of mathematical representation. Each emphasizes only a few aspects of urban organization. If a working model of a generalized city is constructed which has a close enough resemblance to produce realistic behavior in those persons who are "playing" it, then that model constitutes a marked step forward in achieving the synthesis of a common mental image; it would be a general theory of city organization which can at least be communicated without being rejected out of hand by students. Any specialist, such as a demographer, economist, or administrator would be impressed by the superficiality of the model in his area of competence and its complexity in handling unfamiliar variables. For these reasons he is likely to reject it, criticizing its balance and comprehensiveness; but a simulation with these properties of realism for a large population with general education is already one or two notches too complex for the best minds to master (i.e., to play an optimal game, as with a chess master) within a period of days.

When a body of theory has been refined for a decade or two, it is possible to construct a moderately elaborate simulation with only two or three professional man-years of effort. It is possible to represent that aspect of organization theory as a computer program with certain options left open. When the theory is fragmentary, however, a great deal of experimentation is necessary in the course of developing simulations. Most of the experiments are conducted with potential users of the evolving model as the "subjects." The model underlying the resulting simulation should be a significant contribution toward a unified theory.

The deficiency lies in an adequate representation of human ecology. Surprisingly enough, in the accumulated literature on gaming there are no models of ecological conflict. The stochastic model for the expansion of urbanized areas developed by Stuart Chapin and co-workers at North Carolina is useful. Nathan Grundstein at the University of Pittsburgh is working toward a computer simulation.[2] The Penn-Jersey study has already been mentioned. Much work has been done by a colleague, Anatol Rapoport, on the kind of cooperation needed to overcome dilemmas.[3] Studies on the simulation of national economies have appeared in print.[4] It appears now that it would be possible to create two or three quite different kinds of simulations of city organization. They would require different degrees of sophistication on the part of the "decision-makers" about urban processes and would employ different variables.

Thus far, no attention of this kind has been given to the gravest problems in urban organization, those encountered in newly developing countries. Therefore some field work is needed before there is any hope for simulating a city that grows in size, numbers, and wealth, advances in productivity and welfare, establishes political order despite increasing diversity of groups, and enriches its own culture. Any kind of success in producing simulations suitable for developed countries such as the United States would make it vastly easier to construct another one that is representative of the problems and issues in cities that must set the pace in economic growth for newly developing countries.

A Procedure

One approach would be to start from a general model of an idealized metropolis. Its basic structure would include population characteristics (household size, age, fertility, etc.), land use, daily peak traffic flows, social structure, political boundaries, a governmental structure, expenditure and earnings distribution, and a history of regulation. Such data have been collected for cities to a sufficient degree to permit a large amount of borrowing, followed by simplification of relationships so that they hold for more than one city. Even in a simple model, policies for directing growth and development might be instituted and their consequences followed over time. The resultant city form can then be described and compared with outcomes from other policies.

Although this approach has been used repeatedly in the course of simulating other systems, it has certain recognized defects. It tends to freeze into a mold all kinds of adjustments that might be made through time by various firms, public administrators, courts, and voluntary organizations. These units are not permitted to learn from their own experience as the simulation progresses, but tend to make choices by drawing random numbers. Conflict is resolved through bidding for scarce resources or by the toss of a die.

The most noteworthy alternative approach identifies the chief decision centers, constructs a subsystem around them that simulates the real environment encountered there, and then places previously coached neophytes into the decision-making roles at these centers. We know from experience in other game-type simulations that students familiarize themselves with the situation by playing conservative policies first, but later they may sometimes be moved to innovate. The knack of keeping these subsystems simple while still permitting realistic forms of innovation is part of the art of systems design.

The introduction of human behavior, and interactions between choices, requires that much of the detail be shorn away; otherwise, the complexity grows beyond the comprehension of the players. I believe that the essential roles include a political "boss" (together with an aspiring boss), a top city administrator, a planner, a judge, and two or more speculators. A semi-circular urban form seems to offer the best combination of realism, simplicity, and opportunity for variation. There would be elections, an operating budget, a capital budget, and a land use plan or zoning regulation. Miscellaneous events enter from the outer world offering opportunities, threatening catastrophes, and disturbing relationships. The various decision-makers try to work out solutions advantageous to the city but not threatening to the positions they hold. If through poor bargaining or bad luck they fail, then the players are ejected from their posts and may try another role when it is open. (Time should be compressed so that three to four decades of development could be followed.)

In games like this it is possible to change a few maps and rules so as to switch from the simulation of central city to that of suburb. Indeed the two simulations may proceed simultaneously and interact with each other in ways paralleling familiar city-suburb relationships.

Current experience with the simulation of population ecology suggests that it is probably desirable to set up a family of simulations, the simplest of which is at the level of a parlor game, while the most advanced could well be used as a research tool. Then the student, whether child or adult, could progress from one to the next as the necessary concepts are acquired.

Much more experimentation will be needed to develop a set of rules for cities in newly developing countries. This is primarily due to the much greater intervention of the national government in urban affairs in those parts of the world. Urban decision makers have much less freedom to act, as compared to the United States, but the nature of the constraints may be changed more rapidly.

Outcomes

The result of this exploratory experimentation could be a graded series of simulations—two or three adapted to American conditions, and one or more that would be typical of those found in newly developing countries. Each includes several "scenarios," a set of rules for participants, an underlying model, and the specifications of a body of "props" (such as maps that can change over time, computer programs, and specialized communications devices that enrich the interaction), and the like.

The primary justification of simulations is that they provide a novel kind of education which fills a gap in the teaching of the applied social sciences. This gap exists in part because social laboratories are not provided in the educational facilities. Carefully controlled studies to determine what is learned and how rapidly it is acquired would have to be designed after the simulations were completed. In any carefully thought out course of instruction, the time spent "playing games" would probably be significantly less than is employed for laboratory work in science courses.

It is my feeling that a contribution to theory would also be made. But it is a different kind of theory from that which is accepted in the contemporary literature on urbanism, so that this argument is debatable. It is a mode of theorizing that is needed for the *planning* of courses of action, rather than that which is used for analyzing causes and relations, or *past* sequences of action.

References

1. Cohen, K. J., and Rhenman, E., "The Role of Management Games in Education and Research," *Management Sci.*, 7:131-166, 1961.
2. Grundstein, N., "Computer Simulation of a Community for Gaming," paper given at A.A.A.S. Meeting, Denver, Colo., Dec. 28, 1961.
3. See the series of contributions to the Jan. 1962 issue of *Behavioral Science*.
4. Orcutt, G. H., *Microanalysis of Socio-economic Systems—A Simulation Study*, New York: Harper, 1961.

PART FIVE

Ecology of the Social Environment

Two remarkable papers comprise this concluding and summary section.

The first, bý the Dean of the Yale Law School, presents the background of "urban law," constitutional, state, and local, and then moves on to planning and social action. It borrows from Seeley, and takes issue with Poston's reliance on the "grass roots." It raises the basic problem of values, and again calls for pooling the efforts of people from all the relevant disciplines—including "the amateur" who is capable of a "less blinkered" view than most professionals.

The second, by the extraordinary British lawyer and statesman, Sir Geoffrey Vickers, recapitulates in the setting of an ecological image much of what has been said in this book, with reference to specific papers, themes, arguments, and ideas, and to important aspects of the American Dream.

Law, City Planning, and Social Action

28

EUGENE V. ROSTOW
EDNA G. ROSTOW

There are many ways of looking at law, and one's definitional standpoint has consequences. The premise of this paper is that law is necessarily the universal social science, because it is the means for translating social policies into social action. But law is not a neutral mechanism for social engineering. It has its own standards and its own rules of procedure, linked at many crucial points to the morals and experience of society—a society whose first principle, after all, is to govern itself through law. Given our modes of legal action, we can usefully consider the problems presented by the papers in this panel as raw materials of law—a series of comments on a range of related programs and processes, tensions, drives, and situations of conflict, which may, perhaps should, result in adaptations and changes in the existing legal pattern.

In one perspective, the law governing the life of American cities is an integral part of our more general law for national economic planning, which I have sought to outline elsewhere.[1] The tasks of this branch of the law—we might call it "urban law" for convenience—are greatly affected by the successes and failures of our law of national planning. The functioning of our legal institutions for governing the economy at large will define and determine the specific pressures on many or all cities: whether there is much or little unemployment, for example; whether the flow of population from farms to cities is accelerated or slowed down; whether interest rates, or exports, are relatively high or low; whether there is or is not a national program for education, or medical services, or social work, or welfare policies; whether the national road program tears down more housing units per year than the nation can build. Manifestly, the development of national, state, or private programs for retraining workers whose skills have become obsolete, and for subsidizing the movement of labor to areas of manpower shortage, would have a bearing on the welfare and delinquency problems of cities. The economic, social, and human problems which exist within the cities, some of which we now expect the community to resolve, are in part a function of the ways in which our general law for economic and social planning affects the horizons of business, and the environment of the cities.

If the law governing the life of American cities is in one sense part of a larger complex of law addressed to the level of employment, investment, foreign trade, and industrial organization, in another sense it is a separate set of political arrangements and habits, derived from quite a different history. Our cities are creations—artifacts—of law, but of laws which developed in another setting, and which are often outmoded, antiquated, and difficult to harness to what we have come to regard as the needs and duties of our exploding metropolitan communities.

Survey of Urban Law

Like every other part of the law, the law of our cities faithfully mirrors the balance of forces and ideas in American life. As background for the comments I shall venture to offer on the specific subject matter of this conference, I should like to recall four general features of our urban law, viewed as a whole: its position in the constitutional system; its continuity; its quality as the embodiment of doubts, uncertainties, and compromises; and its potentialities for dynamic change.

1. First, let me remind you briefly of the constitutional element in our law of cities, the element which defines them as bodies politic and controls their capacity to act. This feature of our urban law reflects the historical fact that we were originally a rural society, which has only recently become predominantly urban. For a long time, and perhaps still, the prevailing myths of American life looked to the country, to nature, to the rhythm of a farmer's work, as the proper and natural foundation of American democracy; and to the city, the factory, and the office as a source of sin and a betrayal of the American dream. After all, Jefferson and Rousseau were contemporaries, and Thoreau stands for something deep in the American psyche. The constitutional and political systems of the states took form and crys-

tallized while we were still a rural community. The rural interest, sustained by the Jeffersonian belief that those who lived close to the soil were the more faithful guardians of the democratic faith, carefully limited the political freedom of cities, and the effective voice of the cities in the governments of the states. The prevalence of slums and graft in the cities, the revelations of men like Lincoln Steffens, the presence in cities of vast masses of alien immigrants—factors like these reinforced the legal trends and were felt to justify them. The cities were threatening and foreign bodies, to be curbed and endured, not given an equal voice in the political order.

The unreality of the myth has not yet weakened its influence. Slums and graft were and are quite as prevalent in the country as in the city, but they arouse less horror. The president of Yale, Professor A. W. Griswold, once wrote a book, *Farming and Democracy* (1952), in which he punctured the thesis that agriculture is in fact the foundation of democracy. Professor Griswold showed that in three modern democracies, France, Britain, and the United States, progressive ideas and progressive models arise largely in the cities, not the country, and that the tone of agrarian politics seems to become more and more resistant to change as the industrial revolution sweeps many of the most active people from farms to urban centers.

The result today is a paradox, which the Supreme Court has faced directly for almost the first time. The Constitution gives to the states the power to determine "qualifications" for voting, in both state and national elections, and to Congress the power to fix the "manner" in which those rights are exercised in national elections. Thus far in our history, there has been little consideration given to the limits of fairness which may be applied, by the Courts or the Congress, to control the exercise of this fundamental power by the states, save for the primordial requirements of the Fourteenth and Fifteenth amendments as they have been applied to the voting rights of Negroes. The basic power of the states to determine qualifications for voting has been exercised in many parts of the country, as we all know, to give the cities a relatively weak voice in state legislatures and in the House of Representatives—but not in the Senate, whose members are now elected by state-wide constituencies. In local affairs, cities are regarded as arms and agencies of the state governments, deriving their powers by delegation from suspicious legislatures. Since cities are almost everywhere under-represented in the legislatures, they have sought, and obtained, what are in effect direct relations with the national government in their efforts to deal with many problems of modern life—housing and city planning, for example, and many aspects of welfare and education.

Given the character of the constitutional system, in which checks and balances are so evenly divided as to make affirmative government slow and difficult at best, the relative weakness of cities as governmental units is likely to persist. The most likely source of radical change in this pattern is a case decided by the Supreme Court in March, 1962, *Baker v. Carr*. That case had a long background in the history of the Court. The issue arose this time in new perspectives, however, in view of the rapid development in recent years of the Court's ideas about the principles of constitutional fairness and equality embodied in the Fourteenth Amendment, as they have been applied to a wide variety of situations other than voting: criminal trials and proceedings to determine men's right to pursue licensed callings; freedom of speech and the right of peaceful petition; and many others. The Court held that the Fourteenth Amendment, forbidding each state the power to deny "to any person within its jurisdiction the equal protection of the laws," entitled urban voters in Tennessee to proceed before the federal courts, to have those courts determine whether the voting laws of Tennessee treated them unfairly, in the light of the Fourteenth Amendment, as compared with other Tennessee voters. This is not the first time that the Supreme Court, as the keeper of our constitutional conscience, has acted, when the time was ripe, to facilitate the advance of democracy in the United States, even though the political process was incapable in itself of accomplishing the same end through the ordinary methods of voting. If the Court had again refused to pass on problems of fairness in the distribution of voting power, on the ground that they are purely political, the only effective remedy would have been a constitutional amendment —a difficult step on this subject, bound to arouse fierce resistance on grounds of federalism.

2. The second broad feature of the law controlling the authority of our cities is a generalized aspect of the problem we have been considering: the fact that the law of cities, quite apart from its constitutional status, embodies large elements of history and tradition. This quality of law is one of its inevitable and indispensable features as a social institution, assuring continuity and protecting society against

the instability of excessively easy change. As in the physical world, change in law requires the application of considerable force to overcome inertia. Some of the traditional aspects of our laws governing urban life—those requiring the election of mayors, aldermen, and school boards, for example—survive because they correspond both to our mores and to our most cherished aspirations. Others remain on the books because they are ignored in fact, but are harmless. Still others create obstacles to action strongly desired by the community, or by large sections of it. They continue in effect for a variety of reasons: because of inertia or indifference, or because the forces favoring reform cannot agree on what should replace the existing laws, or cannot convince public opinion that they need to be replaced. In this category of historical survivals I should single out for emphasis the property tax as the prevailing foundation of urban finance and the incoherence, in most parts of the country, of the existing boundaries of city governments. The property tax is a capital levy, not a tax on income, and I shall not comment here on its justification in economic theory. Theory apart, it is one of the most influential breeders of waste in the economy, inducing the movement of business and of people from cities to suburbs in flows which involve the premature abandonment and destruction of huge capital resources in the roads, sewers, gas mains, fire stations, houses, schools, and electrical equipment of existing urban areas—investments which then have to be duplicated in the suburbs. The social and political consequences of irrational movements stimulated by the tax system are even more serious than their economic wastefulness. They result in sharper class differences among communities and they often leave older urban areas devoid of leadership, almost incapable of developing as viable communities, in Richard Poston's sense. The property tax is not, of course, the only factor inducing movements of people and of factories. There are others, some—associated with class, status, and racial feelings—of great moment. But the property tax is a factor of importance, whose influence has been neglected. The difficulty of changing the boundaries of governmental units, in most states, is another irrational obstacle to effective urban planning. In many states, it is normally difficult—indeed almost impossible—to obtain a regrouping of communities into metropolitan areas more nearly suited to the functions urban government has to perform, and ought to perform, in the existing climate of social opinion.

3. Some features of the laws which structure our urban environment have a different character. They embody compromises, often shifting compromises, which represent and state the equilibrium of opposing political and social forces, and of opposing ideas, within the life of the city—zoning ordinances and the pattern of exceptions to them, for example; the various paradoxical habits through which we alternately try to treat and to punish juvenile offenders, or send poor alcoholics to jail on endlessly repetitive thirty-day sentences; and school laws, which, in the name of enlightened principle, condemn many of our youth to the traumatic and damaging experience of prolonged failure, and establish in their minds most dangerous self-evaluations of inadequacy, or worse. Even if we could agree on the kind and quality of educational program a modern city should have, which is doubtful, imagine what putting such a program into effect would involve: the conflict over whether teachers should be promoted for merit or for seniority, for example; the laborious task of teaching teachers to learn new methods, and unlearn those with which they have grown up. Do you know any community which has clearly made up its mind whether welfare payments are to be paid of right, or only when the welfare client really can't possibly find a job? In dealing with problems of this kind, the legal tools are perfectly adequate, but there is in fact no effective political consensus on what the law is expected to do, and therefore no political mandate on what should be done.

4. Looking at this kaleidoscope of national, state, and local laws which, in various patterns, constitute the organizing principles of our cities, how can we evaluate our potentialities to act? Does the law, for all its complexity, give us a reasonable chance to guide the development of metropolitan environments in ways which we can persuade ourselves, and our communities, are desirable? Or is the legal system through which we must proceed so anarchic, so confused, and so full of entrenched positions from which minorities can block action desired by majorities that we are condemned to paralysis and frustration? Is it realistic, given our political system, to undertake efforts to improve the environment of the metropolis as a place in which people can live, work, and participate as citizens in the affairs of the community?

I should answer the question in this way. While the inherited structure of the law surely doesn't make it easy to reshape our cities to our hearts' desire, it doesn't make it impossibly difficult, either. We have only to look at the changes accomplished in many cities since Senator Taft's basic statute of 1948 to realize that action is indeed possible, despite all obstacles, if we continue to use the national power, and national funds, as a device to stimulate, guide, encourage, and control effective local planning by the states and the cities. Since the Supreme Court has led the nation to reform its state voting laws, effective procedures of this kind may well be developed by the states acting alone. Many are quite rich enough to redevelop their cities without federal help.

The movement of urban renewal and development, in accordance with approved master plans, is gaining in momentum year by year. Politicians are learning, all over the country, that action on this front, for all its hazards, is good politics. It is a safe prediction that the investment of money in urban planning, somewhat subsidized by the public fisc, will soon become one of the largest economic activities in the country, and one of the most significant. We have spent over $16 billion to this end since 1949, of which the national government provided $2.5 billion. A recent estimate of needs suggests that we could profitably spend $40 billion a year on urban development for an indefinite period—almost the amount of our present defense budget.

Note the decision of social policy reflected by this development. Municipal zoning ordinances, and even city plans adopted by cities, were not unknown to our law as far back as the eighteenth century. They were weakened, and often abandoned, during the heyday of nineteenth-century individualism, and began to gain in strength and effectiveness from the beginning of this century. What our present legal system represents, however, is something else again: a recognition of public and indeed of national responsibility to undertake not merely improved zoning but an affirmative initiative in planning and in building, at least with regard to the physical and economic future of the cities, and perhaps their social and political future as well. That far-reaching step correlatively accepts the proposition that effective action to shape and structure our cities is beyond the power and capacity of private business acting alone, although the plan for urban planning that we are forging utilizes the energies and initiatives of private business at many points. The essence of the matter, however, is an entirely new concept: that the growth of cities should be controlled by public agencies, in this instance by a combination of national and municipal agencies, bringing the national authority directly into the precincts and neighborhoods of urban communities. The idea is not one of uniformity or centralization. In accordance with standards centrally established, and procedures which require a large measure of community initiative and participation, cities are stimulated to organize themselves and to confront and solve a series of economic, social, and aesthetic problems which most of them have been neglecting for a generation, while our urban centers fell apart. This is a process which has galvanized and released a flow of thought and action within cities, to the benefit of the city as a physical and economic entity, and as a more integrated community as well.

Means and Ends in Urban Planning

The real obstacles to successful urban planning, I suggest, are intellectual, not legal or political. If we knew what we wanted to do, I should not despair of findings ways to do it. But do we have a theory of urban planning, and a program for urban planning, which could stir us and our communities to agreement and action?

At the threshold, I should join Professor Seeley in avoiding an answer to the question he posed so brilliantly: Is there any reason to suppose that man would be emotionally healthier than he is if he lived in the city beautiful, planned, organized, and ordered within an inch of its life, devoid of slums, its traffic tamed, full of parks, flowers, museums, and other institutions at a high cultural level? Does modern urban civilization really breed the discontents of men? Can they be mitigated or eliminated by mitigating what Seeley calls "the incredible external chaos men create for each other in the pursuit of lives and careers that may well make sense for each of them severally"?

We know that neurosis, mental illness, crime, and suicide—to say nothing of the cardinal and venial sins—occur frequently in well-ordered universities, monasteries, garden cities, and other planned environments—perhaps as frequently as in malodorous slums. Does it follow that the external environment makes no difference to the mental health of those who live in it? And does it follow equally that attempts to control the environment are futile and self-defeating? I shall start by agreeing with what I take to be Seeley's view: that social efforts of this order are worth undertaking for their own sakes, not because we can be sure that a "good" physical ordering leads towards a "good" society, which produces "good" persons—but because a "good" external order is good in itself. We like to think a "good" external order is more "rational" in some sense, more "scientific," than the teeming confusion of the world we know. Perhaps our preference is no more than the obsessive desire for neatness of compulsive minds. Perhaps, as Seeley suggests, our choice is an act of art, poetry, and instinct, disguised in the more respectable vocabulary of science. More probably, I should guess, it bespeaks that yearning for improvement and for creative self-expression which man cannot repress because he is man.

In any event, I join with Seeley in favoring the effort, and I suppose all of us represented here do. Why else should someone convinced that salvation can be found only on a couch attend a long series of meetings devoted to exploring the impact of different kinds of environments on the emotional lives of people and the social health of communities?

Having made that leap of faith, where do we find ourselves? The second question, equally difficult, is what we mean by a "good" ordering of the external world. Here, to refer again to Seeley's paper, we find ourselves facing the contrast between "scientific" knowledge and other forms of belief. I should suggest that in this, as in other attempts to study physical or social phenomena, the word "science" has, basically, an aesthetic denotation. It is a way of organizing thought and investigation, a matter of establishing a simple, symmetrical relation between hypotheses and data, and of ordering the propositions which shape our knowledge into sets and systems whose ultimate appeal, like that of music, is harmony. We select data out of the infinitude of experience in accordance with hypotheses we must advance and withdraw on the basis of hunch—educated hunch sometimes, but always hunch in the end. The function of "facts," in any body of systematic knowledge, can never be more than that of disproving one or another of the infinite number of possible theories which can be advanced to explain their relationships. No theory can ever be proven to be true.

In what sense, then, is a "good" ordering of the external environment of cities a "rational" ordering? Does the phrase mean more than an ordering which will satisfy the tastes of those who effectively make decisions for the community—its elite of experts and opinion leaders; its voters, who may or may not follow their leaders; its communities, more or less effectively organized—organized perhaps in some depth, but never in much depth—to provide a source and a base for democratic decision-making? Does a "rational" city mean a planned and orderly city, without traffic problems or slums, with large park areas and plenty of places for people to stroll, meet, and have a drink? By that standard, poor Algiers is one of the best ordered environments the world has ever seen, with Leopoldville a close second.

Perhaps the concept of "rationality" in urban planning should be given an economic denotation—and surely the economics of the problem is important. I believe that the prudent use of the enormous capital invested in cities is the largest single economic problem in the country, and that the protection of that capital alone justifies the federal effort to encourage and accelerate urban planning. Should we say, then, that the goal of urban planning is a rational ordering of available space for desired uses at the lowest possible cost? Is this an adequate criterion of "rationality," even if we accept the qualification that the standard for determining what are "desired uses" is not that of competitive bidding on the market place alone, but a mixed process of collective political decision and the working of the market?

But most of the cities which men have loved, and with which their citizens have felt strong bonds of identification, have been profligate, not economical, in their use of space for parks, boulevards, monuments, and other luxuries. A strictly functional approach to city planning is self-defeating in the long run. One has only to contrast attitudes towards the wildly romantic and expensive historical reconstructions of the cities and towns of postwar Poland with the austere, sensible, and prosaic rebuilding of French towns damaged by the war, to appreciate the power of this observation.

There is another element in city planning which may give us a clue to the notion of "rationality" in the process—one of the oldest, in fact—and that is the criterion of public health. From the beginning of time, men have sought to plan cities with deference to the prevailing ideas of doctors about the causes of illness. They have avoided swamps, maximized or minimized sunshine or sea breezes, and otherwise sought to placate their men of medicine—or should I say their medicine men? The trouble with this criterion for rationality, basic as it is, is that it leads us full circle to where we started. If we include psychiatry as well as epidemiology and sanitation among our health sciences, can the experts give us any rules or guides for planning cities in ways which will reduce the burden of emotional illness? Apparently not yet, although we are told we must not despair.

Richard Poston offers another criterion for "rationality" in planning which is quite compatible with a high degree of confusion in traffic, housing, sanitation, and so on. Any environment is good, he tells us—and his test applies to nations and villages as directly as it does to cities—only if it is an active and developed community in whose affairs people participate as citizens, not as experts. "The need," he tells us, "is to build a more vital sense of community in each of the metropolitan areas in which our people live. It is for a deeper and more widespread feeling of local responsibility. It is a need for true community effort as contrasted with the splinter efforts of an assortment of specialized groups." To accomplish this end, he calls for programs "in which all improvements are viewed and carried out in such a way as to make each one of them instrumental in developing an environment in which better problem-solving habits, enriched human relations, and vigorous civic action are dominant characteristics."

Only in this way, he urges, can we overcome the progressive fragmentation of knowledge and expertise—that cancerous process through which the multiplication of books and articles is destroying the possibility of general education, leisure, and perhaps wisdom as well—and achieve a synthesis of expertness and common sense. And only in this way, both Perloff and Webber add, can planning procedures reach decisions addressed to the needs of the community as a social entity—decisions with which considerable numbers of influential citizens will feel identified as participants and will be willing to support.

I hasten to point out that the standard of rationality in Poston's paper is a value choice whose validity can never be tested by the most refined statistical and investigative methods. It appeals strongly to me, as a fervent democrat nurtured in the American system. But do we really know that procedures of this kind will produce the healthiest cities, the most beautiful cities, the cities men enjoy and identify with most enthusiastically, the cities in which they take most pride? Doubt on this score runs throughout Lewis Mumford's books. That generous, idealistic, and mystical prophet is torn by an unresolved conflict. Many of the cities he admires most, both as works of art and as sociological environments he regards as most healthy, were created not by democratic community effort but by ancient or modern patricians, tyrants, or great dreamers endowed by chance with the power of a magic wand. Athens and Rome, he remembers ruefully, became magnificent cities only after their democratic institutions had decayed. Hellenistic and later Roman cities trouble him, because they were imposed on people in order to allay or divert their discontents. Great city plans of the seventeenth century were often aristocratic gestures, imposed by fiat. Washington was planned by an expert—almost a genius—for a non-existent community which is only beginning to have a voice in its own affairs. He never discusses the Paris of Baron Haussman, one of the greatest achievements in the entire history of urban planning—although he refers to it occasionally—I suppose because the clash in that case between his fervent democratic principles and his feeling for the result is too painful. And in the end Mumford expresses great admiration for the British procedure of city planning through autonomous public authorities—public bodies of experts, irrevocably given a good deal of power, and largely immunized from the intense pressures of community opinion on which Poston places all his hopes. Bodies of this kind are in fact functioning in many places to carry out programs of physical development with far-reaching implications for the social shape of cities—those which build roads, for example, or huge water projects, and many agencies which redevelop cities.

In this realm, as in so many others, our law faces the paradox of harnessing the power of experts without abandoning all control over them. The expert, a wise man said, should be on tap, not on top. We should be clear about one general feature of the problem: the reality of democratic control over decision making does not prevent considerable delegations of authority for considerable periods of time—to the Supreme Court and to the Federal Reserve Board, for example; to the President and his ambassadors and generals; to every local chief of police and zoning commission. Democratic theory does not deny the necessity of strong leaders and strong leadership in the process of forming opinion and making decisions. Nor need democracy guarantee the power of commonplace men and prevent the emergence of extraordinary ones to positions of effective leadership. In a generation which has witnessed Roosevelt and Churchill, de Gaulle and Adenauer, we can hardly say that democracy condemns us to mediocrity or denies opportunities for influence to uncommon men—to the elite in fact, to use a word whose social reality we all try to avoid. Democracy is an integrative community process of consultation, of dialogue, of forming a public opinion, and then expressing it through votes. So long as periodic voting remains the ultimate source of power, the principles of democracy do not confine us to the procedures of a town meeting nor require that every decision about the location of a public building or a road within an approved plan be made by referendum. Even Switzerland does not go so far.

We have all come to realize that our cities are disintegrating under the impact of the automobile and the flow of population: disintegrating physically and disintegrating as balanced and viable social organisms. They are dissolving and growing at a rate which challenges the capacity of our institutions to shape and mold the process of social digestion. Communities are more than aggregations of people: they are social entities bound together by the power of shared ideas and shared loyalties. We face the risk, in many places, that such bonds are being destroyed more rapidly than they can be rebuilt, or formed anew. Experts preach decentralization and the appeal of small, beautifully planned cities, capable of becoming integrated civic bodies in the sense of Richard Poston and Harvey Perloff. But people still live, in great masses, by the contrary rule of the old song: "How ya goin' to keep them down on the farm, after they've seen Paree?" Men persist in preferring the variety, excitement, and privacy of great cities to the placid calm of "the sticks." Why?

We are among the various experts concerned with the problem. If we behave like good democrats, faithful to a creed we cannot escape, and do not wish to escape, our first task is to propose, explain, and expound approaches to the problem of metropolis which we can hope will convince our constituents and satisfy that standard.

Yet there is always the residual conflict between what people want and what we, the experts, think is good for them. As Mumford notes, democracies are more stingy than princes in building the city beautiful. If that is our goal, Baron Haussmann's methods must be admitted to be practical, perhaps preferable. We don't know whether the city beautiful contributes to the mental health of the citizens as individuals. Nor, equally, do we really know that the busy processes of social consultation which Poston makes his goal contribute to the emotional well-being of the individual citizens involved. Will family life be better, will children be better nurtured, will they develop as better integrated adolescents, stronger adults, better citizens, if mother and father rush off to committees four nights a week, leaving the children at home with television and a sitter? True, the children could comfort themselves with the thought that their parents are absent at socially constructive and rather dreary meetings, not at entertainments for clients or parties they choose to attend for their own pleasure. Would the rationale really be convincing, at least for children? Are we sure that the emotional development of the community wouldn't be better if there was more delegation to bureaucrats and less mass involvement in the details of the decisional process?

Or do we grasp at democratic urban planning through community participation as a welcome relief from the disturbing problems of the nation and the world, where the individual feels more and more isolated, helpless, and alienated, while his fate is decided by a few regal figures, working with information necessarily secret, almost beyond the reach of parliaments or elections?

I raise these questions to indicate how directly our views on these matters derive from value preferences, and not from demonstrable proofs of rationality in some sense or another of that elusive word. As will be clear, I hope, from what I have said, I do not regard the acceptance of this fact as an objection to action, but as a step toward promoting clarity of thought about the roots of action.

Conclusion

Let me try, by way of conclusion, to sum up where we are now in our new American adventure in planning metropolitan environments.

The goals of such action, like those of our planning system for governing the economy as a whole, should be, as Harvey Perloff stresses, to enlarge the area of freedom for the individual; to enlarge the spectrum of opportunities open to him; and to make him, to as great an extent as proves possible, a free, independent, and responsible agent and citizen within a community favoring his freedom and welcoming his participation in its affairs. This is our choice because we believe in such freedom, despite the fact that we know that the burden of freedom makes many men more lonesome, more isolated, and less secure than they are in societies of status and assured roles—hierarchical societies, static societies, and societies which protect the individual and his security at the expense of his freedom. We feel more comfortable when the plans we propose are those approved in advance by considerable elements within the community affected—plans proposed by experts, it may well be, but then at least submitted to criticism by community groups and ratified by political procedures in which such groups necessarily play an active role.

Procedures for planning apart, what should the content of urban plans be? They should start with the proposition that a city is a social entity within which all sorts of functions are carried out—social functions, political functions, economic functions, and the functions of education, pleasure, and the experience of living. There will necessarily be a strong component of physical planning and artistic dreaming in our programs for cities.

The memory of centuries of experience with cities as the greatest and most complex of man's artistic creations is within us and cannot be exorcised, even if we wanted it to be. We talk about this feature of the city in various ways, in the cold language of the social scientist or the romantic apostrophes of the utopian. In the end, we press for the city beautiful not because we really believe it will be the City of God, or Mumford's City of Love, or the City of Mental Health, but because we can't help doing so. We try to make cities express our ideas of beauty for the same reasons that lead us to make gardens: because it is fun to try and because such cities are a joy to behold. Michaelangelo's plans for Rome were never revised and approved by a citizens' committee, but they have nonetheless touched a chord in Roman hearts ever since.

Senator Taft started a revolution in urban affairs with his statute in 1948. By adding a federal subsidy and federal standards to the urban redevelopment laws which some mayors and city planners had persuaded a few state legislatures to pass before and during the war, he helped establish a legal mechanism of great potency within the boundaries of the constitutional system. The statute has been amended and developed since 1948 and will doubtless be revised again and again. But the basic idea survives—to use the federal power to bypass the weakness of cities in the state legislatures; to use federal funds, raised by income taxes, to supplement local funds, raised by property taxes; to deter and intimidate local graft, in the belief that corrupt politicians have a healthy fear of federal enquiry and federal courts; to encourage and require the formation of local planning and redevelopment agencies, meeting certain standards, and the correlative development of unofficial community organizations to support them.

That revolution—the response of law to a situation in urban affairs society had at last recognized to be dangerous—has only begun. I would suggest that the energy of Senator Taft's revolution should be channelled to make replanning our metropolitan centers an occasion for protecting, developing, and deepening their quality as democratic communities. That procedure in planning could help mitigate the power of the indispensable bureaucrats through the influence of what Mumford calls "autonomous component centers capable of exercising selection, exerting control, above all making autonomous decisions and answering back."

I started this part of my paper by saying that our chief problems were intellectual, not legal. Our pluralist legal system has always proved capable of solving problems if public opinion was clear it wanted them solved. We seem agreed, by faith if not by reason, in opting for democratic methods of reaching planning decisions, at the local level but within a national framework, because we think such methods strengthen the fiber of our civic life and contribute to larger goals of assuring the long-run health of our democratic institutions. In the task of finding goals for that planning process, it is already clear that we must combine the knowledge and the methods of political and behavioral scientists, sociologists, architects, ecologists, economists, and lawyers. And above all, we should involve amateurs, capable of taking a less blinkered view than most professionals, whose minds are swaddled by their training. And we must study the successes and failures, the costs and the benefits, of a wide range of planning efforts, here and abroad. For we really know very little about what we have done and what we are doing as we tear down and rebuild our cities—what we are doing, that is, to people and neighborhoods and to the nearly biological relations of men to their neighbors and their neighborhoods. And, by reason of the scatteration of functions among many agencies, and the scatteration of knowledge among isolated groups of students, we often lose our capacity to distinguish real from imaginary problems and to devise programs for solving them.

Planning methods of synthesis along these lines offers some hope that we may reach plans we like, and plans we should be able to persuade the voters to like.

I don't know a better way.

Reference

1. Rostow, E. V., *Planning for Freedom*, New Haven, Conn.: Yale Univ. Press, 1959.

Ecology, Planning, and the American Dream

29

GEOFFREY VICKERS

I

Here I sit in my rural, ecological niche, metabolizing a breakfast drawn from three continents, and quietly increasing the world's supply of carbon dioxide, which, as Dr. Deevey explains, may be, but probably is not, helping to thaw the polar ice. Across the valley, through the tops of beeches, wych elms, poplars, well grown in a century, I see the crest of the chalk hill, which rose from shallow, warm lagoons some fifty million years ago and which has since mantled itself with humus—that tattered robe, inches deep, which life, dying, has laid over earth's barren nakedness and in which alone new life can root. No longer grazed by sheep or rabbits, it has lost also the fine flora which once found a congenial home in the close-cropped turf; and, being now protected from human "development" by a public trust, it is swiftly reverting to the woodland from which it was cleared in medieval times. Between me and the hill, the Thames follows the course which it took when it broke through these hills after the last ice age; but it is hidden by the multitude of unfolding leaves which compose the slow dream of a single spring.

Along that hill runs a track where I often walk; an old track as human pathways go, for it has been trodden by men and beasts for four thousand years, perhaps far more. Over many miles of grass it leads to the great earth and stone circles of Avebury, where, early in the second millennium before Christ, my predecessors here—including, I may hope, a few linear ancestors—hewed with their antler picks, out of the solid chalk, a ditch twenty feet deep and a mile in circuit to guard their holy place; and piled up an artificial hill three hundred feet high. When they paused in that massive toil to look about them, they saw a landscape different from today's only in a few ways which I know or can guess. The bird voices, the hill contours, the shapes of leaf and tree which are familiar to me were no less familiar to them.

But from what *inner* world those men looked out, what the hill and rampart meant to them, what they saw as meaningful and what escaped their eyes for lack of foothold in their minds, all this I cannot even guess. If I could revisit them, I would expect to find much of their inner world alien or inaccessible. This, however, is equally true, though probably in lesser degree, of the visitor who will stay with me next week. And of them, as of him, I shall at least be sure that, though the objects of their hopes and fears may be beyond my comprehension, their hoping and their fearing will be to them as mine is to me. This conviction is itself odd, for it is unproved and unprovable; yet society in any form we know or value would dissolve if it were not universally held.

My inner world, I can safely say, would be far more strange to them. For at this moment, rooted here in a village community of man, beast, grass, grain, tree, I am equally absorbed in the community of minds which produced the papers in this book—men of other professions on the other side of the world, few of whom I have ever met; men engaged with problems of North American urban ecology, some of which have no counterpart here; yet men whose concerns I share and whose fellowship means much to me in two critical ways.

First, I share with them the excitement of a search for meaning, for understanding of one major aspect of mankind's current predicament: an interest sharpened both by the allure of intellectual challenge and by the need for action, no less here than there. (I live, maybe, in Arcady; but London is less than fifty miles away; and this village has its "amenity association" of anxious citizens, trying to guide, if not to check, the tide of development which is submerging farm and garden and which will flood far more strongly when the projected motorway follows the neolithic track across the hills.)

Secondly, in my incommunicable inner world, I am upheld by the experience of this sharing, of making mine the thoughts of others, and of recognizing from their signals that my signals to them have been received. So, whether or no our activities have made any other contribution to mental health, they have certainly contributed to mine.

These thoughts epitomize the main conceptual framework which these papers have left in my mind.

"Out there" is a "real" world, in which things happen. To be more exact, it is a world of happenings, of relations and interactions: for even a stone in the mud or a brick in the wall may be thought of as an event in time—internally, as a configuration of forces; externally, as one constituent in a set of dynamic relations with its surround. Such a world is, naturally, a world of change; but also a world of stabilities and regularities, reflecting the regularities of its underlying laws. Science offers us at least two ways of thinking about these happenings. If we want to know what science can tell us about the way plants grow, we ask the botanist. If, on the other hand, we want to know why this hill, which fifty years ago was covered with vegetation an inch high, bears rank grass today and will be woodland in a few decades, we ask the ecologist. He will describe the effect on each other of the life cycles of the various denizens of these slopes, from the sheep to the tiniest grasses, and the effect on all of withdrawing one. The sheep and the rabbits kept down whatever plant growth could not renew itself from buds at ground level. The fine herbage flourished under their grazing, whilst the saplings perished. Without sheep or rabbits, the balance was reversed. If pressed to explain the disappearance of the sheep and the rabbits, he would have to widen his field from the hillside to the planet and to take note of a greater variety of interacting forces. His answer, if he tried to make it complete, would take us through the economics of British farming, the response of Australian farmers to a plague of rabbits and of half-urbanized Britons to "urban sprawl," and much else besides—again, the interaction of disparate variables within a single field.

This is the point of view of the ecologist, and of these papers; and the scene before me serves to illustrate its growing complexity. Before life colonized these hills, the physical forces at play there had established their mutual relationships, sometimes self-stabilizing and sometimes not. The great cycle of evaporation and precipitation maintained the planet's water supply in roughly constant balance between the sea, the atmosphere, the land surface, the subsoil, and the deep reservoirs; and the water, in its unceasing circuit, slowly eroded the newly risen hills and carved ever more deeply each gully which it had begun to carve before. On so recent an outcrop, however, the colonizing forces of life would have been soon at work. The seeding plants and grasses were ready to occupy the bare slopes, checking the erosion, deepening the humus in which they rooted, and modifying even the rainfall on which they subsisted. Skip half a million centuries and we are in a familiar world, in which the conspicuous forces in the ecological balance are forces of life, a fully developed threefold hierarchy, through which solar energy and minerals pass into plant form, thence to form and sustain the herbivores, thence to the carnivores and back again, with countless elaborations and short circuits.

Already the ecological balance is being maintained by forms of interaction which were unknown before the scene was animated. Each of these creatures, even the lowliest, can organize matter and energy into new and improbable patterns. Each can for a time preserve stable relations between its transient constituents by new methods of regulation; and each, equally, has new ways of regulating the relations between itself and its milieu, and hence new forms of interaction. In particular, most of these forms, even very lowly ones, can learn. There has been a progressive widening in the *field* of relevant interaction, in the *forces* operating within that field and in the *kinds of interaction* involved.

Then comes the promise, and threat, of a far greater complexity. The track runs across the hill crests to Avebury; the rampart is rising; the men who are moving those millions of tons of earth with muscles and wicker baskets are being fed by the labors of other men who must feed themselves as well. What new forces, interacting in what new field, are setting here their strange, enduring signature?

To understand Avebury, we should need to understand the social and technological organization of these neolithic men, which made possible this vast construction; and also their political and religious ideas, which caused it to take this form. To explain this development, we must admit the existence of a new field, unique within each head yet partly shared, an ill-defined but inescapable "mental" field, which I have called their inner world: a world in which life can be not only lived but experienced and thought about, in which actual and hypothetical, past and future, can be equally present. The forces which operate in this new field, hope, fear, love, hate, ambition, loneliness, obligation, wonder, if not new, are raised to a new power and mediated by new forms of interaction—not only human speech, but all the arts of human intercourse, of mutual support, influence, coercion, manipulation.

This inner world, in which men inescapably live, develops in intimate relationship with the physical world, yet according to its own laws and its own time scale. Human history can be understood only as the interaction of the two worlds. The inner world has its own realities, its own dynamism—and its own ecology. Like the life forms of the physical world, the dreams of men spread and colonize their inner world, clash, excite, modify and destroy each other, or preserve their stability by making strange accommodations with their rivals. The meaning of Avebury, and the reasons why it was built, are to be found not in the ecology of the physical world but in the separate, though so closely related, ecology of the inner world—a world which was old when Avebury was built and which has developed since then far more strongly than the ecology of the surrounding hills.

This is even more true of all the institutions with which these papers deal. Much of the paradox and perplexity which haunt them is due to this essential duality of the world in which we live. Consider in briefest outline the stages of ecological development which this glance has covered. When the first vegetation began to colonize that hill, it found no rivals. There was room, it seemed, for all. Similarly, when the first colonists settled in North America, there must equally have seemed room for all. Actually, in each case there was room not for all but only for the few, rare types which could strike root here and there in such a habitat. As the hillside became one settled home of vegetable and animal life—and equally, as North America became one settled home of human life—the variety of living forms increased; and so did the variety and power of the forces which they brought to bear upon each other, limiting, sometimes eliminating, what had earlier been "successful" types. Increasingly, in both cases, these forces, whether mutually enabling or mutually limiting, were produced by the activities of similar kinds of life, coming, as they multiplied, into ever closer contact with each other. Even in a milieu without man, the result was an increasingly complex pattern of interaction which can be classified, without any teleological implications, as conflict, competition, or cooperation. Trees in a wood mutually stimulated their propensity to climb and mutually inhibited their propensity to spread. Sheep and rabbits maintained for the downland grasses and creeping plants a habitat as "artificial" as the rich man's gardeners provide for his "alpines." With the emergence of man, these interactions of conflict, competition, and cooperation became elaborated in ways new in scale and character. Avebury *could* not have been built except by a society whose food-getting technology was good enough to free large numbers of its members for unproductive work, and whose social technology was good enough to permit elaborate division of labor. These were already achievements possible to human society alone.

Yet these alone do not explain the result. Avebury *would* not have been built, even by such a society, unless the dreams of the decision-takers had taken that form and the total value system of the society had been sufficiently strong and stable to support the implications of that decision for decades. It was a strange dream for men who were little better equipped for digging than the foxes and badgers that shared their native hills. The lonely ring among the brooding hills reminds us that the quality of our dreams is neither masked nor redeemed by the quality of our technology.

And so, as Peter Marris would agree, do the products of the United States Federal Housing Renewal Scheme.

II

The ecologist, in his complex analysis, develops some ideas which are of the greatest importance in assessing the significance of these papers.

He develops first the idea of *interdependence*. In a field of variables so closely and mutually interrelated, any change anywhere will in some degree affect the whole. As fields widen and variables multiply, this insight threatens to make the whole ecological approach too difficult to be useful. Happily, the ecologist finds that some groups of variables can be usefully studied *for some purposes* as if they were isolated. These groups may be local, be the locality as wide as the Amazonian rain forest or as small as the world under a paving stone. Alternatively, their members may be scattered over the planet, be their constituents as numerous as the members of the Roman Catholic Church or as few as the authors of these papers. The developing importance of such non-local groups is a feature of human society, with its unique systems of communication for mediating mutual influence over physical and temporal distances. The individual constituent may be a member of many groups, local and non-local—as I feel myself to be. Whether local or non-local, what makes a group a valid and useful field of study is that the interactions which are the subject of the study are largely confined within the group field. The relevant forces which bear on the members of the group from outside (be they the tropical rains of the Amazon or the traffic problems of North American cities) may be regarded as conditions common to the group.

Next, the ecologist comes to recognize certain *recurring patterns* in his field of study. These are of four main kinds. Perhaps the most interesting, because the least obviously to be expected, is the steady state. In a world of flux, it is constancy, not change, that requires explanation; and the ecologist's world contains a number of patterns which preserve themselves over substantial periods of time with little apparent change. Populations, for example, like organisms, sometimes remain stable for long periods, by exchanging and renewing their transient constituents at a constant rate.

The ecologist also recognizes *change*, in the form of increase or decrease in the magnitude of one or more of the constituents of a field. Decrease is obviously self-limiting. Either the diminishing variable will disappear, as the thyme has disappeared from the scrub-covered hill and the Algonquin Indian from Manhattan island; or the diminution will itself be checked or reversed. Increase, however, is also found to be self-limiting. The period of increase is succeeded by a period of "steady state"; or by a reversed trend, usually resulting in an oscillation; or by a "crash," in which the increase, often accelerating, is terminated by some sudden and radical alteration of the system. The first occurs when, for example, a local bird population is stabilized by a limitation of suitable nesting sites, or the number of lawyers in a small town by the number of their prospective clients. The second is exemplified by those linked oscillations in the numbers of prey and predators which have often caught the notice of ecologists; the lynx and the snowshoe hare in the Arctic tundra are a familiar example. Some forms of predation among humans show similar fluctuations. The third occurs when a tree growing on some steep slope outgrows the point at which its roots can support its weight and crashes down the hill—as once the last barrier crumbled to let the Thames flow through this gap and abandon its former bed. The self-exciting expansion of an arms race between nations, or of sedition and repression within one body politic, usually results in similarly explosive change.

Finally, the ecologist develops the concept of *regulation.* When he observes "steady state," he concludes that the forces interacting in his field of study are so disposed that any departure from the steady state tends to change the balance of forces in such a way as to reverse the departure. When he observes "oscillation," he knows that the span of oscillation defines either the degree of displacement needed to trigger the change which will reverse the process, or the temporal lag before the reversal can become effective. When he observes increase or decrease, he expects it to generate regulative forces which will prevent its continuance in one or other of the familiar ways. Engineers will model for him all the patterns which he can observe in nature and at least some of the devices involved in regulation; in particular, those whereby deviations are "fed back" into the system to check—or sometimes to multiply—the incipient disturbance.

All these concepts are familiar to the social scientist. The anthropologist describes the self-regulating devices which, in "primitive" societies, regulate the size of the population, the exchange of goods, the division of labor and the distribution of power; and he traces the disruptive effects, throughout such a society, of such changes as the introduction of firearms or gin or monogamy or a money economy, as the agricultural ecologist traces the repercussions through the whole rural milieu of chemical fertilizers or insecticides. The sociologist develops general concepts for understanding the dynamics of a social field. The stability of the subculture of West End, as Dr. Ryan has described it, is ensured by the fact that every would-be leader within, every would-be helper from without, even every would-be deviant, is discouraged or neutralized or in the end extruded by built-in responses of the cultural ethic to the threats which the mere existence of such persons implies.

Ecology, as a science of interrelationships, has no use for the concepts of betterment, of value, or of choice. Men may release into the milieu a virus which destroys rabbits, and may develop a fertilizer industry which displaces sheep. No longer destroyed by sheep and rabbits, the coarse growth may displace the finer herbage. Woods may rise to overshadow their own seedbed so densely that only fungus will grow there. The self-destroyed wood may fall to let in the light and destroy the fungus. It is not for the ecologist to prefer beech trees to fungus or thyme to thistle. Equally valueless (at least in theory) to his impartial eye is the process whereby men build cities and cities attract men; cities breed plagues and plagues limit the size of cities; men curb plagues and cities expand into vast and formless aggregates, from which men try to escape. The automobile brings a means of escape for the few; the many follow and choke the roads. The roads multiply and let the traffic through; and roads and traffic carry with them the megalopolis from which they are flying. Ecology gives us a way of describing, not of valuing, the human process and its conscious and unconscious constituents.

Yet the human ecologist must take account, among the facts of his field, that men themselves are *valuers.* They seek and shun; and their seekings and shunnings are to be understood not in terms of the outer world, which the ecologist can observe, but in terms of the inner world which his subjects inhabit and which he may or may not share. In any field in which men function, the relevant facts and forces include not only what is happening but also what men think is going to happen; not only what they are doing to each other but also what they expect, hope, fear, from each other and from themselves. The inner world is fundamentally structured by human values.

It is thus a dynamic structure, a configuration of forces; and it behaves like other dynamic systems. Political beliefs, economic creeds, social attitudes, personal standards, change and develop partly in response to changes in the "real" world and partly through their own dynamic interaction. As Professor Kenneth Boulding has observed, "Such institutions as progressive taxation, inheritance taxes, . . . countercyclical fiscal and monetary policy, and the like, are in part outcomes of the socialist criticism of a pure market economy and in part the result of feedback of experiences. . . ." [1] Nor can the rate of such changes be understood without reference to the resistance of the established ethic to changes of a kind *or at a rate* which would undermine its own coherence. Equally, the dynamic of the inner world may accelerate change. The drive to solve the problems created in America by racial and national minorities, problems which constantly recur in these papers—indeed, even the problems themselves—cannot be described without reference to the development of political and ethical ideas, in particular to the felt need to give adequate and viable meaning to the faith in equality.

In this value-structured world live, inescapably, not only the objects of the ecologist's observations, but also the ecologist himself. The writers of these papers are not only scientists. They are also as Dr. Seeley has eloquently said, human agents, concerned with the "quality" of the civilization in which they live and able to make—unable *not* to make—judgments about it of better and worse.

The most objective observer looks out from an inner world and through an inner world which structures and gives meaning to what he sees. This is as true of an astronomer as of an anthropologist; but the significance of the fact varies with the subject matter. It is worthwhile briefly to follow this variation along its course, which is punctuated with significant changes.

III

From their earliest recorded days men have wondered about the heavenly bodies and have woven around them a great variety of meanings, religious, scientific, and cosmological. Today, a vast body of coherent theory links our solar system with the remotest nebulae and begets increasingly daring speculations, which in turn evoke new observations to confirm or disprove them. This speculative search is an activity of the human mind which seems to grow with exercise; and the body of theory to which it has given rise is a mental artifact, a notable constituent of our inner world. It does not, however, affect, directly or indirectly, the subject matter itself. Whatever may be the realities outside the astronomer's head to which his observations and speculations relate, they are not substantially affected either by his theories or by any action based on his theories—at all events, not yet. The celestial milieu remains an independent variable. For several centuries man's understanding of the solar system was blocked by his assumption that its motions *must* be circular, because circular motion was the most "perfect." The planets maintained orbits no less eliptical on this account; and when men belatedly discovered the fact, they had no means of bringing these orbits into line with their own aesthetic canons. Our inner view of the celestial milieu is a human artifact; but the universe itself certainly is not.

The terrestrial milieu is a different story. In the course of centuries of physical interaction, all intensively colonized land has become in some degree a human artifact. This valley where I sit was a swamp, until the river was controlled with locks and barrages. The depth and constitution of the soil is the product of a specific sequence of agricultural practices. Even the uncultivated spaces usually owe their shape and preservation to the feudal system of land tenure which declared them "commons." This interaction has contributed to and been affected by an inner view far richer and more complex in content than that which we have of the celestial milieu. The changing face of rural England reflected changes not only in agricultural science but also in men's ideas of land as a source of power, of prestige, of security, of aesthetic satisfaction, and much else besides; and itself contributed to these changes.

The physical city, "urbs"—which Dr. Deevey conveniently distinguishes from "civitas," the city of rights and duties—is much more obviously and literally a human artifact. There is scarcely a physical object in it, from the skyscraper to the doormat, that was not born in a human mind and brought to being by human hands. It is also an artifact never finished, always in constant change; and it, too, is represented in our minds by a mental artifact, the body of our knowledge about and attitudes toward it. Between the physical and the mental artifact there exists the same elusive, mutual relation. Our ideas of it constantly change, both through our observations of it and through the development of our conceptions of what it might be and should be; and these changes in turn influence—perhaps very weakly, often mistakenly, and always with a critical time lag—what it will become.

What then of "civitas," the city of rights and duties—not merely legal rights and duties, but all the mutual expectations which make citizens of those who dwell in "urbs"? The mutual expectations which create the subcultures of West End and Harlem and Puerto Rico are there to be studied, as Ryan, Fried, Ellen Lurie, and Hollingshead and Rogler have studied them. They are "facts"; but they are primarily facts of the inner world in which these citizens live, a world which the observer may or may not share. The West End is a slum to the planners, to the residents a home. Which is it *really*? It is both, and much more besides. For these words describe not facts of the physical world but judgments proceeding from the value-structured inner worlds of the observer and the participant.

Thus, as our attention ranges from stars, through the physical world, to men and their doings, the inner world becomes increasingly involved, not merely as the screen through which we look, but as an integral part of the material at which we are looking.

Of what does our inner world consist? Professor Boulding has described our inner view as "the Image" [2] and he has most usefully stressed its importance and its dimensions; but to picture the inner world we must look behind the image and ask what causes an individual or a society to see and value and respond to its situation in ways which are characteristic and enduring, yet capable of growth and change. A national ideology, a professional ethic, an individual personality, resides not in a particular set of images but in a set of *readinesses* to see and value and respond to its situation in particular ways. I will call this an appreciative system.

We know something of the ways in which these readinesses are built up. Even our eyes tell us nothing until we have learned to recognize and classify objects in particular ways; and there is little doubt that our conceptual classifications are built up in the same way. So, equally, are our values and our patterns of action. Our appreciative system grows and changes with every exercise of image formation, a process normally gradual and unconscious; and like all systems, it is resistant to changes of a kind or at a rate which might endanger its own coherence.

These papers are a series of exercises in image formation. Each includes its own individual *realization* of some aspect of the metropolitan environment as an on-going situation and its own *valuation* of what is thus realized. Their major value, as I believe, is to speed in us who read them the development of our own appreciative systems, sharpening and revising our readinesses not only to see but also to value and to respond to the situation in which each of us is involved, in thought and will as well as deed, as agent as well as observer. Such a revision is overdue; for the last two hundred years have left us with an appreciative system peculiarly ill-suited to our needs.

IV

During the past two centuries, men gained knowledge and power, which vastly increased their ability to predict and control; and they used these powers to make a world increasingly unpredictable and uncontrollable. This paradoxical result flowed from the fact that the technologies to which science gave birth enabled man not only to predict but also to alter the course of events in his milieu. Consequently, the outer world began to change in content, form, and complexity at ever-increasing speed, far outstripping the growth rate of any corresponding power of control. Hitherto, learning had meant adapting to the given. Now the very idea of "the given" became suspect and dim.

Nonetheless, the belief persisted that increased power to alter the environment brought increased control over it. This belief, still far from dead, is a manifest delusion. First, as every engineer knows, the difficulty of devising any physical control system lies not only—usually not chiefly—in generating enough power but also in generating enough information. Since the material world is a system, any change in the given is bound to have numberless, often unpredictable, repercussions throughout the system; so even if the effect of the intervention is to bring under control the variable which is directly affected, the total system is likely to be less predictable than before, while all learned skills based on the former "given" are depreciated. Further, these interventions, and the further interventions to which their unpredicted results are bound to lead, are likely to be self-multiplying. The rate of change increases at an accelerating speed, without a corresponding acceleration in the rate at which further responses can be made; and this brings ever nearer the threshold beyond which control is lost.

Even the most liberal legitimate statement of the faith is that men can learn to do anything that can be done by applying energy to material things. But this itself is of depreciating value, far less useful in America today than in the days of the expanding frontier. For the course of human activity in the last two centuries has been not only to change the physical environment from a relatively stable datum to an increasingly unstable artifact but also, and even more importantly, to replace the physical by the social milieu as the most important field of human interaction. It is highly doubtful how far the social environment can be either changed or stabilized by applying energy to material things—even, as these papers show, when the energy is applied to remaking urbs or suburbs.

In consequence, the last two centuries have ushered in a period of instability such as the world has never seen; a period, moreover, in which every new instability was either welcomed as "growth" or accepted as the price of growth. The ecological view was obscured, overlaid, lost, even denied, by the new ideology of "progress," with its implicit faith in the possibility of linear change which would not prove self-limiting. Furthermore, the idea of progress was itself confused by combining too uncritically the ideas of economic expansion and political betterment.

This identification was due at one extreme to mere naivete. "Humanly speaking, the greatest happiness possible for us consists in the greatest possible abundance of objects suitable for our enjoyment and in the greatest liberty to profit by them." So wrote the French economist Mercier de la Rivière in about 1760; and so says Madison Avenue today. At the other extreme, it was the expression of a new, passionate, and comprehensive faith. The wealth of nations was conceived as indefinitely expansible by the division of labor; and free competition was the means whereby the most efficient division of labor would be automatically achieved, internationally as well as nationally. This process would do far more than multiply "objects suitable for our enjoyment." It would eliminate national frontiers, abolish war, and unite the whole world in one great Commercial Republic.

". . . we are living in a period of most wonderful transition, which tends rapidly to accomplish that great end to which all history points —the realization of the unity of mankind." So said Prince Albert, when opening the Great Exhibition in London in 1851; and he was expressing a faith widely shared and more powerfully felt than any that had possessed the British since the days when the great cathedrals were built. Even Marx, who in the same city and at the same time was preparing his great attack on the very foundations of that faith, was sufficiently a child of his time to suppose that, once the victory of the proletariat had removed the cause for the exploitation of persons, history would thereafter become the uneventful administration of things.

There was, however, another and radically different view of political betterment. Society was perfectible because men were plastic; and human institutions were the means by which they could be molded. This view was the heir of a long tradition. The earlier world expected betterment only from good laws; certainly not from blind or selfish interaction. Philosophers from Plato onward based their utopias on the wisdom of a lawgiver—though it was left to the age of hope to conceive of a *progressive* course of education and legislation, leading through ever better institutions to an ever improving polity.

So one way of classifying ideas about progress is to distinguish those which regard it as a form of social evolution from those which regard it as a form of social engineering. Here, to proclaim the first, is Joseph Priestley, prophesying at the end of the eighteenth century:

> . . . nature . . . will be more at our command, men will make their situation in this world abundantly more easy and comfortable . . . and will grow daily more happy . . . whatever was the beginning of the world, the end will be glorious and paradisiacal . . . I think I could show [these views] to be fairly suggested by a true theory of human nature and to arise from the natural course of human affairs.

And here, to express the other view, is T. H. Huxley, writing in 1893:

> Social progress means the checking of the cosmic process at every step and the substitution for it of another which may be called the ethical process. . . . That which lies before the human race is a constant struggle to maintain and improve, in opposition to the state of Nature, the state of Art of an organised policy; in which and by which men may develop a worthy civilization capable of maintaining and improving itself . . .

To temper optimism, he added:

> . . . until the evolution of our globe shall have entered so far upon its downward course that the cosmic process resumes its sway . . . evolution encourages no millenial expectations.

The difference is radical. According to the first view, an acceptable, even a "paradisiacal" future will arise "from the natural course of human affairs," even though it lie the other side of a bloody revolution which we cannot bypass and do well to speed. According to the second view, such a future will arise only as it is conceived by the insight and imposed by the will of men on the recalcitrant material of "the cosmic process." Marx is nearer to the Prince Consort than is Huxley to Priestley or the 1890's to the 1790's.

Yet all these views lack an ecological orientation. Priestley never questions that the natural course of human affairs is linear. Marx seems to have assumed that the dialectical process would "wither away" with the State. Huxley does not envisage that the ethical process will have constantly to wrestle not only with the cosmic process but also with the unexpected results of its own activities. None of them seems to envisage enduring debate about the meaning of betterment, the direction of improvement.

We stand today amid the wreckage of these nineteenth-century hopes and certainties. Though the debate between the two views just illustrated remains unresolved, the second view accords more nearly than the first with the insight and spirit of our age. "A worthy civilisation capable of maintaining and improving itself" will not "arise from the natural course of human affairs." It will need a "constant struggle to maintain and improve it." It will be a state not of nature but of art, man's great, composite work of art; and it can be no more noble than his dreams. We know, however, better than Huxley's generation what is involved in that endless struggle and what are its limitations.

V

The energy at our disposal has been multiplied and is now theoretically limitless. Our technology is sufficient to design and make far more than all the artifacts we are conscious of needing. Our means of communication are sufficient to transmit, store, and handle far more information than we can use. Increasing populations, increasingly urbanized, inhabit cities of increasing size, yet demand more space and more stuff per head with every year that passes. Man-made resources grow; natural resources shrink, especially the three most irreplaceable—clean air, clean water, and empty space. The ancient problem of equating populations with living space and food supply emerges on a planetary scale. The problems of our day are set in ecological terms more strident, more blatant, more urgent, than ever before. They are how to regulate the instabilities inherent in this dizzy expansion; how to keep rates of change within bearable compass; how to choose between so many mutually exclusive possibilities.

Yet neither our institutions nor our ideologies are apt for such problems. Both still bear the shape impressed on them by the epoch that has closed; both resist, as every dynamic system must, changes which threaten their own coherence.

One of the most pervasive products of the ecological view is that every choice has a cost: for every realization precludes a hundred others. We can spend time, attention, life, like money, in only one way at a time; and, unlike money, these precious commodities are not expansible.

The cost inherent in every choice is most obvious in the use of land, for even the most modern technology offers no hope of expanding the surface of the planet. Demand multiplies and scope narrows. North Americans, whose grandfathers were still pushing out the frontier between primal nature and agricultural man, meet a new frontier coming back, an ever-narrowing net woven by their own realized dreams. The cost of every new development rises, not only in money, but in the abandonment, often forever, of all alternatives. Land use illustrates with especial clarity the universal truth that betterment is not the accumulation of recognized "goods" in an ever-increasing heap. It is the realization, within a dynamic system, of some *chosen* set of conditions to the exclusion of countless others.

How are such choices made? And what is the part of the planner in making them? Professor Webber gives a familiar Western answer. The planner helps by making "explicit tracings of the repercussions and of the value implications associated with alternative courses of action." The choice between them is not for the planner but for the agent whom he serves.

When the agent is the government of a large society, a state, or a city, comprising a diversity of "interests," the choice is complex. The individuals concerned do not even know consciously all they want; even their individual wants may be mutually inconsistent; they cannot see ahead even as far as the planner, still less can they see as far as the executive's decision will commit them. How are they to arrive at a collective choice?

Professor Webber states a widespread view when he attributes any difficulties of collective valuation to the lack of a market. Where services are supplied through a market, the individual can express his own choice freely by buying or abstaining from buying; but where services are provided without direct charges, like education and roads and defense, the public must have some alternative means to express its opinion. How else can governments know "what it is that customers prefer and hence what combination of services and facilities would benefit them and the community most"? In practice, governments must rely partly on the poor alternative of the pressure group, partly on their own "value hypotheses" and those of their assistants who are "able to make reasonably good judgments about the current preferences of some of the various publics."

As an account of what actually happens, in America or elsewhere, in the making of collective choices, even through the market but far more in the political field, this account seems to me to miss an essential element. The men and women in England who abolished slavery, created the educational system, or gave women the vote were not acting on hypotheses of what the voters wanted. They were afire with faith in what people ought to want and in the end they persuaded their lethargic compatriots to give them enough support to warrant a change. American presidents, from Lincoln to Kennedy, do not speak with accents of inquirers seeking guidance about other people's preferences. Like most of the authors of these papers, they *criticize* contemporary values, urge *re*valuation, and appeal not to what people are thinking now but to what they ought to be thinking and would be thinking if they exposed themselves with sufficient sensitivity to the subject matter of the debate. A free society is one in which these initiatives spring up freely and in which men are free to espouse or resist them. It depends, like every other society, on the quality and abundance of these initiatives, as well as on the facilities for their debate, facilities which themselves depend partly on institutions and partly on the capacity of the current appreciative system to criticize itself.

Again, as a description of what actually happens, the foregoing account seems to me to underrate what the planner does and must do. A plan, whether it be an architect's plan for the physical rebuilding of a city center or an administrator's plan for a new mental health service, proposes a unique series of concrete, interrelated choices. It is a work of art, having already form but awaiting an executive decision to give it substance. It can be criticized, commended, compared with others; but the choice of the executive as such is limited to the plans before it. It may reject them all and tell the planners to think again; but in the end the planners will decide what alternatives shall be considered—and, by implication, will decide that all others shall be ignored. Only in the capacity of a planner can anyone propose a *new* answer.

"Government of the people, by the people, for the people." How simple it sounds, until we explore the volume of meaning, different in each case, comprised in those words "the people." The responsibilities of "government" are of many kinds and they fall differently on each one of us. We have all some responsibility for action, some area, however small, in which each of us and he alone can play the part of agent. There is a second field, wider and not congruent with the first, in which each of us can contribute to the making of policy. There is a third, wider still, in which each of us has power to give or withhold assent to the policy decisions of others. There is a fourth, yet wider, in which the only responsibility of each of us is the neglected but important responsibility of giving or withholding the trust which supports or inhibits our fellows in the exercise of their inalienable responsibilities, as their trust or distrust supports or inhibits us.

There is, however, a fifth field, sometimes merged in the first or second but in public affairs increasingly separated from them: the responsibility for planning, the creative function which shapes the work thus and not otherwise, whether the work be a building or an institution, a nation's history or a human life. Here lies the possibility for the vision that is manifest, for good or ill, whenever a "state of art" is imposed on a "state of nature," but which is only vaguely missed when it is absent: the authentic signature of the human mind.

Planning thus conceived is viewed askance by Western culture, in measure increasing with its scale in space and time. Large-scale attempts consciously to impose a state of art on human affairs have often ended disastrously; men's most enduring and approved achievements, both in the outer and in the inner worlds, have usually been the fruit of long, unconscious growth, deriving from the unhampered creativity of individuals. To guarantee scope for individual creativity unhampered by limitations physical, historical, or institutional has always been an integral part of the American dream.

An ecological view helps us to understand what this ambition means in the conditions of today and what it will mean in the necessarily changed conditions of tomorrow; and how far these conditions might be controlled and at what cost. It does not encourage either arrogant hopes for social planning or easy optimism about the continuance of individual scope. The environment of the metropolis increasingly conditions us. Since it is man-made, we must acknowledge that through it we condition each other; yet, though it is a collective achievement, it does not represent a collective choice. Both its possibilities and its limitations are largely accidental; and it is a process in rapid change. How far could this process be directed? How far should it be directed—and in what direction? These papers supply no complete or coherent answers to these questions; but they contribute to our image of the process, and thus quicken and enlighten us for the debate from which answers may proceed. In particular, they help to pose those questions of value which are most easily masked.

For value questions do tend to be masked beneath the vast ramifications of our instrumental judgments, judgments of how best to achieve some already agreed end. We are so good at know-how, and so deeply immersed in it, that we scarcely admit, except in the relaxations of leisure, the value of the act done or the work produced for its own sake. Yet, obviously, no instrumental judgment can be final. If A is worth doing only because it leads to B, then why B? And C? Ultimately, this regress must be closed by the judgment that something is worth doing for its own sake. Dean Rostow is right; whether the City Beautiful is or is not likely to breed gracious citizens, it is something which even moderately gracious citizens will want to build, because they will "enjoy" it—and this none the less if they differ passionately in their judgments of beauty.

Again, choices based on major judgments of value tend to be masked behind the frequent threats latent in the instability of our system. Too often, we can justify what we do by some manifest disaster that will otherwise overtake us. Watching a tyro on skates, staggering around in grotesque gyrations, each of which imposes the next, a spectator who asked, "Why is he doing that?" might properly be answered, "He is trying to keep his balance." And indeed the pursuit of balance is enough to absorb the whole of the poor man's energy and attention. If, however, the spectator were to ask the same question about a master skater, weaving arabesques of bird-like elegance on the ice, it would be nonsense to make the same answer. True, the master, like the novice, must constantly seek a balance which must for ever be sought anew; for him, as for the novice, this is an iron law within which alone he can function. But the master has learned it so well that his obedience to it, unconscious for him and invisible to the spectators, is merged in the execution of what he is doing. He is *free* within the world of motion open to men on skates; and as a free man, his choice needs a different explanation.

Similarly a business, a city, a state, which bumps along from one crisis to another can explain and justify each response as the need to evade an imminent and lethal threat; but this is not the state in which human life, individual or collective, bears its most characteristic or its most gracious fruits. The stability of the *milieu intérieur* is only the *condition* of free and independent life. Its absence may explain a breakdown; its presence does not explain the achievement which it makes possible.

It seems to me that we sometimes elude the explicit value judgment also for a more fundamental reason. A hundred years have passed since Marx savagely denounced morality as the rationalized economic self-interest of the strong. Even his critics recognized that there was uncomfortable truth in this. That it was not the whole truth seemed probable, if only from the fact that his theories failed to account for his own moral fervor or for the success of his ideas within the world of ideas. What alternative could his critics offer? Physical scientists who, encapsulated in "objectivity," made increasingly daring excursions into "nature," reported on their return that they found no "values" in the "real world out there." Anthropologists and psychologists, exploring the behavior of men and societies by methods as nearly scientific as might be, saw values as imposed by inner needs and outer circumstances through a determinism less crudely economic but not less rigid than Marx's age imposed on him. Neither physical nor social scientists could find a place for the creative originality of men *as agents* which their own activities so abundantly illustrated.

This was due, I suggest, to their unwillingness to accord even partial autonomy to that inner world which is structured and energized by human values. Happily, this difficulty which beset them as scientists seldom hampered their performance as human agents, for whom the making of responsible value judgments was an accepted major activity of life.

Human mental activity is indeed only part—a small and peripheral part—of the subject matter of science. It is, however, equally true that the whole of science is only a part—a smaller and more peripheral part than we always remember—of human mental activity. Confronted with these two Chinese boxes, each of which claims to contain the other, we may conclude that the human agent is more than he knows and probably more than he can ever know.

To me, at all events, the view implicit in these papers is consistent with, and seems even to require an unshaken faith in, the power and duty of the human mind to make judgments of value—judgments which can never be validated, though they may sometimes be falsified by appeal to any criterion other than another value judgment; faith qualified, nonetheless, by the knowledge that such judgments can never be final, that all dreams—even the American dream—must constantly be dreamed anew.

References

1. Boulding, K., *Conflict and Defense: A General Theory,* New York: Harper, 1961.
2. Boulding, K., *The Image: Knowledge in Life and Society,* Ann Arbor: Univ. of Michigan Press, 1956.

Index